Overcriminalization

Overcriminalization
The Limits of the Criminal Law

Douglas Husak

2008

OXFORD
UNIVERSITY PRESS

Oxford University Press, Inc., publishes works that further
Oxford University's objective of excellence
in research, scholarship, and education.

Oxford   New York

Auckland   Cape Town   Dar es Salaam   Hong Kong   Karachi
Kuala Lumpur   Madrid   Melbourne   Mexico City   Nairobi
New Delhi   Shanghai   Taipei   Toronto

With offices in

Argentina   Austria   Brazil   Chile   Czech Republic   France   Greece
Guatemala   Hungary   Italy   Japan   Poland   Portugal   Singapore
South Korea   Switzerland   Thailand   Turkey   Ukraine   Vietnam

Published by Oxford University Press, Inc.
198 Madison Avenue, New York, New York 10016

www.oup.com

Oxford is a registered trademark of Oxford University Press

Library of Congress Cataloging-in-Publication Data
Husak, Douglas N., 1948–
Overcriminalization : the limits of the criminal law / Douglas Husak.
    p.   cm.
Includes bibliographical references and index.
ISBN 978-0-19-539901-1
1. Criminal law—United States—Philosophy. I. Title. II. Title: Over criminalization.
KF9223.H87 2007
345.73—dc22   2007009297

Printed in the United States of America

Preface

I have two central objectives in this book. Most obviously, I defend a theory of the limits of the penal sanction to combat the problem of overcriminalization. Still, it is important to recognize that this theory has an even broader application. A theory of criminalization is needed to justify the criminal laws we should retain, as well as to provide the criteria by which we should decide whether to enact even more penal legislation. Because I am more interested in retarding overcriminalization than in achieving these latter objectives, however, the theory I present consists in a number of constraints to limit the criminal sanction rather than a set of reasons to extend it. My second objective is to situate my effort in criminal theory and legal philosophy generally. This goal is no less important than the first. Although I frequently contend that too little work on the topic of criminalization has been done, I argue that the resources to produce such a theory can be found in the wealth of scholarship legal theorists have developed—even though these resources have not been exploited for this purpose.

Legal philosophers who specialize in criminal theory are roughly divisible into two camps. The first is composed of academic philosophers who are extraordinarily knowledgeable about moral responsibility and attempt to apply their insights to issues of criminal liability. Some write whole books (allegedly) about the criminal law while barely mentioning a single case or statute. The second camp is composed of law professors who know a great deal about statutes and cases but are not especially conversant with philosophy. Often their philosophical sophistication does not extend beyond their discussion of how their views would be received within the deterrence and retributive traditions. Of course, the writings of any given legal philosopher fall on a continuum between these two extremes. In any event, I believe that this book lies squarely in the middle of these two camps. I try to be firmly anchored in existing criminal law while drawing heavily from contemporary moral, political, and legal philosophy. Along the way, I also borrow freely from the empirical research of criminologists. I hope that my effort captures the best these disciplines have to offer. I aspire to produce a book that it neither too philosophical for legal theorists nor too legalistic for philosophers.

The second of my objectives accounts for my tendency to cite the relevant contributions of philosophers and legal academics. Readers who share my interest in both philosophy and law are well aware that philosophers use footnotes much less frequently than legal commentators. Because my inquiry is located at the intersection between these two disciplines, I initially sought to compromise in the number of my references. Eventually, my efforts became tilted toward the style favored in law. My abundance of footnotes reflects the second of my ambitions. I situate my arguments in criminal law scholarship by building on the thoughts of a host of philosophers and legal theorists.

I have what surely is a fantasy about how a book on the topic of criminalization will be received. Philosophy generally—and legal philosophy as well—has increasingly become a specialized discipline whose practitioners speak exclusively to one another. Issues of relatively minor significance have given rise to an enormous literature while more central topics (like that pursued here) have received virtually no attention. Academic conferences have a predictable dynamic. Arguments are developed; objections are made; counterarguments are defended; everyone goes home to begin the cycle anew. The stakes are low, so no conclusions need be reached. I am persuaded that the topic of criminalization is different. Even if every argument I present is unsound, no reasonable person should contest the gravity of the problems I describe or the need to solve them. I hope that commentators will begin to work together to fill a huge chasm in legal thought: the absence of a respectable theory to help retard the process by which too much criminal law produces too much punishment. The practical need for such a theory is so enormous that legal philosophers cannot afford the luxury of raising objections to existing principles without endeavoring to offer better ideas than those they reject.

I believe my methodology is unremarkable. No one has proposed a means to make progress in normative inquiry without the ample use of thought-experiments. Imaginary cases are described to solicit the judgments of readers, and these responses are used to confirm or reject abstract principles or theories. This device is largely unavoidable, and I occasionally employ it here. Still, I avoid the wildly fanciful and unfamiliar hypothetical cases that have helped to give philosophy a bad reputation among legal theorists. I am skeptical that the reactions of respondents to these extraordinary cases should be given much credibility. Moreover, I do not engage in grand theorizing: the search for a unitary account of the function or purpose of the criminal law.[1] Although I frequently shift from the very general to the very specific, I resist *isms* generally and the most familiar isms in particular. I refer to my theory as criminal law *minimalism,* but I use this term more as a slogan than as the name of a unified account of the criminal law. The theory of criminalization I develop draws from both retributive and consequentialist traditions and proceeds from neither a liberal nor a conservative perspective. I believe that the continued use of these vague labels does a disservice to political and legal debate, and I aspire to produce an argument against overcriminalization that will be persuasive to commentators on all points along the political spectrum. Readers of every ideology are welcome to draw from my theory as they wish. Finally, I do not presuppose the truth of a particular approach to morality. I reject utilitarianism but otherwise remain noncommittal about the details or foundations of moral theory.

---

1. For a discussion of grand theorizing and those commentators who aspire to it, see R. A. Duff: "Theorising Criminal Law: A 25th Anniversary Essay," 25 *Oxford Journal of Legal Studies* 353 (2005).

Despite what is frequently written about "the practical turn" in philosophy, my survey of the landscape convinces me that the scholarship of most academics is decidedly *im*practical. This tendency is especially unfortunate among legal philosophers whose specialty provides us an ideal vantage point to identify injustice. Many of the jurisprudential debates to which we legal philosophers contribute have an abstract and remote application to real-world problems. The endless refinements of various modes of positivism are perhaps the best example of this phenomenon. I am not calling for a return to the days when academics were more directly involved in partisan politics. But our research should be more sensitive to the injustices that surround us.

Much of the impetus for this book was produced by my prior work about the justifiability of drug proscriptions. Over the years, I have struggled mightily to learn why the state might be justified in punishing persons who use drugs for recreational purposes. Clearly, this project cannot be completed unless one has a general idea of what would permit the state to punish anyone for anything. Pursuing this latter idea leads naturally toward the development of a theory of criminalization. I remain persuaded that the state lacks a good reason to punish drug users. In this book, however, drug prohibitions are merely an example of overcriminalization; they are not my central focus.

I have come to believe my thoughts about overcriminalization have been vindicated as a result of presenting my theory to several groups of philosophers and legal theorists. Respondents frequently ask how my theory applies to difficult cases where reasonable minds may differ. Clearly, I cannot explore each such matter in detail here. But I have become confident that the pros and cons of various controversial proposals are debated squarely within the framework I offer. I will have been largely successful in developing a viable theory of criminalization if the issues that are relevant to how particular questions should be resolved are readily expressed within the parameters I develop.

If the central argument of this book is correct, injustice is pervasive throughout the criminal domain. I have tried to maintain a sober and academic tone in describing this sorry state of affairs. Still, I can barely conceal my outrage about what I believe to be an injustice of monstrous proportions. The quality of a criminal justice system is an important measure of the value of a political community. Apart from waging war, no decision made by the state is more significant than its judgment about what conduct should be proscribed and how severely to punish it. Unfortunately, however, contemporary decisions about criminalization conform to no normative principles whatever. The criminal justice system that many commentators have worked so hard to improve is being used for perverse and immoral ends. The passivity of the community of legal philosophers (and the American public at large) in the wake of these atrocities is nothing short of tragic. We seem utterly unconcerned while hundreds of thousands of citizens little different from ourselves spend their most productive years in prison—at taxpayer's expense, I might add. Commentators should not remain silent about these injustices.

An author could use the topic of overcriminalization as the occasion to go almost anywhere in legal and political philosophy. The subject connects fairly directly to many other legal, political, and moral issues. I simply mention one of many possible directions I did not take. Although I complain about injustice in our system of criminal law, I tend not to describe it in socioeconomic terms. It may seem impossible to write a book about injustice in the penal law without paying more attention to the fact that the vast majority of persons punished for criminal behavior are socially and economically disadvantaged. One may wonder, for example, why petty shoplifters are prosecuted vigorously while middle- and upper-income tax evaders are prosecuted infrequently—even though they cheat the government of greater sums of money than petty thieves manage to steal. These issues are of central importance. For the most part, however, I do not pursue them here. I am more anxious to demonstrate how the injustices associated with overcriminalization affect us all, rich and poor alike.

A simple roadmap of this book is as follows. Chapter 1 describes the general problem my theory is designed to address. I discuss the phenomenon of overcriminalization and why we should be worried about it. Although overcriminalization is pernicious for several reasons I mention briefly, its most objectionable consequence is the injustice caused by too much punishment. Chapters 2 and 3 introduce and develop my theory of criminalization. This theory consists in several constraints that limit the use of the criminal sanction. I argue that the constraints described in chapter 2 are internal to criminal law itself, and no respectable theory of the limits of the criminal sanction can afford to disregard them. The constraints defended in chapter 3 are somewhat different; they depend on a controversial normative theory imported from outside the criminal law. This theory describes the conditions under which the state is permitted to infringe the right not to be punished. In chapter 4, I examine three alternative theories of criminalization and argue that my account is superior to each of them. If the competitors to my account are as deficient as I believe, any problems in my theory are likely to seem more manageable. Still, I am painfully aware that many of the crucial arguments I sketch here are inconclusive. A great deal of additional work remains to be done. I only begin the enormous task of formulating a set of constraints to retard the phenomenal growth in the use of the penal sanction.

Acknowledgments

I owe an enormous debt to the legions of criminal theorists who have influenced and shaped my thought. Three deserve to be mentioned by name. George Fletcher originally sparked my interest in the philosophy of criminal law. I continue to believe that his masterful *Rethinking Criminal Law* is the best book in criminal theory to have been written in the last century. It is only a small exaggeration to say that my entire career has addressed the many problems I first confronted in *Rethinking*. My more recent debt—both personally and professionally—is to the two greatest Anglo-American criminal theorists on each side of the Atlantic. Michael Moore has something remarkably sophisticated and thoughtful to say about virtually every problem in the philosophy of criminal law, and his influence extends to almost every idea I defend here. Moreover, Moore's contagious enthusiasm for philosophical discussion is shown by his willingness to organize roundtable discussions in many of the most delightful venues in the United States, including his own home. I have had the privilege to attend several of these wonderful sessions, where many of my arguments were tested and refined. I reserve special praise for Antony Duff. Even a casual reading of this book indicates the extent to which my work is dependent on his deep and humane contributions to criminal theory and the philosophy of punishment. Moreover, Duff first suggested that I collect my haphazard thoughts about criminalization into a (ideally) coherent book. Without his encouragement, I would not have undertaken this effort. Finally, Duff has been instrumental in organizing workshops and colloquia at which criminal theorists from all over the world meet to exchange ideas. The most valuable of these colloquia (to me) was held at the University of Stirling in October 2006, when Duff invited more than a dozen distinguished theorists to read and comment on an earlier draft of this manuscript. Written responses were presented by Sandra Marshall, Scott Veich, James Chalmers, Bob Sullivan, Rowan Cruft, Victor Tadros, and Bjarke Viskum. Unsurprisingly, the most significant insights at that colloquium—both verbal and written—were contributed by Duff himself. It is hard to see how any author could be more indebted to a professional colleague (and friend).

I received enormous assistance from the following commentators, each of whom generously read versions of the entire manuscript: Hugh LaFollette, Roger Shiner, Andrew von Hirsch, Antony Duff (again), Kim Ferzan, Kevin Michaels, and Ken Levy. The latter two scholars were exceptionally careful, calling my attention to mistakes both large and small. I hope these readers recognize the places where their input made a difference to the final draft. I received valuable suggestions on parts of the manuscript from numerous scholars, including Saul Smilansky and Don Regan. Chris Clarkson and Kimberley Brownlee prepared written comments on a chapter I presented at the British Academy in London in January 2007. J. J. Prescott made a response to a version I presented at the University of Michigan Law School. The influence of the late Joel Feinberg should be evident from my style of exposition and reluctance to engage in deep theory. I also thank the audiences in the several colleges and universities at which drafts of this book were presented, as well as students in my seminars in criminal law theory at the Rutgers University Department of Philosophy and the University of Michigan School of Law.

Finally, I acknowledge the support and patience of Linda, the love of my life.

Contents

Overcriminalization

1

The Amount of Criminal Law

The two most distinctive characteristics of both federal and state systems of criminal justice in the United States during the past several years are the dramatic expansion in the substantive criminal law and the extraordinary rise in the use of punishment. My primary interest in this book is with the first of these features: the explosive growth in the size and scope of the criminal law. In short, the most pressing problem with the criminal law today is that we have too much of it. My ultimate ambition is to formulate a *theory of criminalization:* a normative framework to distinguish those criminal laws that are justified from those that are not. Applications of this theory provide a principled basis to reverse the trend toward enacting too many criminal laws. Overcriminalization is pernicious for several reasons I will mention briefly, but the most important of these reasons requires a discussion of the second of the foregoing developments: the massive increase in state punishment. I argue that overcriminalization is objectionable mainly because it produces too much punishment. The central problem with punishment is analogous to the central problem with the criminal law: We have too much of it. I say that we inflict *too much* punishment because many of these punishments are unjust. Punishments may be unjust on different grounds. Most commentators agree that many of the punishments imposed in the United States today are unjust because they are excessive—even when they are imposed for conduct that every reasonable person believes our criminal codes should proscribe. But we also have a great deal of unjust punishment for a more basic reason. A substantial amount of contemporary punishments are unjust because they are inflicted for conduct that should not have been criminalized at all. Or so I will argue.

This chapter contains four sections that show why a theory of criminalization is needed. In the first, I discuss these two distinctive features of our criminal justice system seriatim. We have lots of punishment and lots of criminal law. Although we have enormous amounts of both, we cannot say whether we have *too much* punishment or criminal law without a normative theory to tell us which punishments and criminal laws and justified. I defend a theory to help decide such matters in chapters 2 and 3. At present, I make only a presumptive and intuitive case for my thesis by showing that we have more punishment and more criminal law than seems sensible—and more than at other times or in other places. In the second section, I examine the complex relationship between these two phenomena. Expansions in the criminal law increase levels of punishment in obvious ways: by attaching criminal sanctions to conduct that had been permissible. But the process by which more criminal laws result in more punishments is not always straightforward. More criminal laws cause more punishments because of realities about the penal process that legal philosophers frequently ignore. In the third section, I provide examples of dubious criminal laws and produce a rough classification of some of the new types of offense that legislatures have enacted. Unless a theory of criminalization is to be applied statute by statute, we need to understand the *kinds* of law to which this theory will be applied. In the fourth and final section, I focus in detail on a specific example of how more criminal law produces more punishment. No case can be perfectly representative of the trends I discuss, but the illustration I select contains many of the features that should persuade us of the injustice of overcriminalization. This chapter contains relatively little normative content. But if the arguments in this chapter are sound, I will have set the stage for the normative work that follows by demonstrating the need for a theory of criminalization to help reverse our tendency to enact too many criminal laws and to punish too many persons.

I: TOO MUCH PUNISHMENT, TOO MANY CRIMES

Eventually I will conclude that we have too much punishment and too many crimes in the United States today. We overpunish and overcriminalize. To say that we have *too much* of something implies a standard or baseline by which we can decide whether that amount is too little, not enough, or exactly right. For legal philosophers, *justice* provides the relevant standard. Before defending principles of justice to support my position, however, I must be content to make a presumptive and intuitive case in its favor by showing that we have extraordinarily high levels of punishment and tremendous amounts of criminal law. The fact that we have so much punishment and so many criminal laws is crucial in helping us to appreciate both the enormity and the urgency of the normative task before us. Reasonable persons should anticipate that levels of punishment and amounts of criminal law on this massive scale will prove impossible to justify.

I begin with a brief account of the extent of punishment in the United States today, as data about our punitive practices are widely publicized by contemporary criminologists and are relatively easy to comprehend. Rates of incarceration provide the most familiar measure of the scale of state punishment. About 2.2 million persons were locked up in federal and state jails and prisons in 2005, a rate of 737 inmates per 100,000 residents. As a result, 1 in every 138 residents is incarcerated. An estimated 1 in 20 children born in the United States is destined to serve time in a state or federal prison at some point in his life.[1] Minorities are disproportionately represented behind bars: 12.6% of all black men ages 25 to 29 are in jails or prisons, compared with 1.7% of similarly aged whites.[2]

Although rates of incarceration generally are used to measure the extent to which a society is punitive, a better indication may be the number of persons under

1. These data are drawn from the U.S. Department of Justice, Bureau of Justice Statistics: *Sourcebook of Criminal Justice Statistics* (2005), tables 6.13 and 6.29.
2. For an overview of the racial impact of criminal justice policies, see Michael Tonry: *Malign Neglect: Race, Crime, and Punishment in America* (New York: Oxford University Press, 1995).

the control and supervision of the criminal justice system—a figure that includes probation and parole. Political trends and state budgets have less impact on the number of individuals under correctional supervision, because courts must impose *some* sort of sentence on persons convicted of a crime. Our tendency to ignore probation and parole when assessing the magnitude of punishment probably reflects how accustomed we have become to our punitive policies; many citizens are under the mistaken impression that probation and parole are lenient alternatives to punishment rather than modes or kinds of punishment. In any event, the number of individuals under the control and supervision of the criminal justice system grew rapidly in the last quarter of the 20th century, and continues to grow in the first few years of the 21st. Approximately 4.2 million additional persons are currently on probation, and 784,000 are on parole in the United States—for a grand total of over 7 million.[3] These individuals are subject to incarceration if they violate the terms under which they were placed on probation or paroled.

One way to grasp the magnitude of these figures is to compare them with those at other times and places. The enormous scale of punishment in the United States today is relatively recent. Our rate of imprisonment has soared since 1970, when it stood at 144 inmates per 100,000 residents. The size of the prison population has nearly quadrupled since 1980, an expansion unprecedented in our history.[4] Comparisons with other nations tell a similar story. Although the incidence of incarceration is increasing in many places, the United States has by far the highest rate in the world—nearly five times higher than that of any other Western industrialized country. Because about 8 million people are behind bars throughout the globe, one-quarter of these are jailed or imprisoned in the United States. Probably no nation—and certainly no democracy—has ever tried to govern itself while incarcerating so high a percentage of its citizenry. Commentators have struggled to identify the social and political forces that explain what might be called United States exceptionalism: why we resort to punishment more readily than other countries generally and Western European countries in particular.[5]

The sheer number of persons under the control and supervision of the criminal justice system reveals only part of what is worrisome about our tendency to overcriminalize. Contemporary punishment not only is commonplace in the United States but also is distinctive in its harshness relative to Western European countries. Even at its best, prison life is boring and empty, and overcrowding has made many aspects of incarceration worse. Inmates are assaulted by guards and by other inmates, and homosexual rape is not uncommon.[6] Prisoners retain virtually no

---

3. *Sourcebook: op. cit.*, note 1, table 6.1.

4. Admittedly, one explanation for our historically high rate of incarceration is the fact that institutionalization of the mentally ill is much less routine than in previous eras. See Bernard E. Harcourt: "Should We Aggregate Mental Hospitalization and Prison Population Rates in Empirical Research on the Relationship between Incarceration and Crime, Unemployment, Poverty, and Other Social Indicators?" (forthcoming, available at *http://ssrn.com/abstract_id=880129*).

5. For one such attempt, see James Q. Whitman: *Harsh Justice: Criminal Punishment and the Widening Divide between America and Europe* (Oxford: Oxford University Press, 2003).

6. See Mary Sigler: "By the Light of Virtue: Prison Rape and the Corruption of Character," 91 *Iowa Law Review* 561 (2006).

privacy rights.[7] The unwillingness of citizens to support penal reforms indicates that they welcome or at least tolerate these deplorable conditions as part of the sentence itself. Prison rape, for example, is likely to elicit sarcasm in social circles that express horror at sexual abuse in the outside world.[8]

Between 600,000 and 700,000 inmates are released from prison each year, but the negative effects of their punishments do not end at this time. Ex-offenders lose political, economic, and social rights.[9] Approximately 4 million such persons are currently disqualified from voting; several states also deem them ineligible to be elected to public office or to serve as jurors. Many of these individuals are explicitly denied benefits under welfare and entitlement programs. Ex-offenders face difficulties finding employment and housing. They emerge from prison with financial debts, as increasing numbers of states attempt to offset the expense of operating their criminal justice system by requiring defendants to pay for the costs of trying, incarcerating, and monitoring them.[10] Each of these collateral consequences retards reintegration into society and helps to spin the revolving doors of justice. Almost two-thirds of all ex-offenders convicted in state court are rearrested within three years, and one-third return to prison because of parole violations.

Almost everyone regards punishment as a *necessary* evil. Indeed, some quantum of punishment *is* necessary. But is the vast amount of punishment we inflict really necessary to achieve a greater social good—like crime reduction? Before we become outraged by our eagerness to punish, we must remember that crime remains at unacceptable levels throughout the United States today. Crime exacts a terrible toll both on its victims and on society generally. Still, it is a myth to suppose that we need more punishment than other countries because we suffer from more crime. International crime victim surveys indicate that our offense rates since the 1990s have not tended to be higher than those in other Western countries. *Violent* crime is more prevalent in the United States, although a few other countries suffer from levels that are roughly comparable.[11]

Admittedly, crime rates have plummeted overall since 1992, although no theory has attracted a consensus about why this is so.[12] Even though many laypersons regard the causal link between increased amounts of punishment and decreased amounts of crime as obvious, few criminologists are persuaded that the former has had a major impact on the latter. Most conclude that the policies implemented by our criminal justice system, including increasingly severe sentences, can explain only a small

7. See Donald T. Kramer, et al., eds.: *Rights of Prisoners* (Colorado Springs: McGraw-Hill, 2nd ed., 1993).

8. California Attorney General Bill Lockyer openly joked that he would "love to personally escort [Enron Chairman Kenneth Lay] to an eight-by-ten cell that he could share with a tattooed dude who says, 'Hi, my name is Spike, honey.'" See "Investigating Enron," *Wall Street Journal* (November 30, 2001), p.A14.

9. See Nora V. Demleitner: "Preventing Internal Exile: The Need for Restrictions on Collateral Sentencing Consequences," 11 *Stanford Law & Policy Review* 153 (1999).

10. See Adam Liptak: "Debt to Society Is Least of Costs for Ex-Convicts," *New York Times* (Feb. 23, 2006), p.A1.

11. See Franklin E. Zimring and Gordon Hawkins: *Crime Is Not the Problem: Lethal Violence in America* (New York: Oxford University Press, 1997).

12. For a useful survey of competitive explanations, see Alfred Blumstein and Joel Wallman, eds.: *The Crime Drop in America* (Cambridge: Cambridge University Press, 2000); see also Franklin E. Zimring: *The Great American Crime Decline* (Oxford: Oxford University Press, 2006).

part of the dramatic crime drop in the United States during the past several years. Perhaps the best reason to be skeptical that lengthier punishments have played a central role is the fact that similar decreases in crime have occurred throughout the entire Western industrialized world, yet only the United States has substantially increased its quantum of punishment.[13] Even in the United States, crime rates have fallen just as much in those jurisdictions that have not increased the size of their prison populations so dramatically. Nor are significant amounts of crime prevented by incapacitation, as repeat offenders who become eligible for long sentences tend to be well beyond the age at which they commit the most crimes.[14] Despite initial appearances, these findings may not be counterintuitive. Social scientists have amassed a wealth of evidence to show that people are law-abiding mainly because they internalize social norms, not because they are deterred by their fear of arrest and prosecution.[15] It is hard to see how the immense amount of punishment we inflict could be necessary to achieve a greater social good.

If the extraordinary amount of punishment we impose is not a necessary evil, is it an evil at all? According to utilitarians such as Jeremy Bentham, *all* punishment is an evil.[16] I join retributivists, however, in holding the controversial proposition that deserved punishments are *not* an all-things-considered evil. As I tentatively suggest in chapter 2, deserved punishments implicate but do not violate our rights; no net evil is perpetrated when persons are treated as they deserve. But punishment is deserved only when it is just, and my ambition is to demonstrate that a great many of the punishments we impose are *un*just. Of course, any theory of just and unjust punishments is bound to generate disagreement. In case readers are less persuaded by normative than by economic arguments, it is worth noting that principles of justice are not the only ground on which to oppose the recent growth in rates of incarceration.[17] Commentators who prefer to assess social institutions in terms of their costs and benefits should be equally appalled by the extent of punishment in the United States today, as the price tag of our criminal justice system should disturb any taxpayer who demands to get his money's worth. The cost of federal and state prisons in 2003 was over $185 billion.[18] When the collateral costs on prisoners, their families, and their communities are included in the equation, the money expended on our punitive policies is astronomical. No social benefit can justify this staggering expenditure of resources.

These economic considerations will play only a minor role in the arguments I develop throughout this book. My central focus is on the *injustice* rather than the cost of overcriminalization. Still, no one should underestimate the importance of economic factors in shaping—and ultimately in changing—our policies. Legal philosophers may join me in protesting against injustice, but I predict that the

13. See Michael Tonry: *Thinking about Crime: Sense and Sensibility in American Penal Culture* (New York: Oxford University Press, 2004), p.33.
14. See Daniel S. Nagin: "Deterrence and Incapacitation," in Michael Tonry, ed.: *The Handbook of Crime and Punishment* (Oxford: Oxford University Press, 1998), p.345.
15. See Tom Tyler: *Why People Obey the Law* (New Haven: Yale University Press, 1990).
16. Jeremy Bentham: *Principles of Morals and Legislation* (London: Methuen, 1970), p.158.
17. See Louis Kaplow and Steven Shavell: *Fairness versus Welfare* (Cambridge: Harvard University Press, 2002).
18. See *Sourcebook: op. cit.*, note 1, table 1.1 (2003).

exorbitant costs of our punitive practices will prove to be the more decisive factor in eventually reforming our criminal justice system.[19] It is surprising that more of these changes have not already taken place. Remarkably, our penal policies seem to be immune from the cost-benefit scrutiny that is routinely applied to many other state institutions. Perhaps we must suffer from a major economic recession before we will make significant improvements in our criminal justice system.

In contrast to these familiar statistics about the increase in state punishment throughout the United States, comparable data about the growth of the substantive criminal law are much harder to present and evaluate. The extent of criminalization (and thus of overcriminalization) is largely a function of the breadth or reach of the criminal law, and we have no simple way to measure this variable at a given time or place. That is, no statistic can express whether or to what extent one jurisdiction criminalizes more or less than another.[20] This determination would be possible in extreme cases—as when the prohibitions of one society are a subset of those in another. But in all cases in the real world, no single metric of criminalization exists. Suppose, for example, one country proscribes sodomy but permits the use of alcohol, and a second has the opposite set of laws. Which country has more criminalization? As far as I can see, there is no "right answer" to this question. It is not even clear what additional information might be helpful in trying to resolve it. Might we attempt to decide which of these two societies contains more criminalization by counting the number of people who would like to engage in given illegal behaviors but for their prohibition? Would the strength of their preferences be relevant as well? These variables, at least, might be quantified. But a difficulty with this purported solution is apparent. Existing law shapes the extent and strength of our preferences. One would anticipate that the number of people who like to consume given substances, and the strength of their desire to do so, would be affected by whether this conduct was presently legal or illegal. This same difficulty prevents outsiders from making authoritative judgments about the extent of criminalization in a foreign land.

I do not doubt that political philosophers might defend a normative theory of human rights, an account of what is important to human flourishing, or the like. We can identify states that have better or worse records in using the criminal law to violate whatever interests we take to be central or fundamental. Although all such views are controversial, that is not the main obstacle to using them to measure the extent of criminalization in a given time or place. To my mind, the greater barrier is that relatively little of the conduct proscribed by criminal laws is directly protected by a plausible theory of human rights. Two states can be equally good (or bad) in preserving human rights, even though one contains substantially more criminal law than the other.

---

19. When legislators are made to understand the costs of different punitive policies, they are less likely to prefer sentencing severity. See Rachel E. Barkow: "Administering Crime," 52 *UCLA Law Review* 715 (2005).

20. For an early attempt to gauge the degree of criminalization, see Donald Black: *The Behavior of Law* (London: Academic Press, 1976). For a more recent effort, see Geraldine Szott Moohr: "Defining Overcriminalization Through Cost-Benefit Analysis: The Example of Criminal Copyright Laws," 54 *American University Law Review* 783 (2005).

Without a metric to quantify the degree of criminalization, the sheer number of criminal statutes is often taken to be a surrogate for it. But the volume of criminal statutes, although clearly relevant to my inquiry, is a very imperfect measure of the amount of criminalization. In the first place, it is doubtful that the number of distinct statutes in a jurisdiction maps on to the number of distinct crimes it contains. To illustrate the distinction between the number of crimes and the number of statutes, consider the most frequently enforced law in our federal code today: that pertaining to controlled substances. Intuitively, I suspect that laypersons would regard the distribution of marijuana, for example, as a different crime from the distribution of heroin. One might naturally suppose that the former activity would breach a different statute than the latter. In fact, however, both the distribution of marijuana and the distribution of heroin violate the very same statute. Suppose, however, that a jurisdiction enacted separate laws to proscribe the distribution of each substance it bans. The number of statutes would multiply exponentially, although no more criminalization would result. I doubt that we should say the latter jurisdiction contained more *crimes*, or *criminalized* more than the former. It has created more statutes but has not changed the scope of the conduct prohibited.

Further difficulties arise if we take the number of statutes to be a crude approximation of the amount of criminalization. Surprisingly, no one seems prepared to estimate the number of criminal statutes that currently exist in the United States. This fact alone is cause for alarm. Although the criminal codes of most states gained some semblance of order in the 1960s and 1970s when they became patterned after the influential Model Penal Code, they have steadily deteriorated ever since. Still, they are far more systematic than what is loosely called the Federal Criminal Code, which can only be described as an incoherent mess.[21] It is hard to exaggerate the complete lack of structure in federal law. No instructor's manual for a complex technological gadget can begin to rival the unintelligibility of federal penal law. Ronald Gainer, once Associate Deputy Attorney General in the Department of Justice, describes the current state of federal criminal law as follows:

> Federal statutory law today is set forth in the 50 titles of the United States Code. Those 50 titles encompass roughly 27,000 pages of printed text. Within those 27,000 pages, there appear approximately 3,300 separate provisions that carry criminal sanctions for their violation. Over 1,200 of those provisions are found jumbled together in Title 18, euphemistically referred to as the "Federal Criminal Code."[22]

To compound the problem, many of the most serious federal offenses do not appear in the Federal Criminal Code. Major espionage offenses, for example, are

---

21. The so-called Code is aptly described as a "national disgrace" by Julie R. O'Sullivan: "The Changing Face of White-Collar Crime: The Federal Criminal 'Code' Is a Disgrace: Obstruction Statutes as Case Study," 96 *Journal of Criminal Law and Criminology* 643, 643 (2006).
22. Ronald Gainer: "Federal Criminal Code Reform: Past and Future," 2 *Buffalo Criminal Law Review* 45, 53 (1998).

buried in the midst of regulations pertaining to atomic energy.[23] Federal offenses are hard to find or enumerate. And the situation gets worse each month.

Some commentators hazard greater estimates of the number of federal crimes than Gainer. According to one theorist, approximately 300,000 federal regulations are enforceable through civil or criminal sanctions by the combined efforts of as many as 200 different agencies.[24] New regulations are routinely followed by perfunctory language that indicates that any person who fails to comply is subject to criminal prosecution. The factors that lead regulators to seek criminal rather than civil sanctions when legal rules are broken remain a source of controversy and uncertainty.[25] But whatever the exact numbers of criminal offenses may be, the figure is bound to rise before it falls. Criminal laws are relatively easy to enact but far more difficult to repeal. A criminal statute is more likely to fall into desuetude than to be removed by a deliberate legislative act, as the publicity that would be generated by the prospects of repeal might galvanize whatever support remains in its favor.[26] In any event, counting the number of statutes tends to understate the explosive growth in the scope of the criminal law. Because much of the recent expansion consists in amendments to existing statutes (and, as we will see, may be located outside criminal codes altogether), we cannot meaningfully say that the number of crimes has doubled, tripled, or multiplied tenfold.[27]

Despite the formidable difficulties in measuring the extent of criminalization, we can count the words or pages in criminal codes to illustrate the trend. Paul Robinson and Michael Cahill employ this method to demonstrate the expansion in the criminal code of Illinois—even though commentators (including Robinson himself) tend to rank the overall quality of this state code as well above average.[28] When enacted in 1961, the Illinois Code contained less than 24,000 words. By 2003, that number had swelled to more than 136,000—a sixfold increase in only 42 years.[29] To be sure, greater verbosity does not guarantee that the criminal sphere is expanding. More words may indicate that the scope of liability has narrowed, because offenses may be described with greater specificity. Thus they cover less behavior, even though they contain more words. Conversely, the net of liability can be widened without adding any words—or even without adding any new offenses. More criminalization can result if the

23. *Id.*, p.66.

24. This estimate is attributed to Stanley Arkin in John C. Coffee: "Does 'Unlawful' Mean 'Criminal'?: Reflections on the Disappearing Tort/Crime Distinction in American Law," 71 *Boston University Law Review* 193, 216 n.94 (1991).

25. For a useful study, see Keith Hawkins: *Law as Last Resort: Prosecution Decision-Making in a Regulatory Agency* (Oxford: Oxford University Press, 2002).

26. See Note: "Desuetude," 119 *Harvard Law Review* 2209 (2006).

27. "The amendment process has increasingly degraded American criminal codes." Paul H. Robinson and Michael T. Cahill: "Can a Model Penal Code Second Save the States from Themselves? 1 *Ohio State Journal of Criminal Law* 169, 170 (2003).

28. Paul H. Robinson, et al: "The Five Worst (and Five Best) American Criminal Codes," 95 *Northwestern University Law Review* 1 (2000).

29. Robinson and Cahill: *op. cit.*, note 27, p.172 n.16.

judiciary decides to expand the interpretation of existing offenses.[30] Through this process, greater criminalization may ensue without any legislative action at all.[31]

In fact, the most notorious example of overcriminalization in the past century required painfully few words. The infamous "principle of analogy" in the Soviet Union under Stalin provided "if any socially dangerous act is not directly provided for by the present Code, the basis and limits of responsibility for it shall be determined by application of those articles of the Code which provide for crimes most similar to it in nature."[32] Pursuant to this law, any "socially dangerous act" became a crime. As this example demonstrates, overcriminalization can be a consequence of a single statute. Nothing quite so draconian has taken place in the United States.[33] My general point is that an increase in the number of words contained in criminal codes is but one of many imperfect measures of the unmistakable trend toward greater criminalization. No one figure can tell an accurate story about the size and scope of the criminal law.[34]

Despite the imprecision in quantifying the phenomenon, we have many reasons to be concerned about our tendency to enact so many criminal laws and to punish so much behavior. Only one of these reasons is the central focus of this book, but a comprehensive discussion of overcriminalization would examine several others. I give them only brief attention here. First, commentators have long emphasized the importance of placing prospective defendants on *notice* about whether their conduct is criminal. Persons should not be forced to guess at their peril about whether their behavior has been proscribed, and must be afforded a fair opportunity to refrain from whatever conduct will incur penal liability.[35] Because of the number and complexity of criminal statutes, however, potential lawbreakers may not receive adequate notice of their legal obligations.[36] Law exists largely to guide behavior, but this objective is undermined in our climate of overcriminalization. Who among us

30. *State in the Interest of M.T.S.*, 609 A.2d 1266 (1992), provides one example. A New Jersey sexual assault statute proscribed acts of sexual penetration in which the actor uses physical force or coercion. This statute was interpreted (or reinterpreted) so that its elements were satisfied by any act of nonconsensual sexual penetration, effectively eliminating force as an independent statutory requirement.

Other illustrations of novel statutory interpretation produce grossly disproportionate punishments. In *Michigan v. Waltonen*, 728 n.w.2d 881 (2006), a statute proscribing first-degree criminal sexual conduct whenever "sexual penetration occurs under circumstances involving the commission of any other felony" was construed to authorize a sentence of up to life imprisonment when a man committed adultery by inducing a married woman to engage in consensual sex by giving her Oxycontin pills. Michigan's Supreme Court has held that it is for the legislature, not the courts, to decide when statutory interpretation produces an absurd result.

31. The contribution expansive judicial interpretations of existing statutes makes to the phenomenon of overcriminalization has led some commentators to argue for a rule of lenity in construing criminal statutes. See Zachary Price: "The Rule of Lenity as a Rule of Structure," 72 *Fordham Law Review* 885 (2004).

32. See Harold Berman: *Soviet Criminal Law and Procedure* (Cambridge: Harvard University Press, 2nd ed., 1972), p.22.

33. For a rough analogue in Anglo-American law, consider the common-law offense of "conspiracy to corrupt public morals" as discussed in *Shaw v. DPP,* [1962] A.C. 220.

34. Thus some commentators allege that complaints about overcriminalization suffer from the "I know it when I see it" syndrome. See Moohr: *op. cit.*, note 20, p.784.

35. See *Papachristou v. City of Jacksonville*, 405 U.S. 156 (1972).

36. See Susan Pilcher: "Ignorance, Discretion and the Fairness of Notice: Confronting 'Apparent Innocence' in the Criminal Law," 33 *American Criminal Law Review* 32 (1995).

can pretend to understand the language of criminal offenses? State and federal law have come to resemble the tax code, which is beyond the comprehension of laypersons and can be navigated only with the assistance of a skilled attorney. All too often, expertise is unhelpful in fathoming the contents of the criminal law. Because of the phenomenal growth in the number of offenses, even professors and practicing attorneys who have spent most of their careers wrestling with the intricacies of the criminal law are familiar with only a fraction of the statutes to which we are subject. In the wake of this confusion and uncertainty, the need for a defense of ignorance of law becomes imperative—a defense that would be unnecessary if almost everyone could be expected to know the laws that apply to them.[37] No reasonable person can pretend that this development is for the better.

In addition, our expanding criminal justice system incurs massive opportunity costs. Is there no better use for the enormous resources we expend on criminalization and punishment? Money and manpower are diverted from more urgent needs when police, prosecutors, and courts enforce laws that our best theory of criminalization would not justify. These resources could be to reduce taxes, improve schools, or prevent the crimes we really care about.[38] Criminal justice expenditures in large states such as California already outstrip funding for public education. Except for those who profit from the "prison-industrial complex," everyone agrees that these priorities are misplaced.[39]

Some commentators speculate that lack of respect for law constitutes the most pernicious consequence of overcriminalization. Particular rules and regulations perceived to be stupid are ignored or circumvented by law-abiding citizens. The impact probably extends beyond the single law in question. One would expect public confidence in our entire criminal justice system to wane when individuals are punished for violating laws that a sizable percentage of the citizenry deems to be unfair. Although ample anecdotal evidence supports this hypothesis, the claim that overcriminalization breeds general disrespect for law is surprisingly difficult to confirm empirically. We cannot perform a controlled experiment in which we compare the amount of respect for law in two jurisdictions that differ only in the amount of criminal law they contain. But it is clear that punishments deter partly through the stigmatizing effects of a criminal conviction. Stigma, however, is a scarce resource that dissipates quickly. The state cannot effectively stigmatize persons for engaging in conduct that few condemn and most everyone performs.[40] As the scope of criminal liability expands, stigma is depleted and deterrence most likely is eroded.

---

37. See Douglas Husak and Andrew von Hirsch: "Culpability and Mistake of Law," in Stephen Shute, John Gardner, and Jeremy Horder, eds.: *Action and Value in Criminal Law* (Oxford: Clarendon Press, 1993), p.157. Reasonable mistakes about the content of statutes are so pervasive that one commentator has suggested that ignorance of law might be a justification rather than an excuse. See Re'em Segev: "Justification, Rationality and Mistake: Mistake of Law Is No Excuse? It Might Be a Justification!" 25 *Law and Philosophy* 31 (2006).
38. See Alexander Natapoff: "Underenforcement," 75 *Fordham Law Review* 1715 (2006). Clearly, the phenomenon of underenforcement is more prevalent for some offenses than for others. For example, only six persons have been convicted of perjury for lying to Congress in the last sixty years. See P.J. Meitl: "The Perjury Paradox: The Amazing Under-Enforcement of the Laws Regarding Lying to Congress," 25 *Quinnipiac Law Review* 547 (2007).
39. See Joel Dwyer: *The Perpetual Prison Machine* (Boulder: Westview, 2000).
40. See Douglas Husak: "The 'But Everybody Does That!' Defense," 10 *Public Affairs Quarterly* 307 (1996).

Moreover, the growth in the scope of the criminal law is worrisome even when it does not culminate in conviction and punishment. The number and scope of criminal laws provide police with increased powers to arrest—powers that were exercised on some 14 million occasions in 2004.[41] Arrest shares with punishment many of the features that make the latter so difficult to justify. Even when defendants are not prosecuted, the experience of arrest is embarrassing, costly and inconvenient. The opportunity for unjustified arrests is among the factors that have led courts to find vagrancy and loitering statutes to be unconstitutional. The lives of ordinary citizens are more likely to be unfairly disrupted in any jurisdiction guilty of overcriminalization.[42]

Finally, the increase in criminalization is destructive of the rule of law itself—an important point to which I will return on several occasions. At this time, I mention just one of many ways—by no means the most important—that the quantity of criminal law undermines the principle of legality. Legal theorists typically construe the rule of law to require that criminal statutes be enacted by legislatures and contain an exhaustive description of the conduct proscribed.[43] Increasingly, however, the behavior that is prohibited cannot be ascertained without straying beyond the boundaries of criminal statutes and examining noncriminal laws. In other words, the criminal law *outsources*. I provide just two examples of the need to look beyond criminal codes to identify the content of offenses. First, consider the circumstances under which persons are criminally liable for their *omissions*. Although the Model Penal Code stipulates that "no conduct constitutes an offense unless it is a crime or violation under this Code or another statute of this State,"[44] it subsequently provides that persons may be criminally liable for a failure to act when "a duty to perform the omitted act is otherwise imposed by law."[45] Contract and tort law may provide the source of the duty that is "otherwise imposed." As a result, expansions in the domains of noncriminal law can (and do) enlarge the boundaries of the criminal law as well. Next, consider the countless *possession* offenses contained in criminal codes, such as those that pertain to controlled substances. The public health law, and not the criminal code itself, often specifies whether a particular substance is controlled.[46] Thus amendments to noncriminal laws can (and do) alter the content of the criminal law. Although other examples could be provided,[47] liability for both omissions and possession demonstrates how increasing criminalization jeopardizes the rule of law itself.

41. *Sourcebook: op. cit.*, note 1, table 4.1 (2004).

42. For a nice discussion of how unenforced criminal statutes can have a significant impact in civil law—especially family law—see Hillary Green: "Undead Laws: The Use of Historically Unenforced Criminal Statutes in Non-Criminal Legislation," 16 *Yale Law and Policy Review* 169 (1997).

43. For a critical assessment of the principle of legality in criminal law, see Peter Westen: "Two Rules of Legality in Criminal Law," 26 *Law and Philosophy* 229 (2007).

44. Model Penal Code, §1.05(1).

45. Model Penal Code, §2.01(3)(b).

46. See Markus Dirk Dubber: "The Possession Paradigm: The Special Part and the Police Power Model of the Criminal Process," in Antony Duff and Stuart Green, eds.: *Defining Crimes: Essays on the Special Part of the Criminal Law* (Oxford: Oxford University Press, 2005), p.91.

47. See Paul H. Robinson and Michael T. Cahill: "The Accelerating Degradation of American Criminal Codes," 56 *Hastings Law Journal* 633 (2005).

For each of these reasons (and for many others as well), the phenomenon of overcriminalization should trouble us all. Because the foregoing problems can be so important, I do not allege that excessive punishment is *necessarily* the central objection to overcriminalization. The connection between these two phenomena is contingent. Perhaps my concerns reflect the peculiar American penal context, characterized by its striking reliance on imprisonment. One could easily imagine a regime in which sentences were generally less severe and normally noncustodial, and where the stigma of a criminal conviction was relatively mild when minor offenses are committed. Overcriminalization would still be worrisome for the reasons on which I focus. In such a system, however, other grounds for objecting to this phenomenon would become more salient: for instance, the freedom-limiting, anxiety-producing, and guilt-inducing effects the criminal law may have on those who take its demands seriously, even apart from the threat of punishment. Increased criminalization can deter lawful and even commendable behavior on the margins of the conduct the state intends to prohibit. These factors make overcriminalization troublesome everywhere.

In our current political climate, however, I maintain that overcriminalization is objectionable principally because it produces too much punishment. Thus my foremost complaint is different from those I have briefly described. My central concern is that overcriminalization results in unjust punishments. The primary victims of this injustice are the persons who incur penal liability. That is, the main problem with overcriminalization derives from its impact on those who are punished, rather than from its effects on taxpayers, our culture of compliance, the rule of law, or society generally. Injustice is most glaring when defendants are sentenced for conduct that should not have given rise to criminal liability at all—in other words, when punishments are imposed for conduct that fails to satisfy our best theory of criminalization. If the central argument in this book is correct, a great many of the punishments inflicted in the United States today are unjust according to this criterion.

Overcriminalization often causes substantial injustice even to persons who deserve some degree of punishment for their behavior. An adequate theory of criminalization should include a *principle of proportionality,* according to which the severity of the sentence should be a function of the seriousness of the crime. Injustice occurs when punishments are disproportionate, exceeding what the offender deserves. I claim that overcriminalization frequently produces disproportionate punishments, although this contention will be more difficult to substantiate. No one should profess to know how to *anchor* a penalty scale—how to assign the precise quantum of punishment deserved by particular offenders who commit given offenses such as larceny or rape.[48] Perhaps for this reason, except when the death penalty is at stake, courts have all but abandoned attempts to preclude excessive punishments by applying a principle of proportionality.[49] By any reasonable measure, however, the absence of an effective principle of proportionality has

48. For a discussion of difficulties in anchoring a penalty scale, see Andrew von Hirsch and Andrew Ashworth: *Proportionate Sentencing* (Oxford: Oxford University Press, 2005), pp.141–143.
49. See Youngjae Lee: "The Constitutional Right Against Excessive Punishment," 91 *University of Virginia Law Review* 677 (2005).

produced shocking injustices, and overcriminalization has contributed to these results. I argue that overcriminalization makes disproportionate punishments all but inevitable, however we resolve the formidable problem of anchoring our penalty scale. If my allegations are correct, too much criminal law produces too much punishment. The main reason we should care about this phenomenon is because we should care about injustice and its victims.

Why do we punish so many and criminalize so much? These phenomena are puzzling, because they have come at a time when conventional wisdom favors lesser amounts of governmental intervention. If we hope to reverse these pernicious trends, we must try to understand the forces that have helped to create and sustain them. An adequate account should contain two parts: First, it must identify the sociopolitical factors that have caused our predicament. Second, it must explain why academic commentators have been relatively silent about our plight. I briefly discuss the first matter here and return to the lack of scholarly interest in this topic in chapter 2.

As I have indicated, criminologists debate the empirical realities that contribute to our current situation.[50] Although no consensus has emerged, a hodgepodge of loosely related factors is worth mentioning briefly. Commentators uniformly complain about the extent to which criminal justice in the United States has become *politicized*.[51] The highly democratic character of criminal justice in the United States is the cause of many of its best and worst features.[52] For example, nowhere else do legislatures micromanage decisions about sentencing and parole, and few other Western industrialized countries elect their prosecutors or judges.[53] The input of academic experts rarely is solicited and is likely to be ignored on those few occasions when it is sought.[54] We tend to be unilateralists about criminal justice; we neither know nor care about the successes and failures of other countries, and we feel no need to defend our policies to those who disagree with us.[55] In addition, the extraordinary focus on capital punishment in the United States distracts attention from draconian practices that fall short of the death penalty.[56] Perhaps most important, neither political party has been willing to allow the other to earn the reputation of being tougher on crime. Legislators hope to

50. Older mechanisms of social control have broken down, creating more pressures for criminal sanctions. See David Garland: *Mass Imprisonment in the United States: Social Causes and Consequences* (London: Sage, 2001).

51. See, for example, Sara Sun Beale: "What's Law Got to Do With It? The Political, Social, Psychological and Other Non-Legal Factors Influencing the Development of (Federal) Criminal Law," 1 *Buffalo Criminal Law Review* 23 (1997); Marie Gottschalk: *The Prison and the Gallows: The Politics of Mass Incarceration in America* (New York: Cambridge University Press, 2006); and Sara Sun Beale: "The News Media's Influence on Criminal Justice Policy: How Market-Driven News Promotes Punitiveness," 48 *William & Mary Law Review* 397 (2006).

52. See Samuel Walker: *Popular Justice: A History of American Criminal Justice* (New York: Oxford University Press, 2nd ed., 1999), p.6.

53. Tonry: *op. cit.*, note 13, p.10.

54. "Policy makers in the field of criminal justice should pay more attention to academic criticism." George Fletcher: "The Fall and Rise of Criminal Theory," 1 *Buffalo Criminal Law Review*," 275, 281 (1998).

55. Continental scholars have written more about overcriminalization. See, for example, Nils Jareborg: "What Kind of Criminal Law Do We Want?" in Annika Snare, ed.: *Beware of Punishment* (Oslo: Scandanavian Research Council for Criminology, 1995), p.17.

56. See Dirk van Zyl Smit: *Taking Life Imprisonment Seriously* (The Hague: Kluwer Law International, 2002).

be perceived as "doing something" to combat unwanted behaviors. Tabloids and the popular media thrive on accounts of how offenders "get away" with crime by escaping through loopholes and technicalities. Policies are enacted most easily when they are unopposed, and no significant organization wants to represent the "crime lobby" by protesting our eagerness to resort to criminalization and punishment.[57] Apart from these few random observations, I propose to leave to sociologists and political scientists the surprisingly difficult task of identifying the empirical forces that have led us to punish so many and to criminalize so much. I am more concerned to understand these developments from the perspective of a legal philosopher. In chapter 2, I attempt to explain why academic commentators have tended to neglect our predicament.

Throughout this book, my complaints about too much crime and too much punishment frequently refer to a specific example—the crime of illicit drug possession.[58] I select this example for a simple reason. At the present time, drug offenses constitute the single most important manifestation of our tendency to criminalize too much and to punish too many.[59] A few statistics tell the story. In 2004, approximately 1,745,000 persons were arrested for drug offenses in the United States.[60] About 82% of these were arrested for simple possession.[61] Over 410,000 drug offenders are in jails and prisons across the country—about the same number as the entire prison population in 1980.[62] Nearly one of every five prisoners in America is behind bars for a nonviolent drug offense.[63] This figure has climbed dramatically. In 1986, about 18 of every 100,000 American citizens were imprisoned for a drug offense; that ratio had jumped to 63 a decade later.[64] Persons convicted of drug trafficking account for about 16% of all offenders serving a life sentence. A theory of criminalization has the potential to bring about major reforms in our treatment of drug offenders, with ramifications that would echo throughout the entire system of criminal justice.

To a lesser extent, I focus on gun control. My reasons for selecting this example are very different. Several commentators believe our regime of gun control is woefully inadequate to protect innocent persons from the harms caused by guns, and they favor massive expansions in the criminal law to punish gun owners. Many

---

57. Nonetheless, we should not be quick to conclude that the United States adopts its harsh policies because voters demand them. By 2006, less than 1% of Americans named crime as their top political concern. On this issue, politicians have tended to lead rather than to follow public opinion. In fact, most citizens are remarkably uninformed about the trends I have described. They grossly underestimate the extent of punishments that are imposed and favor greater moderation when educated about the true degree of sentencing severity. See Julian V. Roberts, et al.: *Penal Populism and Public Opinion* (New York: Oxford University Press, 2002).
58. 21 U.S.C. §841(a) (2002). State laws proscribe the same conduct.
59. Drug offenses clearly play this role in the United States, but other examples may provide better illustrations of overcriminalization in other countries. In the United Kingdom, for example, anti-social behavior orders (ASBOs) are a troubling development. These orders extend the reach of the criminal law by making it a criminal offense to breach the terms of what is supposedly not a criminal order. See the several essays in Andrew Simester and Andrew von Hirsch, eds.: *Incivilities: Regulating Offensive Behaviour* (Oxford: Hart Pub. Co., 2006).
60. *Sourcebook: op. cit.*, note 1, table 4.1 (2004).
61. *Id.*, table 4.29.
62. *Id.*, tables 6.0001 and 6.56.
63. *Id.*
64. *Id.*, table 6.30.

reasonable politicians, like former Senator Chafee of Rhode Island, would ban the manufacture, sale, and home possession of all handguns within the United States.[65] This suggestion is not heretical. About 35% of the American public favors a law that would ban the possession of handguns, except by the police or other authorized persons.[66] These proposals would cause a nearly unprecedented expansion in the volume of conduct subjected to criminal liability, as firearms are possessed in about 40% of households throughout the United States today.[67]

Many citizens who enthusiastically favor criminal laws to punish illicit drug users vehemently oppose criminal laws to punish gun possession. The converse is true as well. Many persons who are critical of criminal laws against drug users believe the state should do more to punish gun owners. Principled reservations about employing the criminal sanction in these areas cut across conventional ideological divides. Liberals and conservatives do not really differ about *how often* the state should resort to punishment; instead, they disagree mainly about *what* the state should punish. I focus on the specific examples of drug and gun control because objections to the use of the penal sanction that are widely appreciated in one context tend to be downplayed in the other. A theory of criminalization is needed to help us take a principled approach to both of these controversial and emotionally charged issues.

II: HOW MORE CRIMES PRODUCE INJUSTICE

Few knowledgeable persons contest the existence of the two trends I have described. The rise in the number of persons under the supervision of the criminal justice system as well as the expansion in the scope of the substantive criminal law can scarcely be doubted, even if the latter phenomenon resists precise quantification.[68] What is more difficult to discern, however, is the exact connection between these two developments. Intuitively, the relation seems apparent. As new crimes are enacted, more and more conduct becomes subject to criminal liability. Persons are sentenced for behavior that had been legally permissible at an earlier time. As a result, larger numbers of individuals face arrest, prosecution, and punishment. This simple and intuitive account *does* explain much of the rise in the scale of punishment. But this explanation is incomplete. In this section I describe a more complex mechanism to understand how greater amounts of criminal law produce greater amounts of punishment. I contend that this mechanism is worrisome not only because it causes too much punishment but also because it is destructive of the rule of law.

65. See, for example, Nicholas Dixon: "Why We Should Ban Handguns in the United States," 12 *St. Louis University Public Law Review* 243 (1993).
66. *Sourcebook: op. cit.*, note 1, table 2.65 (2005).
67. See James Jacobs: *Can Gun Control Work?* (Oxford: Oxford University Press, 2002), p.164.
68. Admittedly, some scholars *do* doubt that the criminal law has expanded significantly in size and scope, even though they agree that our criminalization decisions conform to no acceptable normative theory. For the best defense of this skeptical position, see Darryl K. Brown: "Rethinking Overcriminalization" (forthcoming, available at SSRN: *http://ssrn.com/abstract=932667*).

I do not want to overstate my case, so it is best to introduce a few qualifications at the outset. In the first place, the trend toward increasing criminalization is not uniform or constant. The criminal law has contracted as well as expanded; some types of behavior once punished no longer incur criminal liability. Colonial America employed the penal sanction primarily to repress sexuality, preserve religious orthodoxy, and control slaves.[69] Crimes against drunkenness, tippling, and various kinds of extravagances were once relatively common.[70] Obviously, few of these proscriptions still exist. Many "morals" offenses have not been explicitly repealed but rarely are enforced. For example, fornication remains criminal in 11 jurisdictions and adultery in 24—some of which continue to regard the latter as a felony.[71] A surprising number of states retain laws against profanity.[72] Although criminal liability still is used to combat prostitution in most parts of the country, prosecutions are sporadic. Still, many offenses widely enforced a few generations ago have disappeared altogether.[73] The most spectacular example of explicit repeal of a criminal offense is the Twenty-First Amendment, which ended the nation's ill-conceived 14-year experiment with the prohibition of alcohol distribution.

In addition, some of the recent expansions in the size and scope of the criminal sanction are welcome. A few offenses that clearly are desirable are of fairly recent vintage. In England, for example, rape could not be perpetrated between husband and wife until 1991. I am sure there are additional areas in which we still are guilty of *under*criminalization. For the most part, however, I am less concerned to indicate what new crimes are needed than to identify existing offenses that a respectable theory of criminalization would not allow. But even though my primary interest in defending a theory of criminalization is to hold back the tide of criminal law, we should keep in mind that a set of principles is also required to justify those penal offenses we should retain—as well as to identify those we have reason to enact. We need to decide not only whether we have too much criminal law already but also whether we should add even more.

Moreover, I do not allege that the growth of the criminal law is the only or even the most significant factor in explaining the increased size of the prison population. The most important reason our jails and prisons are filled is because punishments for existing offenses have become far more severe.[74] About 132,000 persons are currently serving life sentences; this number has grown at a rate that far outpaces the overall rise in the prison population during the past decade. Approximately 28% of these lifers are denied all chance of parole or early

69. See Samuel Walker: *Popular Justice: A History of American Criminal Justice* (New York: Oxford University Press, 2nd ed., 1999), pp.21–25.
70. See Alan Hunt: *Governing Morals: A Social History of Moral Regulation* (Cambridge: Cambridge University Press, 1999).
71. Melissa J. Mitchell: "Comment: Cleaning Out the Closet: Using Sunset Provisions to Clean up Cluttered Criminal Codes," 54 *Emory Law Journal* 1671, 1676 (2005).
72. See Sara Sun Beale: "The Many Faces of Overcriminalization: From Morals and Mattress Tags to Overfederalization," 54 *American University Law Review* 747 n.6 (2005).
73. A number of examples are provided by Brown: *op. cit.*, note 68.
74. See David M. Zlotnick: "The War Within the War on Crime: The Congressional Assault on Judicial Sentencing Discretion," 57 *Southern Methodist University Law Review* 211 (2004).

release, causing an unprecedented increase in the age of the average inmate.[75] International comparisons reveal the harshness of sentencing in the United States. Terms of incarceration are roughly 5 to 10 times as long as those imposed in France or Germany for similar crimes,[76] and offenses tend to be graded more seriously than in other places.[77] The past 20 years have seen novel changes in sentencing practices not replicated elsewhere in the world. The fate of the most substantial innovation—mandatory sentencing guidelines—remains uncertain.[78] But each of the most significant developments to have survived (at least for now) increases rather than decreases the severity of punishments: "three strikes" laws for recidivists, "truth in sentencing" provisions that prevent early release from prison, and mandatory minimums. The Supreme Court has allowed defendants to be imprisoned for life without possibility of parole for possessing 672 grams of cocaine,[79] and recently has decided that individuals may be jailed for offenses as trivial as driving without a seatbelt.[80] These innovations expand the number of people under the control and supervision of the criminal justice system without the need to enact any new offenses.

Finally, more statutes could not produce more punishment unless other officials in the criminal justice system cooperate to achieve this outcome. No one should make inferences about the size of the prison population simply by reading legal codes. Changes in rates of punishment would not occur unless statutes are enforced. Of course, some offenses are neglected by citizens as well as by officials, even if they are highly publicized. The Violence Against Women Act, passed with great fanfare in 1994, is a case in point. In 1997, the number of prosecutions brought under the Act was exactly zero,[81] even though the incidence of violence against women was probably unchanged. Bans of assault weapons provide another illustration. The initial enactment of (and subsequent failure to renew) this law attracted tremendous media attention. But almost 90% of the owners of the approximately 300,000 assault weapons in California failed to register their arms after the ban became operative. Rates of compliance were even lower in Cleveland, Boston, and New Jersey—where only 947 of between 100,000 and 300,000 assault weapons were registered, despite the dearth of prosecutions.[82] It is difficult, however, to find reliable data about the policies used by police and prosecutors to decide whether to enforce laws in different jurisdictions throughout the United States. Some offenses, like drunk driving and acquaintance rape, almost certainly

---

75. Data about the number of persons serving terms of life imprisonment are from Adam Liptak: "To More Inmates, Life Term Means Dying Behind Bars," *New York Times* (Sunday, October 2, 2005), p.A:1.

76. Whitman: *op. cit.*, note 5, p.57.

77. As Whitman shows, "while the drive in American law has been to reclassify more and more matters of 'disorderly conduct' or 'violations' as crimes, the tendency in continental Europe has been exactly the opposite." *Id.*, p.83.

78. A series of Supreme Court decisions has thrown the constitutionality of mandatory sentencing guidelines into grave doubt. See *United States v. Booker*, 533 U.S. 924 (2005). The guidelines now are said to be advisory. For the most recent (so far) account of what "advisory" means, see *Rita v. U.S.*, 127 S.Ct. 2456 (2007).

79. *Harmelin v. Michigan*, 501 U.S. 957 (1991).

80. *Atwater v. City of Lago Vista*, 533 U.S. 924 (2001).

81. American Bar Association: *The Federalization of Criminal Law* (1998), p.20.

82. See David Kopel and Christopher C. Little: "Communitarians, Neorepublicans, and Guns: Assessing the Case for Firearms Prohibition," 56 *Maryland Law Review* 438, 459 (1997). See also Jacobs: *op. cit.*, note 67, p.164.

are enforced more vigorously than in previous eras. Arrest and prosecution for many other offenses, like drug possession, varies tremendously from one time and place to another. Overall, however, there is little evidence that decreased levels of enforcement have counterbalanced the tendency for greater numbers of crimes to produce greater amounts of punishment.

Despite these cautionary remarks, it is patently clear that more criminalization produces more punishment in a straightforward manner: by expanding the type of conduct subjected to liability. The incidence of punishment is at unprecedented levels partly because defendants are convicted of crimes that did not exist a few generations ago.[83] The majority of those incarcerated under federal law today were sentenced for conduct that was not proscribed in the highly influential Model Penal Code. Indeed, most of the recent growth in our prison population involves nonviolent offenders. Even when more behavior is not punishable, the category of persons who face criminal prosecution has widened. The most obvious examples are juveniles[84] and white-collar offenders,[85] each of whom had relatively little to fear from the criminal justice system until the last quarter of the 20th century, but recently have become more common prosecutorial targets.[86] Moreover, the criminal law now extends deeply into the home, proscribing acts of domestic violence once regarded as private.[87]

In addition, expanded doctrines of joint criminality punish individuals who play a relatively minor role in crimes perpetrated by others. The most notorious example is the *Pinkerton* doctrine, which makes conspirators liable for the offenses committed by their co-conspirators, as long as these offenses are in furtherance of the conspiracy and within the scope of the unlawful project.[88] As a result, the number of substantive crimes committed by conspirators mushrooms out of all proportion to culpability and desert. Like the other crimes or doctrines on which I focus, conspiracy is a familiar weapon in the state's arsenal; perhaps one-quarter of all federal prosecutions involve a conspiracy charge.[89] Yet many commentators deem the offense unnecessary and have called for its abolition.[90]

Some new offenses enlarge the scope of criminalization in ways that are not obvious to laypersons. Most notably, many recent statutes impose *strict liability*—usually defined as an offense containing one or more material elements that do

---

83. Most important, almost no drug offenses existed prior to 1914. See David F. Musto: *The American Disease: Origins of Narcotic Control* (Oxford: Oxford University Press, 3rd ed., 1999).
84. See Franklin E. Zimring: *American Juvenile Justice* (New York: Oxford University Press, 2005). For example, the National Minimum Drinking Age Act, passed in 1984, effectively subjected millions of young drinkers to criminal penalties finally, the net of criminal law has been extended to public schools. See New York Civil Liberties Union: "Criminalizing the Classroom: The Over-Policing of New York City Schools," *http://www.aclu.org/pdfs/racialjustice/overpolicingschools-20070318.pdf.*
85. See Stuart Green: *Lying, Cheating, and Stealing: A Moral Theory of White Collar Crime* (Oxford: Oxford University Press, 2006).
86. According to Whitman, the state of affairs in which all forms of status-immunity to criminal liability are viewed as inegalitarian represents "an expression of an authentic American ideal." *Op. cit.*, note 5, p.46.
87. See Jeannie Suk: "Criminal Law Comes Home," 116 *Yale Law Journal* 2 (2006).
88. *Pinkerton v. United States*, 328 U.S. 640 (1946).
89. See Neil Kumar Katyal: "Conspiracy Theory," 112 *Yale Law Journal* 1307, 1310 (2003).
90. See the references in Joshua Dressler: *Understanding Criminal Law* (Lexis/Nexis, 4th ed., 2006), p.457.

not require culpability or *mens rea*.[91] Many persons are unaware that these crimes exist. But even those who know the law can be liable for these offenses by making a mistake of fact—even a *reasonable* mistake of fact—about whether their conduct falls within the terms of the prohibition. These statutes widen the range of conduct subject to punishment, as long as *conduct* is understood to include the mental as well as the physical dimension of crime. To the chagrin of many commentators, few strict liability crimes allow due diligence of the defendant as an excuse.[92] The proliferation of these offenses is among the primary factors that led Andrew Ashworth to lament that English criminal law has become a "lost cause."[93] This sentiment is equally apt in the United States.

Although this simple explanation of how more crimes produce more punishment suffices in a great many cases, a deeper analysis of the relationship between these two phenomena is needed. A more complete picture emerges if we understand where power *really* is allocated in our criminal justice system today. By inquiring where power really is located, I mean to identify those officials who make the decisions with the greatest impact on outcomes—that is, on whether or to what extent given individuals will actually be punished. The answers, I am sure, are police and prosecutors.[94] Obviously, no one will face punishment unless he is arrested, and the authority to arrest lies almost solely with the police.[95] This power is almost wholly discretionary; only in exceptional circumstances can police be required to make an arrest. Once an arrest has taken place, prosecutors make the crucial decision whether to bring charges.[96] If they proceed, they must determine which charge(s) to bring, whether to allow a plea bargain, and what bargain to accept. Most of these decisions conform to no discernable principle and cannot be reviewed.[97] Efforts to curb *judicial* discretion have been largely successful—perhaps *too* successful, judging by the scholarly opposition to sentencing guidelines. As many theorists have pointed out, however, few institutions are able to eliminate discretion altogether. More typically, discretion shifts from one place to another, finally settling where it is least visible. At the present time, discretion resides largely in police and prosecutors.

Understanding the mechanism by which discretionary powers allow too much law to produce too much punishment requires a more detailed analysis of the

91. According to some commentators, approximately half of all existing crimes in the United Kingdom satisfy this definition of strict liability. See A. P. Simester and G. R. Sullivan: *Criminal Law: Theory and Doctrine* (Oxford: Hart Pub. Co., 2000), p.165.
92. See Jeremy Horder: *Excusing Crime* (Oxford: Oxford University Press, 2004), chap. six.
93. Andrew Ashworth: "Is the Criminal Law a Lost Cause?" 116 *Law Quarterly Review* 225 (2000).
94. These answers are not novel. In 1940, Justice Jackson alleged that a federal prosecutor has "more control over life, liberty, and reputation than any other person in America." See Jackson's "The Federal Prosecutor," 24 *Journal of the American Judicature Society* 18, 18 (1940). For a more contemporary treatment that includes a discussion of administrative agencies with responsibilities of law enforcement, see Andrew Ashworth and Michael Redmayne: *The Criminal Process* (Oxford: Oxford University Press, 3rd ed., 2005), pp.142–146.
95. See Markus Dirk Dubber: *The Police Power: Patriarchy and the Foundations of American Government* (New York: Columbia University Press, 2005).
96. See Michael Edmund O'Neill: "When Prosecutors Don't: Trends in Federal Prosecutorial Declinations," 79 *Notre Dame Law Review* 221 (2003).
97. See Mark Osler: "This Changes Everything: A Call for a Directive, Goal-Oriented Principle to Guide the Exercise of Discretion by Federal Prosecutors," 39 *Valparaiso Law Review* 625 (2005).

realities of the penal process. Our criminal justice system could not survive if the majority of defendants insisted on a trial at which their guilt would have to be proved beyond a reasonable doubt.[98] Many of our policies and practices—including much of the substantive criminal law itself—are designed to facilitate plea bargains by inducing defendants to forego trials and plead guilty.[99] These devices have accomplished their intended effect; roughly 95% of adjudicated cases result in guilty pleas.[100] If defendants were well informed and their lawyers were skilled and experienced, many commentators believe the rate of convictions obtained through guilty pleas would be even higher.[101] Although countless philosophers of law have devoted their careers to formulating principles of justice that protect persons accused of crime, few appear concerned about how the prevalence of plea bargaining blunts the impact of their principles in the real world.[102] When defendants enter guilty pleas, no rule or doctrine can compensate for injustice in the substantive criminal law. In particular, plea bargains remove the power of juries to acquit—perhaps the most important means by which citizens have succeeded in reforming the penal justice system.[103]

Prosecutors have a variety of means to persuade defendants to plead guilty, and increased criminalization provides them with one of their most powerful weapons. As I show in greater detail later, criminal codes include several relatively new overlapping offenses, frequently designed to circumvent problems of obtaining reliable evidence. Some of these recent crimes involve maximum punishments of astonishing severity, despite the fact that they do not seem to be especially serious. As long as these offenses contain distinct elements, no rule or doctrine automatically prevents the state from bringing several charges simultaneously, even though, from the intuitive perspective of a layperson, the defendant has committed but a single crime. Hence these offenses allow prosecutors to *pile on* or *charge stack*—to bring a number of charges against a defendant for the same underlying conduct. Obviously, offenders face a far more severe potential sentence when multiple charges are brought against them. Prosecutors need to make credible threats that these sentences will be imposed if defendants stubbornly assert their innocence. For these threats to accomplish their objective and induce guilty pleas, the punishments defendants receive through plea bargains must be discounted—that is, made considerably more lenient than would be imposed in a trial. Even when a defendant is tried and acquitted on all but one of several charges, he probably will be deemed not to have "accepted responsibility" and may receive a longer sentence

---

98. See George Fisher: *Plea Bargaining's Triumph: A History of Plea Bargaining in America* (Stanford: Stanford University Press, 2003).

99. See Stephanos Bibas: "Plea Bargaining Outside the Shadow of Trial," 117 *Harvard Law Review* 2463 (2004).

100. Rachel E. Barkow: "Separation of Powers and the Criminal Law," 58 *Stanford Law Review* 989, 1047 n.310 (2006).

101. In federal law, William Stuntz says "the rate would approach 100%." See William Stuntz: "Plea Bargaining and Criminal Law's Disappearing Shadow," 117 *Harvard Law Review* 2548, 2568 (2004).

102. See Russell L. Christopher: "The Prosecutor's Dilemma: Bargains and Punishments," 72 *Fordham Law Review* 93 (2003). Christopher describes the incompatibility between plea bargaining and a retributive theory of punishment but defends the novel conclusion that this incompatibility undermines the latter rather than the former.

103. See Thomas Andrew Green: *Verdict According to Conscience: Perspectives on the English Criminal Trial Jury, 1200–1800* (Chicago: University of Chicago Press, 1985).

than would have been imposed if he had pled guilty to the single offense for which he is convicted.[104] Thus defendants who behave rationally have a tremendous incentive to bargain and plead guilty to a subset of the charges in exchange for having the other offenses dropped. As we have seen, most defendants are sufficiently self-interested to respond appropriately to these incentives.[105]

Of course, the Double Jeopardy clause of the Constitution protects defendants from suffering more than one punishment for the same offense. But this protection is limited. In the first place, the Supreme Court allows the imposition of multiple punishments for the same offense if expressly authorized by the legislature.[106] In some contexts—such as drug offenses—legislatures routinely authorize the additional sentence. Moreover, double jeopardy protection is narrowed by judicial decisions about when two offenses are "the same." When the legislature has not made its intention clear, the Supreme Court continues to implement the controversial *Blockburger* test, which provides that offenses are different if and only if each requires proof of some fact that the other does not.[107] This test merges lesser-included offenses into their aggravated counterparts, so prosecutors cannot, for example, charge a defendant with the separate crimes of simple assault and assault with a deadly weapon. Still, this test offers no protection to defendants when prosecutors bring multiple charges that contain distinct elements. For this reason the *Blockburger* test has been roundly criticized by commentators, many of whom favor a less mechanical means to decide when persons may be subjected to more than one punishment for the same offense.[108] At the present time, however, the Double Jeopardy clause is construed to give prosecutors enormous leverage to use the abundance of overlapping offenses to secure guilty pleas from defendants.[109]

Few knowledgeable commentators are prepared to defend the justice of plea bargaining. The practice has been denounced as "absolutely and fundamentally immoral," "a disaster," "unfair and irrational," and "outrageous."[110] Presumably, plea bargaining survives because no one knows how our penal system could function without it. The most glaring injustice occurs when those who plead guilty did not violate the law at all, even though it is impossible to know what percentage of those

104. See Rachel E. Barkow: "Recharging the Jury: The Criminal Jury's Constitutional Role in an Era of Mandatory Sentencing," 152 *University of Pennsylvania Law Review* 33, 98 (2003).
105. In particular, empirical evidence confirms that defendants who are averse to uncertainty are easily exploited by prosecutors and are more likely to plead guilty. See Uzi Segal and Alex Stein: "Ambiguity Aversion and the Criminal Process," 81 *Notre Dame Law Review* 1495 (2006).
106. *Missouri v. Hunter*, 459 U.S. 359 (1983).
107. *United States v. Blockburger*, 284 U.S. 299 (1932).
108. See Michael S. Moore: *Act and Crime* (Oxford: Oxford University Press, 1993); and George Thomas: *Double Jeopardy: The History, the Law* (New York: New York University Press, 1998).
109. The "real offense" provisions of the Federal Sentencing Guidelines sought to block this result by punishing defendants for what really happened. In many cases, the guidelines require multiple counts relating to the same harm to be aggregated, lessening the discretion of prosecutors to increase a defendant's sentence by bringing multiple charges. See Jacqueline E. Ross: "Damned Under Many Headings: The Problem of Multiple Punishment," 29 *American Journal of Criminal Law* 245 (2002). The fact that the Federal Sentencing Guidelines are no longer mandatory provides federal prosecutors with greater opportunities to impose more severe punishments by increasing the number of counts in an indictment.
110. See the references in Christopher: *op. cit.*, note 102, p.96.

punished are actually innocent of all charges.[111] We *do* know, however, that plea-bargaining contains structural features that render it "marvelously designed to secure conviction of the innocent."[112] In any event, many of those who *are* guilty of a crime would receive less severe punishments if each of the offenses with which they were charged were justified by our best theory of criminalization. Even if only *one* of the multiple charges in an indictment includes a statute that is beyond the proper reach of the criminal sanction, more defendants will have reason to plead guilty—and thus be punished—than if *each* statute conformed to our criteria of criminalization. And those who would plead guilty in either event will face more severe punishments in cases in which the indictment includes an offense that fails our test and should not have been criminalized. Defendants are motivated to plead guilty because they are threatened with a sentence that is more severe than could have been imposed if our best theory of criminalization were implemented. *Perhaps*, as a result of pro-longed bargaining, many defendants receive exactly the sentences they deserve—no more and no less. No one should profess to know, as it is hard to say what sever-ity of punishment *is* deserved for particular crimes. If defendants who plead guilty often *are* punished proportionate to their desert, however, defendants who go to trial alleging their innocence are almost certain (if convicted) to be punished excessively. We should not tolerate our criminal justice system if it punishes proportionate to desert only when defendants plead guilty. I conclude that overcriminalization almost inevitably produces disproportionate punishments, even when offenders have actually violated a criminal statute that everyone agrees to be a legitimate use of the penal sanction. Although a theory of criminalization might not reduce the incidence of plea bargaining overall, it might reduce the injustice caused by it.

Of course, too much criminal law leads to too much punishment even without encouraging plea bargains. No commentator has analyzed the connection between these two trends more astutely than William Stuntz, and I draw heavily from his work throughout the next two sections. Stuntz begins by noting that "anyone who studies contemporary state or federal criminal codes is likely to be struck by their scope, by the sheer amount of conduct they render punishable."[113] Offenses are so far-reaching that almost everyone has committed one or more at some time or another; the criminal law no longer distinguishes "us" from "them." Perhaps over 70% of living adult Americans have committed an imprisonable offense at some point in their life.[114] As a result, Stuntz alleges we are steadily moving "closer to a world in which the law on the books makes everyone a felon."[115] Although more criminal law produces more punishment, it could easily produce even more pun-ishment than we have already.

---

111. For some estimates, see Barry Scheck, Peter Neufeld, and Jim Dwyer: *Actual Innocence* (New York: Signet, 2001); see also Samuel R. Gross et al.: "Exonerations in the United States 1989 through 2003," 95 *Journal of Criminal Law and Criminology* 523 (2005).
112. Albert W. Alschuler: "Straining at Gnats and Swallowing Camels: The Selective Morality of Professor Bibas," 88 *Cornell Law Review* 1412, 1414 (2003).
113. William Stuntz: "The Pathological Politics of Criminal Law," 100 *Michigan Law Review* 506, 515 (2001).
114. In addition to the examples I describe, this figure includes shoplifting and driving while intoxicated. See Dwyer: *op. cit.*, note 39, p.188.
115. *Op. cit.*, note 113, p.511.

I cite here just three examples of how the expanding net of criminal liability threatens to ensnare us all. Several possible examples could be used; I select the following because the class of offenders differs markedly in each illustration.[116] First and perhaps most notably, about 90 million living Americans have used an illicit drug, an activity for which many could have been sent to prison if detected and prosecuted. Even occupants of our highest offices have engaged in felonious drug use; recall that George W. Bush dismissed allegations of frequent cocaine abuse as a "youthful indiscretion." Significantly, however, he did not call for an end to criminal penalties for similar indiscretions by the youth of today. Second, astronomical numbers of young adults have engaged in music piracy. According to some estimates, 52% of Internet users between the ages of 18 and 29 commit this crime by illegally downloading approximately 3.6 billion songs each month.[117] The No Electronic Theft Act of 1997 makes the sharing of over $1,000 worth of copyrighted material a federal offense that can result in three years' imprisonment.[118] To date, prosecutions for not-for-profit copyright infringements have been exceedingly rare, but some commentators predict more aggressive enforcement in the future.[119] Internet gambling provides my final example of the ubiquity of criminal behavior. Millions of citizens in the United States place bets from their home computers on Internet casinos. The law on this phenomenon is in a state of flux. Under existing statutes, individuals who gamble online are not guilty of any crime—although Congress periodically entertains bills to proscribe their behavior. But the Unlawful Internet Gambling Enforcement Act of 2006 prohibits American banks from transferring money to Internet gambling sites.[120] Moreover, the very operation of these casinos is unambiguously prohibited under the Federal Wire Act.[121] The ownership of offshore Internet casinos that do business in the United States includes many of the most prestigious investment firms in the world: Fidelity, Merrill Lynch, Goldman Sachs, Morgan Stanley, and others. It is hard to see why these investment companies are not punishable for aiding and abetting these illegal activities. Only prosecutorial discretion prevents criminal liability from extending to the highest reaches of mainstream society. As these examples show, what tends to characterize many of us who have evaded punishment is not our compliance with law but the good fortune not to have been caught, the discretion of authorities in failing to make arrests or bring charges, or the resources to escape criminal penalties in the event we are prosecuted.

---

116. For an additional example, drivers who misinform a police officer that they did not realize how fast they were speeding violate the federal false statement statute. See Alexandra Bak-Boychuk: "Liar Liar: How MPC §241.3 and State Unsworn Falsification Statutes Fix the Flaw in the False Statement Act (18 U.S.C. §1001)," 78 *Temple Law Review* 453 (2005).

117. See Tia Hall: "Music Piracy and the Audio Home Recording Act," *Duke Law and Technology Review* 23 (2002).

118. Public Law No. 105–147, 111 Stat. 2678.

119. See I. Trotter Hardy: "Criminal Copyright Infringement," 11 *William & Mary Bill of Rights Journal* 305 (2002).

120. 31 U.S.C. §5366 (2006).

121. The Wire Act of 1961 makes it illegal to use a "wire communication facility for the transmission in interstate or foreign commerce of bets or wagers." 18 U.S.C. §1084 (2003).

These examples support Stuntz's claim that the substantive criminal law itself rarely functions to define prohibited conduct or the consequences of disobedience. Instead, statutes are mainly "a means of empowering prosecutors"[122]; they serve "as items on a menu from which the prosecutor may order as she wishes."[123] What *do* prosecutors order from the extensive menu legislators prepare? No one should profess to know the answer with any certainty, and generalizations are perilous.[124] Stuntz admits, "there is no developed social science literature on what prosecutors maximize, probably because the solution is too complex to model effectively."[125] In any event, no sensible prosecutor aspires to convict the largest number of people or to impose the harshest sentences authorized by law. Criminal statutes are so pervasive that prosecutors have little choice but to decide which crimes are worth enforcing and which are not. The factors that contribute to the laws prosecutors will enforce and the sentences they will seek through plea bargains include "voters' preferences, courthouse customs, the prosecutor's reputation as a tough or lenient bargainer, [and] her own views about what is a proper sentence for the crime in question."[126] Obviously, these variables will differ from case to case. Whatever their motivations may be, Stuntz concludes that prosecutors rather than legislators are "the criminal justice system's real lawmakers."[127]

Jeffrey Standen offers an excellent example of the array of options made available to federal prosecutors by the maze of criminal statutes.[128] Suppose an officer of a publicly held corporation uses confidential information to make trades in his company's stock over a period of years, yielding more than $100,000 in profits that are deposited in his private bank account. The possible charges that prosecutors may bring include multiple counts of some combination of mail fraud, racketeering offenses, securities violations, money laundering, and a host of others. Possible sentences span from a period of supervised probation to a term of imprisonment of about six years. As this example indicates, the content of criminal statutes does not impose a significant constraint on prosecutors. Their charging decisions give them the power to control whether and to what extent persons will pay for their crimes.[129]

---

122. Stuntz: *op. cit.*, note 101, p.2563.

123. *Id.*, p.2549.

124. Sometimes discretion is used in ways no one could reasonably have anticipated. Martha Stewart provides a well-known example. In 2004, Ms. Stewart was convicted of making false statements to federal officials who were investigating her sale of ImClone stock after her broker advised her that the CEO of ImClone had sold some of his own stock in the company. Ms. Stewart asserted her innocence of insider trading, a crime with which she was not charged. Her allegation of innocence, according to the novel theory adopted by the federal prosecutor, was designed to help prop up the value of stock in her own company, Martha Stewart Omnimedia. I do not claim that prosecutors or judges misconstrued the relevant statutes in this case. The main problem lies in the broad language of the statutes themselves, and thus in the enormous discretion they confer. For a general discussion, see Ellen S. Podgor: "Jose Padilla and Martha Stewart: Who Should Have Been Charged with Criminal Conduct?" 109 *Penn State Law Review* 1059 (2005).

125. Stuntz: *op. cit.*, note 101, p.2554 n6.

126. *Id.*, p.2554.

127. Stuntz: *op. cit.*, note 113, p.506.

128. Jeffrey Standen: "An Economic Perspective on Federal Criminal Law Reform," 2 *Buffalo Criminal Law Review* 249, 252–254 (1998).

129. *Id.*, p.256.

What is worrisome about delegating so much authority to prosecutors? Surely the objection cannot be that prosecutors fail to use their power to punish even more individuals than are sentenced at the present time. From the perspective of a legal philosopher, the answer is simple. Even when exercised wisely, this discretionary power, unchecked and unbalanced by other branches of government, is incompatible with the rule of law. This deterioration in the rule of law produces injustice. Because real power in our criminal justice system is not exercised in conformity with any principle that commentators have been able to formulate, no one is able to answer the question that legal realists like Oliver Wendell Holmes identified as fundamental to understanding what the law *is*. According to Holmes, the law consists in "prophecies of what the courts will do in fact, and nothing more pretentious."[130] Without endorsing the whole school of jurisprudence Holmes sought to defend, he clearly articulated the central concern of laypersons who make inquiries about the law. Holmes recognized that experts who profess to know the law should be able to make a fairly accurate "prediction that if a man does or omits certain things he will be made to suffer in this or that way by judgment of the court."[131] But these predictions become notoriously unreliable in a system in which real power, and the decisions that govern the fate of individuals, is wielded with so much discretion.

Remarkably, few criminal theorists are vocal in protesting this erosion of the principle of legality, despite their enthusiasm about the ideal of establishing a government of laws and not of men. Whatever the ideal of the rule of law might entail, it seemingly means that the distinction between conduct that is and is not punished should depend primarily on the content of the laws that legislatures enact. No one, however, should hazard a prediction about who will be sentenced simply by examining criminal statutes. The *real* law—the law that distinguishes the conduct that leads to punishment from the conduct that does not—cannot be found in criminal codes. Even those police and prosecutors who pledge fidelity to the rule of law could not hope to honor their commitment because they receive almost no guidance from legislators about what they really are expected to do. The number and scope of criminal laws guarantee that neither police nor prosecutors will enforce statutes as written. As Stuntz observes, "the greater the territory substantive criminal law covers, the smaller the role that law plays in allocating criminal punishment."[132] We are already well past the point at which statutes are the dominant factor in explaining who will or will not incur criminal liability. As a result, one might conclude that the substantive criminal law itself is not very important in the context of our system of criminal justice.[133] As Stuntz bluntly concludes, "criminal law is not, in any meaningful sense, law at all."[134]

130. Oliver W. Holmes: "The Path of the Law," X *Harvard Law Review* 457 (1897). Reprinted in Harvard Law Review: *Introduction to Law* (Cambridge: Harvard Law Review Association, 1968), pp.50, 54.
131. *Id.*, p.51.
132. Stuntz: *op. cit.*, note 101, p.2550.
133. See Douglas Husak: "Is the Criminal Law Important?" 1 *Ohio State Journal of Criminal Law* 261 (2003).
134. William J. Stuntz: "Correspondence: Reply: Criminal Law's Pathology," 101 *Michigan Law Review* 828, 833 (2002).

The consequences of this erosion in the rule of law are monumental, jeopard-izing several of the normative principles held dear by legal theorists. Philosophers of law rarely discuss how the discretion of police and prosecutors affects their theories of punishment and criminalization.[135] For example, many commentators believe that criminal justice should implement a theory of desert, which includes (*inter alia*) the principle of proportionality introduced earlier: the severity of the punishment imposed on the offender should be proportionate to the seriousness of his crime. This principle was (and continues to be) a pivotal rationale for adopt-ing guidelines that remove sentencing discretion from judges.[136] Two persons with relevantly similar criminal histories who commit the same offense should receive comparable sentences. Clearly, the principle of proportionality is violated when relevantly similar defendants are punished to different degrees. But violations of this principle can also occur when some but not all relevantly similar offenders are arrested, or when some but not all relevantly similar arrestees are prosecuted. Unfortunately, the latter two deviations from the principle of proportionately are commonplace today.

The relative lack of protest about the violations of proportionality in the lat-ter circumstances probably reflects the long-standing obsession among legal phil-osophers with the judicial branch of government.[137] Although *judicial* discretion has long been recognized to be the enemy of the rule of law,[138] theorists have not tended to apply their reservations about the legitimacy of discretion to other officials in our criminal justice system. Police and prosecutors, no less than judges, are and ought to be subject to the rule of law. Any progress that has been made to ensure that judges impose proportionate sentences is undermined by the failure to take the rule of law seriously at earlier stages of the criminal process. In hindsight, it is doubtful that courts were the best place to find deviations from the principle of legality. Because judicial behavior is so public, it is not surprising that courts have a better track record than other criminal justice institutions in preserving the rule of law.

The drug war provides an example of how the combination of overcriminali-zation and prosecutorial discretion erodes the rule of law and undermines the principle of proportionality. When serving as a federal prosecutor in New York, Rudolph Giuliani sought to keep drug dealers "off balance" by instituting "federal day": one day each week chosen at random in which street-level drug dealers arrested by local police were prosecuted in federal rather than state court, where sentences are far more severe.[139] Despite the notorious difficulties implementing a principle of proportionality, no person would contend that the same criminal behavior becomes more serious and should be punished more harshly because it happens to be perpetrated on a Tuesday rather than on a Wednesday—especially

---

135. For an exception, see Ashworth and Redmayne: *op. cit.*, note 94, chap. 6.
136. See Andrew von Hirsch, Kay A. Knapp, and Michael Tonry: *The Sentencing Commission and Its Guidelines* (Boston: Northeastern University Press, 1987).
137. See Jeremy Waldron: *The Dignity of Legislation* (Cambridge: Cambridge University Press, 1999).
138. See Ronald Dworkin: *Taking Rights Seriously* (Cambridge: Harvard University Press, 1977), pp.31–37.
139. See Beale: *op. cit.*, note 72, p.765 n98.

when notice is deliberately withheld about the date on which the longer sentences will be imposed. I do not allege that this draconian tactic violates the law. Instead, the problem lies with the law to which this strategy conforms.

The incompatibility between the rule of law and the discretionary powers of police and prosecutors may be described more generally. Consider a straightforward and specific question a layperson might pose to someone who professes an expertise in criminal law: How will the law react to a person who uses or sells small quantities of marijuana? Theorists should be embarrassed by their inability to answer this question, because their knowledge of the criminal law—and even their specialty in drug policy—will not enable them to respond confidently. I assume that laypersons are raising Holmes's question when they ask how the law will react to a marijuana offender. I doubt that they are narrowly fixated on what *courts* will do to this individual, but this does not detract from the point I have in mind. Although Holmes defined the law as the set of prophecies of what *judges* will do, I am sure he did not intend to disregard the behavior of other officials in our criminal justice system. I assume Holmes meant only that courts could not act unless police and prosecutors brought a case before them, and judges have the final authority to specify the content of the law by convicting or acquitting. The layperson, then, should be understood to inquire how each stage of the criminal justice system will respond to a marijuana offender. Will he be caught? Will he be arrested? Will he be prosecuted? Will he be punished? If so, how severe will his punishment be? Why are theorists unable to answer these simple questions? I hope no one will reply that the addressees of these questions are only *theorists* who have little familiarity with the nuts and bolts of the criminal law. This reply *cannot* be adequate, because even practitioners with an encyclopedic knowledge of the criminal law would not be able to make a very accurate prediction about the fate of the marijuana offender.[140] The real explanation for their ignorance lies elsewhere.

Of course, knowledgeable commentators may be able to recite a few statistics in addition to those mentioned already. About 25 million Americans use marijuana each month; one is arrested every 42 seconds; 786,000 people were arrested for marijuana violations in 2005, more than double the number in 1993.[141] Of those prosecuted for marijuana offenses, 88% were charged with mere possession and tens of thousands were sent to jail. These data, however, do not reveal how many offenders were not detected at all, or were detected but not arrested because police were willing to look the other way. And what happens after an arrest is made? Here, at least, one would hope that knowledge of the criminal law should come into play. Even at this stage, however, predictions are remarkably tenuous. The variables that lead to decisions about whether an arrestee will be charged are not clear. Some prosecutors believe that low-level offenders are not worth charging; others pursue them with zeal. The charges offenders will face are also difficult

---

140. One commentator describes this state of affairs as producing "'vagueness in practice.' While they are not doctrinally or textually vague, underenforced laws *functionally* raise the same concerns. Citizens receive little or no notice as to what constitutes unlawful (as in 'sanctionable') conduct." Edward K. Cheng: "Structural Laws and the Puzzle of Regulating Behavior," 100 *Northwestern University Law Review* 655, 660–661 (2006).
141. See Federal Bureau of Investigation: *Crime in the United States*, (2005), table 29.

to ascertain. Some prosecutors routinely offer plea bargains to arrestees willing to implicate sellers higher in the distribution chain; others do not. Federal law, at least, purports to remove discretion in sentencing by imposing mandatory minimums on defendants who are guilty of distributing specified quantities of drugs. But mandatory sentences are easily evaded by such devices as fact bargaining and charge bargaining.[142] How frequently do these evasions occur? No one should profess to know with any degree of certainty.

We *do* know that such factors as location and race significantly affect the probability that marijuana users and sellers will be punished. Our system of law practices "justice by geography." There is a wide disparity in the growth of marijuana arrests from one county to another—from a 20% increase in the 1990s in San Diego to a 418% spike in King County, Washington.[143] Contemporary statistics about racial disparities are especially shocking. Although whites and blacks are roughly comparable in their rates of illicit drug use, blacks are arrested, prosecuted, and punished for drug offenses far more frequently and harshly than whites.[144] Recent studies show that African-Americans make up 14% of marijuana users generally but account for nearly one-third of all marijuana arrests. The public does not seem outraged about these inequities; citizens and officials alike are quite complacent about this apparent perversion in the rule of law. In all probability, however, the drug war would have ended long ago but for exercises of discretion that spared suburban whites from prison at the same rate as that for inner-city blacks.

Drug prohibitions are not the only example of how the unfettered exercise of discretion is capable of obliterating the rule of law. Although hardly paradigmatic of serious criminal offenses,[145] the statutes governing motor vehicles can be used to illustrate the same point.[146] Everyone is roughly aware of the scope and complexity of traffic laws. In the state of New Jersey, which is fairly typical in most respects, the Motor Vehicle and Traffic Regulations span some 180 pages of dense text. Although the applicable statutes are relatively easy to find, few drivers are aware of the details of many of the regulations that pertain to them. But widespread ignorance of the law is not the main difficulty on which I focus. Instead, the problem is the remarkable *breadth* of the statutes. Even those who know the law find it is nearly impossible to drive for a period of time without committing some infraction or another.[147] A policeman who follows a driver for several minutes is bound to find probable cause to stop him. Even those few individuals who happen to be familiar with the content of the regulations cannot anticipate what

---

142. Some of the maneuvering around these provisions is described by Stephen J. Schulhofer and Ilene H. Nagel: "Plea Negotiations under the Federal Sentencing Guidelines: Guideline Circumvention and Its Dynamics in the Post-*Mistretta* Period," 91 *Northwestern University Law Review* 1284 (1997).

143. See Ryan S. King and Mark Mauer: "The War on Marijuana: The Transformation of the Drug War in the 1990s" (May, 2005), *http://www.sentencingproject.org/pdfs/waronmarijuana.pdf*.

144. See Jamie Fellner: "Punishment and Prejudice: Racial Disparities in the War on Drugs," 12:2 *Human Rights Watch* (May 2000).

145. Many states construe most traffic offenses as civil infractions rather than misdemeanors.

146. See Illya Lichtenberg: "Police Discretion and Traffic Enforcement: A Government of Men?" 50 *Cleveland State Law Review* 425 (2002–2003).

147. See David Harris: "Car Wars: The Fourth Amendment's Death on the Highway," 66 *George Washington Law Review* 556 (1998).

conduct will lead the police to detain them. After being pulled over, no one can predict what behavior will result in a summons. If cited, it is hard to say whether appearance in traffic court will increase or decrease the penalty.

Speed limits provide an illustration of how the rule of law has been jeopardized. Exactly how fast *is* a driver permitted to travel on a given highway? Posted limits offer little guidance; most motorists exceed them routinely. Even if someone is driving below the posted limit, he may be cited if weather conditions are deemed to be sufficiently hazardous. In other words, the fate of drivers is almost entirely in the hands of police. To make matters worse, the handful of motorists who *do* obey the letter of the law may expose themselves and others to heightened levels of risk, because accidents are minimized when motorists follow the flow of traffic rather than conform to posted speed limits. It is hard to understand why this state of affairs has not given rise to howls of protest from those theorists who take the rule of law (as well as safety) seriously. Perhaps commentators neglect this topic because of the minor penalties that are imposed. In any event, traffic offenses per se are not the phenomenon to which I hope to call attention. The more significant problem is that the criminal law generally has come to resemble traffic offenses in many crucial respects.

Thus I take for granted that those who teach and theorize about the criminal law would be unable to answer the simple and straightforward questions I have borrowed from Holmes. If knowledge of the criminal law consists in the ability to make reliable forecasts about what conduct will be punished, it follows that no one knows the law. Experts in the criminal law cannot make accurate predictions about potential offenders because the fate of such persons is not a function of the law at all. The *real* criminal law, as Holmes would construe it, is formulated by police and prosecutors. The realization that police and prosecutors wield such discretion is nothing new. What *is* new is the power to arrest and prosecute nearly everyone—a power that derives from the ever-expanding scope of criminal statutes as written. The combination of these phenomena—unchecked discretion coupled with all-encompassing offenses—is destructive of the rule of law. This combination produces too much punishment directly, by proscribing conduct that a defensible theory of criminalization would place beyond the reach of the penal sanction. And this combination produces too much punishment indirectly, by allowing prosecutors to stack charges in order to induce defendants to plead guilty by threatening to sentence them in excess of their desert. And all too often, defendants who exercise their right to be tried and found guilty beyond a reasonable doubt *are* punished in excess of their desert. Although unquestionably beneficial to those who enjoy the discretionary authority bestowed, it is impossible to believe that the combination of these phenomena results in justice.[148]

What might be done to enhance the rule of law in the criminal arena?[149] I have no simple advice to give. Clearly, no system of criminal justice can or should aspire

---

148. For a more optimistic view of the effects of overcriminalization, see Kyron Huigens: "What Is and Is Not Pathological in Criminal Law," 101 *Michigan Law Review* 811 (2002).

149. For a survey of some possible solutions, see Donald A. Dripps: "Overcriminalization, Discretion, Waiver: A Survey of Possible Exit Strategies," 109 *Penn State Law Review* 1155 (2005).

to eliminate discretion altogether.[150] But we can hope to eliminate the inevitability that discretion will be exercised without regard for the rule of law.[151] Although realistic progress toward this goal must be incremental, one promising proposal calls for the principled enforcement of the criminal law as written.[152] Police might be required to arrest for the offenses they detect, and prosecutors might be required to charge the most serious provable offense—or be prepared to explain publicly why they have failed to do so.[153] Alternatively, prosecutors might be required to show that some number of other defendants in factually similar cases within the same jurisdiction have been treated similarly.[154] In other words, police and prosecutors might be encouraged to act more like judges. Clearly, however, the number and scope of existing statutes precludes these solutions. A better theory of criminalization can help to address this problem. If we cannot expect authorities to defend their decisions about why given statutes are selectively enforced—like those prohibiting drug use, music piracy, and Internet gambling, for example—we should be reluctant to enact statutes that give authorities this discretion in the first place.

Principled enforcement could help to salvage the rule of law were it not threatened by overcriminalization. It is crucial to recognize, however, that even a good-faith implementation of a minimalist theory of criminalization would represent only a small step toward the ideal of principled enforcement. To a large extent, society is "self-policing." The bulk of police and prosecutorial work is *reactive*, responding to information provided by citizens about the occurrence of criminal activity. Different measures of the incidence of crime—those drawn from victim surveys rather than from law enforcement agencies—reveal that most crimes are unreported. In 2004, for example, over 57% of crimes involving personal and property victimization were not reported to the police.[155] Conformity to principle will not rectify this situation. If we hope to enhance the rule of law, so that the content of offenses provides a more reliable indicator of who will actually be punished or unpunished, the public must be more willing to report crimes to the authorities. In a free society, I have little to say about how to improve this situation—except to speculate that citizens might become more cooperative if they believe the criminal law is just.[156] Improving the substantive criminal law is essential both to reducing the incidence of unjust punishment and to restoring the rule of law itself.

---

150. For the classic account of these matters, see Kenneth Culp Davis: *Discretionary Justice* (Urbana: University of Illinois Press, 3rd ed., 1976).
151. Lessons might be learned from our European neighbors, many of which (allegedly) implement a rule of compulsory prosecution. For some useful observations, see Heike Jung: "Criminal Justice: A European Perspective," *Criminal Law Review* 237 (1993).
152. In a memorandum of September 22, 2003, Attorney General John Ashcroft directed federal prosecutors to "charge and pursue the most serious, readily provable offense" (subject to several exceptions). For a discussion, see Amie N. Ely: "Note: Prosecutorial Discretion As an Ethical Necessity: The Ashcroft Memorandum's Curtailment of the Prosecutor's Duty to 'Seek Justice,'" 90 *Cornell Law Review* 237 (2004).
153. See the model of transparent policing endorsed by Erik Luna: "Principled Enforcement of Penal Codes," 4 *Buffalo Criminal Law Review* 515 (2000).
154. See William J. Stuntz: "The Political Constitution of Criminal Justice," 119 *Harvard Law Review* 780, 838 (2006).
155. *Sourcebook: op. cit.*, note 1, table 3.33 (2004).
156. See Paul H. Robinson and John M. Darley: *Justice, Liability & Blame* (Boulder: Westview Press, 1995).

III: THE CONTENT OF NEW OFFENSES

The criminal law has undergone a remarkable transformation in the past generation. Few philosophers of criminal law seem aware of these developments. One
commentator laments "most criminal law scholars . . . pay surprisingly little attention to the actual state of the law."[157] Penal statutes rarely are read, even by those
who purport to theorize about them.[158] In fact, it is safe to say that virtually *no one*
systematically studies criminal codes. Many of the legislators who vote in favor
of these laws admit to not having read them carefully. Professors seldom assign
them in class, so students are unlikely to examine them. Criminal theorists remain
obsessed with the so-called general part of criminal law, and they are far more fas-
cinated by the philosophical foundations of the criminal law than by the criminal
law itself.[159] As a result, much of their theorizing loses touch with that body of
law they purport to be theorizing *about*. William Stuntz astutely observes that the
criminal law has become "not one field but two. The first consists of a few core
crimes . . . . The second consists of everything else. Criminal law courses, criminal
law literature, and popular conversation about crime focus heavily on the first. The
second dominates criminal codes."[160] Philosophers of law who generalize about
the penal sanction with core crimes in mind are in danger of deriving principles
that do not apply to the bulk of offenses in criminal codes today.

To understand Stuntz's remark, we must clarify the contrast he purports to
draw between two "fields" of criminal law. The only clue he offers about how these
fields might be demarcated is that the first consists of *core* crimes, while the second
does not. What makes a particular crime part of the core of criminal law? George
Fletcher, I believe, was the first to claim that the criminal law contains a core.[161]
Unfortunately, he did not explicate this metaphor in detail, allowing it to remain
intuitive. His claim suggests that the criminal law also includes a periphery that
surrounds its center. But how is the contrast between core and periphery to be
drawn? The answer is not clear, because core offenses might be identified in any
number of ways. The first depends on legal history. Core offenses might be those
that all Anglo-American jurisdictions have contained for centuries, and came to be
adopted in the prestigious Model Penal Code.[162] Of course, the content of many
such offenses has evolved over time. Most contemporary rape statutes, for example, are gender neutral and do not provide for spousal immunity.[163] Still, we easily
recognize a modern rape statute as the product of evolution from an offense that
has long existed at common law. Alternatively, core offenses might be identified

---

157. Gerald E. Lynch: "Revising the Model Penal Code," 1 *Ohio State Journal of Criminal Law* 219, 224 (2003).

158. Stuntz: *op. cit.*, note 113, p.512.

159. See chapter 2, section I.

160. *Op. cit.*, note 113, p.512.

161. George Fletcher: *Rethinking Criminal Law* (Boston: Little, Brown and Co, 1978).

162. Despite accolades from most others, it is noteworthy that no influential criminal theorist seems to be less
enamored with the Model Penal Code than Fletcher. See George P. Fletcher: "Dogmas of the Model Penal Code,"
2 *Buffalo Criminal Law Review* 3 (1998).

163. See Deborah W. Denno: "Why the Model Penal Code's Sexual Offense Provisions Should Be Pulled and
Replaced," 1 *Ohio State Journal of Criminal Law* 207, 213 (2003).

as those that consume the bulk of the workload in our systems of criminal justice.
Our theory of criminal law should not be detached from the actual business of
police, prosecutors, and judges. By this latter criterion, drug offenses—and the
offense of drug possession in particular—should be assigned to the core of criminal law. Under current federal law, more than half as many persons are arrested
and punished for drug offenses as for all other crimes combined.[164]

Here I propose a third and different way to understand the contrast between
offenses in the core of criminal law and those on the periphery. In my judgment,
this contrast is best drawn by examining the *use* to which it is put.[165] In other words,
we must try to understand the *purpose* of consigning some crimes to the core and
relegating others to the periphery. Although many such purposes are possible,
I propose to construe the contrast between core and peripheral offenses *normatively*.
Crimes in the core are those that share whatever features are important from the
standpoint of justice. Virtually all commentators attach enormous normative significance to the requirement of *mens rea*, for example. Statutes that dispense with
mens rea by imposing strict liability should be placed on the periphery, even if
they have an impressive historical pedigree and come to outnumber those that
require culpability for each material element. Crimes outside the core, then—the
"everything else" to which Stuntz refers—are those that are suspect normatively
because they lack the features or characteristics that most theorists regard as crucial
if impositions of criminal liability are to satisfy our principles of justice.

Ultimately, I invoke principles of criminalization to confirm suspicions that
given offenses involve a dubious use of the penal sanction. At this point, however,
my main objective is to understand the content of those crimes largely neglected
by criminal theorists: those that nearly any commentator would regard as problematic from the standpoint of justice and thus would place outside the core of
criminal law. How might we generalize about these offenses? This task is daunting. Many of the principles used to organize criminal law textbooks—such as the
division between crimes against persons and those against property—are unhelpful for this purpose. Existing codes offer no guidance; in the federal code, for
example, statutes are arranged alphabetically rather than according to any sensible
scheme of classification. Commentaries rarely pay much attention to crimes outside the core, so it is not surprising that they lack the conceptual apparatus to
categorize and evaluate them.

Because legislatures have become "offense factories" that churn out new statutes
each week, it is easy to provide illustrations of crimes that seem to have no place in
modern criminal codes.[166] Every few years a popular book appears that lists silly
laws that remain on the books.[167] Many statutes—like the federal government's
ban on using the "Give a hoot, don't pollute" slogan without authorization—seem

---

164. *Sourcebook: op. cit.*, note 1 (2003), table 5.18.
165. For further thoughts, see Douglas Husak: "Crimes Outside the Core," 39 *Tulsa Law Review* 755 (2004).
166. See Robinson and Cahill: *op. cit.*, note 47, p.634.
167. See, for example, Peter McWilliams: *Ain't Nobody's Business If You Do* (Los Angeles: Prelude Press, 1993). In
addition, the Statutory Construction Blog at *http:lawprofessors.typepad.com/statutory* awards a weekly prize to the
"worst statute in the world."

ridiculous. Eric Luna provides several examples of criminal laws that fail what he calls the "laugh test":

> New Mexico makes it a misdemeanor to claim that a product contains honey unless it is made of "pure honey produced by honeybees." Florida criminalizes the display of deformed animals and the peddling of untested sparklers, as well as the mutilation of the Confederate flag for "crass or commercial purposes." Pretending to be a member of the clergy is a misdemeanor in Alabama, and Kentucky bans the use of reptiles during religious services. Maine prohibits the catching of crustaceans with anything but "conventional lobster traps," and Texas declares it a felony to trip a horse or "seriously overwork" an animal. In turn, California forbids "three-card monte" and, as a general rule, cheating at card games, while it's a crime in Illinois to camp on the side of a public highway or offer a movie for rent without clearly displaying its rating.[168]

More recently, Luna expands the foregoing list with additional examples.

> Delaware punishes by up to six months' imprisonment the sale of perfume or lotion as a beverage. In Alabama, it is a felony to maim one's self to "excite sympathy" or to train a bear to wrestle, while Nevada criminalizes the disturbance of a congregation at worship by "engaging in any boisterous or noisy amusement." Tennessee makes it a misdemeanor to hunt wildlife from an aircraft, Indiana bans the coloring of birds and rabbits, Massachusetts punishes those who frighten pigeons from their nests, and Texas declares it a felony to use live animals as lures in dog racing. In turn, spitting in public places is a misdemeanor in Virginia, and anonymously sending an indecent or "suggestive" message in South Carolina is punishable by up to three years' imprisonment."[169]

Ronald Gainer offers comparable examples of equally extraordinary federal legislation. Congress imposes criminal penalties on persons who disturb mud in a cave on federal land, walk a dog on the grounds of a federal building, or sell a mixture of different kinds of turpentine.[170] Although one might quibble about one or another of these illustrations, it is hard to believe that any respectable theory of criminalization would deem many of these laws to be justified. I see no reason to resist the intuition that the majority of these examples represent clear cases of overcriminalization.

But most of these laws, however amusing, are rarely enforced and certainly cannot be blamed for causing the massive increase in punishment throughout the United States today. These statutes may clutter our criminal codes and pose problems for the rule of law. But if the central objection to the enactment of too much criminal law is that it produces too much punishment, we should not allow ourselves to be distracted by these sorts of examples. In what follows, I hope to cite only specific laws that actually are enforced with some degree of regularity. At this point, the challenge for theorists is twofold. We should not simply list peculiar crimes; we must place them into meaningful categories for analysis. Unless a theory of criminalization is to be applied case by case, our project is to decide what

---

168. Eric Luna: "Overextending the Criminal Law," in Gene Healy, ed: *Go Directly to Jail: The Criminalization of Almost Everything* (Washington, D.C.: Cato Institute, 2004), pp.1, 2.
169. Eric Luna: "The Overcriminalization Phenomenon," 54 *American University Law Review* 703, 706 (2005).
170. Gainer: *op. cit.*, note 22, p.74.

general *types* of offense involve dubious applications of the penal sanction. The accomplishment of this task will facilitate the second. We must not be content with ridicule; we must be prepared to say *why* legislatures should not have created these kinds of law. I undertake the first of these projects in the remainder of this section. The subsequent two chapters introduce several constraints on criminalization that are violated by many of these types of law.

Once we move outside the core to the periphery of the criminal law, we lack a familiar conceptual apparatus to classify many of the new types of offense that legislatures have enacted.[171] Historically, commentators have distinguished *mala in se* from *mala prohibita* offenses. Despite its notorious obscurity, this contrast remains useful, and I will raise normative difficulties with *mala prohibita* offenses later.[172] Still, I believe we can improve on this simple classificatory scheme. In what follows, I briefly introduce what I regard as three kinds of fairly recent innovations: overlapping offenses, crimes of risk prevention, and ancillary offenses. I hope this taxonomy will prove more illuminating for analytical purposes than the simple dichotomy between *mala in se* and *mala prohibita*. I make no claim that my categories are precise, novel, exhaustive, or mutually exclusive. My headings are vague and loosely defined; countless examples of these kinds of law have existed for centuries; some new crimes cannot be squeezed into any of these categories; and many statutes probably could be assigned to all three types simultaneously. Nonetheless, I believe that this crude taxonomy will prove helpful both in allowing us to understand the exponential growth in the criminal law and to begin the arduous task of distinguishing legitimate from illegitimate uses of the penal sanction. Despite their lack of conceptual sophistication, these categories will serve as grist for my philosophical mill.

I call the first category *overlapping crimes*. We overcriminalize partly by *re*-criminalizing—by criminalizing the same conduct over and over again. As Stuntz observes, "federal and state codes alike are filled with overlapping crimes, such that a single criminal incident typically violates a half dozen or more prohibitions."[173] We understand the social dynamic that spawns the more notorious of these offenses. A sensationalistic tragedy attracts media attention, and officials solemnly pledge to "do something" to prevent similar events in the future.[174] All too often, this "something" consists in the enactment of a new offense: a crime *du jour*. Additions to codes are welcome and necessary when statutes proscribe harmful and culpable conduct that was previously noncriminal. Such cases, however, are unusual; far more typically, the original conduct was proscribed already, and the new offense simply describes the criminal behavior with greater specificity

---

171. One might have hoped that theorists skilled in the rigors of the economic analysis of law would have produced useful distinctions. But see the unhelpful tripartite scheme recently proposed by Steven Shavell. He claims that the domain of criminal law consists roughly of three kinds of crime: "acts that are intended to do substantial harm;" "acts that are concealed, even if substantial harm was not intended;" and "certain other acts." Steven Shavell: *Foundations of Economic Analysis of Law* (Cambridge: Belknap Press of Harvard University Press, 2004), pp.540–541.

172. See chapter 2, section IV.

173. *Op. cit.*, note 113, p.507.

174. For a discussion of this phenomenon in the context of sexual predators, see Philip Jenkins: *Moral Panic: Changing Concepts of the Child Molester in Modern America* (New Haven: Yale University Press, 1998).

while imposing a more severe sentence. Frequently, the new law involves the use of a technological innovation—a cell phone or computer, for example—as though additional statutes are needed simply because defendants devise ingenious ways to commit existing crimes. In reality, however, relatively few overlapping crimes have originated from the outrage that follows the intense media coverage of a tragedy. The actual process that spawns these offenses is more mysterious. Sometimes they proliferate because legislators appear to be unaware of the prohibitions that already exist in their jurisdictions.[175] Whatever the explanation may be, modern codes contain countless overlapping offenses, with newer, more specific statutes supplementing older, more generic crimes.

Robinson and Cahill provide several mundane examples of overlapping offenses from the Illinois Code. Although Illinois has long contained a general offense of damaging property, recent statutes proscribe damaging library materials, damaging an animal facility, defacing delivery containers, and (their personal favorite) damaging anhydrous ammonia equipment.[176] California contains a generic assault statute but also proscribes assaults against custodial officers, school employees, jurors, and other specific categories of victims. Similar overlapping offenses can be found in every state code throughout the United States and probably are even more prevalent in federal law. Although the federal criminal code includes a general false statement statute that prohibits lies in matters under federal jurisdiction, it also contains a bewildering maze of laws banning lies in specified circumstances. According to one commentator, there are exactly 325 separate federal statutes proscribing fraud or misrepresentation.[177] These statutes vary in subject matter from the general—like mail fraud—to the specific and arcane—like filing a false statement in an affidavit required to accompany a translation of a foreign news article during World War I.[178] Congress has also created approximately 100 offenses involving larceny, theft, and embezzlement,[179] and 99 separate statutes proscribing forgery and counterfeiting,[180] with punishments ranging from the trivial to life imprisonment. This list of overlapping offenses could be extended indefinitely.[181] No reasonable person can believe that each of these additional offenses is necessary or justifiable.

Why are overlapping offenses objectionable? If the conduct proscribed was already criminal, then in one obvious sense these offenses do not contribute to overcriminalization; the reach of the criminal law has not been extended. Still, the proliferation of these statutes leads to increased punishments. As long as overlapping offenses contain distinct elements, no rule or doctrine of the criminal law requires that different counts be merged in order to preclude the state from

---

175. General damage to criminal codes frequently results because "the new offenses tend to be drafted as if the existing general offense(s) did not exist." Robinson and Cahill: *op. cit.*, note 27, p.171.

176. *Id.*, p.170.

177. Standen: *op. cit.*, note 128, p.289.

178. *Id.*, pp.289–290.

179. *Id.*, p.290.

180. Gainer: *op. cit.*, note 22, p.62.

181. See Ellen S. Podgor: "Do We Need a 'Beanie Baby' Fraud Statute?" 49 *American University Law Review* 1031 (2000).

bringing several charges simultaneously—even though the defendant may seem to have committed a single crime.[182] As a result, prosecutors have enormous powers to charge defendants with multiple offenses.[183] Thus, as I have indicated, the main effect of these overlapping statutes is to allow charge stacking that threatens defendants with increasingly severe punishments.[184] Offenders prosecuted for several crimes that cover much the same conduct face more lengthy sentences than could have been imposed had they been charged with only one. Defendants have greater incentives to bargain and plead guilty to a single offense in exchange for having the other charges dropped. Many commentators agree that eliminating overlapping and potentially conflicting criminal laws is among the most important goals of penal code reform.[185]

Offenses of *risk prevention* (or risk creation) are a second category of statute that has contributed to the phenomenal growth of the criminal law. After all, the state has long proscribed just about every possible means of directly causing harm—even if it resorts to *re*criminalization—but there is virtually no limit to how far the state might go in protecting persons from novel ways that harm might be risked. Crimes of risk prevention are examples of *inchoate* offenses. Roughly, an offense is inchoate when not all of its instances cause harm. These offenses do not prohibit harm itself but, rather, the *possibility* of harm—a possibility that need not (and typically does not) materialize when the offense is committed.[186] New crimes of risk prevention can easily be generated by proscribing conduct more and more remote from the ultimate harm to be prevented.

New offenses of risk prevention are enacted each week, and a few generate considerable publicity. The threat of terrorism has provided states around the world with ample excuse to create a multitude of new crimes to reduce risks. But most examples are less politically charged. Most large cities in the United States have enacted juvenile curfew laws. Approximately half of all states prohibit the use of cell phones while driving, or require cell phone users to employ devices that allow them to keep both hands on the wheel. Washington, D.C. goes further; it bans driving while "reading, writing, performing personal grooming, interacting with pets or unsecured cargo" or playing video games. These behaviors are proscribed because they are believed to unjustifiably increase the risk that drivers will cause a crash.[187] Of course, these offenses overlap with existing law; every state already prohibits erratic, dangerous, or reckless driving, even when no accident results. If the use of

182. To be sure, some criminal theorists have tried to block this result by arguing for reforms in the way criminal acts are individuated. See, for example, the references in Moore and in Thomas: *op. cit.*, note 108. To date, their proposals have not been adopted.
183. Of course, this discretionary power may be used to benefit defendants as well as to harm them. See the discussion in Leo Katz: "Is There a Volume Discount for Crime?" (forthcoming).
184. See Stuntz: *op. cit.*, note 113.
185. Kathleen Brickey: "Federal Criminal Code Reform: Hidden Costs, Illusory Benefits," 2 *Buffalo Criminal Law Review* 161, 165 (1998).
186. In some cases, the occurrence of the harm that is risked actually *precludes* liability for the inchoate offense. For example, liability for an attempt merges with the completed offense and thus cannot be imposed if the attempt is successful.
187. See Suzanne P. McEvoy, et al.: "Role of Mobile Phones in Motor Vehicle Crashes Resulting in Hospital Attendance: A Case-Crossover Study," *British Medical Journal* (July 2005) 10.1136/38537.

a cell phone or the application of lipstick while driving does *not* fall under one of these broader offenses—because it is not reckless or dangerous, for example—one wonders why any new statutes are needed. The point of an additional law, one would hope, is to provide concrete notice that a given kind of activity qualifies as reckless or dangerous. If specific notice were not needed, our criminal codes could include a single endangerment offense, proscribing conduct that creates a substantial and unjustifiable risk of a serious harm.[188] Legislatures must always strike a balance between creating too many narrow offenses and creating too few general offenses; there is no formula for how to best accomplish this task.

The harms to be avoided by offenses of risk prevention need not involve personal injury, as many new statutes are designed to lessen the probability of economic loss. Consider, for example, the Sarbanes-Oxley Act of 2002, intended to combat white-collar crime in the wake of the Enron scandal. This Act imposes criminal liability on executives who certify financial statements that prove incorrect, punishes retaliatory action against whistleblowers who alert authorities to corporate criminality, and (*inter alia*) prohibits the destruction of given kinds of documents.[189] The criminalized behaviors are not harmful per se but are proscribed to reduce the risk of substantial economic losses to innocent parties.

Theorists who aspire to retard the trend toward overcriminalization will scrutinize offenses of risk imposition carefully. Criminal liability is more controversial when harm is risked rather than caused. Yet no reasonable person should believe that all offenses of risk imposition are objectionable. If our criminal law required actual harm rather than the risk of harm, we would be forced to repeal the familiar inchoate offenses of attempt, solicitation, and conspiracy. No existing jurisdiction—and no respectable commentator—has called for the abolition of all such crimes. The theoretical challenge is to provide a sophisticated taxonomy of offenses of risk imposition in order to separate the wheat from the chaff.

R. A. Duff has made the most progress in this direction.[190] As Duff demonstrates, crimes of endangerment (or what I call offenses of risk prevention) are a maze of different types, each raising distinct justificatory issues. These crimes may be consummate or nonconsummate, general or specific, direct or indirect, and explicit or implicit. Offenses of risk prevention are consummate "if their commission requires the actualisation of the relevant risk," and nonconsummate if they "do not require the actualisation of the risk."[191] Thus an offense of causing death by dangerous driving is a consummate endangerment offense; dangerous driving itself is a nonconsummate endangerment offense. An offense of risk prevention may be general or specific "as to the interest that is threatened, or as to the way in which it is threatened."[192] Thus an offense of reckless endangerment is general with respect to the kind of conduct that creates the risk as well as to the kind of

---

188. A generic endangerment offense is included in the criminal code proposed by Paul Robinson: *Structure and Function in Criminal Law* (Oxford: Oxford University Press, 1997), p.218.

189. See Kathleen F. Brickey: "Enron's Legacy," 8 *Buffalo Criminal Law Review* 221 (2004).

190. R. A. Duff: "Criminalising Endangerment," in Duff and Green, eds.: *op. cit.*, note 46, p.43.

191. *Id.*, p.55.

192. *Id.*, p.57.

risk created, whereas an offense of risking death by dangerous driving is specific with respect to both.

Each of these distinctions is important, raising interesting analytical and normative issues. In what follows, however, I narrow my focus to Duff's last two contrasts—direct and indirect offenses of risk prevention, and explicit and implicit offenses of risk prevention—because they will figure more prominently in the theory of criminalization I ultimately construct. Endangerment offenses are direct "if the relevant harm would ensue from the criminalized conduct without any intervening wrongful human action"[193]; they are indirect "if the harm would ensue only given further, wrongful actions by the agent or by others."[194] Causing an explosion that endangers life is a direct endangerment offense, whereas carrying a deadly weapon in public is an indirect endangerment offense, because the harm would ensue only if the weapon were misused by the defendant or another. Offenses of risk prevention are explicit "when their commission requires the actual creation of the relevant risk—a risk specified in the offence definition"[195]; they are implicit "if their definition does not specify the relevant risk (the risk that grounds their criminalization), so that they can be committed without creating the risk."[196] Duff lists dangerous driving as an example of an explicit endangerment offense and drug possession as an example of an offense of implicit risk prevention. These offenses are inchoate because a person can (and typically does) commit them without harming anyone—even himself. But no one can drive dangerously without creating a risk, whereas someone might possess an illicit drug while creating no risk at all. I return to these distinctions when defending principles to limit the reach of the penal sanction.[197]

My third and final category of relatively new kinds of crime might be called *ancillary* offenses. This term, I believe, was coined by Norman Abrams—who immediately apologized for its vagueness and imprecision—and I draw heavily from his insights here.[198] Roughly, ancillary offenses function as surrogates for the prosecution of primary or core crimes and bear an indirect relation to them. They are created mostly for situations in which a defendant is believed to have committed a primary or core offense, but prosecution is unlikely to be successful or is otherwise thought to be undesirable. On some occasions, the state cannot prove the commission of the core offense, or its evidence of this offense is inadmissible because it has been obtained illegally. These occasions have led to the enactment of growing numbers of ancillary offenses that surround core crimes. Because most of these statutes have neither common-law analogues nor well-established public meanings, legislators have broad authority to define them as expansively as they wish. As a result, many of these laws venture into the "gray zone of socially acceptable and economically justifiable business conduct."[199] The features of many of

193. *Id.*, p.62.
194. *Id.*, p.62.
195. *Id.*, p.59.
196. *Id.*, p.59.
197. See chapter 3, section III.
198. Norman Abrams: "The New Ancillary Offenses," 1 *Criminal Law Forum* 1 (1989).
199. *United States v. United States Gypsum Co,* 438 U.S. 422, 441 (1978).

these offenses—the absence of culpability requirements, the shifting of burdens of proof, the imposition of liability for omissions, and the implicit trust in prosecutorial discretion to prevent abuse—compromise fundamental principles long held sacrosanct by criminal theorists.[200] These crimes lie far outside the core of criminal law and seem unlikely to satisfy the criteria in a theory of criminalization.

Abrams divides ancillary offenses into several kinds.[201] The first are *derivative crimes*, defined as "crimes an element of which involves proof that a primary harm offense was committed or intended to be committed."[202] Many derivative crimes proscribe "aid-like" conduct that occurs after the commission of a core offense. Money laundering statutes provide an example.[203] Prior to the enactment of federal money laundering statutes, a defendant committed a single crime by robbing a bank and depositing his ill-gotten gains in an account. Subsequently, he may be guilty of at least two crimes. As Abrams explains, "the activity that is made the subject of criminal sanctions is, at bottom, nothing more than ordinary commercial activity"; what transforms it into an offense is "the criminal knowledge of the participants and the fact, as required under the statute, that the money has been generated by specified kinds of criminal activity."[204] Abrams's second category is *enforcement and information-gathering offenses*. These crimes are committed in the course of a law enforcement investigation directed toward a core offense or involve a failure to provide required information that might have led to an investigation of such an offense. Federal regulations often proscribe the failure to submit given forms or maintain specified records. Abrams's example is the Bank Secrecy Act,[205] which makes it a crime for a financial institution to omit to file a report about a bank transaction that exceeds a given amount. Bank employees may be processing a fairly routine and innocent activity, but the statute criminalizes their failure to report it to the proper authorities.

The number of these crimes has increased dramatically since the appearance of Abrams's seminal article. In particular, recent statutes punish the failure to report one's awareness of crimes perpetrated by others—such as child abuse, abuse of the elderly, the discharge of hazardous waste, and other kinds of suspicious activity.[206] These laws differ considerably about *who* must report, *what* must be reported, and *when* or *to whom* the report must be made. These statutes are reminiscent of the common-law offense of misprision of felony, which punished the nondisclosure of a felony by *anyone* who knew of its commission. Although an offense of this name still exists in federal criminal law, it has been revised to prohibit only the active concealment of a felony committed by another rather than the passive failure to report such a crime.[207] Many of the more recent statutes, however, proscribe

200. See Ashworth: *op. cit.*, note 93.
201. In addition to the two categories of ancillary offense I mention here, Abrams includes a third, which he unhelpfully names *catchall crimes*. *Op. cit.*, note 198, p.24.
202. *Id.*, pp.5–6.
203. 18 U.S.C. §§1956–1957.
204. Abrams: *op. cit.*, note 198, pp.8–9.
205. 18 U.S.C. §§5311–5326.
206. See Sandra Guerra Thompson: "The White-Collar Police Force: 'Duty to Report' Statutes in Criminal Law Theory," 11 *William & Mary Bill of Rights Journal* 3 (2002).
207. 18 U.S.C. §4.

both passive and active behavior. One commentator has wondered how the proliferation of these new statutes can be reconciled with the steadfast refusal of the
criminal law to impose liability on bad Samaritans—those who fail to provide
reasonable assistance to strangers in need.[208]

Theorists raise grave doubts about these ancillary offenses. Abrams himself
frequently indicates his reservations, yet he admits that "it is difficult to grab hold
of the specific objection that underlies such an intuition."[209] Ronald Gainer is
less reticent, and he expresses his dissatisfaction with these ancillary offenses as
follows:

> Sometimes the operating philosophy seems to be that, if government cannot pros-
> ecute what it wishes to penalize, it will penalize what it wishes to prosecute. . . .
> Moving beyond penalization of collateral misconduct to the penalization of collat-
> eral, seemingly innocent conduct, that causes no real independent harm but that may
> be associated with either lawful or unlawful actions, raises jurisprudential questions
> that lawmakers have not frequently chosen to face.[210]

Despite the cogency of his analysis, I do not think that Gainer quite captures the
"jurisprudential questions" raised by the ancillary crimes to which he refers. His
main concern seems to be that the punishment of relatively innocuous conduct
will contribute to the trivialization of the criminal sanction and thereby erode
respect for law, undermining its general efficacy as a deterrent.[211] Any number of
commentators have voiced similar concerns,[212] although solid empirical evidence
for this conjecture is not readily available. In any event, I do not believe that empirical speculation is needed to understand why many of these ancillary offenses are
objectionable. My own position is not that these statutes erode respect for law but
that the case for including them in a just penal code will be difficult to defend. If
I am correct, the primary injustice is done to the unfortunate individuals who are
punished, and not to society generally. Had Abrams or Gainer developed a theory
of criminalization, their misgivings might have been easier to articulate. If each
criminal offense must be justified by stringent criteria—a reasonable assumption
I will defend at length—many of these ancillary offenses will be jeopardized.

One feature of my taxonomy of relatively new offenses merits special attention.
We will be hard-pressed to decide whether crimes in these categories satisfy a
theory of criminalization without examining *other* crimes. By definition, a given
offense cannot be overlapping or ancillary in the absence of a different offense
with which it overlaps or to which it is ancillary. Somewhat less obviously, much
the same is true of offenses of risk prevention. An offense does not prohibit conduct that creates a risk of harm X unless some other offense proscribes conduct
that directly and deliberately causes harm X. For example, an offense of driving
while intoxicated prohibits conduct that increases the risk of a crash; conduct that

208. See Thompson: *op. cit.*, note 206.
209. Abrams: *op. cit.*, note 198, p.29.
210. Gainer: *op. cit.*, note 22, p.63 n.38.
211. *Id.*, p.78.
212. See, for example, Robinson and Darley: *op. cit.*, note 156.

directly and deliberately causes a crash is proscribed as well.[213] The important point is that questions of justification cannot afford to remain fixated on single offenses if a theory of criminalization is to help retard the phenomenon of over-criminalization. To decide whether given offenses are justified, we may need to consider additional statutes a jurisdiction contains. This observation falls short of supporting what might be called *justificatory holism*—the view that normative judgments must be applied to entire criminal codes as a whole rather than to individual statutes. But it does indicate that our justificatory inquiry cannot be narrow.

Although these three kinds of offense complete my rough taxonomy, we can only imagine what novel forms of criminal liability are on the horizon if a theory of criminalization does not retard the growth of the penal sanction. Several distinct trends might be detected, and very different schemes to categorize new kinds of statute might be proposed. In particular, legislators have been tempted to enact crimes of *vicarious liability* whenever they believe objectionable behavior is best deterred by punishing someone other than the person who actually engages in it. Some of these crimes exist already, and there is every reason to think they will become more prevalent. In England, for example, parents are guilty of an offense for failing to ensure their children attend school regularly.[214] Although the statute provides for a number of defenses, "due diligence" is not among them. Thus a parent who could not have done more to ensure his child's regular attendance but cannot use one of the specific defenses is simply out of luck.[215] In the United States, the so-called Rave Act, recently defeated in Congress, would have punished anyone who "knowingly promotes any rave, dance, music, or other entertainment event, that takes place under circumstances where the promoter knows or reasonably ought to know that a controlled substance will be used or distributed."[216] It is hard to see how any concert that attracts masses of adolescents could hope to comply with this statute. One concern is that the Act might induce promoters to use extreme measures to ensure that their patrons do not use or distribute drugs, although even the most conscientious efforts to avoid liability would not seem to amount to a defense. Commentators express little enthusiasm for these examples of vicarious liability.

I repeat that my efforts to categorize the massive numbers of new criminal offenses do not demonstrate much sophistication or ingenuity. Some offenses that raise troubling justificatory issues—such as those regulating sexual activity between consenting adults—do not fall neatly into any of my categories. More important for present purposes, the distinctions between overlapping crimes, offenses of risk prevention, and ancillary offenses are vague and imprecise, and a

---

213. In the case of offenses of risk prevention, however, the connection between the offense in question and other offenses is normative rather than conceptual. In other words, no offense of risk prevention *should* be enacted unless the foregoing condition is satisfied. I call this normative condition the *consummate harm requirement* in chapter 3, section III.
214. Education Act of 1996, §444(5).
215. See Horder: *op. cit.*, note 92, p.256.
216. H.R. 834, §305.

few statutes seem to be instances of each of these three types of offense. Consider crimes of possession, for example. These offenses typically overlap with those that proscribe use, are designed to prevent the risk of harm rather than harm itself, and qualify as ancillary because possession is easier than use or acquisition to detect and prove. Thus many possession statutes serve as excellent illustrations of the phenomenon of overcriminalization.

No commentator has done more than Marcus Dubber to describe both the sheer number as well as the conceptual peculiarities of crimes of possession. According to Dubber, New York State contains over 150 possession offenses, ranging from minor violations to the most serious category of felony punishable by life imprisonment.[217] These include possession of a toy gun, graffiti instruments, public benefit cards, credit card embossing machines, gambling records, usurious loan records, obscene materials, eavesdropping devices, noxious materials, and a host of others.[218] Fictions of constructive possession dramatically expand the number of persons who commit these crimes. In most jurisdictions, for example, each occupant of a car is presumed to knowingly possess any drug or gun found in that car. Moreover, possession may trigger a presumption of other offenses both past and future, such as manufacture, importation, or distribution. To compound the oddity of these crimes, some jurisdictions prohibit what is colloquially referred to as internal possession. In other words, the offense of possession extends to banned substances already consumed and inside the defendant's body. Arizona, for example, makes it unlawful "for a person under the age of twenty-one years to have in the person's body any spirituous liquor." South Dakota extends the definition of an "illegal controlled substance" to include "an altered state of a drug or substance . . . absorbed into the human body."[219] Obviously, these offenses are enormously useful to police and prosecutors, even if they get a chilly reception from criminal theorists.

Drug policy, which includes many crimes of possession, plays a major role in any systematic treatment of the phenomenon of overcriminalization. The drug offenses in New Jersey provide excellent illustrations. In addition to the familiar offenses of possession and distribution, New Jersey prohibits the possession of drug paraphernalia—items used for a variety of purposes, such as storing or containing drugs.[220] Defendants may be convicted without knowing that the items that qualify as drug paraphernalia are typically used to commit drug offenses.[221] New Jersey also criminalizes the possession of substances known *not* to be drugs by both the seller and the buyer—when these substances are possessed under circumstances that would lead a reasonable person to *believe* they are drugs. Evidence of such circumstances exists whenever the physical appearance of the substance resembles that of a drug.[222] Punishments can be severe; violations carry a fine of up to $200,000.

217. Dubber: *op. cit.*, note 46.
218. *Id.*, pp.96–97.
219. See David A. Fahrenthold: "In N.H., a Beer in the Belly Can Get Youths Arrested," *The Washington Post* (February 5, 2006), p.A8.
220. New Jersey Criminal Code 2C:36–1 (2005).
221. See *Posters 'N' Things v. United States*, 511 U.S. 513 (1994).
222. New Jersey Criminal Code 2C:35–11(a)(3)(c) (2005).

Whatever categories of relatively new offense are ultimately developed and found to be useful, I hope to have shown that something has gone seriously wrong with the legislative process in the criminal domain. Thus I have made a presumptive and intuitive case for the urgent need to develop a theory of criminalization to retard the explosive growth of the penal law. Any such theory should have implications for the novel kinds of crime that legislatures have recently enacted. I encourage commentators to refine and improve on the crude categories of offense I have described. The test of any such scheme is whether it contributes to an understanding of the varieties of criminal law and facilitates an application of principles to limit the scope of the penal sanction.

IV: AN EXAMPLE OF OVERCRIMINALIZATION

As I have indicated, no judicial decision can begin to illustrate the way that too much crime causes too much punishment. In the first place, no single example can prove a generalization. More to the point, no case brought before a court can be representative of the phenomenon I have described here, because the vast majority of sentences are imposed pursuant to guilty pleas. The best example would involve a situation in which a person engages in conduct that arguably should not have been prohibited by the criminal law at all, is arrested and charged with multiple offenses, agrees to plead guilty in exchange for having one or more charges dropped, and receives a substantial punishment, albeit less severe than would have been imposed had he gone to trial. This scenario is routine, happening literally hundreds of thousands of times in jurisdictions throughout the United States each year. Too much criminal law would not have succeeded in producing too much punishment if this situation were unusual. Despite the difficulties of using a judicial decision to illustrate the phenomenon I have described, it is helpful to move beyond generalities and become specific. In this section I recount in detail a particular case that helps to understand the pernicious effects of overcriminalization.

The story begins in May 1988 in the state of New Jersey, when Susan Hendricks and Fred Bennett came to the apartment of Carlos Rodriguez for the purpose of buying cocaine.[223] Immediately after their purchase, Hendricks and Bennett proceeded to weigh and place the cocaine into smaller bags for resale. At that moment, police burst into Rodriguez's apartment. In an attempt to destroy the evidence, Hendricks and Bennett each swallowed several of the smaller bags. Within minutes, Hendricks collapsed in convulsions on the floor. Emergency medical workers were summoned to try to resuscitate her. They asked whether anyone else in the room had swallowed drugs; Bennett denied having done so. About half an hour later, Bennett also went into convulsions and died at the scene. Hendricks subsequently died in the hospital.

---

223. *New Jersey v. Rodriguez*, 645 A.2d 1165 (1994). The opinion includes a companion case—*New Jersey v. Maldonado*—in which the facts are not quite so unusual. With only slight hyperbole, the court described *Maldonado* as "a straightforward drug distribution and strict-liability-death case." *Id.*, p.1169.

I claimed that the best example of the phenomenon I propose to illustrate would involve a situation in which a person engages in conduct that arguably should not be prohibited by the criminal law at all. Later, and in more detail, I indicate why the foregoing example qualifies.[224] At this time, I point out only that the tragic story I have recounted helps to demonstrate the folly of the war on drugs. Many commentators have alleged that drug prohibitions are counterproductive, causing greater harms than they reduce.[225] This allegation is difficult to assess, however, unless we can identify the ultimate harm(s) these offenses are designed to prevent. Although legal officials disagree about the nature of these harms, the physical and psychological injuries suffered by drug abusers certainly are among them.[226] Government statistics listed the deaths of Hendricks and Bennett as caused by acute cocaine overdose. These statistics are routinely cited to indicate the perils of illicit drug use. When the full story is told, however, these statistics reveal little about the dangers of cocaine and much about the dangers of cocaine prohibitions.[227] Clearly, the deaths of Hendricks and Bennett would not have occurred but for the regime of drug proscriptions. Ironically, the very harms that drug proscriptions are designed to prevent were caused by the proscriptions themselves.

Although I hope that the foregoing point raises suspicions about the justifiability of drug proscriptions, a more extensive critique of these offenses must await the development and application of a theory of criminalization.[228] In what follows, I propose to use this case to further illustrate the process by which too much criminal law causes too much punishment. The remainder of my argument does not depend on my claim that the conduct for which the police sought to arrest Rodriguez involves a dubious imposition of the penal sanction. For present purposes, I will assume that the crimes of cocaine possession and distribution are justified by our theory of criminalization.

Suppose that laypersons were asked to identify the crime committed by Rodriguez. I believe they would answer that he was guilty of distributing cocaine. Clearly, Rodriguez was guilty of this offense under positive law. In an ideal system of criminal justice, he should have been punished with whatever degree of severity is proportionate to the seriousness of this crime. In the real world, however—the world of overcriminalization—Rodriguez was charged with a number of additional offenses: possession of a controlled substance, possession of a controlled substance with intent to distribute, and distribution of a controlled substance within 1,000 feet of a school zone. Rodriguez may have been fortunate; he could have been

224. See chapter 3, section III.
225. For the brief but classic argument, see Ethan Nadelmann: "Drug Prohibition in the United States: Costs, Consequences, and Alternatives," 245 *Science* 939 (1989).
226. Courts have not begun to reach a consensus about the harms drug offenses are designed to prevent. See Douglas Husak and Stanton Peele: "'One of the Major Problems of Our Society': Imagery and Evidence of Drug Harms in U.S. Supreme Court Decisions," 25 *Contemporary Drug Problems* 191 (1998).
227. The National Institute on Drug Abuse lists over 25,000 fatalities from illicit drug use. But a majority of these deaths are more properly attributed to drug prohibition than to drug use. Some 14,300 fatalities are due to hepatitis and AIDS—diseases that are not caused by illicit drugs but (almost exclusively) by the dirty needles that heroin addicts tend to share. Needle exchange programs could prevent many of these fatalities.
228. I return to a discussion of strict liability and *Rodriguez* in chapter 2, section I.

charged with literally twice as many offenses, since each of these behaviors is also criminalized under federal law, and the "dual sovereignty" doctrine allows both federal and state charges to be brought simultaneously without breaching the Double Jeopardy clause.[229] But the federal government did not intervene, so I propose to restrict my comments to the state charges brought against Rodriguez in light of the taxonomy of crimes I sketched earlier.

I claimed that the dramatic expansion in the number of criminal offenses exists largely in three categories of offense: offenses of risk prevention, ancillary offenses, and overlapping crimes. It is obvious that the additional charges brought against Rodriguez involve *each* of these three categories. Clearly, most drug offenses are intended to reduce the risk of some subsequent (but unspecified) harm. Moreover, many of these offenses are ancillary, designed to facilitate proof of those crimes that cause whatever ultimate harms the regime of drug proscriptions is designed to prevent. Even though it is not altogether clear what these ultimate harms *are*, no one can doubt that many of the charges brought against Rodriguez involve offenses that were created because proof of the conduct that causes these ultimate harms is difficult to obtain. Use is harder to prove than possession; the latter is an ongoing (or continuous) offense that is not limited to a specific time and place. Finally, most of the charges brought against Rodriguez overlap with one another. The offense of possessing an illicit drug overlaps with the offense of distribution, as it is probably impossible to distribute something without possessing it. This overlap is equally apparent with the offense of possession with intent to distribute. Again, virtually no one distributes a drug without a prior act of possession with intent to distribute. Finally, the crime of distribution within 1,000 feet of a school zone overlaps with most of these other offenses; to distribute within a particular place implies (or all but implies) possession with intent to distribute, and possession. Thus the charges brought against Rodriguez involve clear examples of each of the relatively new kinds of crime I distinguished earlier.

Moreover, school zone statutes impose strict liability with respect to their crucial element; even a reasonable mistake of fact about the existence of the school zone or its proximity to the place where the defendant is found is not a defense to the charge. Two examples illustrate how defendants may be guilty despite their absence of culpability for this element. In one case, a defendant riding his bicycle near a public park was convicted under a statute proscribing possession of drugs with intent to distribute within 1,000 feet of a school zone, even though the state did not prove that he intended to sell drugs near school property, even though the state did not prove he had any reason to know the park was school property, and even though the park, owned by a parochial school, had been leased to the city and regularly used for general recreational purposes.[230] In another case, a defendant was convicted under the same statute even though she distributed drugs within a prison that happened to be near a school.[231] It is important to add that New Jersey

229. See Thomas: *op. cit.*, note 108, pp.188–194.
230. *New Jersey v. Ivory*, 592 A.2d 205 (1991).
231. *New Jersey v. Ogar*, 551 A.2d 1037 (1989).

is not unusual in enacting such offenses. Most states prohibit drug possession and/or distribution in proximity to a school zone; none appears to require that a defendant believe or have any reason to believe that his possession or distribution took place within the proscribed area.[232]

Thus several of the drug offenses with which Rodriguez was charged involve fairly new and novel forms of criminal liability. Nonetheless, under normal circumstances, Rodriguez's case would never have gone to trial. In this event, his situation would have been no more illustrative than countless others of the phenomenon by which too much criminal law produces too much punishment. Rodriguez would have been prosecuted for each of these offenses and been allowed to plead guilty in exchange for dropping one or more of the charges. It is hard to predict how severe his sentence would have been. Estimates are always tenuous, especially because the prosecutor might have promised leniency in exchange for Rodriguez's willingness to implicate someone higher in the chain of cocaine distribution. The judicial opinion offers no hint about whether Rodriguez actually had any such information, or whether he would have been prepared to provide it in exchange for a reduced sentence.

Most important for present purposes, these normal circumstances did not obtain. This case came before the Supreme Court of New Jersey because Rodriguez was prosecuted and convicted not simply for the foregoing offenses but also for *homicide*—for causing the death of Fred Bennett.[233] He could not have been found guilty of any of the familiar kinds of homicide—murder, manslaughter, or negligent homicide—that have long existed in criminal codes throughout the United States. Instead, Rodriguez was prosecuted and convicted of a wholly *new* kind of homicide created by the Comprehensive Drug Reform Act of 1986.[234] I argue that the statute that creates this new kind of homicide is a monstrosity, serving as an excellent illustration of the phenomenon of overcriminalization. Because I concentrate on this statute in the remainder of this section, its relevant portions are worth quoting at length.

> a. Any person who manufactures, distributes or dispenses . . . any . . . controlled dangerous substance classified in Schedules I or II . . . is strictly liable for a death which . . . results from the injection, inhalation or ingestion of that substance, and is guilty of a crime of the first degree.

> b. The provisions . . . (governing the causal relationship between conduct and result) shall not apply in a prosecution under this section. For purposes of this section, the defendant's act of manufacturing, distributing or dispensing a substance is the cause of a death when:

---

232. See Tracey Bateman: "Annotation, Validity, Construction, and Application of State Statutes Prohibiting Sale or Possession of Controlled Substances within Specified Distance of School," 27 *A.L.R. 5th* 593 (2000).
233. The opinion does not indicate why the defendant was not also charged with a second count of homicide—for causing the death of Susan Hendricks.
234. "What is created is an additional species of homicide, akin to felony-murder." *New Jersey Statutes Annotated:* Official Comment to 2C:35–9 (2004). This new kind of homicide is not peculiar to New Jersey. At least 13 other states impose strict criminal liability for a death resulting from the distribution or manufacture of drugs. Two states subject defendants to capital punishment when convicted under their drug death statutes, and two others impose life imprisonment. See the references in *Rodriguez*, op. cit., note 223, p.1175.

(1) The injection, inhalation or ingestion of the substance is an antecedent but for which the death would not have occurred; and

(2) The death was not:

(a) too remote in its occurrence as to have a just bearing on the defendant's liability; or

(b) too dependent upon conduct of another person which was unrelated to the injection, inhalation or ingestion of the substance or its effect as to have a just bearing on the defendant's liability.

(c) It shall not be a defense to a prosecution under this section that the decedent contributed to his own death by his purposeful, knowing, reckless or negligent injection, inhalation or ingestion of the substance, or by his consenting to the administration of the substance by another.

(d) Nothing in this section shall be construed to preclude or limit any prosecution for homicide . . . [235]

In *New Jersey v. Rodriguez*, the Supreme Court of New Jersey unanimously upheld the constitutionality of this strict liability drug homicide statute and affirmed Rodriguez's conviction.

I have alleged that most of the charges brought against Rodriguez involve dubious uses of the criminal sanction and thus represent plausible examples of overcriminalization. Even if I am correct, there is no obvious reason to suppose that statutes must be unconstitutional when they fail to satisfy our theory of criminalization. Rodriguez, however, was persuaded to challenge the constitutionality of this new homicide statute because it imposed strict liability with regard to its crucial element. Under this statute, "no culpability is required for the deadly result. A defendant is guilty whether the defendant intends the death or has absolutely no idea that it may occur."[236] Why did Rodriguez believe his constitutional challenge to this homicide statute might succeed? His prospects appeared to be bleak. Almost no one contends that strict liability itself is unconstitutional throughout the criminal law.[237] Moreover, as I have indicated, Rodriguez was charged with an offense other than homicide that also imposed strict liability. Yet he did not challenge the constitutionality of the school zone statute. Finally, strict liability has played a prominent historical role in combating the dangers of drug abuse.[238] Without contesting any of these points, Rodriguez argued that strict liability was objectionable in his case—a case of serious crime. Because he faced a lengthy term of imprisonment if convicted of homicide, he contended that liability without culpability was unconstitutional, inflicting cruel and unusual punishment and violating due process of law. Commentators provided Rodriguez with some basis for optimism. Although theorists are somewhat divided about the *justice* of strict liability,[239] their protests are more vocal as sentences become more substantial.

---

235. New Jersey Criminal Code 2C:35–9 (2004).
236. *Rodriguez*, op. cit., note 223, p.1170.
237. For a dissenting view about the constitutionality of strict liability, see Richard Singer: "The Resurgence of Mens Rea III—The Rise and Fall of Strict Criminal Liability," 30 *Boston College Law Review* 337 (1989).
238. See *United States v. Balint*, 258 U.S. 250 (1922).
239. See, for example, A. P. Simester: "Is Strict Liability Always Wrong?" in A. P. Simester, ed.: *Appraising Strict Liability* (Oxford: Oxford University Press, 2005), p.21.

Concerns about the severity of punishments have been a persistent theme among courts and commentators who express reservations about the justifiability of strict liability in the criminal law.[240]

Nonetheless, the court flatly rejected Rodriguez's constitutional challenge to the strict liability drug homicide statute, showing extreme deference to the authority of the legislature to enact crimes and impose punishments. "Case after case, almost without exception, has upheld the power of the states to impose strict criminal liability not only in a regulatory setting but for serious offenses as well."[241] According to the court, virtually all that is needed to uphold strict liability is "the legislator's rational conclusion that the safety of the public requires such draconian measures."[242] In this case, the court entertained no doubt about the rationality of the legislature's decision. This statute was said to have a "conceivable rational basis" because legislatures are entitled to suppose that greater deterrence would result from holding drug offenders strictly liable for the deaths they cause.[243] As I explain in more detail later, this "conceivable rational basis" test is generally applied to assess the constitutionality of criminal legislation throughout the United States today; its permissive standards almost always result in a finding that the challenged law is constitutional.[244] If a higher standard of criminalization were in place, however, we might not be satisfied with mere conjecture. Instead, we might demand empirical evidence that some defendants who might otherwise distribute cocaine would be deterred by the threat of being punished for homicide if their customers happened to die from the drugs they had purchased. I am skeptical that such empirical evidence would be forthcoming. If the unbelievably severe sentences already in place for cocaine distribution do not succeed in deterring dealers, it is hard to believe that they will be persuaded to desist by additional statutes imposing even more severe punishments in the highly unlikely event that a death occurs. Without questioning the bare rationality of the contrary judgment, many commentators offer several reasons to doubt that such statutes produce any marginal gains in deterrence.[245]

No one should be surprised to learn that courts show extreme deference to legislatures in the criminal arena. Without this deference, we would not be in the predicament I describe throughout this book. What is more remarkable, however, is the court's claim that "the Constitution places a lesser burden on the states to justify strict liability for serious criminal offenses than for regulatory offenses."[246] In supporting this contention, the court relied heavily on similarities between the strict liability drug homicide statute and the felony-murder rule—the common-law rule that allows persons to be convicted of murder when their felonious behavior

240. See Simester and Sullivan: *op. cit.*, note 91, p.165. The Model Penal Code bars strict liability when defendants are subject to imprisonment. See §6.02(4).
241. *Rodriguez*, op. cit., note 223, p.1171.
242. *Id.*, p.1172.
243. *Id.*, p.1172.
244. See chapter 3, section I.
245. See Paul H. Robinson and John M. Darley: "The Role of Deterrence in the Formulation of Criminal Law Rules: At Its Worst When Doing Its Best," 91 *Georgetown Law Journal* 949 (2003).
246. *Rodriguez*, op. cit., note 223, p.1171.

causes death, even if the death is unforeseeable.[247] These similarities, of course, will not persuade those many commentators who believe the felony-murder rule to be equally pernicious.[248] Indeed, the court noted that even though the felony-murder rule demonstrated "the power of the states to create strict liability crimes," it has been "bombarded by intense criticism and constitutional attack" since its inception.[249] Nonetheless, the court concluded that the continued survival of the felony-murder rule served as "a strong indicator of states' power to impose strict criminal liability,"[250] even when punishments are severe.

I am not especially concerned with the *constitutionality* of strict liability in the criminal law.[251] Still, it is important to notice two significant differences between the felony-murder rule and the strict liability drug homicide statute upheld in *Rodriguez*. First, the application of New Jersey's felony-murder rule, like that in many states, is restricted to a small number of specifically enumerated felonies—robbery, sexual assault, arson, burglary, kidnapping, or criminal escape.[252] Whatever considerations led jurisdictions to restrict the felony-murder rule to these felonies—perhaps the view that they are inherently dangerous—should have militated against applying the rule to the facts of *Rodriguez*. The dangers inherent in crimes such as arson and robbery need not be belabored. But persons manufacture, distribute, or dispense illicit drugs on literally billions of occasions, and death rarely ensues.[253] Indeed, the consumption of some illicit Schedule I drugs (such as marijuana) has never been known to kill anyone.[254]

Second, the felony-murder rule, unlike the challenged strict liability drug homicide statute, preserves the usual test of causation applied to other offenses. New Jersey's statute governing causation provides that "when causing a particular result is a material element of an offense for which absolute liability is imposed by law, the element is not established unless the actual result is a probable consequence of the actor's conduct."[255] Had this statute been applied, the court might

247. William Blackstone's classic formulation of the felony-murder rule is as follows: "And if one intends to do another felony, and undesignedly kills a man, this is also murder." William Blackstone: *Commentaries on the Laws of England,* vol. 4, (1765–1769), pp.200–201.

248. According to some commentators, "criticism of the [felony-murder] rule constitutes a lexicon of everything that scholars and jurists can find wrong with a legal doctrine." Nelson E. Roth and Scott E. Sundby: "The Felony-Murder Rule: A Doctrine at Constitutional Crossroads," 70 *Cornell Law Review* 446, 446 (1985).

249. *Rodriguez,* op. cit., note 223, p.1171.

250. *Id.*

251. The strict liability drug homicide statute satisfies tests recently articulated by commentators who have sought to assess the constitutionality of strict liability. See Alan C. Michaels: "Constitutional Innocence," 112 *Harvard Law Review* 828 (1999).

252. New Jersey Criminal Code: 2C:11–3(3) (2004).

253. The court disagrees. Remarkably, it alleged that "the conduct sought to be deterred—illegal drug manufacturing and drug distribution—is also widely regarded as constituting the most substantial threat to public safety that now exists." *Rodriguez,* op. cit., note 223, p.1172. To support this claim, the court indicated that in 1986 "more than 37,000 people suffered drug-related deaths." *Id.,* p.1173. In 1988, the names of Susan Hendricks and Fred Bennett were added to this total. Admittedly, a minority of states have held that the distribution of cocaine is inherently dangerous and triggers application of the felony-murder rule. For example, see *Heacock v. Commonwealth,* 323 S.E.2d 90 (Va. 1984).

254. See Mitch Earlywine: *Understanding Marijuana: A New Look at the Scientific Evidence* (Oxford: Oxford University Press, 2002), pp.143–144.

255. New Jersey Criminal Code 2C:2–3(2)(e) (2004).

have concluded that Rodriguez's act of selling cocaine did not cause the death of Hendricks or Bennett. By any reasonable measure, death is not (beyond a reasonable doubt) a "probable consequence" of cocaine distribution. In addition, the victims would not have died but for their own intervention; they decided to consume the drugs in order to avoid arrest—a situation that Rodriguez could not have been expected to anticipate. But the ordinary statute governing causation was *not* applied in Rodriguez's strict liability drug homicide prosecution. Under the strict liability drug homicide statute, a defendant can be liable even if death is *not* a probable consequence of his manufacture, distribution, or dispensing of drugs[256]—an important point to which I soon return. At this juncture, I simply note that the policy considerations included in most tests of proximate causation can function as a surrogate for culpability under many applications of the felony-murder rule.

What is unjust about the strict liability drug homicide statute upheld in *Rodriguez*?[257] One answer is that the defendant's conviction misrepresents the nature of what he *did*—what he is blameworthy *for*. Clearly, Rodriguez distributed cocaine. But the strict liability drug homicide statute punishes him for something quite different: the death of Fred Bennett. No one should be criminally liable for a state of affairs for which he does not deserve to be blamed. Unless persons are culpable for a state of affairs—at least negligent—no censure *for* that state of affairs is deserved. Among my claims, then, is that Rodriguez's conviction involves a kind of deception. Rodriguez may not be blameless altogether, but he is not blameworthy *for* the result for which he was convicted. But why shouldn't he be blamed for Bennett's death? Is the only answer that Rodriguez is not culpable for this result? Moral and legal philosophers have long debated the precise nature of the relationship that must obtain between a defendant's action and a state of affairs before he deserves to be blamed for it. Typically, this relationship is said to be *causal*.[258] Assume this position is correct; assume that Rodriguez does not deserve to be blamed *for* the death of Bennett unless he *caused* that death. *Did* Rodriguez cause Bennett's death? No philosopher has defended a theory of causation that should inspire much confidence about how to settle this complex issue.[259] Nonetheless, I believe there are several reasons to doubt that it should be answered affirmatively.

First, suppose that the legislature is generally correct about the conditions under which persons cause results for which negligence is not required. For other strict liability offenses, we have seen that the result must be "a probable consequence of the actor's conduct."[260] The strict liability drug homicide statute does not retain this general test; it relaxes the ordinary rules of causation that usually are applied

256. See *New Jersey v. Martin*, 573 A.2d 1359, 1372 (1990).
257. I return to this question in chapter 2, section I
258. But see Douglas Husak: "Omissions, Causation, and Liability," 30 *Philosophical Quarterly* 316 (1980).
259. See Michael Moore: *Legal Causation* (New York: Oxford University Press, forthcoming).
260. New Jersey Criminal Code 2C:2–3(2)(e) (2004).

to strict liability result crimes.[261] To be sure, the statute preserves the so-called cause in fact component of causation. Still, the legislature decided to fashion a wholly new rule of *proximate* causation for strict liability drug homicide cases. But if the usual test of causation is adequate in other contexts—when a consequence is brought about by using a gun, for example—I cannot comprehend why it would be *in*adequate when that same consequence is brought about by using a different instrument, such as a drug.[262] Deaths frequently ensue from ingesting medications, even when patients conform to the terms of their prescriptions.[263] Why should the test of causation vary depending on whether death follows from taking a drug the legislature has proscribed? Unless the test of causation is defective across the board, we are entitled to conclude that it is defective in this case.

This conclusion is important for the topic at hand because judgments about causation are not wholly independent of those pertaining to culpability and thus to criminalization itself. As I have indicated, the policy considerations many theorists contend to be inherent in tests of proximate causation often serve to mitigate the harshness of doctrines in the criminal law that dispense with culpability—like the felony-murder rule. In other words, proximate causation frequently functions as a surrogate for culpability. In *King v. Commonwealth*,[264] for example, a felony-murder conviction was reversed when a co-pilot survived after his airplane, transporting marijuana, crashed into a mountainside in dense fog. The court reasoned that the felonious nature of the defendant's conduct was not the proximate cause of the pilot's death, because the plane would have hit the mountain even if its cargo had not contained contraband. The court noted that the outcome might have been different if the crash had occurred because the pilot had been trying to avoid detection by flying at a low altitude. I am not suggesting that the very same reasoning would support an acquittal in *Rodriguez*. In suspending the usual test of proximate causation, however, some of the kinds of considerations adduced in *King* become unavailable to defendants like Rodriguez. After all, deaths like that suffered by Bennett do not provide the state with a reason to proscribe drug distribution. No legislature would enact a drug offense in order to dissuade buyers from swallowing large quantities of cocaine to avoid arrest and prosecution. Indeed, as I have noted, Bennett's fate provides a reason *not* to proscribe drug distribution. The special provisions applicable to strict liability drug homicide cases limit our opportunity to employ causal language to convey our skepticism that Rodriguez deserves to be blamed for Bennett's death. For these reasons, I conclude that Rodriguez probably did *not* cause death, and he clearly did not do

261. Remarkably, the court did not appear to believe that the new statutory provision regarding causation was needed to impose liability. In commenting on the nature of the causal connection between Rodriguez's sale and the ensuing deaths, the Court indicated that "no case could be more direct....Rodriguez provided cocaine to Bennett, he died from the ingestion." *Rodriguez*, op. cit., note 223, p.1178. According to this analysis, the intervention of the police or the effort of Bennett to avoid arrest played no causal role.

262. I take the fact that lesser standards of causation apply to drug offenses as further evidence for what might be called "drug exceptionalism" in the substantive criminal law. See Erik Luna: "Drug Exceptionalism," 47 *Villanova Law Review* 753 (2002).

263. See Jay S. Cohen: *Overdose* (New York: Jeremy P. Tarcher/Putnam, 2001).

264. 368 S.E.2d 704 (1988).

so beyond a reasonable doubt. If I am correct, and a defendant does not deserve to be blamed for an outcome he did not cause, Rodriguez does not deserve to be blamed for Bennett's death.

I have not yet identified the most serious allegation of injustice that might be brought against the strict liability drug homicide statute upheld in *Rodriguez*. Earlier, I expressed my commitment to the principle of proportionality, which requires the severity of the punishment to be a function of the seriousness of the crime. I claim that the sentence imposed on Rodriguez was almost certainly disproportionate. Thus far, my description of *Rodriguez* has not provided sufficient information on which to base this allegation. Yet we naturally assume that the strict liability drug homicide offense for which Rodriguez was convicted involves a more severe sentence than the several other crimes he unquestionably committed. Why *else* would the legislature have created an additional species of homicide— especially when its inclusion in the criminal code gives rise to the misrepresentation I mentioned earlier? Indeed, this assumption is correct. In New Jersey, a defendant convicted of distributing cocaine is guilty of an offense of the second or third degree, while a defendant who is convicted of strict liability drug homicide is guilty of an offense of the first degree.[265] Specifically, Rodriguez was sentenced to an additional 18 years for his homicide.[266] The severity of punishment inflicted for this offense is comparable to that imposed on murderers—one of the few other crimes of the first degree in New Jersey. Even without a detailed theory to match the severity of punishments with the seriousness of crimes, it is hard to believe that Rodriguez deserves a sentence comparable to that imposed on persons who deliberately kill. I conclude that Rodriguez was punished excessively.

I hope that my extended examination of *Rodriguez* helps to illustrate the phenomenon of overcriminalization and why it is worrisome. Too much punishment is produced by a criminal law that is monstrous. I describe the strict liability drug homicide statute as monstrous because it dispenses with culpability for its crucial element of death, misrepresents the nature of the defendant's wrongful act, blames him for a result he probably did not cause, and punishes him in excess of his desert. I repeat, however, that the typical mechanism by which too much criminal law causes too much punishment does not involve a judicial decision at all. More frequently, objectionable laws like the strict liability drug homicide statute upheld in *Rodriguez* are included in a lengthy indictment, and defendants agree to plead guilty if one or more of the additional charges are dropped. Sentences would be less severe and more likely to be deserved if codes contained only justified laws to include in indictments. Although no judicial decision can illustrate this more typical mechanism, *New Jersey v. Rodriguez* exemplifies much of what is unjust about the criminal law today.

265. *Rodriguez*, op. cit., note 223, p.1168.
266. The court initially merged the counts for possession and possession with intent to distribute into the distribution count, for which Rodriguez was sentenced to a five-year term. On the school zone count, Rodriguez was sentenced to an additional term of four years. The Appellate Division affirmed Rodriguez's convictions, merged the distribution conviction into the school zone conviction, and ordered that the sentences for the drug death and the school zone conviction run concurrently. The court rejected Rodriguez's contention that his school distribution conviction should merge into his strict liability drug homicide conviction. *Id.*, p.1170. The principles on which these decisions are based remain mysterious.

2

Internal Constraints on Criminalization

I hope to have made a presumptive case in favor of my central claims: The United States presently suffers from too much criminal law and too much punishment, and these phenomena, although distinct, are intimately related. Unless these normative claims are to remain wholly intuitive, a theory of criminalization is needed to provide a principled basis for combating these trends. My initial efforts to provide such a theory remain at a fairly high level of abstraction. I will not begin to attempt to offer a justified criminal code, for example.[1] Instead, the theory of criminalization I ultimately defend consists in a total of seven general principles or constraints designed to limit the authority of the state to enact penal offenses.[2] No single constraint will prove adequate for the task at hand. Several distinct constraints are needed because given criminal statutes exceed the boundaries of legitimate state authority for different reasons. As we see in chapter 4, the complexity of my account provides the resources lacked by simpler theories to slow the growth of the criminal law.[3]

I sort these constraints into two rough categories. I call one set of constraints *external;* they depend on a controversial normative theory imported from outside the criminal law itself. I defend a number (three, to be exact) of external restrictions on the scope of the criminal sanction in chapter 3. I describe the other set of constraints as *internal* inasmuch as I derive them from the criminal law itself. I maintain that *any* respectable theory of criminalization must include these internal constraints; no adequate criteria to limit the penal sanction can afford to reject them. My primary goal in this chapter—which I believe will prove relatively easy to accomplish—is to identify and defend four such constraints: what I call the *nontrivial harm or evil* constraint, the *wrongfulness* constraint, the *desert* constraint, and the *burden of proof* constraint.

How might we defend constraints on criminalization? Different approaches could be taken. An ambitious answer might try to extract each of the several limitations on the criminal law from a general view about the conditions under

---

1. For an admirable attempt to produce a better criminal code, see Paul Robinson: *Structure and Function in Criminal Law* (Oxford: Oxford University Press, 1997). Robinson, however, is less concerned to implement a theory of criminalization than to reorganize criminal codes and to rewrite statutes in clear and accessible language.

2. I do not believe that we can or should seek to understand criminal law only as a matter of principle. But the principles of criminalization I defend establish the parameters within which policies and economic objectives may be pursued.

3. I describe what follows as a *theory* of criminalization even though it might be construed as a *decision procedure* for justifying criminal laws. Although it is not exactly clear what makes a set of principles qualify as a theory, my account consists in more than a single consideration and aspires to be reasonably comprehensive.

which political authority is legitimate. A follower of John Rawls, for example, might insist that exercises of coercive state power in a liberal democracy are justified only if all members of society would accept them under appropriate conditions of rational choice.[4] I agree that further connections between penal liability and political philosophy must be developed.[5] One might reasonably expect that the topic of what kinds of conduct may be proscribed by the state, on pain of punishment, would be among the most central and widely debated issues in political philosophy.[6] Indeed, controversies that have generated a more extensive literature presuppose a satisfactory answer to this question. To cite a single example, consider the voluminous commentary on the general question of political obligation—specifically, on the obligation to obey the law.[7] How could one hope to decide whether persons have an obligation to obey the law without attending to the content of the law to which one supposedly is obligated?[8] This issue might be evaded by stipulating that the laws in question must be "basically just." If so, however, we need to know the criteria by which we should decide whether the laws are basically just so that persons might have an obligation to obey them. In any event, the strategy I pursue here is more modest, avoiding deep connections to political philosophy. I propose to sort constraints into two kinds, and derive what I call the internal constraints on the penal sanction from within the criminal law itself. I presuppose the existence of a legitimate state, and ask what must be true before that state is permitted to resort to the criminal sanction in particular. Although legal philosophers have said disappointingly little about the topic, much of the content of the theory of criminalization I ultimately defend is drawn from issues about which penal theorists have said a great deal.

This chapter contains four sections. In the first, I attempt to explain why legal philosophy in its present form suffers from its neglect of the topic of criminalization. Although I briefly mention a number of contributing factors, the main problem among academic theorists is their narrow focus on the several difficulties that arise within the so-called *general part* of criminal law. Few theorists who write about the general part appear to have much interest in principles that limit the scope of criminal statutes. I argue, however, that some constraints on the power of states to impose penal sanctions can be derived from the general part of criminal

---

4. John Rawls: *Political Liberalism* (New York: Columbia University Press, 1993).

5. See Guyora Binder: "Punishment Theory: Moral or Political?" 5 *Buffalo Criminal Law Review* 321 (2002). One commentator speculates "this lack of attention by philosophers of punishment to [questions about political authority] is an artifact of the extent to which the punishment debate has been dominated by moral philosophers, while political theorists for the most part have been disinclined to participate." Sharon Dolovich: "Legitimate Punishment in Liberal Democracy," 7 *Buffalo Criminal Law Review* 307, 323 n.36 (2004).

6. See John Braithwaite and Philip Pettit: *Not Just Deserts* (Oxford: Oxford University Press, 1990).

7. See, for example, William A. Edmundson: *The Duty to Obey the Law* (Lanham, Md.: Rowman & Littlefield, 1999).

8. Few contemporary philosophers attempt to defend an obligation to obey the law that is *content-independent*, that is, an obligation that "does not depend on the morally worthy tenor of a legal system as a whole or on the morally worthy substance of any specific laws within the system." See Matthew H. Kramer: "Legal and Moral Obligation," in Martin P. Golding and William A. Edmundson, eds.: *The Blackwell Guide to the Philosophy of Law and Legal Theory* (Oxford: Blackwell Publishing, 2005), pp.179, 180.

law. In the second section, I explain how justifications of punishment provide an important source of restrictions on penal laws. No adequate theory of *how* punishment is justified can pretend to be neutral about *what* conduct is punished. If I am correct, widely accepted principles about the justification of punishment have important implications for criminalization. In the third section, I identify what it is about punishment—and thus about criminal liability—that requires justification. State punishments include two problematic components: deliberate inflictions of hard treatment and impositions of stigma. Persons generally have a *right* not to be subjected to intentional deprivation and censure through state action. Because ordinary utilitarian gains do not justify impositions of hard treatment and stigma, I tentatively propose that persons have a right not to be punished. Although this right is overridden by whatever considerations justify punishment, penal liability violates rights when this rationale is absent. If we keep this point in mind, we should be receptive to my claim that impositions of the criminal sanction must satisfy demanding criteria of justification. In the fourth and final section, I begin to apply some of these internal constraints to existing legislation. In particular, I ask whether punishments are defensible when persons commit *mala prohibita* offenses. My discussion here will be almost entirely critical; I will respond to the heroic efforts undertaken by a handful of contemporary legal philosophers who have endeavored to show why criminal liability is justified when persons perpetrate *mala prohibita* offenses.

My overall conclusion in this chapter is that the resources for identifying four constraints in a theory of criminalization can be found within the boundaries of criminal theory as it is presently conceptualized, even though these resources have not been explicitly utilized for this purpose. If I am correct, many of the principles in a theory of criminalization can be derived from positions on issues with which legal philosophers are certain to be conversant. Thus my secondary and more ambitious goal is to explore some of the connections between a theory of the limits of the penal sanction and criminal theory as traditionally construed. To achieve this objective, my discussion occasionally focuses as much on criminal theory generally as on criminalization in particular.

A word of caution is advisable before I begin. The distinction I draw between internal and external constraints is somewhat crude. I contend that several limitations on the penal sanction are internal to criminal law itself, and thus they must be included in any respectable theory of criminalization. The source of these constraints—positive law and our thoughts about punishment—leads me to describe them as internal.[9] But I do not pretend that debates about the *content* of these constraints can be resolved by attending to the nature of the criminal law. The

---

9. The connection to Lon Fuller is apparent. In his *The Morality of Law* (Cambridge: Harvard University Press, 1968), Fuller famously argued in favor of a morality internal to law itself. My position differs in three significant respects. First and perhaps least important, I claim that limitations on the criminal sanction are internal to the criminal law, and not to law generally. Second, I derive no implications from my position for the jurisprudential debate between natural law and positivism. I do not allege that a system of norms that did not conform to my constraints could not possibly qualify as a system of law. Finally, Fuller's internal morality of law is procedural rather than substantive, whereas the internal constraints I identify are substantive in any meaningful sense.

task of interpreting and applying these internal constraints—where much of the real substantive work must be done—involves no less controversy than is needed to defend the external constraints I introduce in chapter 3. Thus I admit that reflection on the nature of the criminal law does not take us very far in producing a theory of criminalization. In addition, the internal and external constraints overlap to a significant degree; many unjust laws violate several constraints simultaneously, and it is not always clear which particular constraint is doing the work when an injustice in the criminal law is detected.[10] For these reasons, the contrast I draw between these two kinds of constraints is a bit artificial. Fortunately, nothing of deep significance depends on my claim that limitations on the criminal sanction are of two kinds and derive from distinct sources. I will regard my project in this chapter as successful if I am able to show, first, that criminal laws should be required to satisfy each of the four constraints I identify and, next, that the growth of the criminal sanction will be slowed if penal statutes are made to conform to these constraints.

I: THE "GENERAL PART" OF CRIMINAL LAW

Too much criminal law will continue to produce too much punishment until we have a principled means to limit the scope of the criminal sanction. The absence of a viable account of criminalization constitutes the single most glaring failure of penal theory as it has developed on both sides of the Atlantic. In my judgment, the leading commentators of our era who specialize in criminal theory have been too complacent about the two trends I have discussed. Admittedly, a number of distinguished criminologists have protested our willingness to inflict too much punishment.[11] But the phenomenon of enacting too many criminal laws has not received the attention it deserves from philosophers of the criminal law. I have already speculated briefly about some of the sociopolitical causes of these trends. But why have so few academic theorists been passionate about the problems that result when too much criminal law produces too much punishment? I have no entirely satisfactory answer to this question; at the end of the day, I find the lack of scholarly interest in the topic of criminalization to be baffling. But I am not content merely to express bewilderment. In this section, I begin by mentioning a few factors that have contributed to our predicament and end by focusing on one in particular: the fixation among theorists on the *general part* of criminal law. If my arguments are cogent, however, criminal theory as traditionally construed has the resources to yield constraints on the reach of the penal sanction. I will show that two internal limitations can be extracted from what is called the general part of criminal law.

---

10. Joel Feinberg, for example, subsumes the wrongfulness requirement under the harm requirement. See his *Harm to Others: The Moral Limits of the Criminal Law* (Oxford: Oxford University Press, 1984), p.34. By contrast, I treat these constraints as distinct.
11. See, for example, Michael Tonry: *Thinking about Crime: Sense and Sensibility in American Penal Culture* (New York: Oxford University Press, 2004).

Knowledgeable commentators may respond to my query by denying that legal theorists *have* neglected these matters.[12] After all, two of the most prominent theorists of the latter half of the 20th century complained bitterly about overcriminalization.[13] In the late 1960s, Herbert Packer[14] and Sanford Kadish[15] famously argued that a range of behavior roughly classified as "private" should be exempted from penal liability. Although I cannot fault the conclusions these theorists defended, their arguments were quite unlike those I develop here. Both Packer and Kadish stressed the negative *consequences* of overcriminalization for an effective system of criminal justice. They were worried mostly about such problems as corruption among legal officials and disrespect for law among citizens, and they insisted that efforts to curb consensual behavior like gambling or drug transactions were likely to be futile and counterproductive. History has confirmed their fears. From the perspective of a legal philosopher, however, these consequentialist concerns do not get to the heart of the matter. Neither Packer nor Kadish emphasized how overcriminalization produces injustice to the very persons who become subject to a widened net of liability. Because their positions were grounded in utilitarian considerations rather than in principles of justice, one critic responded that the arguments of Packer and Kadish "are parasites in search of a host: they derive the persuasive power they seem to possess from the unstated and unproven proposition that private behavior ought not to be prohibited by the criminal law. What is missing is the principle or set of principles from which this latter proposition may be derived."[16] In other words, neither Packer nor Kadish developed a normative theory of criminalization: a set of principles to narrow the reach of the substantive criminal law.

Even if I am too dismissive of the work of Packer and Kadish on the topic of overcriminalization in the late 1960s, it remains true that their contributions are dated, and no legal philosopher in the United States has emerged to carry

12. Libertarians are among those commentators who have protested against overcriminalization with the most vehemence. Generally, see Randy Barnett: "Restitution: A New Paradigm of Criminal Justice," in Randy Barnett and John Hagel III, eds.: *Assessing the Criminal: Restitution, Retribution, and the Legal Process* (Cambridge: Ballinger Pub. Co., 1977), p.349. Many of these theorists are mainly opposed to *overfederalization* and are less critical of the expansion in the scope of state codes. From my perspective, however, questions about federalism are relatively unimportant. What is most worrisome about overcriminalization is that it produces too much punishment, and we should be largely indifferent to whether punishment is imposed by the states or by the federal government. Still, libertarians are nearly alone in the United States in having objected to overcriminalization generally. The Heritage Foundation even provides its own website: *http://www.overcriminalized.com.*

13. I do not mean to suggest that all concern about overcriminalization is new. Clarence Darrow wrote in his autobiography: "Among the bills that I always tried to kill, and generally with good success, were laws increasing penalties and creating new crimes. Congress and every State legislature are always beset with this sort of legislation. Judges and State's attorneys constantly cudgel their brains to think of new things to punish, and severer penalties to inflict on others. Reform associations are likewise active in this regard. And many citizens who think that they have been unjustly dealt with, or have witnessed something that provoked their anger are always seeking to send some one to jail; so that I am satisfied that at least half the men in prison to-day are there for crimes that did not exist thirty years ago—violations of the Volstead Act, confidence games, conspiracy and offenses against many other statutes comparatively new." Clarence Darrow: *The Story of My Life* (New York: Charles Scribner's Sons, 1932), p.122.

14. Herbert Packer: *The Limits of the Criminal Sanction* (Stanford: Stanford University Press, 1968).

15. Sanford Kadish: "The Crisis of Overcriminalization," 374 *Annals of the American Academy of Political and Social Science* 157 (1967).

16. John M. Junker: "Criminalization and Criminogenesis," 19 *UCLA Law Review* 697, 700 (1972).

their torch forward. In 1978, the publication of George Fletcher's monumental *Rethinking Criminal Law* set the agenda for a whole generation of criminal theorists.[17] Unfortunately, it contained nary a word about criminalization within its 932 pages.[18] The second major work of that decade—Hyman Gross's *A Theory of Criminal Justice*—mentions criminalization in its preface, only to apologize for subsequently ignoring it.[19] Among leading contemporary theorists of the criminal law, Andrew Ashworth deserves the most credit for having defended general limitations on the imposition of the penal sanction. Ashworth laments the "tendency" among "writings on English criminal law" to "devote little attention to the rightness or wrongness of criminalizing certain conduct."[20] This observation is equally apt about the American counterparts of English writers: textbooks in the United States generally omit the topic of criminalization altogether. Ashworth counters the tendency he detects by embracing a *minimalist* approach to criminal law—a term I gratefully borrow.[21] His efforts to defend minimalism are welcome, and they cohere nicely with my endeavors here. But even Ashworth, by his own admission, advances only a handful of relevant principles and explicitly disavows the search for "some general theory which will enable us to tell whether or not certain conduct should be criminalized."[22] Despite my survey of alternative theories of criminalization in chapter 4, *no* contemporary theorist in the United States or Great Britain is closely associated with a theory of criminalization.[23]

Vehement controversies about the criminalization of given kinds of behavior still occur, of course. The specific topics most frequently debated have changed surprisingly little since the time of Packer and Kadish. Disagreement continues to swirl around the issues raised some 40 years ago in the well-known exchange about the "enforcement of morality" between Lord Devlin[24] and H. L. A. Hart.[25] This debate is seemingly relevant to so-called morals offenses such as homosexuality and prostitution. But much of the disagreement about the justifiability of these offenses can be attributed to a difference of opinion about whether these behaviors are indeed immoral. Thus, Ronald Dworkin trenchantly responds: "What is shocking and wrong is not [Devlin's] idea that the community's morality counts, but his idea of what counts as the community's morality."[26] Remnants of the Hart–Devlin debate still engage legal philosophers.[27] Nonetheless, resolution of this debate would do little to address the problem of overcriminalization

17. George Fletcher: *Rethinking Criminal Law* (Boston: Little, Brown & Co., 1978).
18. For an argument that Fletcher's opus contains the resources to develop principles of criminalization, see Douglas Husak: "Crimes Outside the Core," 39 *Tulsa Law Review* 755 (2004).
19. Hyman Gross: *A Theory of Criminal Justice* (New York: Oxford University Press, 1979), p.xvi.
20. Andrew Ashworth: *Principles of Criminal Law* (Oxford: Clarendon Press, 4th ed., 2003), p.24.
21. *Id.*, pp.33 ff.
22. *Id.*, p.24.
23. For a possible exception, see Jonathan Schonsheck: *On Criminalization* (Dordrecht: Kluwer Academic Publishers, 1994).
24. Patrick Devlin: *The Enforcement of Morals* (London: Oxford University Press, 1965).
25. H. L. A. Hart: *Law, Liberty, and Morality* (New York: Vintage Books, 1963).
26. Ronald Dworkin: "Lord Devlin and the Enforcement of Morals," in his *Taking Rights Seriously* (Cambridge: Harvard University Press, 1977), pp.240, 255.
27. See, for example, Gerald Dworkin: "Devlin Was Right: Law and the Enforcement of Morality," 40 *William and Mary Law Review* 927 (1999).

as I conceive it. As we have seen, most of the recent expansion of criminal liability has little to do with anything that plausibly can be construed as the enforcement of morality. Theorists might agree about whether the criminal law should enforce morality while continuing to disagree about whether overlapping offenses, crimes of risk imposition, or ancillary offenses involve a proper use of the penal sanction.

A few contemporary commentators *are* disturbed about the twin phenomena of too much crime and too much punishment but have proposed a very different kind of solution than I defend here. Donald Dripps, for example, is motivated to search for "content-neutral" norms to limit the criminal sanction primarily because he is frustrated by previous efforts to find principled constraints.[28] In particular, he expresses exasperation about the potential of the "harm principle" to impose meaningful curbs on the scope of criminal liability. If my efforts in this book are even partly successful, however, progress in identifying principled limits on the penal sanction does not depend solely on whether the harm principle can be salvaged. In any event, Dripps endeavors to combat overcriminalization through reforms in criminal procedure rather than by implementing normative constraints. His most intriguing proposal is to require all penal laws to be passed by a "supermajority" of two-thirds of the legislature. Why, he asks pointedly, can a "bare majority . . . authorize prison for private conduct while a two-thirds majority is required to ratify a treaty setting tariffs on winter wheat"?[29] I have no quarrel with Dripps's ideas. His proposals might supplement my own; we need not be forced to choose between procedural and substantive solutions to the difficulties I have described. I readily admit that normative restrictions on the scope of the criminal law are not the only possible means to address the problem of overcriminalization. Still, all the procedural protections in the world—the presumption of innocence, the requirement of proof beyond a reasonable doubt, the privilege against self-incrimination and the like—cannot compensate for the injustice that occurs when bad laws are enacted. The principles I ultimately defend might be violated even if a bill could not become law without the unanimous support of legislators.

Suppose, then, I am correct to conclude that too little is said about the phenomenon of overcriminalization or the need for principled limits on the penal sanction. Why in particular have criminal theorists neglected this important topic? Several miscellaneous factors are worth mentioning briefly. Courses in criminal law taught throughout the United States tend not to cover this issue. Students typically begin their analysis with a statute or case; they have little occasion to raise the prior issue of why the statute is as it is. The instructor's manual to the most widely adopted casebook in criminal law recommends that the brief materials on "What to Punish?" should be skipped in a one-semester course.[30] Of course, few if any schools require more than a single semester of criminal law. And perhaps these materials *should* be skipped; they would lead one to believe that the only

28. Donald A. Dripps: "The Liberal Critique of the Harm Principle," 17 *Criminal Justice Ethics* 3 (1998).
29. *Id.*, p.12.
30. Instructor's Manual to Sanford Kadish and Stephen Schulhofer: *Criminal Law and Its Processes* (New York: Aspen, 7th ed., 2001), p.34.

major controversies about criminalization involve sexual morality. Sentencing and punishment—issues that might lead to matters of criminalization—are neglected as well. As one commentator observes, professors expend great effort analyzing the standards by which instances of killing should be categorized as manslaughter or murder but generally fail to discuss the sentencing consequences of either verdict.[31] If my arguments are sound, this failure is important, as increases in the severity of punishment are among the most pernicious effects of overcriminalization. The central reason to oppose the strict liability drug homicide statute upheld in *Rodriguez*, for example, is because it produces a sentence that is disproportionate to the seriousness of the crime.

In addition, criminal law scholarship has become overly specialized. Those commentators who are most knowledgeable about the substantive criminal law are not especially conversant with the latest developments in criminology or criminal justice. In particular, as we will see, applications of a theory of criminalization require a willingness to wrestle with empirical issues, and few legal philosophers are proficient in the social sciences. Moreover, many of the most talented thinkers in the United States concentrate on criminal procedure, where change has been even faster than in the substantive criminal law itself.[32] Largely in response to the threat of terrorism, commentators have expressed reservations about the increased powers of law enforcement (and of racial profiling in particular) authorized under such provisions as the Patriot Act.[33] To be sure, we should be alarmed about the greater authority of the state to use wiretaps, obtain search warrants, and employ other surveillance techniques that undermine our privacy. Yet these legitimate worries should not blind us to the urgent need for principled restraints on the *content* of criminal statutes.

Yet another explanation is the long-standing obsession among legal philosophers with the judiciary and, in the United States, with the Constitution. What passes for a general theory of *law* in jurisprudence often is nothing more than a theory of how courts should decide hard cases. Commentators tend to focus on those issues that can be debated before a judge. In a criminal proceeding in the United States, one can argue that the legislature has overstepped its bounds only by citing some constitutional provision that has been breached. As we will see, however, few of these provisions limit the substantive criminal law itself.[34] Because of this fixation on the Constitution, relatively little systematic work has been done on the issue of whether given kinds of conduct should or should not be criminalized.

Perhaps the best explanation for this lacuna is simpler: The topic of criminalization is just too hard. If my subsequent efforts are less persuasive than I believe, I may unwittingly reinforce the suspicion that attempts to defend

31. See Gerald E. Lynch: "Towards a Model Penal Code, Second (Federal?): The Challenge of the Special Part," 2 *Buffalo Criminal Law Review* 297, 301 (1998).
32. For a critical discussion of recent changes in England, see Andrew Ashworth and Lucia Zedner: "Defending the Criminal Law: Reflections on the Changing Character of Crime, Procedure, and Sanctions" (forthcoming).
33. For a defense of some of these measures, see Shlomit Wallerstein: "The State's Duty of Self-Defence: Justifying the Expansion of Criminal Law" (forthcoming, *Oxford Legal Studies Research Paper No. 56/2006*).
34. See chapter 3, section I.

principled restrictions on the scope of penal liability are hopeless. Theorists may have resigned themselves to the sad reality of overcriminalization. We should not expect to return to a (real or imaginary) time when the criminal law conformed to the normative standards legal philosophers hold dear. Why bother to tackle a difficult project if the task cannot be accomplished?

Although each of these several factors may help to explain our predicament, I believe we must understand how the discipline of criminal theory is conceptualized by legal philosophers if we hope to appreciate why a theory of criminalization has not been produced. Due largely to the extraordinary influence of Glanville Williams, commentators typically carve their subject matter into two halves: the *general* and the *special* parts of criminal law.[35] The vast majority of scholars focus on issues in the general part: roughly, on those rules and doctrines that apply to a broad range of offenses rather than to particular crimes. A small sampling of the difficult questions that consume theorists in the general part are as follows.[36] How does the principle of legality apply to the criminal law? Why should all crimes include a voluntary act? When may persons be punished for their omissions? What mental states make agents culpable for their criminal conduct? Should persons ever be punished for their negligence? What conditions must be satisfied before an agent can be said to have caused a result, and should results ever be relevant for criminal liability? How should justifications be differentiated from excuses, and is this contrast between types of defense important? When should mistakes about justifications or excuses justify or excuse? Why should the state recognize any excuses, and which excuses should it allow? Positions on each of these matters invite further questions that have spawned a massive literature.

The quantity and quality of scholarship in the general part is far more impressive than comparable work in the special part of criminal law.[37] Obviously, examples of the issues pursued in the special part are peculiar to individual offenses. Consider the crime of rape—a topic on which a great deal of critical commentary and legal reform has recently taken place.[38] Theorists ponder such matters as whether nonconsent should be an element in a rape statute or whether consent should function as an affirmative defense. Does force have independent significance above and beyond nonconsent? Should frauds in the inducement be differentiated from frauds in the factum? What is the exact nature of the wrong of rape, and what harm is this crime designed to proscribe? What degree of culpability should attach to each material element in a rape statute? Again, these questions have given rise to a lively debate. The important point, however, is that few of the

35. Glanville Williams: *Criminal Law: The General Part* (London: Stevens & Sons, 1961).
36. For an overview of these issues, see Douglas Husak: *Philosophy of Criminal Law* (Totowa, N.J.: Rowman & Allanheld, 1987). More recently, see Larry Alexander: "The Philosophy of Criminal Law," in Jules Coleman and Scott Shapiro, eds.: *The Oxford Handbook of Jurisprudence & Philosophy of Law* (Oxford: Oxford University Press, 2002), p.815.
37. For a recent exception to the narrow focus on the general part of criminal law, see the collection of essays in Stuart Green and R. A. Duff, eds.: *Defining Crimes: Essays on the Special Part of Criminal Law* (Oxford: Oxford University Press, 2005).
38. See, for example, Jennifer Temkin: *Rape and the Legal Process* (Oxford: Oxford University Press, 2nd ed., 2002); and Alan Wertheimer: *Consent to Sexual Relations* (Cambridge: Cambridge University Press, 2003).

issues I have listed in either the general or special parts of criminal law appear to
have more than a remote relation to the topic of criminalization.

I certainly do not mean to denigrate the significance of scholarship in both
the general and the special parts of criminal law; I have contributed to it myself.
Conspicuously absent from this literature, however, is comparable research on the
scope and limits of the criminal sanction. My hypothesis is that the familiar division between the general and special parts of criminal law tends to inhibit work
on this central topic. When the domain of criminal theory is divided between its
general and special parts, controversies about the limits of penal liability seem destined to fall between the cracks. To which half of criminal theory should we assign
this issue? Principles of criminalization cannot easily be located in the special
part of criminal law—in that part that deals with specific crimes such as burglary
or arson. If these limitations are not included in the general part, they will have
a hard time finding a home in criminal theory at all.[39] It is scandalous to think
that professors might teach and students might learn about both the general and
special parts of criminal law without paying attention to the crucial issue of what
conduct should or should not be criminalized.

I suspect that the very contrast between the general and special parts of criminal law is unhelpful and has outlived whatever usefulness it may have had. Why
presuppose that all interesting questions in criminal theory must fall on one side
or the other of this artificial divide? But I need not challenge the viability of this
entrenched contrast to make my case for the importance of the topic of criminalization or the reason for its neglect. In the remainder of this section, I argue that
this familiar conceptualization of the domain of criminal theory, and the scholarly
preoccupation with the general part of criminal law, cannot excuse the lack of
attention to this issue. My thesis is that at least two internal constraints on the
penal sanction can be found in the general part of criminal law.[40] Those who hope
to find a place for this topic within the parameters of criminal theory as traditionally construed should be receptive to my thesis that some such limitations can be
derived from the general part.[41]

---

39. I do not deny that many restrictions on criminalization may be found in disciplines other than criminal theory
itself. As I have suggested, some such limitations might be located within political philosophy. Many political theorists, for example, defend *liberalism*, which some construe to require the state to remain *neutral* with respect to conceptions of the good. This claim gives rise to significant limitations on criminalization.
40. In other words, I reject the *content-neutrality thesis:* that the doctrines in the general part must lack implications
for the question of what conduct may be punished. Although I am indebted to Michael Moore for the name of this
thesis, I am less sure that Moore himself actually *holds* it. He describes "what an area of law must possess if it is to
have a distinction between a general part and a special part. It must possess a content-neutral theory—analogous to
the theory of responsibility.... To have such a content-neutral theory, an area of law must have a contrasting, content-
laden theory.... Criminal law has such a structure." Michael Moore: *Placing Blame* (Oxford: Clarendon Press, 1997),
p.34. I have reservations about attributing the content-neutrality thesis to Moore because I do not understand why
he would believe that the distinction between a general and a special part of law *requires* the former to be neutral
with respect to the latter.
41. According to some commentators, doctrines in the general part are more likely to have implications for criminalization when they exert "homogenizing, rather than diversifying pressure." For reasons to doubt that these doctrines
exert homogenizing pressure, see John Gardner: "On the General Part of the Criminal Law," in Antony Duff, ed.:
Philosophy and the Criminal Law (Cambridge: Cambridge University Press, 1998), p.205. At the same time, Gardner
explicitly allows doctrines in what he calls the *supervisory* general part to have a "bearing on...criminalisation...it-
self." *Id.*, p.208.

Clearly, my thesis cannot be defended (much less attacked) without a conception of what the general part of criminal law *is*. Theorists have reached no consensus about this matter,[42] offering very different rationales for what the general part of criminal law should include or exclude.[43] Most scholarly contributions simply ignore this conceptual uncertainty and proceed directly to a particular topic that has long been treated within the general part. I do not pretend to resolve this difficult issue here. My thesis is plausible even without a detailed account of the nature of the general part.[44] Whatever else the general part of criminal law may be, it consists in *generalizations*. These generalizations are (in some sense) *about* the particular offenses that comprise the special part of criminal law. Why aren't the rules and doctrines of crimininalization just as general, and just as applicable to a broad range of offenses, as those that are universally agreed to belong to the general part? Because all justified criminal statutes must conform to the constraints I describe, their status as generalizations about particular offenses is secure.

More important, the *significance* of scholarship in the general part presupposes that the content of the penal law is reasonably just. Few of the issues explored in the general part would be worth pursuing if our theory of criminalization were radically defective. For example, why should we agonize about the mental states that make persons culpable unless the government has made appropriate decisions about what conduct to proscribe?[45] The importance of virtually any topic in the general part assumes the state has criminalized conduct that is worthy of penal liability. We have little reason to struggle to preserve the principles in the general part if injustice is pervasive throughout the special part. Deviations from these hallowed principles might actually rectify rather than compound the more basic injustice caused by a defective theory of criminalization. The normative value of our criminal justice system does not end with its special part, but surely it begins there.

But I need not defend these sweeping claims to make my case. I argue that positive law itself involves a commitment to two constraints on the scope of the criminal law: what I call the *nontrivial harm or evil* constraint and the *wrongfulness* constraint. In other words, the statutes and defenses about which the general part generalizes are the source of two principles that limit the reach of the criminal sanction. I provide four distinct illustrations of my thesis, each two of which support a different constraint. First, I show that often we cannot decide whether a defendant

---

42. Reluctance to be precise about these generalizations is reflected in James Stephen's barely intelligible account of "the general doctrines pervading the whole subject [of criminal law]." According to Stephen, these general doctrines consist in a number of "positive and negative" conditions, "*some* of which enter *more or less* into the definition of *nearly* all offenses." James Stephen: *A History of the Criminal Law of England* (vol. II, 1883), p.3 (emphasis added).
43. See Nicola Lacey: "Contingency, Coherence, and Conceptualism" in Duff: *op. cit.*, note 41, p.9.
44. For earlier thoughts, see Douglas Husak: "Limitations on Criminalization and the General Part of Criminal Law," in Stephen Shute and A. P. Simester, eds.: *Criminal Law Theory: Doctrines of the General Part* (Oxford: Oxford University Press, 2002), p.13.
45. To cite another example, why should criminal theorists care about whether a defendant has caused a given result unless we believe that the state should prohibit acts that cause that result? A legion of criminal theorists—roughly half, by my count—hold that the results caused by criminal acts should not be relevant to liability. Intuitions divide sharply on this question. Those who subscribe to this school of thought need not solve hard problems of causation. See Stephen J. Morse: "Reasons, Results, and Criminal Responsibility," *University of Illinois Law Review* 363 (2004).

is *justified* in breaching a statute without adopting a position on criminalization. I examine three distinct justification defenses and explain how attempts to interpret and apply them entail a constraint on the conduct that can be proscribed in the special part of criminal law. Although theorists have disagreed about the matter,[46] I assume that all defenses should be placed in the general part, so any limitations on criminalization that result from interpreting and applying defenses should be assigned to the general part as well.[47] Second, I suggest that often we cannot decide whether persons satisfy the degree of culpability required for liability without supposing the existence of this same constraint on the penal sanction. In the situations I describe, the defendant is charged with breaching a statute that requires intentional action, even though the defendant's intention is *conditional*. Whether the condition on which his intention depends allows liability to be imposed cannot be determined without making inferences about the content of the statute in question. Each of these illustrations supports my claim that the general part of criminal law includes the *nontrivial harm or evil* constraint: Criminal liability may not be imposed unless statutes are designed to prohibit a nontrivial harm or evil.

My third and fourth illustrations support a second internal constraint on what criminal laws may proscribe. I call this the *wrongfulness* constraint: Criminal liability may not be imposed unless the defendant's conduct is (in some sense) wrongful.[48] I argue that we cannot understand whether or under what conditions defendants should be *excused* from criminal liability unless this constraint applies throughout the criminal domain. Excuses cast criminal behavior in a more favorable light; it follows that criminal behavior is cast in a less favorable light when it is not excused. Finally, I suggest that the best account of scholarly opposition to *strict liability* in the criminal law presupposes that this same constraint limits the reach of the criminal sanction. As I have indicated, countless theorists have denounced strict liability offenses.[49] But commentators cannot identify what is generally objectionable about strict liability unless penal sanctions require wrongdoing. In combination, these four illustrations provide powerful support for my thesis that restrictions on criminalization can be found within the general part of criminal law.

My first argument in favor of my thesis shows that three familiar justification defenses are unintelligible unless criminal offenses are designed to proscribe a nontrivial harm or evil. My first example is the defense alternatively named "lesser evil," "necessity," or "justification generally." This defense is available when "the harm or evil sought to be avoided . . . is greater than that sought to be prevented by

---

46. Disagreement surrounds justifications rather than excuses. See Moore: *op. cit.*, note 40. Justifications are available when persons are permitted to engage in criminal conduct. If the special part fully describes the conduct that gives rise to criminal liability, justifications would belong to the special rather than to the general part. Still, the constraints I identify would remain internal to the criminal law.

47. Some defenses may pertain only to a single offense and thus may be assigned to the special part. Doctrines regarding provocation, for example, may suffice only to reduce a grade of homicide from murder to manslaughter. They typically appear in homicide statutes in the special part of criminal law. The defenses I consider in this section, however, apply to virtually all offenses.

48. Although criminal liability is imposed only for *conduct*, I do mot mean to rule out the possibility that other subject matters, such as traits of character, might also be assessed as wrongful. See George Sher: *In Praise of Blame* (Oxford: Oxford University Press, 2006).

49. See chapter 1, section IV.

the law defining the offense charged."[50] Next, consider the defense of consent.[51] Consent bars liability when it "precludes the infliction of the harm or evil sought to be prevented by the law defining the offense"—unless that harm or evil is "serious," in which case consent is not a defense at all.[52] My final example is the defense of *de minimis*.[53] This defense applies when the defendant's conduct "did not actually cause or threaten the harm or evil sought to be prevented by the law defining the offense or did so only to an extent too trivial to warrant the condemnation of conviction."[54] Of course, specific formulations of each of these three defenses may vary from one jurisdiction to another. Yet it is hard to see how any version could avoid referring to the point or objective of the offense with which the defendant is charged and for which a defense is needed. Because the Model Penal Code describes this point or objective as the "harm or evil sought to be prevented [or avoided]" by the offense, my subsequent discussion adopts this terminology.

At least two judgments are needed to decide whether these defenses should be granted in particular cases. First, one must identify the harm or evil the offense in question is designed to prevent. The second judgment is somewhat different for each of the three defenses but involves an assessment of the magnitude or severity of the harm or evil described in the first judgment. In the case of necessity, one must determine whether the harm or evil the defendant sought to avoid is greater than that to be prevented by the offense; in the case of consent, one must determine that the defendant has consented to that very harm or evil, and that this harm or evil is not serious; and, in the case of *de minimis,* one must determine that the defendant did not really cause or threaten that harm or evil, or did so only to a trivial degree. Each of these two judgments is made by law; the defendant's own views about these matters are not decisive.[55] In other words, judges or juries should not defer to the opinion of the defendant about this first judgment; his conjecture about the nature of the harm or evil a given statute is designed to prevent can be mistaken. Neither should judges or juries defer to the opinion of the defendant about the second judgment; his assessment of the magnitude or severity of this harm or evil might be mistaken as well. Suppose, for example, a defendant believes that the harm or evil to be prevented by a theft offense is trivial when he takes office supplies from his employer. His own views about this matter should not be decisive as a matter of law.

None of these three justification defenses can be interpreted or applied unless each penal statute is designed to prevent a nontrivial harm or evil. Thus it is clear that positive law itself entails the nontrivial harm or evil constraint. This conclusion is important. Although many commentators hold harm or evil to

50. Model Penal Code, §3.02(1)(a). Subsequent clauses narrow the availability of the defense, but these are unimportant for present purposes.

51. For the seminal discussion, see Peter Westen: *The Logic of Consent* (Burlington, Vt.: Ashgate, 2004).

52 Model Penal Code, §§2.11(1) and 2.11(2)(a).

53. Admittedly, it is unclear whether the defense of *de minimis* should be categorized as a justification. I assume that *de minimis* infractions simply are not wrongful, or at least are not *sufficiently* wrongful to merit criminal liability. Ultimately, however, nothing of consequence turns on whether this defense is properly conceptualized as a justification.

54 Model Penal Code, §2.12(2).

55. See Model Penal Code, Comments to §3.02, pp.9–14.

be prerequisites for the imposition of criminal sanctions, none appears to have noticed that the foregoing defenses are unintelligible unless their belief is true.[56] No respectable theory of criminalization can reject this constraint; we simply cannot understand or apply many of the defenses in the general part unless criminal statutes are designed to prevent a nontrivial harm or evil. I doubt that we can reformulate these defenses to delete reference to harm or evil or anything equivalent to them. Short of abolishing these defenses altogether—a preposterous suggestion that would only magnify the injustice in our penal system—this constraint is inherent in the general part of criminal law.[57]

Admittedly, there may be some crimes that cannot be justified: genocide, torture, and perhaps murder, for example. But these crimes do not provide counterexamples to my claim that the criminal law contains a harm or evil requirement. These crimes cannot be justified because the enormity of the harm or evil cannot be outweighed, not because they involve no harm or evil. Thus the existence of these crimes confirms rather than undermines my thesis. In addition, there may be offenses for which consent is not a defense. For example, consent is not a defense to statutes supported by a paternalistic rationale. Again, however, these offenses do not undermine my thesis. Consent is not a defense in such cases because the harm or evil the statute is designed to prevent persists *despite* consent, not because there *is* no harm or evil to be prevented.

Clearly, however, attempts to identify the nature and severity of the harm or evil a given law is designed to prevent can be extraordinarily problematic—perhaps more problematic than any single difficulty that will plague efforts to implement a minimalist theory of criminalization. A few examples illustrate the uncertainty.[58] Consider the defense of necessity when a defendant is charged with the use or possession of an illicit drug. Suppose he pleads a justification for using a controlled substance in the course of a religious ritual,[59] to treat a disease or illness,[60] or to display in an educational program.[61] No one can hope to decide whether a defendant is justified in possessing drugs under these circumstances without forming a belief about the nature and severity of the harm or evil the statute seeks to avoid. Much the same is true of the defense of consent. Consider the ongoing controversy about ordinances requiring motorcyclists to wear helmets. Suppose this law is intended to protect the taxpaying public from the various expenses

---

56. Joel Feinberg is the most celebrated such commentator. See *op. cit.*, note 10. Remarkably, however, Feinberg does not really try to explain *why* the harm principle should be accepted—at least, not directly. Rather, he assumes rather than defends the claim that the prevention of harm should be needed to impose penal liability. His strategy is to present the harm principle in its best light. Once explicated in this way, he hopes this principle will seem sufficiently attractive to fair-minded readers.
57. Of course, the *scope* of these defenses may vary somewhat from one code to another. In addition, I admit that a jurisdiction need not have an explicit defense of *de minimis* at all. In these jurisdictions, however, it is likely that some other rule or doctrine is invoked to accomplish the same results.
58. Additional examples could be provided. For example, courts differ about the justifiability of prison escape when inmates seek to avoid homosexual rape. If courts must consider how their decision will affect subsequent escapes, it would be much more difficult—and perhaps impossible—to construe a statute proscribing prison break to justify a particular act of escape. See *United States v. Bailey*, 444 U.S. 394 (1980).
59. See *Employment Division v. Smith*, 494 U.S. 872 (1990).
60. See *Commonwealth v. Hutchins*, 575 N.E.2d 741 (Mass. 1991).
61. See *People v. Mijares*, 491 P.2d 1115 (Cal. 1971).

incurred in motorcycle accidents. If so, consent would be a plausible defense when a motorcyclist has purchased adequate insurance. Suppose, however, that this law has a paternalistic rationale and is designed to minimize injuries to the motorcyclist himself. Insurance would be irrelevant on the latter assumption, and consent would not be a defense.[62] Finally, consider the defense of *de minimis*. Imagine a case in which an illicit drug cannot cause a psychoactive effect because its quantity is minuscule.[63] If the offense of possession is intended to prohibit harm to oneself and others when drugs are used, the *de minimis* defense would apply when the amount of the drug is too small for the body to detect. But if the offense is designed to serve expressive functions—to send a message about the evils of drugs—the case for the defense is weakened.

How can we identify the harm or evil a given law is designed to proscribe? This question is incredibly difficult, because legislators need not articulate a rationale or objective for the statutes they enact.[64] Controversies about the availability of the foregoing defenses—not to mention the implementation of a theory of criminalization generally—would be ameliorated if legislatures were made to identify explicitly the harm or evil they hope to avoid. This requirement not only would assist determinations of whether the above defenses apply but also might yield important collateral benefits. The very need to articulate a rationale for a statute could go a surprisingly long way toward retarding overcriminalization. Judges, after all, write opinions to explain their reasoning, and this exercise is bound to improve the quality of the judgments they render. Why shouldn't something roughly comparable be demanded of legislators? I suspect that laws generally—and unjust laws in particular—would become more difficult to enact if legislators were encouraged to commit themselves to a reasonably specific description of the purpose they intend these laws to serve.

A second reason to suppose that criminal laws must prohibit a harm or evil derives from uncertainty about whether given defendants possess the *mens rea* required for penal liability. The cases I have in mind arise when a statute requires intentional (or purposeful) action, but the intention of the defendant is *conditional*. These cases are common; nearly all intentions are conditional. Suppose, for example, a defendant intends to commit robbery, but only if his victim carries cash. If he is apprehended while accosting a victim, should a court construe his conditional intention as equivalent to an unconditional intention that suffices for liability for attempted robbery? Under the Model Penal Code's response, a conditional purpose to commit an offense qualifies as a purpose to commit that offense unless the condition "negatives the harm or evil sought to be prevented" by the

---

62. The Commentaries to the Model Penal Code consent statute indicate "what is required in the discrete case, therefore, is an isolation of the societal objectives of the offense in order to determine the effect to be given consent." Model Penal Code, Comments to §2.11, p.395. The draftsmen do not specify, however, how this task is to be accomplished.

63. See Note: "Criminal Liability for Possession of Nonusable Amounts of Controlled Substances," 77 *Columbia Law Review* 596 (1977).

64. "This Court never has insisted that a legislative body articulate its reasons for enacting a statute." *United States Railroad Retirement Board v. Fritz*, 449 U.S. 1, 179 (1980).

offense.[65] Obviously, no one could make sense of this provision unless statutes *are* designed to prevent a harm or evil. Thus decisions about whether given conditional intentions amount to *mens rea* presuppose the harm or evil constraint.[66]

My example of robbery is easy. But the Supreme Court has been bedeviled by controversy about the harm or evil given statutes are designed to prevent when the intention of a defendant is conditional. Consider, for example, the federal carjacking statute, which makes an act of hijacking an instance of the more serious crime of carjacking when it is performed with the intention to kill or inflict serious bodily injury on the driver.[67] Suppose a defendant hijacks cars and threatens to kill drivers unless they hand over their keys. When apprehended, he contends that he lacks the intention required by the carjacking statute.[68] He alleges his intention is very different from that of hijackers who intend to kill unconditionally, that is, who intend to kill drivers whether or not they comply with the hijacker's demands. We cannot decide whether this defendant is liable for carjacking (or merely for hijacking) without adopting a position on the harm or evil the statute is designed to prevent—which, of course, supposes that the statute *is* designed to prevent a harm or evil. In a recent case in which this issue was posed, the Court affirmed a defendant's conviction for carjacking, alleging, "of course, in this case the condition that the driver surrenders the car was the precise evil Congress wanted to prevent."[69] But this description of the harm or evil to be prevented by the carjacking statute is by no means as obvious as the Court pretends. If the Court were correct, the purpose of carjacking laws would appear to be identical to that of hijacking laws. Instead, the federal carjacking statute is probably designed to prevent drivers from facing risks of serious bodily harm when their cars are taken—risks beyond those posed by mere hijackers. A statement of statutory purpose by Congress could have helped the Court resolve this uncertainty.

I have provided two distinct illustrations of my thesis that the nontrivial harm or evil constraint on criminalization can be found within the general part of criminal law. Although this constraint has the potential to be an important restriction on the content of criminal offenses, it also has the potential to be relatively insignificant. Obviously, everything depends on exactly what is meant by *harm* or *evil*. The Model Penal Code does not define these terms, or indicate whether or how "harm" differs from "evil."[70] The concept of harm has received more analysis than that of evil. Still, only two points are clear. First, on any plausible interpretation, a harm constraint should not be construed to preclude the state from prohibiting conduct that causes a *risk* of harm rather than harm per se.[71] Second, harm refers

---

65. Model Penal Code, §2.02(6).
66. Of course, the Model Penal Code position could be challenged. For a critical discussion, see Gideon Yaffe: "Conditional Intent and *Mens Rea*," 10 *Legal Theory* 273 (2004).
67. 18 U.S.C. §2119.
68. *Holloway v. United States*, 526 U.S. 1 (1999).
69. *Id.*, p.11 n.11.
70. For this reason, sometimes I refer to the nontrivial harm or evil constraint simply as the harm constraint. Presumably, however, the reference to *evil* is designed to allow the proscription of harmless immoralities—a topic to which I return. See my discussion of expressive functions of law in chapter 2, section II, and my treatment of legal moralism in chapter 4, section III.
71. See chapter 3, section III.

to the effect of conduct on a person or institution; it is not a property of conduct itself. Almost everything else we might want to know about harm is unresolved. Because of this uncertainty, many commentators are skeptical that the harm constraint can play a significant role in limiting the scope of criminal liability. They note that nearly any result that anyone has ever wanted to prevent could be construed as harmful.[72] On these "deflationary" accounts, the harm principle merely requires that criminal laws aim toward a legitimate state objective. Because the overwhelming majority of state objectives probably are legitimate, this constraint does not amount to much.[73]

If we adopt the influential analysis of "the harm principle" defended by Joel Feinberg, however, the ramifications of this constraint could be far-reaching. According to Feinberg, harm generally is a "thwarting, setting back, or defeating of an interest."[74] But "the sense of 'harm' as that term is used in the harm principle must represent the overlap of [normative and non-normative senses]: only setbacks of interests that are wrongs, and wrongs that are setbacks to interest, are to count as harms in the appropriate sense." In the "normative" sense of harm, A harms B "by wronging B, or by treating him unjustly"[75]; in the "non-normative" sense of harm, A harms B "by invading, and thereby setting back, his interest."[76] The need for an overlap between these two senses should be apparent. Person A might set back the interests of B—thereby placing B in a "harmed condition"—through a legitimate competition, for example. But A's conduct should not be criminalized because B has not been wronged or treated unjustly. Conversely, harmless but impermissible conduct is not eligible for criminal liability because it does not set back anyone's interests. Person A might behave wrongfully without victimizing anyone,[77] but his conduct should not be criminalized because no one has been harmed. The "overlap" between these two senses of harm can be expressed by invoking the concept of rights: All wrongful conduct that sets back the interests of others violates their rights.[78] Thus Feinberg's liberal framework establishes the moral limits of the criminal law by reference to the rights of persons. As expressed succinctly, "criminal prohibitions are legitimate only when they protect individual rights."[79]

If we accept this analysis, a detailed account of the specific instances of legislation that should be rejected as incompatible with the harm principle requires two supplementary theories: (1) a theory of moral rights; and (2) a theory of wrongful conduct. Feinberg is well aware of the need for each of these supplementary theories.[80] He is equally aware that neither of these theories will be easy to produce,

---

72. See Fletcher: *op. cit.*, note 17, pp.402–406; also Bernard E. Harcourt: "The Collapse of the Harm Principle," 90 *Journal of Criminal Law and Criminology* 109 (1999); also Stephen D. Smith: "Is the Harm Principle Illiberal?" 51 *American Journal of Jurisprudence* 1 (2006).

73. See chapter 3, section I for a discussion of the legitimacy of state objectives.

74. *Op. cit.*, note 10, p.33.

75. *Id.*, p.34.

76. *Id.*

77. Examples are presented and discussed in Joel Feinberg: *Harmless Wrongdoing: The Moral Limits of the Criminal Law* (New York: Oxford University Press, 1988).

78. Feinberg: *op. cit.*, note 10, p.34.

79. *Id.*, p.144.

80. Feinberg acknowledges the need for a moral theory at *id.*, pp.17–18 and his lack of "a theory of 'moral rights' that are independent and antecedent to law" at *id.*, p.111.

and he admits he has made little or no progress in completing the job. Are persons harmed when they are deeply offended, for example?[81] I will not try to answer such questions by filling in the huge gaps in Feinberg's account. The theory of criminalization I develop will place surprisingly little weight on this first internal constraint. I describe my lack of reliance on this constraint as surprising because the harm principle has played a major role in previous attempts by legal philosophers to limit the scope of the penal sanction. Despite my failure to provide substantive theories of rights or of wrongdoing, I simply note that Feinberg's views have enormous potential to retard the growth of the criminal law.[82]

The defenses I have mentioned thus far are instances of justification, but a second constraint on the content of penal statutes emerges from the general part of criminal law by considering the nature of *excuses*. In the most comprehensive and sophisticated treatment of excuses produced by an Anglo-American commentator, Jeremy Horder argues that any claim to excuse "is an explanation for engagement in wrongdoing . . . that [make it seem] entirely wrong to convict, at least for the full offence."[83] These defenses, in other words, "excuse the act or omission amounting to wrongdoing, by shedding favourable moral light on what D did through a focus on the reasons that D committed that wrongdoing."[84] I believe Horder is basically correct.[85] According to his view, legal excuses can be understood only against a background of criminal wrongdoing: If the defendant is not guilty of wrongdoing, there is nothing to excuse.[86] Because wrongdoing is included in this concept of excusing conditions, it presupposes the *second* internal

81. Feinberg thinks not, and appeals to a separate principle to allow the proscription of offensive behavior. See Joel Feinberg: *Offense to Others* (New York: Oxford University Press, 1985). But see A. P. Simester and Andrew von Hirsch: "Rethinking the Offense Principle," 8 *Legal Theory* 269 (2002).

82. Or perhaps not; we need to understand not only how harm but also the harm *principle* (or *requirement*) should be construed. This question is posed in John Gardner and Stephen Shute: "The Wrongness of Rape," in Jeremy Horder, ed.: *Oxford Essays in Jurisprudence* (4th Series, 2000), p.193. These authors describe what they take to be a case of harmless rape and try to show why the defendant should be punished even though his action caused no harm. These theorists do not explain what harm *is*, such that they believe harm is *not* caused in the case they describe. More important, despite their belief that the defendant caused no harm in this case, Gardner and Shute claim that the imposition of liability is consistent with their understanding of how the harm principle should be formulated. They write, "it is no objection under the harm principle that a harmless action was criminalized, nor even that an action with no tendency to cause harm was criminalized. It is enough to meet the demands of the harm principle that, if the action were not criminalized, *that* would be harmful." *Id.*, p.216. Depending on how this idea is explicated, a great deal of criminal legislation might turn out to be compatible with the harm principle. Suppose citizens were inclined to retaliate violently against persons who were perceived as having escaped their just deserts by engaging in conduct the state had refrained from criminalizing—by obtaining abortions, for example. Can the desirability of preventing this violence possibly show that abortion (for example) may be criminalized under the harm principle? This cannot be the result that Gardner and Shute intend. But such questions indicate how their interpretation of the harm requirement has the potential to expand the scope of the criminal law exponentially.

83. Jeremy Horder: *Excusing Crime* (Oxford: Oxford University Press, 2004), pp.8–9. Specifically, Horder believes an excuse "is an explanation for engagement in wrongdoing...that sheds such a favourable moral light on D's conduct that it seems entirely wrong to convict, at least for the full offence."

84. *Id.*, p.9.

85. For some quibbles, see Douglas Husak: "A Liberal Theory of Excuses," 3 *Ohio State Journal of Criminal Law* 287 (2005).

86. Admittedly, *some* theories of excuse may not require wrongful action by the defendant. H. L. A. Hart famously argued in favor of excuses (and against strict liability) on the ground that it is unjust to subject a person to criminal liability unless he had the capacity and fair opportunity to obey the law. This capacity and opportunity may be absent even when the conduct proscribed is not wrongful. See his *Punishment and Responsibility* (Oxford: Oxford University Press, 1969).

constraint to be included in a theory of criminalization: Penal liability may not be imposed unless the defendant's conduct is (in some sense) wrongful. I call this the *wrongfulness constraint*.

We understand how to apply Horder's view of excuses when criminal behavior unquestionably is wrongful. If a defendant drives a getaway car under duress, for example, we would agree that his reason for assisting in the crime would make his conviction unjust. When the wrongfulness constraint is breached, however, we have no idea how to apply this theory to particular examples. The difficulty emerges when we ask what could possibly be said about a statute that did not proscribe wrongdoing at all. Should we deem such a crime to be inexcusable? This position seems completely misguided. But what answer should we give? Suppose, for example, a jurisdiction prohibits users of prescription drugs from removing their medicines from their original containers, and a defendant commits this ancillary offense prior to his vacation to spare himself the inconvenience of carrying several different bottles. Is this defendant wholly or partially excused; does his reason for breaking the law cast his behavior in a favorable moral light? This question is nearly impossible to answer one way or the other, as the conduct proscribed does not appear to be wrongful in the first place. If an offense does not satisfy the wrongfulness constraint, it makes little sense to inquire whether the defendant's reasons for committing it cast his behavior in a favorable moral light.

I conclude that criminal theorists who provide accounts of specific defenses—either justifications or excuses—must assume that their accounts will be applied to defendants who commit criminal offenses that proscribe wrongdoing and are designed to prevent a nontrivial harm or evil. Clearly, these two assumptions involve principles of criminalization. If so, theorists must undertake a more basic inquiry into the conditions under which given offenses satisfy these constraints. This inquiry about criminalization proceeds squarely within the general part of criminal law.

A second reason to believe that the wrongfulness constraint can be found in the general part of criminal law is more complex, and draws from our prior discussion of strict liability and the drug homicide statute upheld in *Rodriguez*.[87] Criminal theorists typically treat issues about culpability as central to the general part. Thus questions about whether it is ever appropriate to impose liability in the *absence* of culpability should be central to the general part as well. Whether or not their reservations are based on constitutional interpretation, nearly all theorists regard strict liability offenses as morally problematic and recognize limits on the state's authority to enact them.[88] They differ, however, in their accounts of what is objectionable about strict liability, or how these difficulties might be overcome.[89] The court in *Rodriguez*, for example, recognized "limitations on strict liability criminal statutes" when "the underlying conduct is so passive, so unworthy of blame, that the persons violating the proscription would have had no notice that they were

---

87. See chapter 1, section IV.
88. See Alan C. Michaels: "Constitutional Innocence," 112 *Harvard Law Review* 828 (1999).
89. See the essays in A. P. Simester, ed.: *Appraising Strict Liability* (Oxford: Oxford University Press, 2005).

breaking the law."[90] The strict liability drug homicide statute that was challenged, however, was said not to fall under this limitation. As the court explained, "to the extent moral culpability is a desirable element of a criminal offense, it is inextricably embedded in the drug death statute."[91] I construe these words as follows. Because the mere act of distributing drugs is (alleged to be) wrongful, the court felt no need to demand any additional culpability for statutes requiring this act to cause death. Suppose, however, that the defendant had distributed peanuts, and a purchaser died from an unforeseen allergic reaction. In this event, a statute that imposed liability for the consumer's death would punish him despite his lack of wrongdoing—which the strict liability drug homicide statute in *Rodriguez* (arguably) did not do.

Of course, judgments about whether persons act wrongfully are bound to be controversial.[92] I am puzzled, for example, why the *Rodriguez* court singled out cases as "unworthy of blame" when defendants are "passive" and given "no notice" that their behavior is illegal.[93] Conduct may be permissible even though it is active rather than passive, and adequate notice that conduct is prohibited hardly ensures that it is wrongful.[94] Neither passivity nor the absence of notice need be the problem with my hypothetical offense that punishes persons who cause death by distributing peanuts. But whatever the details of a theory of wrongdoing may be, strict liability for death should not be imposed when persons engage in *any* conduct that happens to result in a fatality; it should be reserved for situations in which the underlying conduct that causes death is wrongful. Strict liability is unjustified when the wrongfulness constraint is violated.

These observations help us to appreciate what is typically objectionable about strict liability—and the main source of the injustice I claimed to find in *Rodriguez*.[95] Although the most notorious instances of strict liability dispense with wrongdoing altogether, we cannot say that *all* do so. As the drug homicide statute upheld in *Rodriguez* suggests, many impositions of strict liability appear to satisfy the wrongfulness constraint. What, then, is generally unjust about examples of strict liability—about statutes that allow defendants to be convicted, even though they need not be culpable with respect to each material element? The answer, I think, is that even though a given strict liability offense requires wrongdoing, it may not require *enough* wrongdoing. This answer invites the further question: *Enough wrongdoing for what?* To my mind, this is both the most important as well as the most difficult question to answer in attempts to understand the normative problems associated with strict liability. The answer I propose is that the extent of wrongdoing in cases of strict liability is (typically but not necessarily) insufficient to merit the *degree* of punishment imposed on the offender. If I am correct, the

90. *New Jersey v. Rodriguez*, 645 A.2d 1165, 1174 (1994).
91. *Id.*, p.1174.
92. For further thoughts, see Richard Singer and Douglas Husak: "Of Innocence and Innocents: The Supreme Court and *Mens Rea* Since Herbert Packer," 2 *Buffalo Criminal Law Review* 859 (1999).
93. The obvious reference is to *Lambert v. California*, 355 U.S. 225 (1957).
94. Even when conduct *is* wrongful, notice may not be the heart of the problem. The real difficulty is that there may be little that persons can reasonably *do* with notice to avoid liability.
95. See chapter 1, section IV.

most general complaint about strict liability is that it results in excessive punishments that violate the principle of proportionality.[96] As I have argued, this answer accurately describes the injustice done to Rodriguez himself.

But—assuming the justifiability of drug proscriptions—didn't Rodriguez act wrongfully? Doesn't he thereby deserve to be punished to the full extent of the law? The trouble with this train of thought is that it disregards proportionality, supposing that no sentence can be excessive when conduct is wrongful. I want to digress to discuss a metaphor that may help to understand what is superficially attractive but ultimately unacceptable about most impositions of strict liability. A "thin-ice" principle sheds light on some of my claims about how too much criminal law can produce too much punishment. According to this principle, a person who skates on thin ice has no cause for complaint when he falls through.[97] An important qualification must be added before this principle becomes plausible. No one should be blamed for falling *through* thin ice unless he had reason to believe he was *on* it. Suppose a person reasonably believes (somehow) that he is not skating on ice at all, or (more plausibly) that the ice on which he is skating is not thin. Under these circumstances, I doubt that he deserves blame for his misfortune. Suppose, however, that our skater *is* at least negligent about whether he is on thin ice. On this assumption, he will merit little sympathy if he falls through. Perhaps this metaphor helps to explain why so many commentators turn a deaf ear to Rodriguez's complaint. The thin-ice principle enables us to appreciate why a criminal defendant who acts wrongfully garners little sympathy when his punishment is more severe than he might have expected it to be.

How helpful is the thin-ice principle? Although the metaphor is useful, it may obscure as much as it illuminates. After all, we are not told exactly what happens to our unfortunate skater. What exactly *does* he deserve when he falls through thin ice? To get wet? To suffer from pneumonia or hyperthermia? To pay for his own rescue? To drown? Can he deserve the latter fate even if he had no reason to believe that the waters were sufficiently deep to make drowning a realistic possibility? As far as I can tell, the thin-ice principle provides no guidance about how these questions should be answered; it does not specify the *amount* of misfortune our skater deserves. In other words, the principle totally disregards issues of proportionality. Surely there must be *some* limit to the blame persons typically merit when they fall through thin ice; I see no reason to deem each of them to be morally equivalent to thrill-seekers who *knowingly* or *purposely* plunge into icy waters, or who skate fully aware that the waters are deep and dangerous. Similarly, Rodriguez could not deserve whatever fate the law might choose to inflict on him—a fate comparable to that deserved by deliberate killers. If my observations are cogent, questions of proportionality raise the central difficulty with strict liability offenses. Penal statutes are unjustified unless they proscribe conduct that is (in some sense) wrongful. But even when the wrongfulness constraint is satisfied by a particular strict liability offense, defendants frequently face disproportionate punishments.

---

96. For further thoughts, see Douglas Husak: "Strict Liability, Justice, and Proportionality," in Simester, ed.: *op. cit.*, note 89, p.81.
97. See Ashworth: *op. cit.*, note 20, pp.71–72. The metaphor is drawn from an opinion by Lord Morris in *Knuller v. DPP,* (1973) AC 435, 463.

Suppose I am correct that the wrongfulness constraint is internal to the general part of criminal law. How important is this constraint in a theory of criminalization? Although the general answer is unclear, three brief remarks may be helpful. First, I say that conduct must be wrongful in *some* sense because no internal constraint should preclude the possibility that punishments may be justified in cases of *mala prohibita*. Significantly, *malum prohibitum* offenses are still said to be *mala*—even if the supposed wrongfulness of these crimes will prove difficult to understand. Whether and under what conditions this internal constraint is satisfied when persons are punished for violating a *malum prohibitum* offense is a topic of sufficient complexity to require separate treatment in a theoretical examination of overcriminalization.[98] Second, "wrongfulness" should not be confused with "culpability" as that term is narrowly used in criminal law. Agents may act culpably even though their conduct is permissible. A statute punishing the act of purposely scratching one's head, for example, would require the highest degree of culpability known to the criminal law—purpose (or intention)—but clearly would not proscribe wrongdoing in any intelligible sense. Finally, I admit that the real challenge for legal philosophers is not to demonstrate the bare existence of the wrongfulness constraint, but to infuse it with substantive content. Although I endeavor to provide a bit more substance to this constraint later, I do not defend general criteria to decide when conduct is wrongful. Throughout this book, I appeal to specific intuitions rather than to abstract principles to defend my judgments that an action is or is not wrongful. Fortunately, the intuitions I invoke do not involve unusual or bizarre cases that are a staple among some moral and political philosophers; they involve familiar, everyday situations with which readers have ample experience. Although I concede that any intuition may be controversial, they are no more controversial than principles or theories.

I have argued that two constraints can be derived from the general part of criminal law: the nontrivial harm or evil constraint and the wrongfulness constraint. I acknowledge the tension in claiming that we can extract normatively defensible constraints on criminalization from a system of criminal law that has serious normative deficiencies. How has the criminal law been able to function coherently in light of this tension? My answer is that it functions mechanically, with little awareness of the tension I have mentioned. Suppose, for example, a defendant pleads insanity after committing an offense that fails to satisfy the wrongfulness constraint. Practitioners should have no more than the usual difficulty in deciding whether he qualifies for an insanity defense. The tension emerges only if we are self-consciously reflective about what we are doing and ask why his insanity should amount to a defense. Insanity should be a defense, I contend, because it excuses his conduct. It excuses his conduct because it precludes blame (or perhaps responsibility, a prerequisite for blame). An excuse can preclude blame only if there is blame to preclude, which requires wrongdoing. If the offense does not involve wrongdoing, we should be puzzled about how insanity can excuse. If we do not ask these questions—as few professionals involved in criminal practice are

98. See section IV *infra*.

inclined to do—we can proceed merrily with the day-to-day business of criminal justice, unaware of the incoherence.

If I am correct to conclude that two constraints can be derived from the general part of criminal law, the obsession among theorists with the general part provides no reason to neglect issues of criminalization. Theorists need not retool to find constraints on the reach of the criminal sanction. Admittedly, the political forces that contribute to overcriminalization may be resistant to the pleas of legal philosophers. Nonetheless, commentators can identify principles to limit the scope of penal liability without redirecting their focus from the general part of criminal law.

II: FROM PUNISHMENT TO CRIMINALIZATION

The nontrivial harm or evil and wrongfulness constraints can be found in the general part of criminal law. But the general part is not the only place in positive law from which we might derive restrictions on the content of offenses. Normative defenses of punishment also provide an important source of constraints. A theory of criminalization must identify the special reasons to limit the *criminal* law in particular. In other words, what is special—and especially troublesome—about criminal liability? Why should it be required to proscribe a nontrivial harm or evil? Why should the penal sanction be unjustifiable in the absence of wrongdoing? More generally, why do citizens have particular reason to be concerned when state authority is exercised through the criminal law? As we will see, two additional constraints on the penal sanction emerge by addressing these questions.

The most important difference between the criminal law and other bodies of law, or between the criminal law and systems of social control that are not modes of law at all, is that the former subjects offenders to *state punishment*.[99] Unless the state is authorized to punish persons believed to have violated given rules, we should not categorize those rules as belonging to the criminal law.[100] The converse is true as well. Punishment may not be imposed by the state unless individuals are believed to have committed a crime. We should not describe sanctions as punishments when the state inflicts them on persons who are known not to have engaged in criminal conduct. Although not entirely unproblematic, this thesis linking the criminal law with state punishment has the advantage of resolving two problems simultaneously. It not only identifies the distinguishing mark of the criminal law but also provides a plausible explanation of why a theory of criminalization is needed. A theory of criminalization provides the set of conditions under which the state is permitted to resort to punishment. We seek principles to limit the criminal law because we seek principles to limit the circumstances under which the state is allowed to inflict punitive sanctions.

---

99. The connection between punishment and the criminal law may be easier to appreciate in languages other than English: German, *Strafrecht;* Spanish, *Derecho Penal,* French, *Droit Penale,* and Italian, *Diritto Penale.* I owe this observation to Leo Zaibert.
100. "The institution of punishment provides the distinguishing features of the criminal law." George P. Fletcher: *Basic Concepts of Criminal Law* (New York: Oxford University Press, 1998), p.25.

Of course, my thesis that conduct is criminal if and only if it subjects persons to state punishment does not entail that offenders actually will *be* punished. Even those offenders who are detected may avoid arrest and prosecution through corruption or exercises of discretion. When criminal laws are enacted, however, it is nearly inevitable that *some* punishments will need to be imposed. This inevitability stems from the fact that rarely is the criminal law completely efficacious. Criminalized conduct is *proscribed* or *prohibited* but almost never wholly *prevented*. Some persons will persist in the prohibited behavior, whatever the law may say. If indeed the law in question is criminal, these offenders will become eligible for state punishment. Is the punishment of these persons *justified?* This question would be moot if the mere act of passing a law could effectively prevent persons from breaking it. In an imaginary world of perfect compliance, no one would commit the offense, so no one would have to be sentenced. In the real world of imperfect compliance, however, implications for criminalization become apparent. Before legislators enact a criminal offense, they had better be confident that the state would be justified in punishing persons who breach it. The state should not create crimes that will subject offenders to punishment without good reason to believe that the punishment to which such persons will become subject would be justified. If the punishment of those who commit a given offense cannot be justified, the state should not have enacted that offense in the first place. Such legislation would require the state to neglect its own proscriptions, impose punishments that cannot be justified, or renege on its classification of that law as criminal. It is hard to know which of these options is the least unpalatable.

But is the criminal law *really* special—for this or for any other reason? Should I remain fixated on the justifiability of criminal laws in particular, rather than on the legitimacy of state authority in general?[101] I *think* so; criminalization remains my central focus. I regard the identity of the criminal law with the susceptibility to state punishment as something approximating a conceptual truth: A law simply is not criminal unless persons who break it become subject to state punishment, and what the state does to persons is not punishment unless it is imposed for a criminal offense.[102] But no appeal to a supposed conceptual truth should persuade skeptics. I readily admit to lack a decisive argument in favor of my thesis. But what might these skeptics offer in its place? Frankly, few serious rivals exist; no one pretends

---

101. As I discuss further in chapter 3, section I, part of my motivation for singling out the criminal sanction as special is to require more than a rational basis to justify criminal offenses. For an argument that *all* laws—including those that are noncriminal—should be made to satisfy more than the rational basis test, see Randy E. Barnett: *Restoring the Lost Constitution: The Presumption of Liberty* (Princeton: Princeton University Press, 2004).

102. I do not doubt the logical coherence of a proscription without a sanction; I only deny that the proscription would belong to the criminal law. The question whether the criminal law can survive without punishment is posed vividly in assessing *abolitionist* theories. Herman Bianchi, for example, believes that punishment cannot be justified and recommends it should be allowed to "wither away completely." Herman Bianchi: "Abolition: Assensus and Sanctuary," in Antony Duff and David Garland, eds.: *A Reader on Punishment* (Oxford: Oxford University Press, 1994), pp.336, 341. Abolitionists do not always think of themselves as doing away with the criminal law so much as doing away with a punitive response to crime. My thesis, of course, alleges that the abolition of punishment *is* the abolition of the criminal law; what remains after punishment ceases to exist is a body of law that no longer merits the name *criminal*. In any event, abolitionists have won few converts, at least among Anglo-Americans. I remain persuaded that punishments for violations of *some* laws are justified. I applaud those who would allow punishment to wither—but not those who would allow it to wither away.

that the criminal law can be identified by reference to its content.[103] Whatever the case in recent jurisprudential history,[104] contemporary theorists more often evade than address the problem of identifying the distinguishing characteristic(s) of the criminal law.[105] Some commentators openly despair about the prospects of identifying the criminal sanction at all.[106] Even those who equate the criminal law with a distinctive set of procedures do not advance a genuine alternative to my thesis.[107] To be sure, many constitutional safeguards apply only penal laws.[108] The Fifth Amendment privilege against self-incrimination, for example, is reserved for criminal cases; the right to proof beyond a reasonable doubt applies only to penal prosecutions. But the procedural protections that surround the criminal sanction cannot provide a satisfactory account of what the criminal law *is*. In fact, these extraordinary provisions are defensible only on the assumption that criminal laws are special and more difficult to justify than other kinds of law.[109] As Henry Hart pointedly asked some 50 years ago, "what sense does it make to insist upon procedural safeguards in criminal prosecutions if anything whatever can be made a crime in the first place?"[110] Any serious attempt to identify the nature of the criminal law should not leave us puzzled about why so many commentators have thought that these procedural guarantees are important to preserve throughout the domain to which they apply.

Clearly, the hardest task in applying my thesis that the criminal law is special is to decide which state responses are modes of punishment. If we do not know whether the sanction for which offenders become eligible is a type of punishment, we will be unsure about whether an offense that authorizes it is criminal, and thus we will be unclear about whether that offense must be made to satisfy the higher standard of justification a theory of criminalization should demand. An array of novel sanctions compounds the problem of identifying those offenses that qualify as criminal.[111] These sanctions include asset forfeiture, expatriation, punitive

---

103. As Henry M. Hart, Jr., once lamented, a crime seems to be "anything which is called a crime." See H. M. Hart, Jr.: "The Aims of the Criminal Law," 23 *Law & Contemporary Problems* 404, 410 (1958).

104. For a nice discussion of C. S. Kenny's eight definitions of crime in the 19 editions of his *Outlines of Criminal Law*, see Lindsay Farmer: *Criminal Law, Tradition and Legal Order: Crime and the Genius of Scots Law* (Cambridge: Cambridge University Press, 1977), pp.176–177.

105. See Claire O. Finkelstein: "Positivism and the Notion of an Offense," 88 *California Law Review* 335 (2000).

106. The quest for a definition of the criminal law was labeled a "sterile and useless exercise" by P. J. Fitzgerald: "A Concept of Crime," *Criminal Law Review* 257 (1960).

107. See, for example, Rollin M. Perkins and Ronald N. Boyce: *Criminal Law* (Mineola, N.Y.: Foundation Press, 3rd ed., 1982), pp.11–12: "A definition of the term crime cannot practically be separated from the nature of proceedings used to determine criminal conduct." As support, the authors cite Glanville Williams, who once defined a crime as "an act capable of being followed by criminal proceedings having a criminal outcome." See his: "The Definition of Crime," 8 *Current Legal Problems* 107, 125 (1955). Williams's subsequent definitions of crime, however, clarify the nature of this "criminal outcome" by including an explicit reference to punishment. See: *Textbook of Criminal Law* (London: Stevens & Sons, 1983), p.27.

108. See Stephen J. Schulhofer: "Two Systems of Social Protection," 7 *Journal of Contemporary Legal Issues* 69 (1996).

109. See William Stuntz: "Substance, Process, and the Civil-Criminal Line," 7 *Journal of Contemporary Legal Issues* 1 (1996).

110. Hart: *op. cit.*, note 103, p.431.

111. The use of these sanctions contributes to "the civilization of the criminal law and the criminalization of the civil law." See Thomas Koenig and Michael Rustad: "'Crimtorts' as Corporate Just Deserts," 31 *University of Michigan Journal of Law Reform* 289, 297 (1998).

damages, deportation, denaturalization, revocation of privileges, antisocial behavior orders, confinement of juvenile delinquents, pretrial detention, shaming rituals, civil contempt orders, protection orders, and the like.[112] Many measures employed against white-collar offenders also straddle the criminal–civil divide. Pursuant to "deferred prosecution agreements," for example, the state charges a company with criminal conduct but delays prosecution in exchange for a promise of reform. The potential charges expire if these reforms are implemented by a specified date. But perhaps the greatest current controversy has swirled around various sexual predator statutes that authorize (what are called) civil proceedings that often result in the confinement of persons who are deemed to be dangerous to the community because of their sexual disorder.[113] The status of provisions requiring the registration of convicted sex offenders is hotly contested as well.[114] Are these sanctions types of punishment that are imposed for violations of the *criminal* law?

Uncertainty about what types of state response are kinds of punishment looms large in debates about how states deal—and should deal—with drug offenders. Fueled by the explosive growth in the number of drug courts throughout the United States, the movement to treat rather than to incarcerate drug users continues to gain momentum.[115] Consider, for example, Proposition 36, approved by a three-to-two margin among California voters in 2000, which requires many individuals caught using illicit drugs to subject themselves to treatment. Failure to comply, or to undergo treatment successfully, makes users eligible for jail. The trend toward treating instead of imprisoning drug users is not peculiar to California. Throughout the United States today, somewhere between 1 and 1.5 million persons enter 12-step alcohol and drug treatment programs, often because they "choose" to participate rather than to endure a more conventional punishment.[116] Treatment is an option some states offer as a way to avoid imprisonment for, say, drunk driving. Many reformers package such proposals as humane and cost-effective alternatives to punishment—and perhaps they are correct.[117] The issue, of course, is whether these devices simply amount to punishment under a different name.

My characterization of the criminal law as that body of law that subjects offenders to state punishment turns out to be easier to articulate than to apply. How should we decide when a sanction is punitive? The Supreme Court classifies a proceeding as civil rather than as criminal primarily as a result of statutory

112. For a discussion, see Susan R. Klein: "Redrawing the Criminal-Civil Boundary," 2 *Buffalo Criminal Law Review* 679 (1999). See also Carol S. Steiker: "Punishment and Procedure: Punishment Theory and the Criminal-Civil Divide," 85 *Georgia Law Journal* 775 (1997).
113. See *Kansas v. Hendricks*, 521 U.S. 346 (1997). For a critical discussion, see Stephen J. Morse: "Uncontrollable Urges and Irrational People," 88 *Virginia Law Review* 1025 (2002).
114. See *Smith v. Doe*, 538 U.S. 84 (2003), which decided whether the Alaskan version of "Megan's Law," the Sex Offender Registration Act, is so punitive either in purpose or effect as to negate the State's description of the Act as civil.
115. See James L. Nolan, Jr.: *Reinventing Justice: The American Drug Court Movement* (Princeton: Princeton University Press, 2001). Similar movements are even more widespread outside the United States.
116. See Stanton Peele and Charles Bufe with Archie Brodsky: *Resisting 12-Step Coercion* (Tucson: Sharp Press, 2000).
117. Or perhaps not. For a less favorable assessment, see Eric J. Miller: "Embracing Addiction: Drug Courts and the False Promise of Judicial Interventionism," 65 *Ohio State Law Journal* 1479 (2004).

interpretation.[118] Judges show enormous deference to how legislatures describe the proceedings they have authorized. But the label attached by the state is not conclusive. If the statute is "so punitive in purpose or effect as to negate [the State's] intention" to deem it civil, courts may pronounce the law to be criminal, and thus treat the sanction as a form of punishment.[119] Needless to say, applications of this standard cause headaches among courts and commentators alike. One theorist describes the Court's attempt to distinguish punishments from civil sanctions as "an incoherent muddle . . . so inconsistent that it borders on the unintelligible."[120]

Although confusion is unavoidable, I do not believe it undermines my thesis.[121] *Any* account of the nature of the criminal law must strain to accommodate unusual or nonstandard examples, and we should not always expect a definitive answer to the question whether each sanction is or is not an instance of punishment.[122] The concept of punishment, like nearly all concepts, is vague and admits of borderline cases. And the number of these borderline cases is bound to proliferate, because states have ample incentive to devise novel types of sanction that are not clearly punitive in order to circumvent the need for those procedural safeguards that apply only throughout the criminal domain. It is likely that the most philosophically sophisticated analysis would treat the contrast between criminal and noncriminal sanctions as a difference of degree and not of kind.[123] Perhaps we should be content simply to say that some types of state response deviate further from paradigm cases of punishment than others: The greater the deviation, the fewer protections that are needed. Unfortunately, most of the jurisprudential work to which the concept of punishment is put cannot readily accept the conclusion that given sanctions are impossible to categorize and can only be regarded as somewhat like while also somewhat unlike paradigm cases of punishment. Ultimately, the practical realities of the legal process demand that borderline examples be pigeonholed into one classification or the other. But the concept of punishment will always resist facile categorization. A theory about the limits of the criminal law is not deficient because it reluctantly treats this contrast as one of kind.[124]

---

118. *Allen v. Illinois*, 478 U.S. 364 (1986).

119. *United States v. Ward*, 448 U.S. 242, 248–249 (1980).

120. Wayne Logan: "The Ex Post Facto Clause and the Jurisprudence of Punishment," 35 *American Criminal Law Review* 1261, 1268, 1280 (1998).

121. Admittedly, contracting the size and scope of the criminal law would be a less impressive achievement if it resulted in a corresponding expansion in the use of sanctions that are close to but not quite punitive.

122. H. L. A. Hart coped with (or perhaps evaded) this problem by identifying what he called secondary or substandard cases of punishment. See *op. cit.*, note 86, p.5.

123. "Even on a theoretical plane, fixing the proper boundaries of the criminal law is likely to involve not sharp distinctions and clearly-defined categories, but rather judgements of degree." Ashworth: *op. Cit.*, note 20, p.27.

124. Perhaps some of the uneasiness about my failure to draw a bright line between the criminal and noncriminal spheres can be addressed. I readily concede that legal rules that are not quite criminal must satisfy stringent but lesser standards of justification. Many practices that are not paradigm forms of punishment are objectionable for much the same reason that would apply if they *were* punishment. Consider, for example, *Department of Housing and Urban Development v. Rucker*, 535 U.S. 125 (2002), in which tenants were evicted from public housing for failing to "assure that . . . any member of the household, a guest, or another person under the tenant's control, shall not engage in . . . any drug-related criminal activity on or near the premises." The regulations authorized eviction even if the tenant did not know, could not foresee, or could not control the drug-related activity of other occupants. Such proceedings impose hardship and stigma that seem roughly equivalent to that of criminal sanctions, so powerful reasons are required to justify them.

Even though the distinction between punishments and other forms of unwanted deprivations is hard to draw, I will continue to suppose that the criminal law is special because it makes offenders eligible for state punishment. If I am correct, the most basic question to be answered by a theory of criminalization is: *For what conduct may the state subject persons to punishment?* As a result, limitations on the penal sanction can be found by deciding when persons are *in*eligible for punishment.[125] This inquiry plunges us directly into one of the deepest quagmires in the history of political and legal philosophy: the justification of state punishment. Punishment has proven incredibly difficult to defend.[126] Disagreement among philosophers is profound, is radical, and takes place at the deepest level of moral intuition. Some theorists hold premises to be self-evident and humane that others regard as counterintuitive and barbaric. It is unrealistic to expect these disputes to be resolved any time soon. Fortunately, we need not await a comprehensive justification of punishment; ample progress in the matter at hand is possible with only a few modest suppositions. First, notice that all legal philosophers concur that inflictions of punishment require a justification. That is, even though they disagree about *how* punishment is justified, they do not disagree *that* a justification is needed.[127] In the absence of whatever rationale they favor, they must regard punishments as *un*justified. If we can identify one or more constraints that any acceptable defense of punishment must satisfy, we might be able to show that some (real or imaginary) criminal laws should be placed beyond the reach of the punitive sanction. Penal statutes that fail to satisfy these constraints will make offenders eligible for punishments that cannot be justified. No respectable theory of criminalization should tolerate this result.

I have already identified two constraints on criminalization: Penal liability is unjustified unless it is imposed for an offense designed to proscribe a nontrivial harm or evil, and may not be inflicted unless the defendant's conduct is (in some sense) wrongful. In this section I introduce a third principle, which I call the *desert* constraint: Punishment is justified only when and to the extent it is deserved. In other words, undeserved punishments are unjustified. Of course, this latter constraint, like any other, lacks content in the absence of a substantive theory of desert. I make little effort to offer such a theory here.[128] On any plausible conception, however, it is clear that the wrongfulness and desert constraints overlap significantly; most criminal laws that violate one will violate the other as well. But the overlap between these two principles should not be mistaken for an identity; for three reasons, we should not think that punishments are undeserved if and only if

---

125. This conceptualization of the problem has antecedents in Kantian legal philosophy, according to which the fundamental question for a theory of criminalization is whether the state is permitted to resort to force.

126. One commentator describes the assumption that punishment *can* be justified as "the fallacy of begging the institution." See Mary Margaret Mackenzie: *Plato on Punishment* (Berkeley: University of California Press, 1981), p.41.

127. John Rawls remarks that it "is rather surprising" that "only a few have rejected punishment entirely" in light of "all that can be said against it." See "Two Concepts of Rules," 64 *Philosophical Review* 3 (1955).

128. The collected works of Andrew von Hirsch provide an excellent account of desert in the criminal domain. In particular, see *Past Or Future Crimes?* (New Brunswick, N.J.: Rutgers University Press, 1987).

they are imposed for conduct that is permissible. The existence of excusing conditions provides the first demonstration that these constraints are different. Punishments are undeserved even when imposed for wrongful conduct if the defendant is excused.[129] Moreover, punishments may be undeserved when they are excessive. The desert constraint underlies the principle of proportionality—a principle that nearly every theorist regards as central to the philosophy of criminal law. But the desert and wrongfulness constraints diverge for a third and less obvious reason. As we will see, not all wrongdoing makes persons eligible for punishment imposed by the state. *Private* wrongdoing, however identified, does not render persons deserving of state punishment. Obviously, these observations provide only the smallest of steps toward producing a theory of deserved punishments. My subsequent (and admittedly meager) efforts to provide content to this constraint will proceed by developing intuitions I am confident are widely shared.

No adequate theory of punishment can reject the three internal constraints I have identified. As a matter of fact, they are compatible with virtually all theories of punishment that philosophers have tried to defend. It may seem that these constraints are less plausible if punishment is thought to be justified because of its beneficial consequences. But the vast majority of consequentialists, as I understand them, are anxious to show that their attempts to justify punishment preserve these constraints. That is, these theorists do not explicitly reject these constraints but merely construe them differently than nonconsequentialists. For example, a consequentialist might hold (roughly) that conduct is wrongful when it is intended to cause a harm or evil the state may legitimately deter, and that persons deserve to be punished whenever they (inexcusably) engage in such conduct. I concede, however, that a few attempts to justify punishment might reject these constraints; I do not insist that they are neutral with respect to every possible defense of punishment that has ever been devised. I hope this lack of neutrality is not too problematic. Philosophical inquiry must begin somewhere; mine begins here.

I also admit that a persuasive *argument* for these constraints is difficult to construct. I would have little idea how to respond to a theorist who alleges that punishments are justified even when they are *not* deserved, are imposed for conduct that is *not* wrongful, or are inflicted for violations of statutes that are *not* designed to proscribe a nontrivial harm or evil. Perhaps the best we can do is to inquire: What would a justification of punishment be like if it dispensed with these constraints? Suppose a given individual were about to be punished, demanded a justification for his treatment, and was assured that a justification was needed. He might ask: "What harm or evil is the state seeking to prohibit by punishing me?" or, "What have I done wrong to justify my punishment?" or, "Why do I deserve to be punished?" Suppose the state were to respond: "We aim to proscribe no harm or evil by punishing you," or, "You have done nothing wrong, but your punishment is justified nonetheless," or, "Your punishment is not deserved, but still it is justified." These replies are so peculiar that further dialogue between the individual and the state is unlikely to be fruitful.

---

129. See Horder: *op. cit.*, note 83.

Do I hold that existing criminal law conforms to these constraints? Of course not; that is precisely what is wrong with it. Many offenses on the periphery of the criminal law—those outside its core—are incompatible with them. Some commentators report almost as a revelation that legislators show little regard for these constraints. Legal philosophers are chided for fostering the "myth" that "personal moral culpability and blameworthiness delineate modern criminal law."[130] Others point out that "criminal law is not nearly the stickler for individualized moral blameworthiness that [Henry] Hart mythicized."[131] I concede that no principle can function as an accurate generalization about positive law when exceptions become too numerous. It is hard to identify the exact point at which these constraints no longer describe the criminal law we actually have instead of the criminal law we would prefer to have. At this late stage, political inertia may prevent us from reversing the trend toward overcriminalization by requiring the state to proscribe only wrongful conduct that causes (or risks) a nontrivial harm or evil for which persons deserve to be punished—constraints we have increasingly less reason to suppose accurately pertain to the criminal law as it presently exists. The criminal law already may have become a "lost cause."[132] But the point of my project is not to describe the criminal law as it is but to defend a normative theory of criminalization to limit it. At the same time, I have tried to show that this normative theory can be found within the criminal law itself. We should not tolerate deviations from these internal constraints because violations of criminal statutes subject offenders to state punishment, and punishments must be justified. When any of these constraints is breached, criminal liability and punishment are *un*justified. If *this* is the reality we are chided for not accepting, legal philosophers should fold our tents and abandon normative inquiry altogether.

Because punishment should be inflicted only for violations of laws that conform to these constraints, it follows that punitive sanctions cannot possibly be justified in the absence of presuppositions about the behavior for which they are imposed. Admittedly, a great many philosophers *appear* to have sought a justification of punishment without attending to the nature of the conduct to be punished. But this appearance is misleading. When attempts to justify punishment are examined carefully, philosophers can be seen to assume (often implicitly) that their accounts will be applied only when given normative conditions are satisfied. Typically, these conditions pertain either to the legal system as a whole—as when the purported justification is confined to a "basically just legal system"—or to individual statutes—as when a theorist stipulates that the law in question must be "basically just."[133] It is easy to miss this crucial assumption in light of the controversy that inevitably surrounds the defense of punishment that follows. But a moment's reflection demonstrates that complex normative accounts of whether

130. John L. Diamond: "The Myth of Morality and Fault in Criminal Law Doctrine," 34 *American Criminal Law Review* 111, 112 (1996).
131. Louis D. Bilionis: "Process, the Constitution, and Substantive Criminal Law," 96 *Michigan Law Review* 1269, 1279 (1998). Bilionis hastens to add, however, that he is "among the many who find [Hart's account of the criminal law] normatively attractive." *Id.,* p.1278.
132. See Andrew Ashworth: "Is The Criminal Law a Lost Cause?" 116 *Law Quarterly Review* 225 (2000).
133. See, for example, Herbert Morris: "Persons and Punishment," 53 *Monist* 474, 478–480 (1968).

and under what conditions punishment is deserved would not be needed if criminal sanctions may be imposed irrespective of the content of the criminal law.

Although some theorists who attempt to defend punishment purport to confine their normative assumptions to *systems* of law rather than to *individual* statutes, the latter restriction is necessary, whatever may be true of the former. That is, punitive sanctions are unjustified when we have principled reasons to conclude that the particular conduct for which they are imposed should not have been criminalized—subjected to punishment—in the first place.[134] This is true even when the law in question is part of a "basically just" legal system (whatever exactly that may mean). Can it possibly be true, for example, that persons who broke fugitive slave laws prior to the Civil War deserve to be punished simply because the legal system at that time was basically just? This result would follow unless the immorality of slavery destroyed the "basic justness" of slave-owning societies and rendered theories of punishment inapplicable to them.

Thus when philosophers assume that their justifications of punishment will be applied only when given normative conditions are satisfied, I assume these conditions pertain to individual statutes rather than (solely) to entire systems of law. Because an adequate theory of punishment must specify the conditions under which criminal sanctions are *un*justified, a theory of punishment has implications for the content of the criminal law. In the remainder of this section, I illustrate how justifications of punishment impose constraints on criminalization by briefly discussing the probable implications of a few theories of punishment that have been defended by some prominent philosophers. Although I am confident that my points can be generalized to any plausible theory whatever, I focus on a handful of retributive accounts.[135] A given retributive theory must be explicated in reasonable detail before its consequences for criminalization can be discerned.[136] A retributivist must specify *why* criminals deserve to be punished; he must identify *what* it is about criminal conduct that makes punishments deserved.[137] Several philosophers have tried to meet this formidable challenge. My goal in quickly surveying a small sampling of their answers is not to defend or attack their efforts; an enormous critical literature on such matters is available elsewhere.[138] Instead, my aim is to

---

134. I am not the first legal philosopher to make this claim, although its implications for criminalization remain largely undeveloped. For example, Herbert Packer indicated that we cannot sensibly talk about the limits of the criminal sanction without settling on a rationale of punishment. See Packer: *op. cit.*, note 14, p.4. See also the brief remarks in Jeffrie Murphy and Jules Coleman: *The Philosophy of Law* (Totowa, N.J.: Rowman & Allanheld, 1984), p.114.

135. I make no effort to defend a conception that would show each of the theories I subsequently discuss to be varieties of retributivism. Generally, see John Cottingham: "Varieties of Retribution," 29 *Philosophical Quarterly* 116 (1979).

136. According to Jules Coleman, however, "retributivism is not a theory of criminality; it is a theory about what ought to be, or at least what may legitimately be done by the state in those cases where a criminal misdeed has been committed." Jules Coleman: *The Practice of Principle* (Oxford: Oxford University Press, 2001), p.33. Coleman is half right and half wrong. Particular varieties of retributivism may not provide whole theories of criminalization. Nonetheless, most are more than justifications of what the state may do to those who commit misdeeds; they limit what counts as a misdeed in the first place.

137. As R. A. Duff indicates, "anti-retributivists make quite a meal…about the general idea that crimes 'deserve' punishment." See R. A. Duff: "Punishment, Communication, and Community" in Matt Matravers, ed.: *Punishment and Political Theory* (Oxford: Hart Pub. Co., 1999), pp.48, 50.

138. Among the best critiques of retributive theories is Russell L. Christopher: "Deterring Retributivism: The Injustice of 'Just' Punishment," 96 *Northwestern University Law Review* 843 (2002).

demonstrate that each of these theories has significant implications for criminalization. If all theories of punishment entail constraints on criminal statutes, and criminal statutes are that body of law that subject offenders to state punishment, it follows that constraints on criminalization are internal to the criminal law itself.

Many retributivists, for example, defend *benefits-and-burdens* theories.[139] According to this general approach, a person gains an unfair advantage relative to law-abiding citizens when he breaks the law. Punishment is deserved because it somehow removes or negates this gain; it restores the prior equilibrium of benefits and burdens. The ramifications of these theories for the substantive criminal law depend mostly on the nature of the advantage alleged to be gained through criminal behavior.[140] On the least plausible account, the unfair benefit to the offender is his material acquisition—the fruits of his crime. He prospers, relative to citizens who do not resort to theft, for example, by not having to pay for whatever he has stolen. This characterization of the benefit of criminality seems apt for property offenses but fails to explain why offenders deserve punishment when they commit crimes from which they derive no material advantage. Philosophers might try to salvage this account through either of two strategies. First, they might argue that, appearances notwithstanding, this version of a benefits-and-burdens theory *can* show why persons deserve criminal sanctions for committing offenses with no apparent material gain.[141] Alternatively, they can concede that these offenses lie beyond the legitimate reach of the penal sanction. Although neither of these options is promising, my point is more basic: Either strategy presupposes that this theory has implications for the substantive criminal law.

Most theorists, however, deny that the unfair advantage to the criminal is his material gain. Instead, criminals are said to benefit by renouncing the burden of self-restraint, a burden law-abiding citizens continue to bear.[142] This characterization solves the foregoing problem; persons who derive no direct gain from their crimes nonetheless renounce a burden assumed by law-abiding citizens. As the unfair advantage is alleged to follow simply from breaking the law—*any* law—this account may seem to lack implications for criminalization. But does it? If so, it seemingly justifies the punishment of those who renounce the burden of self-restraint by surrendering to their humane desire to harbor runaway slaves in the antebellum South. Any effort to block this sort of counterexample reveals that implications for the content of the substantive criminal law must exist.

What might these implications be? Return briefly to the relatively new kinds of offense that fill criminal codes: overlapping crimes, ancillary offenses, and crimes of risk prevention.[143] Offenses of risk prevention are the easiest of my three

---

139. Not so long ago, such theories could be said to be the most influential versions of retributivism. See David Dolinko: "Some Thoughts About Retributivism," 101 *Ethics* 537 (1991).
140. Various interpretations of the unfair advantage gained by criminality are distinguished in Richard Burgh: "Do the Guilty Deserve Punishment?" 79 *Journal of Philosophy* 193 (1982).
141. A few theorists have tried to solve such problems. See, for example, Michael Davis: "Why Attempts Deserve Less Punishment than Complete Crimes," 5 *Law and Philosophy* 1 (1986).
142. See Morris: *op. cit.*, note 133.
143. See chapter 1, section III.

categories to justify under a benefits-and-burdens theory. Drivers who create risks by speeding, for example, unquestionably gain an advantage relative to motorists who comply with traffic laws and take a longer time to reach their destinations. Because respectable theories of punishment are seemingly compatible with many of these offenses, my theory of criminalization addresses questions about their justifiability separately.[144] Consider, however, the application of a benefits-and-burdens theory to overlapping offenses. When someone commits a criminal act, it is hard to see how his benefit is greater if he happens to live in a jurisdiction that has enacted several overlapping statutes that proscribe his conduct. No plausible measure of his benefit should be responsive to the sheer number of overlapping laws he manages to breach. Similarly, the burdens of self-restraint borne by law-abiding members of society are not increased when legislatures pass additional overlapping offenses. Although it is tempting to think that those who refrain from criminal activity are disadvantaged by their restraint, it seems fantastic to suppose that their burden is greater in a jurisdiction in which the conduct from which they refrain transgresses four statutes rather than three. Implications for many ancillary offenses are less straightforward. As we have seen, the point of these laws is to enable the state to gather information of other crimes or to criminalize behavior that can be detected more easily than the conduct it really seeks to prevent. Admittedly, some of these offenses impose burdens on those who comply with them. Obviously, corporate officers who file tedious reports and monitor their accountants undertake burdens that law-breaking officers do not. Still, it is not altogether clear how offenders can be said to benefit relative to non-offenders when they engage in behavior the state has no real interest in deterring but has prohibited because of its evidentiary relation to a core or primary offense. If a defendant commits an ancillary offense *without* engaging in the behavior the statute really is designed to prevent—as when he neglects to file a form even though he has not cheated or stolen, for example—has a gain that could justify punishment accrued to him? The answer is not obvious.

Expressive theories of punishment have become somewhat more popular among philosophers than benefits-and-burdens theories. This label includes many variants under its broad umbrella.[145] Although expressivists differ about exactly what it is that punishment expresses, Joel Feinberg's influential account might be taken as representative. Feinberg claims that "punishment is a conventional device for the expression of attitudes of resentment and indignation, and of judgments of disapproval and reprobation, on the part either of the punishing authority himself or of those 'in whose name' the punishment is inflicted."[146] This view, like almost any other, has implications for criminalization. Expressivism cannot be thought to provide even a partial justification of punishment without attending to the nature of the criminal acts that trigger the expression of the attitudes Feinberg

144. See chapter 3, section III.
145. For an ambitious attempt to explain what makes a theory of law (including a theory of punishment) expressive, see Matthew Adler: "Expressive Theories of Law: A Skeptical Overview," 148 *University of Pennsylvania Law Review* 1363 (2000).
146. Joel Feinberg: "The Expressive Theory of Punishment," in his *Doing and Deserving* (Princeton: Princeton University Press, 1970), pp.95, 99.

describes. Unless resentment and indignation were *appropriate* responses to given kinds of conduct, conventional devices to express these attitudes would only baffle those to whom they were directed. Feinberg concurs. He holds that an expressive theory demands "that the crime be of a kind that is truly worthy of reprobation."[147] Thus his expressivism would deem punishment to be *un*justified when the crime for which it is inflicted is *not* "truly worthy of reprobation." This sensible demand is hard to square with many of the new kinds of offense that clutter our criminal codes. Which existing crimes fail to satisfy this criterion? Do any *mala prohibita* offenses qualify? Can expressions of resentment and indignation possibly be appropriate when someone violates the ancillary laws that recently have been enacted? Do persons become worthy of more reprobation when their conduct happens to breach several overlapping statutes? Probably not. Among the new kinds of offense I have distinguished, only persons who commit (some) crimes of risk prevention are likely to be "truly worthy of reprobation."

Finally, consider the probable implications of *paternalistic* theories of punishment. According to Herbert Morris, education is among the primary aims of punitive sanctions.[148] Jean Hampton goes further; she regards moral education as the *sole* justifying aim of punishment.[149] Again, the content of the criminal law must meet rigid criteria before punishment has any prospect of being educational.[150] If punishment exists to provide moral education, each offense in the criminal law must have a moral basis. Unless offenders behave wrongfully when committing given crimes, what could be the rationale for requiring them to undergo education characterized as moral? Thus, Hampton indicates that the subject matter of a criminal law "ought to be drawn either from ethical imperatives, of the form 'don't steal' or 'don't murder.' or else from imperatives made necessary for moral reasons, for example, 'drive on the right.'"[151] I have more to say about the latter kind of example in the final section of this chapter. At this time, I simply note that the increased punishments imposed for violations of ancillary or overlapping offenses appear to satisfy neither of Hampton's disjuncts. The same conclusion can be reached by applying her description of the lesson supposedly taught by moral education. Hampton writes that punishment should be designed to inform "the wrongdoer that her victim suffered, so that the wrongdoer can appreciate the harmfulness of her action."[152] Is suffering thus to be a necessary condition for the legitimate imposition of criminal sanctions? If not, Hampton has incorrectly described the lesson offenders should learn through punishment. If so, however, the implications for criminalization are far-reaching indeed.

147. *Id.*, p.118.
148. Herbert Morris: "A Paternalistic Theory of Punishment," 18 *American Philosophical Quarterly* 263 (1981).
149. Jean Hampton: "The Moral Education Theory of Punishment," 13 *Philosophy and Public Affairs* 208 (1984). Hampton subsequently revised her views about the rationale of punishment in Jeffrie J. Murphy and Jean Hampton: *Forgiveness and Mercy* (Cambridge: Cambridge University Press, 1988).
150. See Russ Shafer-Landau: "Can Punishment Morally Educate?" 10 *Law and Philosophy* 189 (1991).
151. Hampton: *op. cit.*, note 149, p.210.
152. *Id.*, p.227.

Despite its brevity, I hope the foregoing survey is sufficient to support my general conclusion: Any *plausible* theory of when punishment is deserved has implications for criminalization. We should reject the few philosophical attempts to justify punishment that stand as exceptions to my claim and clearly lack implications for criminalization. The most prominent such theory, which might be called *legalistic retributivism*, was defended by J. D. Mabbott.[153] Legalistic retributivists hold that the punishment of criminals is justified simply because they have broken the law.[154] Mabbott explicitly indicates that the goodness or badness of either the government or the law is wholly irrelevant to whether punishment is justified.[155] Almost no philosopher has been persuaded by Mabbott's approach. The most trenchant criticism is that legalistic retributivism allows punishment *whatever* the criminal law happens to proscribe. It is hard to believe, for example, that courts in Afghanistan would be justified in punishing Muslims (by death, no less) who commit the offense of converting to Christianity. Someone is bound to object that this counterexample would be unconstitutional in the United States, but this response reinforces my point. The unconstitutionality of this law is a function of its content, and Mabbott's theory holds that punishment may be justified without attending to the substance of the law for which it is imposed. The fundamental difficulty, in other words, is the very feature that makes legalistic retributivism so distinctive: its lack of implications for the criminal sanction.[156] I believe we are entitled to conclude that any plausible theory of punishment *must* constrain the substantive criminal law.

Legal philosophers who aspire to develop a minimalist theory of criminalization can only lament the fact that the implications of given theories are not always traced explicitly. Several legal scholars miss golden opportunities to explore the ramifications of their views about punishment for questions about the reach of the criminal sanction. For example, some theorists who believe that a central desideratum of punishment is to motivate voluntary compliance with the law have concluded that this objective is best achieved when the state pays attention to community attitudes about justice. Paul Robinson and John Darley undertake the most well-known defense of this approach.[157] They argue that society will lose faith in the penal law if it is perceived as criminalizing conduct unjustly. Conversely, the state runs the risk of extralegal vigilante actions if it fails to criminalize conduct the community believes should be proscribed. Either failure causes the criminal law to forfeit some of its moral credibility, with a corresponding loss of voluntary compliance.

This view has obvious implications for criminalization. No defect in the criminal law is likely to erode confidence among citizens more rapidly than the perception that the wrong acts are punished or unpunished. Curiously, however, Robinson

153. J. D. Mabbott: "Punishment," in H. B. Acton, ed.: *The Philosophy of Punishment* (Macmillan: St. Martin's Press, 1969), p.39.
154. *Id.*, p.42.
155. *Id.*, p.48.
156. In a subsequent response to his critics, Mabbott allows that countervailing obligations should lead a judge *not* to impose a justified punishment. See J. D. Mabbott: "Professor Flew on Punishment," in Acton: *op. cit.*, note 153, pp.115, 124. This response raises the difficult issue of exactly what is meant by describing a punishment as *justified*.
157. Paul H. Robinson and John Darley: *Justice, Liability & Blame* (Boulder: Westview Press, 1995).

and Darley embellish their thesis while paying virtually no attention to the topic of criminalization itself. Admittedly, the first chapter of their book is titled "Doctrines of Criminalization: What Conduct Should Be Criminal?" They begin this chapter by noting the extent of social disagreement about the prohibition of "victimless crimes" like "prostitution, gambling, or distribution of certain drugs."[158] But their discussion of these controversies is confined to a single paragraph; they do not bother to solicit community views about any of the offenses they label as controversial. Instead, they immediately direct their attention to the implications of their theory for "secondary prohibitions," that is, extensions of criminal liability to cases of attempts, complicity, and the like. Remarkably, the community attitudes that matter most to Robinson and Darley tend to involve relatively esoteric doctrines in the general part of criminal law. Any discrepancy between lay intuitions and these arcane topics is unlikely to cause citizens to lose faith in our criminal justice system.[159] The public is almost certainly uninformed about these doctrines, and nothing can affect compliance unless citizens are aware of it. Surely *primary* offenses provide the more fundamental application of their thesis.[160] Thus, Robinson and Darley fail to explore the most significant implications of their project.

What would these scholars have discovered if they had tried to solicit the views of the community about the (so-called) victimless crimes they mention? The offense of drug possession—the most commonly punished crime in the United States today—surely would be jeopardized. Not surprisingly, different polls elicit different responses about this offense. In recent surveys, 36% of all Americans said they believed that "the use of marijuana should be made legal."[161] This finding might have led Robinson and Darley to clarify their view in two crucial respects. First, they might have tried to decide not only *whether* community views are relevant to criminal liability but also *what degree* of social consensus is needed before the state may resort to punishment. What percentage of the public must regard given statutes as unjust before the entire system of law begins to lose credibility? Second, Robinson and Darley might have attempted to specify *who* counts as the relevant community.[162] Attitudes about the offense of drug possession vary significantly with demographic characteristics. Respondents are more likely to favor marijuana decriminalization if they are better educated and less religious.[163] In addition, although minorities tend to have more negative attitudes about illicit drugs, they have greater reservations about the wisdom of enforcing drug prohibitions.[164] Are attitudes in communities in which punishment is commonplace more or less important than those in communities

---

158. *Id.*
159. See Christopher Slobogin: "Is Justice Just Us? Using Social Science to Inform Substantive Criminal Law," 87 *Journal of Criminal Law & Criminology* 315 (1996).
160. I suspect that respect for law is influenced more by one's personal experience with the legal system than by the rules or doctrines promulgated by legal officials. Anyone who has participated in everyday altercations in local municipal court, for example, is unlikely to emerge with his respect for law intact.
161. U.S. Department of Justice: *Sourcebook of Criminal Justice Statistics* (2005), table 2.67.
162. See Deborah Denno: "The Perils of Public Opinion," 28 *Hofstra Law Review* 741 (2000).
163. *Sourcebook: op. cit.*, note 161, table 2.68 (2003).
164. Drug policy toward minorities is explored in Tracey Meares: "Social Organization and Drug Law Enforcement," 35 *American Criminal Law Review* 191 (1998).

in which punishment is infrequent? How do these factors affect a justification of punishment based on community reactions?[165] If these questions had been raised, Robinson and Darley might have refined their theory.

The foregoing remarks are designed merely to scratch the surface of a huge issue. I am aware that my survey of attempts to justify punishment is superficial and cursory, and that several plausible theories have not been mentioned at all. Still, I hope to have said enough to support my basic claim: Efforts to justify punishment have important implications for criminalization. Hence the voluminous literature about punishment—with which criminal theorists are certain to be familiar—provides a fertile source of constraints on the penal sanction. In particular, criminal liability may be imposed only for conduct for which punishment is deserved. Philosophers who advance a particular theory of deserved punishment should be encouraged to supply the details of how their accounts limit the content of the criminal law. Those who accept this invitation are likely to improve their theory of punishment while helping to develop constraints internal to a theory of criminalization.

Admittedly, any progress I have achieved to this point is modest. An attempt to combat the problem of overcriminalization by developing a set of principles to confine the criminal sanction requires four analytically distinct steps. We must (1) identify, (2) defend, (3) explicate, and (4) apply each constraint. Almost all of my efforts here involve tasks (1) and (2). That is, I am mostly content to identify and defend constraints on the scope of penal statutes. I am aware that any reasonable person would be impatient to advance to steps (3) and (4). These constraints must be given *content,* and we must illustrate how they retard the phenomenon of overcriminalization by their application to particular examples. I understand and sympathize with this impatience. Still, before proceeding to these crucial stages, we need to know *what* to explicate and apply, and *why* we should do so. I pursue these two objectives here.

In any event, the arguments I have offered help us to resist a very seductive train of thought. It is tempting to suppose that we should withhold judgment about whether the criminal law should include a desert constraint (or a nontrivial harm or evil constraint, or a wrongfulness constraint) until we see the particular account of desert (or of harm or evil, or of wrongfulness) that the criminal law should include. Why should we accept something until we are told exactly what it is we are to accept? Still, I believe this supposition is misguided. If someone produces a theory of desert (or of harm or evil, or of wrongfulness) that she argues the criminal law should include, her opponent may reply that her particular theory is mistaken. Obviously, disagreement on this level should be expected. What her opponent *cannot* claim, however, is that no theory of desert (or of harm or evil, or of wrongfulness) is required, because no reason has been given to conclude that the criminal law need conform to these constraints. If my arguments are sound, we *must* produce these theories. These constraints are internal to the criminal law itself.

---

165. Some theories of punishment have been faulted for their insensitivity to social context, as they struggle to explain why the content of the criminal law should vary from one jurisdiction to another. See Kenneth Simons: "The Relevance of Community Values to Just Deserts: Criminal Law, Punishment Rationales, and Democracy," 28 *Hofstra Law Review* 635, 639 (2000).

III: A RIGHT NOT TO BE PUNISHED?

The criminal law is that body of law that subjects offenders to state punishment. To be justified, punishments must be deserved, should be imposed only for offenses designed to proscribe a nontrivial harm or evil, and may not be inflicted on persons unless their conduct is wrongful. The punishments that satisfy these three internal constraints—a topic of enormous dispute—will have profound implications for matters of criminalization. But why should punitive sanctions be so difficult to justify? After all, we have seen that punishments are inflicted routinely in the United States today, and even legal philosophers do not appear to be overly upset by this trend. An answer to this important question must attend to the nature of state punishment itself.[166] In this section I argue that state punishment is hard to justify because it involves two essential features: hard treatment and censure. Under normal circumstances, impositions of hard treatment and censure violate important personal interests. Because ordinary utilitarian reasons do not allow the government to infringe these important interests, we have reason to countenance a *right not to be punished*. When punishments are justified—when they are imposed for violations of laws that pass our test of criminalization—the state may infringe this right. Thus the key to a theory of criminalization is to determine when the state is permitted to infringe the right not to be punished. A more complete account of when this right may be infringed conjoins what I have called the internal and the external constraints into a single theory of criminalization.[167]

I begin by focusing on what it is about punishment that requires justification. Although legal philosophers obviously disagree about *how* to defend punishment, they also disagree about *what* it is about punishment that must be defended. The difficulty of justifying punishment is so great that many commentators are attracted to accounts that render it mysterious why punishment needs much of a justification at all. The temptation to construe punishment as based on consent,[168] or as designed to benefit those on whom it is imposed,[169] partly reflects the difficulty of defending state punishment as I propose to understand it here. But we should not take these easy ways out. I contend that state punishment requires a justification because it contains two problematic features: what I call *hard treatment* (or *deprivation*) and *censure*.[170]

Few will deny that punishment includes the first of these ingredients. As H. L. A. Hart recognized long ago, a state response to conduct does not qualify

166. My account is intended to apply to *state* punishments, not to punishments that may be inflicted by private persons or other institutions. For reasons to think that theorists should begin by producing a more general account of punishment, see Leo Zaibert: *Punishment and Retribution* (Burlington, Vt.: Ashgate Pub. Co., 2006).

167. I should not be understood to say that satisfying the internal and external constraints is *sufficient* to justify penal legislation. Many procedural considerations not discussed here are important as well. As a matter of substance, however, I can think of no statute that satisfies each of these constraints but is unjustified.

168. See C. S. Nino: "A Consensual Theory of Punishment," 12 *Philosophy and Public Affairs* 289 (1983).

169. See Morris: *op. cit.*, note 148; and Hampton: *op. cit.*, note 149.

170. I do not hazard a *definition* of punishment, because the conditions I identify are not conjointly sufficient. Instead, I merely describe what it is about punishment that requires justification. I concur that an attempt to define punishment "is doomed to futility if it is intended to...[capture] all and only those practices that properly count as 'punishment.'" R. A. Duff: *Punishment. Communication, and Community* (Oxford: Oxford University Press, 2001), p.xiv.

as punitive unless it involves "pain or other consequences normally considered unpleasant."[171] These consequences might be of various kinds: Persons might be killed, imprisoned, mutilated, fined, deported, banished, or the like. For simplicity, I generalize by saying that all modes of punishment involve hard treatment or deprivation. Hart also appreciated, however, that not all state inflictions of consequences normally considered unpleasant are modes of punishment. Consider, for example, taxes, license revocations, benefit terminations, and other disqualifications. These deprivations do not typically count as punitive, despite the severe hardship they may cause. Thus a second condition must be satisfied before a sanction should be categorized as a punishment, although there is far more controversy about how this additional condition should be formulated. I contend that a state response to conduct does not qualify as punitive unless it is designed to censure and to stigmatize.[172] For this reason, I concur with those many legal philosophers who believe that punishment has an important expressive dimension.

Each of these two conditions must be brought about deliberately rather than accidentally. In other word, state sanctions do not amount to punishment because they *happen* to impose deprivations and stigmatize their recipients. The very *purpose* of a punitive state sanction is to inflict a stigmatizing hardship on an offender. Perhaps the state has ulterior motives in resorting to punishment. A punitive response to criminal behavior may be the most effective way to deter future crimes, promote social cohesion, protect the rights of law-abiding citizens, and so forth. But the existence of these ulterior motives does not undermine my claim that a sanction is not a punishment without a purpose to deprive and censure. No other state institution is comparable in this respect. Many state sanctions result in hardships and several others stigmatize. Some state practices, like involuntary confinement of the dangerous mentally ill, probably do both simultaneously.[173] But these sanctions differ from punishment because they lack a punitive intention. Although they *knowingly* cause deprivations, that is not their point or purpose. We would prefer a different response that neither stigmatized nor imposed a hardship on these unfortunate souls if a suitable alternative could be found. That is why we should be reluctant to say that dangerous mentally abnormal offenders are *punished*, even though the *effects* of their treatment may be indistinguishable from genuine punishments. What differs is the intention of those who impose the sanction.

The requirement that punishments express censure is of monumental importance for a theory of criminalization.[174] The expressive dimension of punishment

171. H. L. A. Hart: *op. cit.*, note 86, p.4.

172. For an impressive defense of the view that punishment includes both hard treatment and censure, see Andrew von Hirsch: *Censure and Sanctions* (Oxford: Clarendon Press, 1993).

173. The stigmatizing effect of civil commitment is conceded in *Addington v. Texas*, 441 U.S. 418 (1979).

174. And for many other purposes as well. For example, Dan Kahan argues that state responses to criminality simply are not accepted by the public as genuine modes of punishment unless they involve censure. Given kinds of sanctions must stigmatize if they are to be recognized as punitive. See "What Do Alternative Sanctions Mean?" 63 *University of Chicago Law Review* 591 (1996). In addition, the requirement that punishments express censure is important in showing what is deficient about the economic analysis of crime. See chapter 4, section I.

helps to explain why an adequate theory of criminalization must satisfy the internal constraints I have described. When persons are found guilty of committing a crime, their conduct should render a set of reactive attitudes appropriate. The state must ensure that individuals labeled "criminals" merit the disapprobation this term connotes. Some commentators endeavor to derive fairly specific implications for the content of offenses from the set of reactive attitudes that become warranted when persons are guilty of criminal conduct. According to Victor Tadros, judgments of criminal responsibility express moral indignation, which are appropriate only when agents display improper regard for a significant interest of another.[175] It seems to follow that conduct should not be criminalized unless offenders betray a disregard for others. Tadros may well be correct, but my claim is more modest. I hold only that expressions of censure and impositions of stigma must be appropriate if punishments are to be justified, and that these responses are inappropriate unless offenders deserve to be stigmatized. I withhold further judgment on the *kind* of conduct that merits state censure.

The stigmatizing dimension of punishment also lends support to the principle of proportionality. As Andrew von Hirsch and Andrew Ashworth have argued, the requirement of proportionate sentencing can be

> derived directly from the censuring implications of the criminal sanction. Once one has created an institution with the condemnatory connotations that punishment has, then it is a requirement of justice, not merely of efficient law enforcement, to punish offenders according to the degree of reprehensibleness of their conduct. Disproportionate punishments are unjust not because they possibly may be ineffectual or possibly counterproductive, but because they purport to condemn the actor for his conduct and yet visit more or less censure on him than the degree of blameworthiness of that conduct would warrant.[176]

A theory of criminalization must be sensitive to these considerations; it should help us to decide not only *whether* but also *to what extent* persons deserve to be punished. As I have suggested repeatedly, too much criminal law produces too much punishment partly because many sentences are disproportionate to the seriousness of the crime. My main point in emphasizing the expressive dimension of punishment, however, is to indicate that it, no less than hardship, requires a justification.[177] Persons who are stigmatized by the state have every right to demand a justification for how they have been treated.

My central project is to defend a theory of criminalization that would justify punishment as I have characterized it. A theory of criminalization must ensure that persons who commit offenses qualify for both hard treatment and censure.[178] The nature of my endeavor might be clarified by considering how it differs from an undertaking that a number of legal philosophers have recently pursued. Some

---

175. Victor Tadros: *Criminal Responsibility* (Oxford: Oxford University Press, 2005), pp.82–83.
176. Andrew von Hirsch and Andrew Ashworth: *Proportionate Sentencing: Exploring the Principles* (Oxford: Oxford University Press, 2005), p.134.
177. Several legal philosophers neglect censure and claim that punishment requires justification simply because it inflicts suffering. For example, see Burgh: *op. cit.*, note 140.
178. Of course, hard treatment and censure are inappropriate if persons have a defense.

commentators take the content of the substantive criminal law as more or less given, and ask what the state is permitted to do to persons who break these laws. Many conclude that a justified state response would be quite unlike punishment as we know it. These humane reformers propose to alter our response to criminal conduct by reducing or eliminating its hardship and/or by removing its stigma.[179] Alternatively, they call for fundamental reforms in the nature of society that would help to make impositions of criminal liability easier to defend.[180] Unfortunately, these approaches leave my inquiry up in the air. Is there any kind of behavior that may be subjected to punishment *as it presently exists?* Should we conclude that no conduct should be proscribed until we improve our social institutions and rethink the nature of punishment? What should we do to offenders in the meantime, while we are waiting for these reforms to be implemented?[181] My project, then, is quite different; I do not attempt to describe a better state response to crime than punishment as we know it. Instead, I take both the structure of society and the nature of punishment as more or less given and ask what conditions the criminal law would have to satisfy before a punitive response could be justified. If we hope to defend the punishments we actually have, we must try to identify the kinds of conduct that would allow the state to subject offenders to hard treatment and censure. If I am correct that we have far too much criminal law, a code that would allow offenders to be punished would differ markedly from the criminal codes that exist today.[182]

In light of the foregoing characterization of our current state response to crime—the intentional infliction of a stigmatizing deprivation—it is easy to see why punishment is so difficult to justify. The criminal sanction is the most powerful weapon in the state arsenal; the government can do nothing worse to its citizens than to punish them. I do not mean, of course, that each particular instance of punishment is necessarily worse than any alternative mode of treatment. As a *type* of response, however, criminal sanctions are the most severe and therefore the most in need of justification. It is a gross understatement to say that punishments treat persons in a manner that typically is wrongful. More to the point, punishments treat persons in a manner that implicates their moral rights.[183] In addition, as I explain below, ordinary utilitarian gains do not provide an adequate justification for imposing punishments. If these claims are correct, I believe we should tentatively conclude that persons have a *right not to be punished.* Much of

---

179. Despite their many differences, I tend to place models of restorative justice in this category. See the essays in Andrew von Hirsch, et al., eds.: *Restorative Justice & Criminal Justice: Competing or Reconcilable Paradigms?* (Oxford: Hart Publishing, 2003).

180. To cite just one of many examples, see Jeffrie Murphy: "Marxism and Retribution," 2 *Philosophy and Public Affairs* 217 (1973).

181. For thoughts on these matters, see Duff: *op. cit.*, note 170, chap. 5. He coins (at p.30) the term "contingent abolitionists" to describe those commentators who believe that punishment should be abolished until social reforms are implemented.

182. Even though my goal is to identify what the content of the substantive criminal law would have to be like before punishment would be justified, I hasten to express my agreement with those many reformers who argue that our existing institution of punishment should be rendered more humane. But that is a topic for another day.

183. No standard terminology about rights has taken hold. Actions *implicate* a right when they are contrary to that right. I intend this term to be neutral about whether those actions are or are not permissible.

the remainder of this section explores what might be said in favor of supposing this right exists.[184]

Admittedly, this alleged right is unfamiliar. We are accustomed to the rights of freedom of religion or freedom of speech, for example, but few if any contemporary theorists explicitly countenance a right not to be punished. Remarkably, philosophers have been more receptive to a right *to* be punished.[185] But the novelty of the right not to be punished is not a good reason to deny its existence. Imagine any state practice deliberately designed to express censure and to deprive. No example other than punishment comes to mind, because any such practice would *be* a mode of punishment. But any example that was not a punishment would be held to implicate rights. The only reason we tend to lack a similar reaction to this state practice when it involves a punishment is because we assume this punishment is justified. But we would not hesitate to say that *un*justified punishments violate rights. Of course, many punishments *are* justified, as I will indicate by drawing a distinction well-known to moral and political philosophers. When an action implicates our rights justifiably, I will say that our rights are *infringed*. When an action implicates our rights *un*justifiably, I will say that our rights are *violated*.[186] If a punishment is justified—if it is imposed for breaking a law that satisfies our test of criminalization—I will say that the right not to be punished is infringed rather than violated. But infringements, no less than violations, implicate rights.[187]

Philosophers concede that punishments *ordinarily* or *typically* treat persons in ways that are contrary to their rights. But this consensus unravels when they try to explain what happens to these rights when punishments are justified.[188] No account of the fate of these rights is unproblematic. According to the view I tend to favor, rights are implicated by all punishments. Rights are infringed even when defendants are treated exactly as they deserve. The very same considerations that show a punishment to be justified show our right not to be punished is infringed rather than violated. But this view is controversial. Admittedly, justified punishments do not implicate all possible formulations of the right not to be punished. No right is implicated if the correct formulation of our right vis-à-vis punishment denies that persons possess a right not to be punished *simpliciter*. Perhaps persons have a *conditional* right not to be punished, that is, a right not to be punished *unless*. . . . Let us call conditional formulations of our right not to punished—those that contain an *unless* clause—*specifications*. The *unless* clause in specifications of

184. I am not persuaded that anyone has provided a conclusive demonstration for how our rights vis-à-vis punishment should be formulated. At the very least, my project might be construed as a model that exhibits the attractions of supposing that persons possess a right not to be punished *simpliciter*—a right that is infringed when punishments are justified.

185. See Morris: *op. cit.*, note 133.

186. The distinction between rights infringements and rights violations was first drawn in Judith Thomson: "Some Ruminations on Rights," 19 *Arizona Law Review* 45 (1977).

187. For a challenge to my use of the distinction between infringements and violations of rights, see John Oberdiek: "Lost in Moral Space: On the Infringing/Violating Distinction and its Place in the Theory of Rights," 23 *Law and Philosophy* 325 (2004).

188. For a penetrating discussion, see Mitchell N. Berman: "Punishment and Justification" (forthcoming, available at SSRN: *http://ssrn.com/abstract=956610*).

our right not to be punished might be completed in different ways.[189] Suppose we complete this conditional clause by saying that persons have a right not to be punished *unless their punishments are justified*. On this formulation of our right, justified punishments turn out not to implicate a fully specified right at all. I have no definitive argument against specifying our right not to be punished in this way.[190] Theorists who take the specificationist alternative are welcome to build my theory of criminalization into the *unless* clause on which the right not to be punished is conditioned. Of course, my preferred formulation of this right is simpler: Persons possess a right not to be punished *simpliciter*.

Even if I am correct that persons have an unconditional right not to be punished, it does not follow that we must conceptualize the considerations that serve to justify punishment as overriding this right. The right not to be punished might be *cancelled* rather than *overridden* by the considerations that justify it. The contrast between cancellations and infringements is aptly described by Joseph Raz.[191] You have a right to be taken to the airport if I have promised to do so. But if you release me from my promise, your right has been canceled rather than overridden. Your release entails that your right to be taken to the airport ceases to exist. But not all cases are comparable. You have a right that I not take your car. But if my friend is bleeding to death and must be driven to the emergency room immediately, and your car is the only way to get him there on time, I am justified in taking your car. Your right that I not take your car is overridden, not canceled.

Does a justified punishment infringe or cancel the right not to be punished? When a right is canceled, it ceases to exist. When a right is overridden, it is plausible to think that it somehow leaves a residue, surviving to play a further role in moral argument.[192] Thus our decision to conceptualize a justified punishment as overriding rather than as canceling the right not to be punished may turn on whether that right survives when a punishment is justified. When a right survives its infringement, something seems to be owed to the person who possesses it. What might this be? Surely the person whose punishment is justified is not owed compensation—as you are owed compensation when I take your car to help my wounded friend.[193] What else might he be owed? I suggest that the person whose right not to be punished is overridden is owed a rationale or justification for the way she is treated. If her right has been canceled and no longer exists—or is specified and thus was not really implicated in the first place—it is unclear why we owe anyone an explanation for making her suffer a stigmatizing deprivation. In particular, it is unclear why we owe this explanation

---

189. The *unless* clause might be completed with a *moral* or a *factual* statement, or with some combination of each. See Thomson: *op. cit.*, note 186.

190. Some attempts to formulate our rights as conditionals seem vacuous and unhelpful. They say that a right is implicated in the absence of the conditions under which it is not implicated, thus telling us nothing more than we knew already.

191. Joseph Raz: *Practical Reasons and Norms* (Princeton: Princeton University Press, 2nd ed., 1990), p.27.

192. *Id.*, pp.202–203.

193. See Duff: *op. cit.*, note 170, p.15. When rights are overridden, Duff alleges that the right-holder typically is owed compensation and/or an apology.

to *her*. Surely the person who releases me from my promise to take him to the airport is not entitled to an explanation for why I went to the beach on the day of his flight.

Again, I concede that the foregoing issues are controversial and unsettled. Although unjustified punishments clearly violate our rights, no conclusive argument establishes what happens to these rights when punishments are justified. Fortunately, little of practical significance depends on the precise formulation of the right not to be punished, or on whether it leaves a residue when a punishment is justified. I will continue to use the terms *override* or *infringe* to describe what happens to the right not to be punished when a punishment is justified. On the view I tend to favor, the very considerations that show a punishment is justified are those that show the right not to be punished is infringed. Those who prefer to think that the right ceases to exist when a punishment is justified should still be amenable to the theory of criminalization I defend.

If I am correct that punishments implicate rights, it is clear that the rights that are implicated are important. Any support for this contention is bound to be controversial, as no criteria to rank the relative value of rights has attracted a consensus among moral and political philosophers. One possible measure of the relative importance of given rights is as follows. If offered the choice, rational persons surely would prefer a violation of any number of their other rights than to be punished. Many theorists struggle to show why given rights are widely believed to be valuable even though citizens care about them so little. Freedom of speech is a good example.[194] However this puzzle might be resolved in the context of freedom of speech, it certainly does not arise in connection with the right not to be punished. We all care very much about whether we are deliberately subjected to hard treatment and censure by our government. I assume that rational persons who hypothetically consent to state authority would allow infringements of the right not to be punished only under narrowly defined conditions.

Another of the many possible ways to gauge the relative value of a right is to assess its contribution to the attainment of some other good. Personal autonomy is one of the several goods to which particular rights might contribute.[195] According to the influential account of autonomy defended by Joseph Raz, "an autonomous person is part author of his own life. His life is, in part, of his own making."[196] On this self-authorship conception, autonomy requires a "variety of acceptable options to choose from."[197] It is hard to think of types of state action that limit available options more than punishment. Even though the *mode* of punishment is a crucial factor in measuring the degree of incompatibility between the two, *all* stigmatizing deprivations threaten personal autonomy as so construed. For this reason, Raz concludes that criminal liability may be imposed only for conduct

---

194. See Joseph Raz: "Free Expression and Personal Identification," in his *Ethics in the Public Domain: Essays in the Morality of Law and Politics* (Oxford: Clarendon Press, 1994), p.146.
195. Various conceptions of personal autonomy are explored in the essays in James Stacey Taylor, ed.: *Personal Autonomy* (Cambridge: Cambridge University Press, 2005).
196. Joseph Raz: *The Morality of Freedom* (Oxford: Clarendon Press, 1986), p.204.
197. *Id.*

that is harmful.[198] Even if this latter argument is unsound, no one should dispute the significance of remaining unpunished for the prospects of attaining personal autonomy.

Still, it may be debatable whether the right not to be punished really *is* very valuable—even if I am correct about the nature of punishment itself. What is precious, it might be contended, is the right not to be *incarcerated*, and only *some* criminal laws implicate this right. This position has been ably defended by Sherry Colb.[199] If she is correct, I should not endeavor to present a general theory of criminalization, but rather a theory to limit the scope of those criminal laws that are backed by incarceration. Perhaps I should not be unhappy if what I have called a theory of criminalization were better construed as a theory of incarceration. By any standard, incarceration is more severe than other modes of punishment and thus must meet a higher standard of justification before it may be imposed.[200] Nonetheless, I continue to seek a general theory of criminalization. Surely the state must justify the threshold decision whether to punish at all. Only then can we turn to the question whether the severity of the punishment is proportionate to the seriousness of the offense. If imprisonment is unduly severe in light of the gravity of the crime, an analytically distinct principle—proportionality—is breached. Thus I am inclined to think that the right not to be punished is as important as many rights widely acknowledged to be valuable. The fact that some state actions involve worse violations of this right hardly shows that other state actions—those not involving jail or prison—implicate a different right, or do not implicate a right at all. Although we have special reasons to ensure that statutes are justified when their enforcement leads to incarceration, I will continue to suppose that we need a theoretical justification for all criminal laws.

Employing the language of rights to describe what is morally problematic about punishment is not designed to beg questions in favor of a minimalist theory of criminalization by making penal statutes nearly impossible to justify. *All* rights—even our most valuable, such as the right to life—probably are subject to infringement.[201] But my decision to describe what is worrisome about punishment in terms of rights helps to combat the problem of overcriminalization by reminding us that laws backed by the penal sanction are presumptively unjust. If we hold that rights are implicated by each punishment, we may be more vigilant to ensure that punishments are justified. As we will see, applications of the theory of criminalization I ultimately defend require a number of difficult and controversial determinations. The risk that punishment is unjustified is almost always present. We should prefer formulations of our right vis-à-vis punishment that minimizes these risks. These risks are minimized by supposing that rights always are implicated by punishment. The burden of proof in justifying the infringement

---

198. Joseph Raz: "Autonomy, Toleration, and the Harm Principle," in Ruth Gavison, ed: *Issues in Contemporary Legal Philosophy* (Oxford: Oxford University Press, 1987), p.313.
199. Sherry F. Colb: "Freedom from Incarceration: Why Is This Right Different from All Other Rights?" 69 *New York University Law Review* 781 (1994).
200. I leave aside the death penalty—as well as other possible modes of punishment that are unacceptable.
201. But see Alan Gewirth: "Are There Any Absolute Rights?" 31 *Philosophical Quarterly* 1 (1981).

of rights is generally placed on those who would potentially violate them—in this case, on a state that resorts to penal sanctions. If I am correct, expressing what is problematic about punishment in terms of rights is important because it suggests a fourth and final constraint internal to a theory of criminalization. Because punishments implicate and potentially violate important rights—the right not to be deliberately subjected to hard treatment and censure by the state—the burden of proof should be placed on those who favor criminal legislation.

Clearly, this fourth internal constraint on the penal sanction differs categorically from those defended thus far. Although particular offenses might violate one or more of the previous three constraints, allocations of the burden of proof cannot show any given statute to be unjustified. Still, I believe this principle is sufficiently important to include explicitly in a theory of criminalization. If the burden of proof is assigned to the state, those who propose to enact a criminal offense must provide reason to believe that it satisfies our test of criminalization. They may not assume a criminal statute to be justified unless someone establishes the contrary position. If those who favor passing a criminal law fail to make their case—or if the considerations adduced on each side balance each other exactly—the law should not be enacted.[202]

Moreover, expressing what is problematic about punishment in terms of rights helps us to resist the tendency to accept some *kinds* of reason as sufficient to justify a criminal offense. A long tradition holds that rights protect persons from the application of policies supported by mere utilitarian considerations.[203] In most cases, utilitarian calculations justify state actions that treat persons in ways they dislike. I assume, for example, that a utilitarian analysis can yield the best system of licensing or taxation. The situation is otherwise, however, if a person has a *right* not to be treated in a given way. We should not invoke the familiar metaphor of *trumps* to express how rights withstand competitive utilitarian considerations. I do not mean to suggest that utilitarian reasons cannot *possibly* justify state actions that implicate rights. No right—including the right not to be punished—should be protected come what may. If the stakes are sufficiently high, even our most important rights must give way.[204] Unfortunately, it is hard to be precise about exactly how *much* disutility is needed before a right may be overridden.[205] But *mere* utilitarian gains, as I have been saying, are insufficient. My point is that utilitarian advantages do not transform state actions that implicate rights from violations into infringements.

Perhaps even *violations* of rights must be tolerated in the most extreme cases philosophers might imagine. No moral consideration is absolute, and the same is true of the internal constraints in a theory of criminalization. Even large utilitarian gains will not allow the state to inflict undeserved punishments, to attach criminal liability to conduct that is permissible, or to punish persons for behavior

202. I do not discuss the crucial question of the quantum of evidence that must be produced to satisfy the burden of proof in justifying criminal statutes.
203. See Ronald Dworkin: "Taking Rights Seriously," in *op. cit.*, note 26, p.184.
204. This view might be called *threshold deontology*. See Moore: *op. cit.*, note 40, p.158, n.13.
205. Opponents of threshold deontology have pressed this difficulty. See Larry Alexander: "Deontology at the Threshold," *37 San Diego Law Review* 893 (2000).

that does not cause or risk a nontrivial harm or evil. But even these principles might give way if extremely important state purposes simply cannot be achieved without violating them. I am agnostic about whether such cases actually exist. Controversial though this matter may be, I insist on one point. We must be candid about when these constraints are violated; we should not pretend that a rationale for imposing undeserved punishments or for punishing persons who do not act wrongfully entails that punishments really are deserved or that conduct really is wrongful after all. Any deviation from these constraints should be recognized as an occasion for extreme regret that should not be glossed over or disguised.

Although I admit that I have not provided a definitive argument in favor of the right not to be punished, the foregoing considerations help to identify the probable commitments of those who deny its existence. All philosophers believe that punishments require a justification. Anyone who is unwilling to countenance a right not to be punished—the details of its formulation aside—will have difficulty showing why mere utilitarian advantages fail to provide an adequate reason to impose criminal sanctions. Admittedly, my claim that the interests implicated by punishment rise to the level of rights because they may not be overridden for small utilitarian gains rests upon a moral intuition—an intuition rejected by consistent utilitarians. No argument has succeeded in persuading these philosophers to acknowledge the existence of rights that may not be overridden for mere utilitarian benefits. I concede that I cannot produce such an argument here. Fortunately, the moral intuition that small utilitarian gains do not justify punishment is widely shared. Perhaps the most frequently cited and intuitively powerful counterexample to utilitarianism involves a situation in which a person is punished for utilitarian advantages.[206] In the famous counterexample, a highly publicized crime has occurred, and a single individual known by the authorities to be innocent is punished in order to prevent the unsuspecting public from committing acts of vigilantism that would victimize innocent persons. If *these* consequences do not justify punishment—as most (but not all) philosophers agree—it is hard to see why (what I have called) *mere* utilitarian gains would do so. A more robust theoretical defense of the right not to be punished must address the thorny problem of how the existence of *any* right can be supported.[207] I do not tackle that difficult issue here.

Let me be more explicit about how rights figure in a theory of criminalization—rights that are not implicated when other kinds of law are employed. To this point, I have spoken simply of a right not to be punished. But all punishments are imposed *for* something. When persons become subject to punishment—as is the case when any criminal law is enacted—more important interests are at stake than the liberty to perform whatever conduct has been proscribed. An example (to which I will return) is helpful in illustrating this point. Suppose the state decides

---

206. See H. J. McCloskey: "A Non-Utilitarian Approach to Punishment," 8 *Inquiry* 249 (1965). For further discussion, see chapter 4, section II *infra*.

207. One way to proceed is by determining whether a right not to be punished is consistent with any of the leading theories about the *function* of rights. I believe a right not to be punished can be analyzed within any of these traditions. For a nice discussion, see Leif Wenar: "The Nature of Rights," 33 *Philosophy & Public Affairs* 223 (2005).

to curb the problem of obesity by criminalizing the consumption of doughnuts.[208] If we assume that the liberty to eat doughnuts is not especially valuable, the state should need only a minimal reason to dissuade persons from doing so. Clearly, the fact that doughnuts are unhealthy provides such a reason. This reason might justify *non*criminal means to discourage consumption—increased taxation, bans on advertising, educational programs, and the like. But the interests implicated by a *criminal* law against eating doughnuts are much more significant. Persons not only have an interest in eating doughnuts but also have an interest in not being punished if and when they disregard the proscription. This latter interest is far more important than the former, and qualifies as a right. Even though the state may have a good enough reason to discourage the consumption of doughnuts, it may lack a good enough reason to subject those who persist in this conduct to the hard treatment and censure inherent in punishment. Generally, the state may have adequate reasons to proscribe given kinds of behavior while lacking sufficient reasons to punish those who engage in them. Thus the crucial question to be asked about my imaginary crime is not whether persons have a right to eat doughnuts. They do not. Instead, the crucial question is whether persons have a more complex right: a right not to be punished for eating doughnuts. An affirmative answer to this latter question is far more plausible. If I am correct, important rights are implicated by each and every piece of criminal legislation. Once this point is grasped, we should be less persuaded by the familiar democratic rationale for vesting broad authority in legislatures to enact criminal laws. The mere fact that a majority (or even a supermajority) may approve of a law that would subject persons to hard treatment and censure for eating doughnuts provides an inadequate justification for infringing our rights.[209] To express the matter somewhat differently, judgments about overcriminalization are normative and presuppose a baseline. Because rights are implicated in all criminal legislation, the preferences of the majority as expressed through democratic procedures should not be used to identify this baseline.

These points require further elaboration. As I have indicated, theorists should not suppose that the criminal law operates by preventing given forms of conduct. If prevention were effective, the only substantive consideration that would be relevant to criminalization would be the value of the liberty that is lost when conduct is prohibited. According to this supposition, questions about the legitimacy of the criminal sanction could be resolved by pretending that the state could eliminate the incidence of the proscribed behavior. Presumably, nothing of deep significance

208. I intend this example to involve an outrageous extension of the scope of the criminal law. Still, it is noteworthy that, according to some estimates, about 400,000 Americans die each year from diseases caused or worsened by obesity, a toll that soon may overtake tobacco as the chief cause of preventable death. See Kelly D. Brownell and Katherine Battle Horgen: *Food Fight* (New York: McGraw-Hill, 2004).

209. Perhaps my claims appear plausible mainly because of the peculiar example I have chosen. It is not so hard to believe that persons lack a right to eat doughnuts but have a right not to be punished for eating doughnuts. But can the same be said of other criminal prohibitions—those that obviously satisfy the criteria in any theory of criminalization? Should we say, for example, that persons lack a right to kill but have a right not to be punished for killing? I am willing to accept this result, albeit reluctantly. We should not make the mistake of supposing that a right does not exist because it is overridden easily.

would be lost if no one ever ate a doughnut again. In reality, of course, the criminal law rarely succeeds in prevention, and the punishment of those whose conduct is not prevented must be justified. This justificatory task is more difficult than in a possible world in which the state could eliminate criminality altogether. Most commentators would be quick to differentiate the worlds of perfect and imperfect compliance on the ground that the latter involves enforcement costs and other expenses. Although they clearly are correct, that is not the principled point I am making here. My point is that the real world of criminalization gives rise to *punishments*. Punishments have proved remarkably difficult to justify because they implicate rights by subjecting persons to deliberate impositions of hard treatment and censure by the state.

Let me quickly summarize my argument to this point. I have tried to derive constraints on the reach of the penal sanction from within criminal theory itself: from the general part of criminal law, and from reflection about the nature and justification of punishment. Criminal laws implicate valuable rights by subjecting offenders to state punishment. Because mere utilitarian reasons do not justify infringements of these rights, and rights are valuable moral considerations that withstand countervailing utilitarian reasons, I tentatively conclude that we should countenance a right not to be punished. Because all criminal laws implicate this right, I contend that a stringent test of justification must be applied to decide when this right is overridden. In other words, a demanding test of justification must be applied to all penal legislation. I have identified four internal constraints in this stringent test; the state should not deliberately subject persons to hard treatment and stigma unless each of these conditions is satisfied. The most pressing difficulty, as I have said, is to provide *content* to these constraints. I now begin to address this problem by turning to matters of application—to a critical discussion of whether a given kind of offense is compatible with the internal constraints an adequate theory of criminalization must include.

IV: MALUM PROHIBITUM

To be justified, criminal laws must satisfy each of the four internal constraints I have articulated. Penal statutes must proscribe a nontrivial harm or evil; hardship and stigma may be imposed only for conduct that is in some sense wrongful; violations of criminal laws must result in punishments that are deserved; and the burden of proof should be placed on those who advocate the imposition of criminal sanctions. I introduce additional constraints—external to the criminal law itself—in chapter 3.

The foregoing internal constraints may appear to be fairly innocuous. It might seem that their application would do little to retard the phenomenon of overcriminalization I described in chapter 1. The concepts of harm, wrongdoing, and desert are notoriously elastic; they may be (and have been) stretched to cover just about anything that one would want to proscribe. My goal in this section is to dispel this impression by applying these constraints to a huge class of criminal prohibitions. Specifically, I inquire whether these constraints are satisfied by the class of crimes

known as *mala prohibita*. The following questions must be addressed in deciding whether and under what conditions a theory of criminalization should allow
punishment for *mala prohibita* offenses. In *what* sense must conduct be wrongful
before it may be criminalized? What harm or evil do these proscriptions prevent?
Can persons deserve hardship and censure for committing *mala prohibita* offenses?
Do the arguments on behalf of these laws overcome the burden of proof placed
on those who favor the imposition of criminal liability? These questions are easy
to answer when persons commit core *mala in se* offenses such as rape or murder.
These crimes are harmful and wrongful in the most obvious sense, and persons
who commit them deserve to be punished. But the constraints I have described
create far greater obstacles for the justifiability of *mala prohibita* offenses.

To this point, I have barely mentioned the ancient contrast between *mala in
se* and *mala prohibita* or the contributions the latter have made to the problem of
overcriminalization. Other commentators may be less reticent; it is plausible to
allege that the proliferation of *mala prohibita* offenses is the most important factor
causing the exponential growth in the size and scope of the criminal law today.
While this observation is almost certainly correct, I have tried to offer a slightly
more refined taxonomy of the new kinds of offense that fill our criminal codes.
My categories include overlapping offenses, crimes of risk prevention, and ancillary offenses. Clearly, these categories cut across the contrast between *mala in se*
and *mala prohibita* offenses. The great majority of ancillary offenses are *mala prohibita*. Overlapping crimes may belong in either category, depending on the kind
of offense with which they overlap. Many but not all crimes of risk prevention are
mala in se. In any event, if my categories are as helpful as I believe them to be, why
invoke a different distinction that duplicates much of the progress made already?
The answer is that we may gain additional insights into the probable implications
of a theory of criminalization by applying it to more familiar categories of offense.
As we will see, a few prominent commentators have endeavored to show why the
state is justified in punishing persons who commit *mala prohibita* offenses, and we
have much to learn from their successes and failures.

How should we draw the contrast between these two kinds of crime? I will not
try to describe and critique the various efforts commentators have made to answer
this question. Because the difference between *malum in se* and *malum prohibitum* is
so elusive, many theorists appear to have abandoned this distinction altogether.[210]
No one needs to offer an account of a nonexistent contrast.[211] But even though
the definitional question is difficult, I hope it does not detract from the problem at hand. For present purposes, I construe an offense as an instance of *malum*

---

210. For example, Glanville Williams dismisses the distinction in a number of footnotes to his influential treatise in
op. cit., note 35. A cursory discussion of *malum prohibitum* appears in the text of his subsequent *Textbook of Criminal
Law* (London: Stevens & Sons, 2nd ed., 1983). Here, Williams apparently equates (at p.936) *mala prohibita* with
"quasi-criminal offences," "public welfare offences," and "regulatory offences," and laments "the difficulty with trying
to establish a category of this kind is to say exactly what it means."

211. Some commentators claim that "the difficulty of classifying particular crimes as *mala in se* or *mala prohibita*
suggests further that the classification should be abandoned." See Wayne R. LaFave: *Criminal Law* (St. Paul: West
Pub. Co., 3rd ed., 2000), pp.35–36.

prohibitum when the conduct proscribed is not wrongful prior to or independent of law. I hope that this rough characterization captures how most theorists understand the nature of *malum prohibitum*.[212] Most important, this simplified description enables us to move directly to the normative issue of whether and under what circumstances these offenses are justifiable.

An example of a *malum prohibitum* offense will prove helpful. In light of the notorious difficulty contrasting *malum in se* from *malum prohibitum*, no case can be expected to be wholly beyond controversy.[213] An illustration should satisfy two desiderata. First, it should not be patently objectionable; it should not be a crime that no sensible theorist would defend as a legitimate exercise of the criminal sanction. In addition, it should not contain features that clearly are unrepresentative of the entire category of *mala prohibita* offenses. An example that satisfies these desiderata—to which I return frequently—is the federal statute proscribing money laundering. This ancillary offense imposes up to 10 years' imprisonment on persons who engage in a monetary transaction of funds greater than $10,000 known to be derived from a specified form of unlawful activity.[214] This offense is not *malum in se;* although it is obviously wrongful to profit from illegal conduct, it is hard to see why a person who merely deposits his profits in a bank commits a *second* wrong that is prior to and independent of law. Moreover, unlike other possible examples of *mala prohibita* offenses that rarely if ever are enforced through criminal sanctions,[215] charges of money laundering are a staple in the ongoing war on drugs.[216]

Because *mala prohibita* offenses such as money laundering are so ubiquitous, one would expect criminal theorists to have expended considerable ingenuity in justifying the punishment of persons who commit these crimes. In fact, however, surprisingly few such efforts have been undertaken. This oversight demands an explanation. One possibility is that theorists are reluctant to concede that *mala prohibita* offenses are "true crimes" for which "real punishments" are imposed.[217] This tack is suggested by the Model Penal Code, which creates a category of

212. I am aware of several problems with this account, none of which (I believe and hope) raises grave difficulties for my project. One problem is that even *mala in se* offenses often have a *malum prohibitum* component. The application of a homicide statute, for example, must specify when a victim is dead and when that death has been caused by the defendant. Some such determinations, such as the "year-and-a-day" rule, are partly stipulative.

213. Some candidates seem peculiar. Consider, for instance, Joshua Dressler's curious example of a *malum prohibitum* offense: selling adulterated foods. I trust that Dressler cannot believe that there is nothing wrongful about this conduct independent of and prior to law. Thus he must presuppose a different conception of *malum prohibitum* than I invoke here. See Joshua Dressler: *Understanding Criminal Law* (New York: Lexis Publishing, 4th ed., 2006), p.157.

214. 18 U.S.C. §1957. For a discussion, see J. Kelly Strader: *Understanding White Collar Crime* (Lexis-Nexis, 2nd ed., 2006), pp.290–291.

215. Ironically, Stuart P. Green admits that the example he chooses to defend the justifiability of punishment for *mala prohibita* offenders—the crime of tearing a tag off a mattress—has never actually been used to impose criminal sanctions. See: "Why It's a Crime to Tear the Tag Off a Mattress: Overcriminalization and the Moral Content of Regulatory Offenses," 46 *Emory Law Journal* 1533, 1540–1541 n.7 (1997).

216. Presumably this statute is almost never construed as written but is applied against those who act furtively or secretively. I have little doubt that exercises of prosecutorial discretion help to salvage many *mala prohibita* offenses. But prosecutorial discretion is a poor substitute for correctly formulating statutes in the first place.

217. Some commentators state emphatically: "An offense *malum prohibitum* is not a crime." See Perkins and Boyce: *op. cit.,* note 107, p.886. I am sure that persons serving lengthy prison terms for money laundering would be surprised to learn that they had not been convicted of a crime.

"violations" that are differentiated from crimes and are exempted from many of the doctrines in the general part.[218] I am skeptical of this evasion. Punishments require a justification even when they are not especially severe. In any event, this explanation clearly fails when applied to all *mala prohibita* offenses. No one can deny that a great many such offenses *do* subject perpetrators to real punishments. As I have indicated, persons convicted of money laundering may be imprisoned for as many as 10 years.

How *might* a given *malum prohibitum* offense satisfy the internal constraints in a theory of criminalization and thus make perpetrators eligible for state punishment? In particular, why should we believe that *mala prohibita* offenses are really *mala* and satisfy the wrongfulness constraint?[219] This constraint cannot be infinitely elastic; unless it is utterly vacuous, crimes that satisfy our criteria of criminalization must be wrongful in some intelligible sense. But how? No single answer to this question will suffice. The beginning of wisdom is to recognize the existence of several different *kinds* of *mala prohibita* offense.[220] What makes individual offenses members of a given kind? If our objective is to reconcile *mala prohibita* offenses with the wrongfulness constraint, the basis for classifying various offenses into a single group is relatively straightforward. Crimes should be assigned to the same category because they are wrongful for the same reason. Once we have listed all the possible reasons an offense can be wrongful (without being an instance of *malum in se*), we will have produced an exhaustive inventory of the kinds of *mala prohibita* offense that are needed for present purposes.[221] In this section I describe three such categories—what I call hybrid offenses, proscriptions based on a promise, and those supported by a principle of fair play. I attempt to decide whether defendants act wrongfully when they commit crimes in these categories. I do not allege that these three categories exhaust the universe of *mala prohibita* offense. But if we conclude that persons do not act wrongfully in perpetrating these kinds of offense, we are entitled to doubt that our theory of criminalization will allow them to be enacted.

Antony Duff has made heroic attempts to address the general problem I have raised. Although he does not pretend to offer a comprehensive account of how *mala prohibita* offenses might be justified, he defends what he regards as a solution for one important kind of offense: a category of crime he alleges to be "neither purely *malum prohibita* nor purely *malum in se*."[222] Instances of the kind of offense he has in mind "involve a more or less artificial, stipulative determination of a genuine *malum in se*."[223] Since Duff himself does not give this category of proscriptions a name, I propose to call them *hybrid* offenses. His examples of hybrid

218. Model Penal Code, §1.04(5). Although the Code generally refrains from using the word "punishment," violations are contrasted from crimes in that they do not subject offenders to terms of imprisonment. It is not hard to interpret the draftsmen as believing that violations, unlike crimes, do not authorize punishment.

219. Most of the arguments I present in this section would be sound if they applied constraints other than the wrongfulness constraint.

220. Admittedly, without a more precise distinction between *malum in se* and *malum prohibitum*, we may be unable to provide a complete account of the many ways that instances of the latter might be wrongful.

221. A single *malum prohibitum* offense might be justified by distinct rationales and thus be assigned to several different categories simultaneously.

222. R. A. Duff: "Crime, Prohibition, and Punishment," 19 *Journal of Applied Philosophy* 97, 102 (2002).

223. *Id.*

offenses—statutory rape and drunk driving—are illustrative. Duff contends that the genuine *mala in se* that correspond to these respective hybrids are (roughly) "having sexual intercourse with a young person who is not yet mature enough to be capable of making rational decisions about such matters," and "driving when one's capacities are impaired by alcohol or drugs." Instead of explicitly criminalizing these behaviors, however, the criminal law proscribes "sexual intercourse with anyone under a specified age" or driving "with more than a specified amount of alcohol in one's blood."[224] When fully specified, these latter offenses are hybrids—neither purely *malum in se* nor purely *malum prohibitum*.[225] They are similar to but different from wholly *mala in se* or *mala prohibita* offenses in the following respect. Persons can (and frequently do) commit these offenses without doing anything wrongful prior to or independent of law. This is not the case with pure *mala in se* offenses. But some instances of these offenses *are* wrongful prior to or independent of law.[226] This is not the case with pure *mala prohibita* offenses.

Punishment is easy to justify when the conduct of a given defendant is both *malum in se* as well as *malum prohibitum*. That is, no difficulty arises when the sexual partner of a defendant is *both* below the age at which she is too immature to consent *and* below the age stipulated by the statute. The fundamental problem emerges, however, when the latter but not the former is true—when the conduct of the defendant is *malum prohibitum* without simultaneously being *malum in se*.[227] Some individuals, in other words, commit a hybrid offense despite the fact that their conduct is not a *malum in se*. Because these offenses are hybrids, this outcome is inevitable. When the law proscribes sexual intercourse with anyone under a specified age, Duff admits "we know that there are some individuals under that age who are fully capable of rational consent (more so than some above that age)."[228] Similarly, when the law proscribes driving with a given blood alcohol content, "we know that some people could still drive safely (more safely than many of those who are under the legal limit) when they are above the limit."[229] In these circumstances—when a defendant commits a hybrid offense by engaging in conduct that is *malum prohibitum* although not simultaneously *malum in se*—how can punishment be justified within a theory of criminalization that includes the wrongfulness constraint? As I have argued that any respectable theory of criminalization must include this constraint, my question can be expressed more generally. In the circumstances I have described, how can punishment be justified at all?

---

224. *Id.*

225. Notice that it may not be clear *what* particular *malum in se* is allegedly specified by a hybrid offense, or whether a genuine *malum in se* is specified at all. The first of the examples provided by Duff gives rise to this worry. Duff purports to "leave aside the issue of whether [the act of having sexual intercourse with a young person who is not yet mature enough to be capable of making rational decisions about such matters] really is a *malum* that should concern the criminal law." *Id.*

226. Or so I assume. Some theorists contend that crimes of risk prevention—such as drunk driving—are not wrongful in cases in which the risk does not materialize. For example, see Heidi Hurd: "What in the World Is Wrong?" 5 *Journal of Contemporary Legal Issues* 157 (1994).

227. In other words, hybrid offenses are *overinclusive*—perhaps necessarily so. I provide a more detailed discussion of overinclusion in the criminal arena in chapter 3, sections II and III.

228. Duff: *op. cit.*, note 222, p.102.

229. *Id.*

Duff's response invites us to consider why legislatures formulate these offenses as hybrids rather than as "genuine *mala in se*." He begins by mentioning that the foregoing "artificial, stipulative determinations" achieve valuable objectives, such as facilitating convictions, curbing discretion, and reducing abuse in law enforcement. But these advantages are mostly consequentialist; they should not satisfy a theorist who (like Duff) contends that punishment must be grounded in the desert of the offender. The crucial issue, as he recognizes, involves "considerations of principle. Our first question must be whether breaches of such regulations should *in principle* be made a criminal matter."[230] Thus Duff advances what he calls "a better reason [for criminalization]—that in these kinds of situations people should not try to decide for themselves whether what they would like to do is safe, since they cannot be trusted (and should not trust themselves) to do so."[231] Specifically, "a man excited at the prospect of sex with a young woman is ill placed to judge her maturity, and "someone relaxing in a pub is ill placed to judge whether another drink might impair his capacity to drive safely."[232]

How do these observations help to justify punishment? Consider a person who has breached one of the hybrid laws Duff describes, even though his sexual partner is sufficiently mature to consent, or his driving is not seriously impaired. The difficulty is to show why such persons act wrongfully. Duff offers an original answer to this problem. He contends that punishment in such cases is justified because the defendant displays "what we can call a kind of *civic arrogance*, which merits public censure and punishment."[233] His position on this issue is worth quoting in full:

> Someone who insists that his sexual partner, although under the legal age of consent, is mature enough to decide about her own sex life, or that he can safely drive . . . after drinking an amount that puts him over the alcohol limit, might in fact be right. Indeed, he might *know* that his action is safe: his belief that it is safe might be true and well grounded. Nonetheless, if the assumption which underpins the law is correct, that these are contexts in which people cannot be trusted, and should not trust themselves, to make rational judgements, then this person arrogantly claims to be an exception to that rule. He claims that he can trust himself, and that we should therefore trust him, to make such judgements; but he has no adequate basis for that claim. He might know that his conduct is safe—that it does not endanger the relevant interests: but he does not *know* that he knows this, and therefore cannot justifiably claim to be sure that he is not endangering any such interest. So even if his action does not in fact endanger any such interest, he takes an unjustified risk that it will do so; and he arrogantly claims the right to decide for himself on matters which he, like the rest of us, should not trust himself to decide. His claim is arrogant because it is unjustified—but also because it seeks to set him above his fellow citizens, in matters which affect their legally protected interests; and that is what merits the censure of the criminal law.[234]

---

230. *Id.*, p.103 (emphasis in original).
231. *Id.*
232. *Id.*
233. *Id.*, p. 104 (emphasis in original).
234. *Id.* (emphasis in original).

I will refer to the foregoing contention as the *civic arrogance* argument for punishing persons who commit hybrid offenses in circumstances in which their conduct is not a *malum in se*.

Of course, the importance of Duff's civic arrogance argument in a comprehensive justification for enacting *mala prohibita* offenses depends on how *many* crimes can plausibly be construed as hybrids—a matter of considerable dispute. It is hard to see how the crime of money laundering, for example, could be interpreted as specifying the content of a genuine *malum in se*. In any event, I question whether this argument justifies punishment for those offenses that unquestionably *are* hybrids. I conclude that Duff's civic arrogance argument probably succeeds in only a handful of cases—in only a small minority of the crimes to which it might apply.

First, notice that Duff's position rests on a comparative empirical claim for which no evidence is offered. Presumably, he regards his claim as uncontroversial, but I am less certain. He assumes that the legislature is in a better position than the defendant to decide, for example, if a woman of a given age is sufficiently mature to make a rational decision about sex, or if a specified amount of alcohol seriously impairs one's ability to drive. A long tradition, dating at least to John Stuart Mill, holds that the individual himself, in his own circumstances, is in the better position to make these sorts of determinations.[235] Of course, Duff reminds us of the distortion in judgment produced by self-interest and wishful thinking. But we should not be persuaded to accept the civic arrogance argument by comparing nonrational defendants with ideal legislatures: the philosopher-kings described by Plato.[236] A fair comparison must remain mindful of the factors that infect the quality of legislative determinations. Even the most casual experience with the political processes that have led states to lower the blood alcohol level required by the hybrid offense of drunk driving, for example, does not inspire confidence that legislatures have drawn the line in the right place for the right reasons.[237]

Moreover, both of the examples Duff selects involve what might be called *temptation* cases—situations in which a person's self-interest urges him to proceed while his judgment is clouded by lust, intoxication, or the like. In these kinds of situation, we all recognize the human tendency to err on the side of permitting our own behavior. But temptation is not present in all cases in which the legislature provides content to a *malum in se* by enacting a hybrid offense. In fact, relatively few hybrid offenses are designed to compensate for temptation. Federal law, for example, bars doctors from prescribing marijuana to their patients. The relevant *malum in se* consists (roughly) in prescribing substances that are ineffective as medicines and may even be harmful to those who ingest them. The law provides

---

235. Mill expresses these reservations in the context of rejecting paternalism. See John Stuart Mill: *On Liberty* (E. P. Dutton: Everyman's Edition, 1951), p.188. Joseph Raz makes similar remarks in the context of his discussions of authority. See *op. cit.*, note 191, pp.74–78.

236. "In law, the rules are designed by legislators or other authorities who are not any better at practical reasoning, by and large, than other individuals." Philip Soper: "Legal Theory and the Claim of Authority," 18 *Philosophy & Public Affairs* 209, 226 (1989).

237. See the discussion of the politics of drunk driving described by H. Laurence Ross: *Confronting Drunk Driving* (New Haven: Yale University Press, 1992), pp.173–184.

content to this *malum in se* by identifying the specific substances that allegedly meet this description. Regardless of whether the specification that precludes marijuana is correct or incorrect, there is no reason to believe that the judgments of physicians are clouded by temptation. In such a case, we need a better reason than Duff provides to conclude that doctors are less able than legislatures to identify those instances of conduct that are *mala in se*. As a general matter, why should we concede that the legislature is better situated than the defendant to draw lines in the right place?

And where *is* the right place? This question goes right to the heart of my inquiry. No one could deny that *some* attempts to provide an "artificial, stipulative determination of a genuine *malum in se*" are deficient. An adequate theory of criminalization must identify when a given *malum prohibitum* offense would *not* be justified. At some point, persons become sufficiently mature to consent to sexual relations; not just any degree of intoxication seriously impairs drivers.[238] The task of line drawing is not arbitrary in the sense that any position is as good as any other; some specifications clearly are indefensible.[239] Where should we draw these lines? Expressed concretely, how should the state decide where to set the specific blood alcohol concentration of drunk driving, or the precise age at which adolescents cannot convey effective consent to sexual relations?[240] More abstractly, how should legislatures give content to the *malum in se* of a hybrid offense? Duff responds with only the following hint: "If the laws defining such offences are to be justified at all, it must be true that most of those who commit such offences will commit a *malum in se* of the appropriate kind."[241] I construe Duff to mean that hybrid offenses should be specified so that the majority of those who commit them will also be guilty of a *malum in se*. In other words, more than half of those who commit the offense of statutory rape or drunk driving, for example, must be guilty of a *malum in se*. Let us call this proposal for specifying the content of a hybrid offense the *majoritarian condition*.

Recall that the point of my inquiry is to understand how persons who commit hybrid offenses act wrongfully and thus become eligible for state punishment. With this focus in mind, I believe that the majoritarian condition is inadequate to justify impositions of the criminal sanction.[242] Should we really conclude that a given individual acts wrongfully when he commits a hybrid offense the content of which conforms to this condition? If the majoritarian condition were implemented, nearly half of all persons who are guilty of hybrid offenses could commit

238. In many states, however, *any* amount of blood alcohol concentration is sufficient to allow adolescents (who are too young to drink alcohol legally) to be convicted of impaired driving. Presumably, these "no tolerance" statutes fail (what I will soon call) the *majoritarian* condition.

239. Some commentators suggest that a *malum prohibitum* offense can become *malum in se* "depending on the degree of the violation." See LaFave: *op. cit.*, note 211, p.34.

240. I leave aside such difficult questions as whether the specification of the offense of drunk driving should consist in a blood alcohol concentration (BAC) at all. There is no obvious reason why the degree to which a driver's ability is impaired by intoxication should be defined by the amount of alcohol in his blood. See James B. Jacobs: *Drunk Driving: An American Dilemma* (Chicago: University of Chicago Press, 1989), pp.61–62.

241. Duff: *op. cit.*, note 222, p.102.

242. Of course, Duff explicitly advances the majoritarian condition only as a *necessary* condition for deciding whether a hybrid offense is justified.

a *malum prohibitum* that is not also a *malum in se*. This condition casts the net of punishment far too widely, and no theorist who hopes to construct a minimalist theory of criminalization should welcome this result. Generally, we regard punishing the innocent as far more objectionable than not punishing the guilty.[243] A person's act is not wrongful because it tokens a type that is wrongful when performed by the majority of agents. Only *personal* wrongdoing can render persons eligible for punishment.

Moreover, the distribution of persons who commit hybrid offenses that conform to the majoritarian condition without simultaneously perpetrating a *malum in se* is not likely to be random. Some persons have excellent reason to believe that their *malum prohibitum* is not wrongful prior to or independent of law. In fact, some such persons actually *know* that their conduct is not a genuine *malum in se*.[244] Duff is aware that given individuals may know their act-tokens are not a *malum in se* even though they are a type of act that is wrongful more often than not. What is perhaps most intriguing about his argument from civic arrogance is his contention that the wrongfulness constraint is satisfied when criminal liability is imposed on these individuals. Duff alleges that these agents act wrongfully despite knowing that their conduct is not *malum in se* because they do not *know* that they know this.[245] It is not entirely clear why the agents in question do *not* know that they know their conduct is not a *malum in se*. Epistemologists offer different analyses of the state of knowing that one knows. On some influential accounts, many of these agents *do* know that they know their conduct is not a *malum in se*.[246] But I will not press this point. The more important question is whether persons who fail to meet this lofty standard act wrongfully and thus become eligible for punishment. Why, in other words, should we conclude that an agent who knows his act is not wrongful prior to and independent of law nonetheless acts wrongfully simply because he does not know that he knows this?[247] As far as I can tell, this extraordinary epistemic standard is not applied elsewhere in the criminal law. In the well-known debate about whether a defendant can be justified in violating a law unless he knows he has a justification, for example, has anyone ever thought that the defendant in question not only must know but also must know that he knows he has a justification?

---

243. See Vidor Halvorsen: "Is it Better that Ten Guilty Persons Go Free Than that One Innocent Person Be Convicted?" 23 *Criminal Justice Ethics* 3 (2004).
244. I will describe this state as *epistemic privilege* in chapter 3, section III.
245. Duff: *op. cit.*, note 222, p.104.
246. The accounts I have in mind are *internalist*. On *externalist* accounts of knowledge, on the other hand, it is not uncommon for persons to know without knowing that they know. They may believe a true proposition p, have whatever justification for p is needed to elevate their justified true belief to knowledge, but not believe their justification to be adequate. In such a case, the agent would know without even believing that he knows; he certainly would not know that he knows. See Michael Bergman: *Justification Without Awareness: A Defense of Epistemic Externalism* (Oxford: Oxford University Press, 2006).
247. Duff alleges (at *op. cit.*, note 222, p.104) that the claim of this defendant is "unjustified;" indeed, his supposed lack of justification is crucial to why his claim is thought to be arrogant. But the defendant who knows his conduct is not a *malum in se* must (on standard accounts of knowledge) have a justification for his true belief; why doesn't whatever justifies him in believing that his conduct is not a *malum in se* furnish the justification Duff alleges to be absent?

By hypothesis, Duff maintains that a defendant manifests *civic arrogance* when he commits a hybrid offense while knowing but not knowing that he knows his conduct is not a genuine *malum in se*. But four problems arise. First, where exactly is the arrogance? Duff alleges that our defendant claims an exception to a rule that others must follow and seeks to set himself above his fellow citizens.[248] But no such exception need be claimed. A defendant could allow anyone who knows his conduct is not a *malum in se* to perpetrate the hybrid offense as well.[249] Second, why think that arrogance merits punishment? Civic arrogance itself is not an offense, and no one, to my knowledge, has proposed to criminalize it. Third, I fear that the appeal to civic arrogance may prove too much. It is hard to understand why a defendant who commits a hybrid offense that is specified in violation of the majoritarian condition displays any less civic arrogance than a defendant who commits a hybrid offense that conforms to this condition. If I am correct, Duff's only constraint on the justifiability of hybrid offenses cannot be reconciled with his general argument for punishing persons who commit these crimes. Finally, assuming that civic arrogance does merit some degree of punishment, how *much* punishment could it possibly merit? Because civic arrogance itself is not a crime, our defendant is punished *for* his hybrid offense, not for his civic arrogance. The punishments imposed for some such offenses—like that for statutory rape—are severe. But civic arrogance, if it should be punished at all, does not seem especially serious. How can such severe punishments satisfy any reasonable concern for proportionality?

I propose to illustrate this latter problem of proportionality by contrasting two statutory rapists, Jack and Jim. Jack has sex with a young woman he knows to be too immature to consent to sex. Jim has sex with a woman of the same age, but his partner is *not* too immature to consent. In addition, Jim actually knows that his partner is sufficiently mature to consent. Jack commits a *malum in se*; Duff holds that Jim acts wrongfully as well, not because his conduct is a *malum in se* but because he displays civic arrogance. As a result, both Jack and Jim are guilty of the very same hybrid offense, and (presumably) become eligible for comparable punishments.[250] This outcome seems manifestly unjust. Whatever quantum of punishment (if any) may be appropriate for displays of arrogance, it surely should be less severe than that deserved by statutory rapists who (like Jack) knowingly perpetrate a serious *malum in se*. Unless a theorist can improve on Duff's account, we should remain skeptical that persons who commit hybrid offenses behave wrongfully when their conduct is *malum prohibitum* without also being *mala in se*.

Thus far, I fail to understand why persons behave wrongfully when their conduct is *malum prohibitum* but not *malum in se*. In some cases, however, it is virtually impossible to commit a hybrid offense without simultaneously committing

248. *Id.*, p.104 (emphasis in original).
249. Duff is aware of this possibility. See *id.*, p.108, n.19.
250. Of course, Duff might claim that Jim but not Jack qualifies for mitigation. But no one has ever explained why some circumstances that bear on culpability make defendants eligible for reduced punishments, while others preclude punishment altogether. Generally, see Douglas Husak: "Partial Defenses," XI *Canadian Journal of Law & Jurisprudence* 167 (1998).

a *malum in se*. To understand why, consider the class of *coordination offenses*— criminal laws designed to solve coordination (or collective action) problems. Extravagant claims have been made about the jurisprudential significance of this category of crime. John Finnis, for example, has famously argued that the point or function of law is to coordinate activities for the common good, and that this objective supports a version of natural law theory as opposed to positivism.[251] Finnis's thesis, of course, is compatible with the belief that a great many criminal laws do *not* serve this function. The immediate question is not whether entire *systems* of law should be construed as solutions to coordination problems but to what extent this function helps to show that many *mala prohibita* offenses satisfy the wrongfulness constraint needed to justify punishment.[252]

We cannot hope to resolve this matter unless we are clear about what a coordination problem *is*. According to Leslie Green's influential account, agents have a coordination problem "where each must choose between exclusively alternative courses of action, the directly consequentialist returns of which each depend on both his own choices and those of others."[253] Green holds that a regularity R in the behavior of members of a population P in a recurring situation S represents a *solution* to a coordination problem if and only if, "in (almost) any instance of S: (1) it is common knowledge in P that (2) (almost) everyone conforms to R because (2a) (almost everyone expects (almost) everyone else to conform to R; (2b) (almost) everyone prefers that any one conform to R on the condition that (almost) everyone conform to R; (2c) (almost) everyone prefers that everyone conform to some R rather than not conform to any R."[254] The need for a rule requiring motorists to drive on a given side of the road is a favorite example of a coordination problem. When a solution to this problem is proposed, each motorist increases his utility by driving on whatever side is required, and (almost) none could do better (and most would do worse) by driving in the opposite direction.

This account helps us to understand the relationship between coordination offenses and hybrid offenses. The categories overlap substantially. Many traffic offenses, like those requiring drivers to stop at red lights at busy intersections, seem to be examples of both categories; they solve a coordination problem while providing content to the *malum in se* of reckless or dangerous driving. Criminal liability is justified in these cases. Notice, however, that there is little need for punishment if adopting a solution to a coordination problem really is beneficial to all.[255] If the obvious risks of deviating from the coordination solution by driving through a red light are insufficient to motivate compliance, it is unclear how threats of penal sanctions would help to do so.

251. John Finnis: *Natural Law and Natural Rights* (Oxford: Clarendon Press, 1980).

252. Some theorists appear to have endorsed the claim that concerns us here. William S. Boardman, for example, maintains that "the law typically works by solving coordination problems." See W. S. Boardman: "Coordination and the Moral Obligation to Obey the Law," 97 *Ethics* 546, 549 (1987).

253. Leslie Green: "Law, Co-ordination, and the Common Good," 3 *Oxford Journal of Legal Studies* 299, 301 (1983).

254. *Id.*, p.302.

255. See David Lewis: *Convention* (Cambridge: Harvard University Press, 1969), p.38.

As I agree that punishments may be justified when the solution to a coordination problem specifies the content of a *malum in se*, it is crucial to point out that few hybrids are coordination offenses. No crime can qualify as an instance of a coordination offense in the absence of a preexisting coordination problem. The crimes of statutory rape and drunk driving, for example, do not solve preexisting coordination problems. Moreover, many solutions to coordination problems do not specify the content of a *malum in se*. Persons do not act wrongfully when they deviate from the solution to a coordination problem by, say, speaking a different language, ignoring the conventional calendar, or resorting to barter instead of using the common currency. I admit—as any reasonable commentator must—that it is wrongful to drive on the wrong side of the road. But we should not be too quick to generalize from this example and infer that we have identified what is wrongful about most *mala prohibita* offenses. The generalization applies only to solutions of coordination problems that specify the content of a *malum in se*.

What should be said about pure *mala prohibita* offenses—those that are *not* hybrids? Stuart Green has made the most ambitious attempt to show that punishments may be deserved when persons commit crimes of this type. According to Green, the wrongfulness of breaking a promise or violating a duty of fair play "frequently" explains why it is wrongful to commit a pure *malum prohibitum* offense.[256] Partly because of the well-known difficulties in distinguishing obligations that originate in promises from those that arise from fair play,[257] I examine each of these arguments together. I conclude that these arguments may succeed occasionally but do not support punishment for a great many *mala prohibita* offenders.

I begin with promises—surely the least controversial way to undertake a moral commitment the breach of which is *prima facie* wrongful. Green asks us to consider, for example, many of the criminal laws that govern an activity—like those pertaining to fishing, hunting, or driving. He observes that individuals who apply for permits or licenses typically "make an explicit promise to abide by certain applicable rules and regulations."[258] Green concludes that the wrongfulness of conduct that deviates from the terms or conditions of these permits and licenses can be derived from the immorality of breaking this earlier promise. He is careful to disassociate his position from that of theorists in the social contract tradition who aspire to defend a general obligation to obey the law. As global accounts of the wrongfulness of criminal behavior, social contract theories encounter many well-known difficulties to which Green's view may seem immune. In particular, he need not worry about how a binding promise might be inferred from non-verbal behavior or could arise from what a rational person would do under ideal circumstances. The kinds of promise on which Green relies are *explicit*, not tacit or hypothetical. Nonetheless, I believe that many of the familiar objections to social contract theory also count against Green's more modest endeavor to explain why persons often are said to act wrongfully in committing *mala prohibita* offenses.

---

256. Green: *op. cit.*, note 215, p.1586.
257. For difficulties in categorizing John Locke's theory of political obligation, see A. John Simmons: *Moral Principles and Political Obligations* (Princeton: Princeton University Press, 1979), pp.83–95.
258. Green: *op. cit.*, note 215, p.1587.

Admittedly, many persons *do* make explicit agreements in order to receive permission to engage in an activity. Notice, however, that individuals who fish or hunt *without* a permit or license, for example, have made no such promise. At best, Green's account pertains only to persons who breach the terms or conditions of the permits or licenses they have obtained. Thus it has no conceivable application to the most egregious violators—those who fish or drive without ever having bothered to get a license they know is required. Only those individuals who have taken the crucial step of applying for a permit could possibly be said to have promised to conform to its terms or conditions.[259]

Is Green's argument persuasive even for that class of persons who breach the terms or conditions of a permit they *have* obtained? Perhaps his strategy succeeds in a handful of cases. Still, consider the content of the promise that persons who receive a driver's license, for example, are likely to have made. Clearly, applicants do not explicitly agree to comply with each and every specific law that pertains to driving. At best, they make a generic promise like "the holder of this permit hereby agrees to conform to all of the current provisions in the Code of Motor Vehicles." For several reasons, I am dubious that such generic promises can give rise to obligations. Consider, for example, a driver who fails to affix a validated inspection sticker he has obtained on the precise spot of the windshield of his car. Can his generic promise to abide by the terms of his license possibly explain why his conduct is wrongful and renders him eligible for punishment? Notice that our driver would not be held to have breached a contract by neglecting to display his sticker. He may not even be aware of the particular regulation he has violated. This possibility is hardly remote. Almost no driver knows more than a fraction of the literally thousands of rules to which he is subject. Ignorance of law may not excuse criminal liability generally, but it creates an insuperable obstacle to any attempt to invoke an explicit promise to explain why such conduct is wrongful.

Perhaps more important, even those individuals who *are* aware of a specific term or condition would rarely be held to have breached a contract in the event of noncompliance. My skepticism draws from the philosophical foundations of contract law. The terms in a driving or fishing license might be described as "adhesive" or "boiler-plate," offered to applicants on a "take-it-or-leave-it" basis. For this reason, virtually all of the enforceable regulations governing fishing or driving are and ought to be a product of law, not of agreement.[260] The fact that these promises would not give rise to liability under contract law may not be *fatal* to Green's proposal.[261] Surely, however, it is peculiar to hold that a promise that would not

---

259. Although Green is aware of this problem—see *id.*, p.1590—he does not indicate how he purports to solve it. It is odd to think that persons act wrongfully only when they deviate from the terms of the licenses they have obtained rather than when they engage in the same type of conduct but have not applied for a license at all. It is also peculiar to suppose that a different account of the wrongfulness of their conduct must be given in the two types of case.

260. For the classic account, see Todd D. Rakoff: "Contracts of Adhesion: An Essay in Reconstruction," 96 *Harvard Law Review* 1174 (1983).

261. Green is not persuaded. He subsequently replies "the fact that one is required to make a promise to abide by the laws of the local jurisdiction *in order to* obtain the privilege of fishing in its waters need not significantly diminish the force of the promise. If the would-be fisherman is uncomfortable with the prospect of binding himself to the terms of the required promise, he is free to withdraw from the application process." See Stuart P. Green: *Lying, Cheating, and Stealing: A Moral Theory of White-Collar Crime* (Oxford: Oxford University Press, 2006), pp.252–253.

create an enforceable obligation in civil law would suffice to justify punishment in a criminal context. One would think that the standard of justification needed for criminal liability would be at least as high, if not higher than what is required in the civil domain. Moreover, the criminal law rarely attaches a sanction to breaches of promise. Of course, Green is well aware of this fact but contends that such statutes as the Mail Fraud Act and the Hobbs Act serve as models for punishing persons who default on their agreements.[262] But the fact that there is precedent for imposing criminal liability on those who break their promises does not establish that this approach should be adopted more broadly. Green does not recommend that *all* breaches of contract should be treated as criminal wrongs.[263] On what ground would he (or anyone else) propose to be selective?

My final worry is that Green's analysis proves too much. If a person behaves wrongfully in violating a term in a permit because he has defaulted on his agreement, how could *any* condition in a license *not* provide the basis for satisfying the wrongfulness constraint? Green readily admits that the failure to comply with some *mala prohibita* offenses might *not* be wrongful, but he does not explain why this concession does not undermine his entire account. His examples include "nonsensical regulations prohibiting pineapple chunks from being colored green, honey from being added to peanut butter, and vitamins from being added to chocolate bars."[264] It is easy to imagine, however, that a person might be required to promise not to add color or honey in order to be allowed to sell pineapple or peanut butter. Even these "nonsensical regulations" are amenable to exactly the same analysis Green provides for those laws he argues persons have promised to obey.

I do not deny that promissory obligations might occasionally provide an adequate account of the wrongfulness of *mala prohibita* offenses. But I suspect that such an explanation will succeed infrequently; it cannot justify punishment for the vast majority of *malum prohibitum* offenders. It cannot explain the wrongfulness of violating the great bulk of motor vehicle regulations. Nor can it explain the wrongfulness of many other *mala prohibita*, such as my example of money laundering. Thus I turn to a related account—the principle of fair play that Green alleges to underlie the wrongfulness of several other *mala prohibita* offenses.[265]

In its most general formulation, the principle of fair play states that "those who benefit from the good-faith sacrifices of others, made in support of a mutually beneficial cooperative venture, have a moral obligation to do their parts as well (that is, to make reciprocal sacrifices) within the venture."[266] Persons who break the law could be said to act unfairly by benefiting from the conformity of others; they are *free riders*. The free rider need not directly harm anyone or endanger the

262. *Op. cit.*, note 215, p.1600.
263. Green is certainly correct (at *id.*, p.1601) to note that "the line between criminal law and civil law is not, and never has been, impermeable." But this observation does not go very far toward establishing the general justifiability of punishment for breaches of contract.
264. *Id.*, p.1582, n.157.
265. "Even when there has been no promise to obey the law, a moral obligation might be derived from notions of fair play." *Id.*, p.1589.
266 A. John Simmons: *Justification & Legitimacy: Essays on Rights and Obligations* (Cambridge: Cambridge University Press, 2001), p.29.

entire cooperative enterprise, but he acts unfairly by taking a privilege that cannot be extended to everyone who is similarly situated. Philosophers disagree about the circumstances under which the principle of fair play creates an obligation of reciprocity, but nearly all concur that the mere *receipt* of a benefit, although necessary, is not sufficient.[267] Whatever requirements (such as the option to reject the benefit) are added to this condition almost certainly disqualify the principle from serving as an adequate account of political obligation generally.[268] It may be true, however, that *some* of the benefits conferred by *mala prohibita* offenses will satisfy whatever set of conditions is ultimately deemed sufficient to generate a duty of fair play. For example, the principle of fair play might explain the wrongfulness of driving in the "breakdown lane" or on the soft shoulder of a highway. But such examples seem relatively unusual; many of the benefits conferred by *mala prohibita* offenses will not satisfy each of the necessary conditions. Admittedly, this conclusion cannot be supported without a more complete account of the principle of fair play than I try to provide here. Still, I suspect that this principle will succeed in explaining the wrongfulness of *mala prohibita* offenses in only a small number of cases, leaving unresolved our central question of why persons deserve punishment in committing the majority of such crimes. Yet again, persons guilty of money laundering cannot be portrayed as free riders who benefit from the sacrifices of those who support a mutually beneficial cooperative venture. Presumably, those who violate this statute would be willing to allow similarly situated persons to deposit or withdraw their ill-gotten gains.

Stuart Green believes otherwise, and he relies as much on the principle of fair play as on explicit promises in his efforts to account for the alleged wrongfulness of many *mala prohibita* offenses.[269] His example is instructive, revealing what is defective about his analysis generally. He discusses taverns that violate a local ordinance by selling alcohol on Sundays. According to Green, the owners who profit from these sales act wrongfully because they are *cheaters*.[270] "Such establishments are profiting at the expense of, and obtaining an unfair advantage over, their law-abiding competitors."[271] Clearly, Green is correct that these taverns "increase their revenues in relation to their law-abiding rivals."[272] But why do their profits not simply represent the fruits of capitalistic competition; what is the basis for describing the advantage gained by those establishments that sell alcohol on Sunday as an "unfair" case of "cheating"? Green's account may explain the wrongfulness of a few offenses, such as paying subminimum wages to employees. But the particular example of the *malum prohibitum* regulation he selects probably has less to do with fair competition than with an attempt to enforce religious morality. Persons who break this law are not free riders who exploit a system of mutual forbearance by

267. But see Richard Arneson: "The Principle of Fairness and Free-Rider Problems," 92 *Ethics* 624 (1982).
268. See Simmons: *op. cit.*, note 266, pp.31–36.
269. Green: *op. cit.*, note 215, p.1589.
270. See Stuart Green: "Cheating," 23 *Law and Philosophy* 137 (2004).
271. Green: *op. cit.*, note 215, p.1589.
272. *Id.*, p.1590.

taking a privilege they withhold from others who are similarly situated. Again, they would allow (even though they would not prefer) all taverns to sell alcohol on Sundays.

If we suppose that the law *stipulates* or *defines* the parameters of fair competition, we could conclude that establishments that profit by breaching these conditions gain an advantage that is unfair. But where is the argument that these parameters are defined by law generally, or by this law in particular? Recall Green's examples of nonsensical laws that are not wrongful to disobey. He writes: "to the extent that such laws exist for no reason other than to give an unfair advantage to one or more market participants or to satisfy the whims of some regulator, it seems likely that there is no moral obligation to obey such laws."[273] It is revealing that Green admits that some regulations might be objectionable if they are designed "to give an unfair advantage to one or more market participants." This concession indicates that Green could not believe that the terms of fair competition simply *are* those regulations the competitors are legally required to obey. Some such regulations actually make the terms of competition *un*fair. Thus, there must be an antecedent standard of fairness to which these regulations may or may not conform. If so, defendants need not breach these conditions simply by committing a *malum prohibitum* offense.

Finally, I want to note an oddity and even an irony in appealing to the principle of fair play to explain why it is allegedly wrong to violate many *mala prohibita* statutes. After all, the principle of fair play is supposed to enhance fairness. It furthers this objective by distributing burdens more equitably. But my earlier discussion of the impact of overcriminalization on the principle of legality was designed to show that criminal offenses are so numerous and far-reaching that they cannot be enforced fairly.[274] As a result, enforcement is highly selective and discretionary. When a particular *malum prohibitum* law is widely disregarded and grossly underenforced, those few persons who comply are placed at a distinct disadvantage relative to others. If law-abiding individuals could somehow be assured that compliance would become more widespread, the resulting state of affairs might well be more just for everyone. In the real world of police and prosecutorial discretion, however—where the rule of law is virtually nonexistent—it is likely that a marginal increase in conformity to *mala prohibita* laws would only exacerbate unfairness. Legal philosophers who invoke the principle of fair play should resist this outcome. If we really want the principle of fair play to enhance fairness, we should begin by combating the phenomenon of overcriminalization. Ironically, however, the proliferation of *mala prohibita* offenses is among the main causes of our current predicament.

I have critically discussed the few attempts undertaken by legal philosophers to explain why the punishment of persons who commit *mala prohibita* offenses might conform to the wrongfulness constraint in a theory of criminalization. My initial effort to solve this problem construed *mala prohibita* offenses as hybrids, designed to provide specific content to a vague *malum in se*. Then I sought to ground the wrongfulness of pure *mala prohibita* offenses in promissory obligation or the principle of fair play. Each of these efforts might succeed in a small number

273. *Id.*, pp.1582–1583.
274. See chapter 1, section II.

of cases. If my criticisms are cogent, however, none of these attempts justifies punishing those who commit the vast majority of *mala prohibita* offenses. They fail, for example, to provide a persuasive rationale for punishing persons convicted of money laundering. Perhaps other theorists will solve the problems I have raised.[275] As I have indicated, disappointingly few theorists have addressed the challenges Duff and Green are willing to confront. Unless better explanations can be offered, however, placement of the burden of proof on those who favor criminal liability allows us to conclude that punishments are unjustified when many *mala prohibita* offenses are enforced.

I must be clear about what I hope to have accomplished. I do not conclude that the conduct prevented by unjustified *mala prohibita* offenses lies wholly beyond the limits of state authority. The state has perfectly good reasons to discourage retailers from tearing tags off mattresses, for example. These reasons, however, do not appear to justify the enactment of a criminal law that implicates the right not to be punished. A more ambitious project than I undertake here would go on to describe the conditions under which legitimate state interests should be pursued through free markets, systems of taxation, civil law, state-sponsored advertising campaigns, and the like. According to Roger Shiner, "a normative theory that says only 'This should not be criminalized' misses the opportunity to recommend positively to legislators how otherwise to proceed."[276] I agree that these matters are supremely important, despite the fact that I do not address them here. I lack a comprehensive theory of the state, a general theory of law, or a set of criteria to decide how given state interests are best pursued. My goal is more modest. I have argued that no one has shown why the good reasons to discourage the conduct proscribed by many *mala prohibita* offenses justify state impositions of hard treatment and stigma. The criminal law is special, and many of these offenses breach constraints that any respectable theory of criminalization should include. This conclusion is only a first step in the larger project Shiner describes.

If my arguments are persuasive, the internal constraints I have articulated in this chapter are not so innocuous after all, as many existing statutes appear to violate them. I hope to have begun to develop a theory to show that the state criminalizes too much. It overcriminalizes. Moreover, I contend that the resources to combat this phenomenon can be derived from the criminal law itself. The general part of criminal law and the wealth of scholarship about the nature and justification of punishment are the source of principled constraints to limit the reach of the penal sanction. In particular, many *mala prohibita* offenses prove difficult to reconcile with the wrongfulness constraint, a principle that any respectable theory of criminalization should include. Reducing the number of *mala prohibita* offenses would represent major progress toward achieving a minimalist criminal law.

275. I do not pretend to have exhausted the possibilities. See, for example, Philip Soper: *The Ethics of Deference* (Cambridge: Cambridge University Press, 2002). Soper hopes to ground the wrongfulness of noncompliance to law in the ethics of deference—"a requirement for giving weight to the normative judgments of others even against one's own judgment about the correct action to take" (p.169). He purports to base the ethics of deference "not simply on respect for others, but also on respect for one self and one's own values and choices" (p.170). Whatever the general merits of this endeavor, Soper admits it is least plausible when trying to justify *mala prohibita* offenses—the very proscriptions that are most likely to breach the wrongfulness constraint. See *id.*, p.177.
276. Roger Shiner: "The De- and Re-construction of Criminal Law Theory" (forthcoming).

3

External Constraints on Criminalization

If my arguments thus far are sound, a theory of criminalization is needed to provide a principled basis to reverse the tendency for more and more criminal law to produce more and more punishment. Any such theory will consist in a number of constraints that limit the authority of the state to enact penal offenses. These constraints derive from two sources. In chapter 2, I argued that four constraints are internal to criminal law itself: statutes must proscribe a nontrivial harm or evil; hardship and stigma may be imposed only for conduct that is wrongful; punishments must be deserved; and the burden of proof should be assigned to those who advocate the imposition of penal sanctions. Any respectable theory of criminalization must include these restrictions. Even though they may appear to be innocuous, these internal constraints have the potential to retard the phenomenon of overcriminalization by jeopardizing many of the new kinds of offense that clutter our criminal codes. In particular, applications of these constraints may reduce the number of *mala prohibita* offenses.

In this chapter, I take a different, more controversial approach and introduce a second set of constraints to supplement the first. I do not allege that these limitations inhere in the criminal law itself, or that any theory of criminalization that rejects them is obviously deficient. Criminal law could (and indeed does) function coherently in their absence. Instead, the constraints I defend here are external to the criminal law and derive from a political theory about the conditions that must be satisfied in order to justify infringements of a valuable right: the right not to be punished. My central objective in this chapter is to sketch these external constraints. I describe my efforts as a *sketch* because I am painfully aware that it is incomplete in several important respects. The details of a comprehensive theory of criminalization require nothing less than a theory of the state, so it hardly is surprising that a more complete account is not forthcoming. At some crucial points, I pose more questions than answers. My claim is not that the theory I sketch is unproblematic but that it clearly is superior both to the status quo and to any of the alternatives I canvass in chapter 4. Uncertainties notwithstanding, the conjunction of the internal and external constraints I identify would go a long way toward achieving criminal law minimalism by imposing severe limits on the authority of the state to enact penal offenses.

The external constraints in a theory of criminalization differ from the internal constraints in some interesting respects. Both are involved in *justifying* the criminal law. But justifications, I think, are *relational*. They do not exist in the abstract, but are addressed *to* someone—to those who have standing to demand a justification for what is otherwise objectionable. The internal constraints are best construed as addressed to the individuals who are punished. If they ask why their punishments are justified, it is appropriate to reply that their conduct is wrongful and harmful, and their punishments are deserved. By contrast, the external constraints address not only the persons who are punished but also the citizens who are asked to create and maintain a system of punitive sanctions. As I describe further in chapter 4, members of communities need good reasons to establish an institution of criminal justice. The external constraints provide these reasons. One constraint, for example, requires criminal laws to promote substantial state interests. If citizens ask why given penal laws are justified, it is relevant to point out that important state interests are achieved by subjecting persons to criminal liability. Despite this difference between the two sets of constraints, I contend that both must be satisfied before the state is permitted to infringe the right not to be punished.

I have little else to say about how the internal and external constraints relate in a single theory of criminalization. I have no doubt that they overlap enormously; any statute that clearly is unjust will breach both kinds of constraint at once. Still, these constraints are not wholly redundant; it is easy to imagine unjust laws that violate constraints from one source but not the other. But I do not dwell on these matters, largely because the content of these constraints is so indeterminate. I have not proposed substantive theories of desert, wrongfulness, harm, or evil. Without these theories, it is hard to know how much we should expect the internal constraints to accomplish on their own. To this point, I have tried to apply these constraints to existing law by relying on intuitions that I believe are widely shared. Unfortunately, this methodology can take us only so far in combating the problem of overcriminalization. Many questions will remain unanswered unless we carefully analyze the central concepts in the theory of criminalization I defend.

This chapter contains three sections. I begin section I by describing what passes for a theory of criminalization in constitutional law today. This theory is obviously deficient, and has helped to cause the problem of overcriminalization from which we now suffer. Despite its shortcomings, I will describe how we might construct a better account of criminalization from its foundations. I then introduce the external constraints I believe must be satisfied before the state should be permitted to infringe the right not to be punished. Although constitutional law in the United States offers too little protection to this right, it contains a wealth of experience in deciding when rights of comparable value may be infringed. The key to developing a theory of criminalization is to adapt these insights throughout the criminal law generally. In section II, I embellish these constraints and suggest how they might apply to a few particular cases. There is room for wide disagreement here, and many of the details of this theory will remain unexplored. Further progress will result as commentators struggle to decide how these principles should be interpreted and applied. In the third and final section, I discuss the legitimacy of crimes of risk prevention (or risk creation)—the single type of relatively new offense that a theory of criminalization is most likely to justify. Criteria to determine when offenses of this type may be enacted are sufficiently complex to require treatment in a separate section. Some but not all of these laws will satisfy the theory of criminalization I sketch.

I: INFRINGING THE RIGHT NOT TO BE PUNISHED

Although the internal constraints on criminalization I have identified thus far may not appear to be radical, we have seen that they create serious complications for the justifiability of *mala prohibita* offenses. Commentators who disagree with my position must bear the burden of showing why the state is permitted to resort to penal sanctions by enacting these statutes. Because even these relatively innocuous restrictions on the scope of the substantive criminal law appear to have far-reaching repercussions for many of the offenses that fill our criminal codes, it may be instructive to reflect yet again on our current predicament. Surely there must be *some* limits on the content of the criminal statutes states may enact. What *are* these limits? What theory of criminalization is actually in place in the United States today?

We might begin by asking what considerations prevent the state from enacting any outlandish crime one might imagine. Perhaps the most straightforward answer is that legislators would not, as a matter of fact, pass any such law. Subject to the few qualifications I describe, the most important practical limitation on the content of criminal statutes is the need for a majority of legislators to vote in favor of whatever offenses are proposed. In the present state of our democracy, no legislature would dare to prohibit the consumption of popular foods like doughnuts. But legal philosophers should not be satisfied with this answer, and the inquiry must be pressed further. I have claimed that rights are implicated by all criminal legislation. The most important consequence of this claim is that criminal laws are not justified for mere utilitarian reasons, or simply because majorities have chosen to enact them. If a sufficient number of legislators somehow *were* persuaded to enact an outrageous offense, what *principle(s)*, if any, would stand in their way?

In the absence of a normative theory of criminalization to restrain legislatures, the Constitution provides the only principled source of limitations on the scope of criminal statutes.[1] Significantly, however, the Constitution leaves states nearly absolute authority to enact criminal laws.[2] Although the Constitution imposes many significant constraints on criminal *procedure*, only five or six of its provisions directly affect the content of the substantive criminal law by disabling majorities from creating offenses.[3] The Eighth Amendment ban on cruel and unusual punishment, for example, apparently precludes so-called status crimes, that is, offenses that punish persons for what they are rather than for what they do.[4]

---

1. State constitutions may provide a source of constraints in addition to those derived from the federal Constitution, especially in the domain of privacy. See Neil Colman McCabe: "State Constitutions and Substantive Criminal Law," 71 *Temple Law Review* 521 (1998).

2. A handful of theorists have attempted to locate a more robust theory of criminalization in the Constitution. See, for example, Markus Dirk Dubber: "Toward a Constitutional Law of Crime and Punishment," 55 *Hastings Law Journal* 509 (2004).

3. See Stephen Shute: "With and without Constitutional Restraints: A Comparison between the Criminal Law of England and America," 1 *Buffalo Criminal Law Review* 329 (1998). Shute contends that these provisions include the First Amendment, the Eighth Amendment, the Fourteenth Amendment, the Fifth Amendment, and Sections 9[3] and 10[1] of Article 1. It is interesting that Shute neglects to mention the Second Amendment.

4. *Robinson v. California*, 370 U.S. 660 (1962).

Substantive readings of the Due Process clause, to cite another example, probably limit the conditions under which liability can be imposed for omissions.[5] Various "penumbras" of constitutional rights forbid invasions of privacy.[6] The scope of these restrictions is notoriously unclear—as unclear as any of the constraints in the theory of criminalization I defend here. Commentators debate their continued vitality, and disagree profoundly in their interpretations of the judicial opinions in which these constitutional limitations first were recognized.[7] More important, no one believes these provisions can or do play a major role in combating the problem of overcriminalization. In what follows, I do not dwell on these isolated, unimportant, and uncertain constitutional restrictions on state authority. Instead, I generalize about what passes for a theory of criminalization under constitutional law today. I describe this theory not only to demonstrate its inadequacies—which I take to be glaring—but also to suggest how we might build a better account of criminalization upon its foundations.[8]

Suppose a given law limits or restricts our liberties. If the constitutionality of this law were challenged, courts have traditionally responded by identifying the liberty in question and categorizing it as one of two kinds: *fundamental* or *nonfundamental*.[9] Some liberties (e.g., speech) are fundamental because they are explicitly enumerated in the Constitution. Other liberties (e.g., marriage) are fundamental not because they are mentioned in the Constitution, but because they are said to be "deeply rooted in [our] history and tradition"[10] or "implicit in the concept of ordered liberty."[11] The constitutionality of legislation that restricts a fundamental liberty is subjected to *strict scrutiny* and is evaluated by applying the onerous *compelling state interest* test. Under this test, the challenged law will be upheld only if it is necessary to achieve a compelling government purpose. In other words, the government's objective must be essential, and the law must be the least restrictive means to attain it. The constitutionality of legislation that restricts a nonfundamental liberty, on the other hand, is evaluated by applying the much less demanding *rational basis* test. Under this test, the challenged law will be upheld only if it is substantially related to a legitimate government purpose. The legitimate government purpose need not be the *actual* aim of the legislation—only its *conceivable* objective. Because only those laws that lack a substantial relation to a conceivable legitimate purpose will fail this test, courts almost never hold a law to be unconstitutional when nonfundamental liberties are implicated.

The great bulk of criminal laws—like the examples of *mala prohibita* I mentioned in chapter 2—limit nonfundamental liberties and thus are assessed by

---

    5. *Lambert v. California*, 355 U.S. 225 (1957).

    6. *Griswold v. Connecticut*, 381 U.S. 479 (1965); *Roe v Wade*, 410 U.S. 959 (1973).

    7. See, for example, the novel interpretation of *Lambert* in Alan C. Michaels: "Constitutional Innocence," 112 *Harvard Law Review* 828 (1999).

    8. Because I build on the foundations of this theory, I discuss it here rather than in chapter 4, which I devote entirely to competitive theories of criminalization.

    9. For a more detailed elaboration, see Erwin Chemerinsky: *Constitutional Law: Principles and Policies* (New York: Aspen, 1997), pp.414–417 and 533–545. Constitutional law now subjects statutes to *three* tiers of review—a point that will play a major role in the theory of criminalization I ultimately defend.

    10. See *Moore v. City of E. Cleveland*, 431 U.S. 494, 503 (1977).

    11. See *Palko v. Connecticut*, 302 U.S. 319, 326 (1937).

applying the rational basis test. As a result, courts show extraordinary deference to nearly all legislative decisions to criminalize conduct; the state needs only a conceivable legitimate purpose to enact the vast majority of criminal statutes on our books today. Persons who break these laws can be punished simply because the government has a rational basis to do so. Moreover, their punishments can be (and often are) unbelievably harsh.[12] Despite scholarly opposition,[13] courts almost never invoke a principle of proportionality to ensure that the severity of the punishment reflects the seriousness of the offense.[14] Applications of the rational basis test produce a startling departure from the level of justification we should demand before allowing the state to resort to penal sanctions. A person can spend his remaining years in prison because he engaged in conduct the state had only a rational basis to proscribe.[15]

Of course, the state needs an extraordinary rationale to punish persons who exercise fundamental liberties. The Constitution effectively precludes the government from criminalizing travel, prayer, or political speech, for example. Outside the narrow range of fundamental liberties, however, it is only a slight exaggeration to say that the state can decide to criminalize almost anything. The "bare congressional desire to harm a politically unpopular group"[16] or the mere "animus" or "moral disapproval" the Court claimed to motivate given kinds of discrimination against disfavored groups such as homosexuals are prominent exceptions to this generalization.[17] Even these examples remain somewhat controversial, however, as a few justices believe that the state has a legitimate interest in proscribing conduct simply because society regards it as immoral.[18] I return to this dubious contention later.

I embellish my earlier example to demonstrate the potential injustice of the incredible power wielded by majorities in the criminal domain.[19] Suppose that legislators, alarmed by the fact that too many citizens are overweight, decided to prohibit—on pain of criminal liability—the consumption of designated unhealthy foods such as doughnuts. The rational basis test would be applied to assess the constitutionality of this statute, as the liberty to eat doughnuts does not seem to qualify as a fundamental right. Therefore, nothing in the Constitution prevents a state from enacting this hypothetical offense. The government has an uncontested interest in protecting health, and surely it is at least conceivable that proscribing the consumption of doughnuts would bear a substantial relation to this interest. Of

---

12. See *Ewing v. California*, 538 U.S. 11 (2003).

13. See Youngjae Lee: "The Constitutional Right Against Excessive Punishment," 91 *Virginia Law Review* 677 (2005).

14. Capital punishment is an exception to this generalization. Proportionality review is alive and well when the death sentence is imposed. See, for example, *Coker v. Georgia*, 433 U.S. 584 (1977).

15. See *Harmelin v. Michigan*, 501 U.S. 957 (1991).

16. *U.S. Dept. of Agriculture v. Moreno*, 413 U.S. 528, 534 (1973).

17. See *Romer v. Evans*, 517 U.S. 620, 644 (1996), and *Lawrence v. Texas*, 539 U.S. 558 (2003).

18. "Society's belief that certain forms of sexual behavior are 'immoral and unacceptable,'...is the same justification that supports many other laws regulating sexual behavior that make a distinction based upon the identity of the partner—for example, laws against adultery, fornication, and adult incest, and laws refusing to recognize homosexual marriage." *Lawrence, op. cit.*, note 17, p.600 (Scalia, J., dissenting).

19. See chapter 2, section III.

course, many foods may be more detrimental to health than doughnuts, and not all doughnuts need be detrimental to health. Because the rational basis test requires only a substantial relation to a legitimate state purpose, however, these facts are irrelevant to the inquiry. In other words, a law need not proscribe each instance of conduct that contributes to the statutory objective, and it may proscribe some instances of conduct that do not contribute to the statutory objective.[20] Indeed, it is doubtful that the Constitution as it is presently construed disables the state from sentencing persons to life imprisonment for the newly minted crime of eating doughnuts.[21] I doubt that this imaginary offense would conform to each of the internal constraints I have identified. But such doubts are immaterial in the real world, because these internal constraints need not be satisfied under the rational basis test employed in constitutional law today.

If I am correct that any respectable theory of criminalization must include the internal constraints I have defended, but that the rational basis test disregards them, it follows that our constitutional theory of criminalization does not qualify as respectable. Sadly, its deficiencies are even more glaring. The most remarkable feature of this constitutional theory is its complete indifference to the contrast between criminal and noncriminal legislation. It is one thing for *non*criminal regulations to be evaluated by the rational basis test. But it is quite another when *criminal* legislation is assessed by that same standard. I have contended that the criminal law is *special*—critically dissimilar from other kinds of law. Despite the considerable difficulty of deciding which sanctions qualify as punitive, the criminal law is special in subjecting persons to state punishment. I have tentatively supposed that rights are implicated by the hardship and censure inherent in punishment, and that penal statutes are unjustified unless these rights are overridden. If I am correct thus far, a theory of criminalization should impose stringent constraints on the kinds of conduct that make persons eligible for punitive sanctions. As the right not to be punished is valuable, no law that implicates it is justified simply because it has a rational basis. A higher standard of justification should be applied throughout the criminal arena. The theory of criminalization accepted within constitutional law today is defective because it fails to afford the criminal law the significance it merits. Regardless of the standards that pertain to the justifiability of nonpenal sanctions, the right not to be subjected to hard treatment and censure should not be overridden simply because majorities have a rational basis to enact a criminal offense. Legislatures should recognize constraints on the justifiability of penal statutes beyond those derived solely from the Constitution as it is presently construed.

20. See Chemerinsky: *op. cit.*, note 9, p.543.
21. I suspect, however, that the Court would devise *some* constitutional impediment to imposing an extreme punishment for violations of my hypothetical crime. In dicta, the Supreme Court has stressed that its decisions should not be construed so "that a proportionality principle would not come into play...if a legislature made overtime parking a felony punishable by life imprisonment." *Runnel v. Estelle*, 445 U.S. 263, 274 n.11 (1980). The constitutional basis for this exception, however, remains obscure. In any event, my central point is that the Constitution would allow states to enact this imaginary statute, even if courts would find some way to limit the quantum of punishment inflicted on persons who violate it.

I have tentatively suggested that punishment, by its very nature, implicates a valuable right: the right not to be punished. Under ordinary circumstances, persons have a right against the state not to be subjected to deliberate inflictions of hard treatment and censure. What could possibly allow the state to treat persons so badly? Fortunately, our legal system has accumulated a wealth of experience in deciding whether and under what circumstances a law is justified even though it implicates a valuable right. The key to identifying the external constraints in a theory of criminalization, I believe, is to adapt this wealth of experience to the issue of when criminal legislation is justified.[22] Recall that the great bulk of laws are constitutionally acceptable when they meet the "rational basis" test, that is, when they bear a rational relation to a legitimate state interest. An exception to this generalization is acknowledged, however, when statutes implicate a significant right. My central contention is that this exception should encompass *all* of the substantive criminal law. In developing a theory of criminalization that is preferable to any of the alternatives I survey in chapter 4, it would be helpful to find a body of thought in which a definable type of conduct is believed to implicate a right sufficiently important to merit a heightened level of protection. In other words, we should identify a right the state needs more than a rational basis to infringe, and we should try to understand how courts decide which state actions that implicate this right are justified. For my purposes, it is not especially relevant whether constitutional scholars believe the particular right we select really *is* very important. A given right may serve as a useful model to adapt throughout the substantive criminal law, even if many commentators doubt that laws that interfere with it should be made to satisfy such stringent criteria of justification.

The most obvious candidates are those rights that constitutional law has deemed to be fundamental. As we have seen, rights may be fundamental because they are explicitly mentioned in the Constitution or because they are said to be deeply rooted in our history and tradition or implicit in the concept of ordered liberty. When laws implicate a right deemed fundamental for either reason, they are subjected to *strict scrutiny*. A challenged law that attracts strict scrutiny will be upheld only if it is necessary to advance a compelling or overriding government purpose. To be justified, the law in question must be narrowly tailored; it must be the least restrictive means to further its objective. I sympathize with the proposal to apply this test to *each* criminal law. It is not the least bit implausible to suppose that the right not to be punished is just as important as many of those rights categorized as fundamental. Why concede that each of these fundamental rights is more valuable and thus entitled to a greater degree of protection than the right not to be punished? If we agree that the right not to be punished has the same normative status, *all* criminal laws should be made to satisfy the same stringent justificatory criteria that apply to deprivations of our fundamental rights. By examining what counts as an adequate reason to restrict these fundamental rights,

---

22. For earlier thoughts in this direction—to which I am greatly indebted—see Sherry F. Colb: "Freedom from Incarceration: Why Is This Right Different from All Other Rights?" 69 *New York University Law Review* 781 (1994).

we could begin to develop standards for subjecting persons to criminal liability and punishment. If this proposal were adopted, state actions that implicate the right not to be punished—the whole of the criminal law—would be required to satisfy the onerous compelling state interest test.

This proposal, however, would be radical—probably *too* radical. To be sure, implementing the compelling state interest test throughout the entire criminal domain would best promote my minimalist agenda. Arguably, the right not to be punished should be protected as zealously as any right persons possess. The difficulty with this proposal, however, is that the compelling state interest test is probably too onerous in practice and might come close to obliterating the criminal law altogether. Constitutional scholars have long described applications of the compelling state interest test as strict in theory but fatal in fact.[23] Precious few laws survive strict scrutiny. Requiring a compelling interest before allowing the state to resort to punishment may prove a recipe for paralysis. If we hope to retain a fair amount of the criminal law—minimalist sympathies notwithstanding—given offenses should be held to a somewhat less demanding standard. Thus a more moderate and cautious approach is advisable. I propose to implement throughout the criminal arena that body of thought that has been developed to justify infringements of rights that are important but not regarded as absolutely fundamental. I suggest that those rights that should be deemed relevantly similar to the right not to be punished are those that attract what has come to be known as an *intermediate* level of scrutiny. Applications of this test, as I hope to show, will not be fatal to the criminal law but will afford the appropriate degree of protection to the right not to be punished. Thus we avoid the twin perils of too much and too little criminal law. Commentators who reject this test because it is too permissive should describe intuitively unjust impositions of the penal sanction that pass this level of scrutiny. Commentators who reject this test because it is too restrictive should describe intuitively just impositions of the penal sanction that fail this level of scrutiny.

Because constitutional law has applied intermediate levels of review to only a handful of specific rights, we should be prepared to look in unusual places to find examples that have received a degree of protection appropriate for the task at hand. We are unlikely to find much help within the criminal arena, because the state now allows the right not to be punished to be overridden for the most trivial of reasons. Most of the specific rights that courts guard with a reasonable degree of vigilance are far removed from the criminal domain and seem to have little in common with the right not to be punished. Two such rights are prominent: the right against discrimination on the basis of gender[24] and the right to engage in commercial speech.[25] The body of thought surrounding laws that implicate these

---

23. See Gerald Gunther: "The Supreme Court, 1971 Term—Forward: In Search of Evolving Doctrine on a Changing Court: A Model for a Newer Equal Protection," 86 *Harvard Law Review* 1, 8 (1972).

24. Applications of intermediate levels of scrutiny for gender-based discrimination can be traced to *Craig v. Boren*, 429 U.S. 190 (1976).

25. "From a strict doctrinal or institutional perspective, freedom of commercial speech is now an established right in the United States...[A]n intermediate level of constitutional protection for commercial speech has become standard operating procedure." Roger A. Shiner: *Freedom of Commercial Expression* (Oxford: Oxford University Press, 2003), p.69.

rights is useful in developing external constraints in a theory of criminalization. I pay special attention here to the standards governing infringements of the latter right. For the past several decades, courts in the United States have applied more than the rational basis test but less than the compelling interest test when states attempt to regulate commercial speech—that is, speech that merely proposes that parties enter into a commercial transaction.[26] In other words, commercial speech presently occupies a middle position between fully protected rights like political association and the myriad activities that do not implicate rights at all, or do so only incidentally. Thus a brief digression into the constitutional law of commercial speech is helpful in identifying the external constraints that form the more controversial part of a theory of criminalization.

Again, I should not be misconstrued to assert that the level of deference presently shown to gender-based discrimination or to commercial speech is defensible as a matter of political morality. In particular, some commentators have argued that the body of law governing commercial expression is confused and profoundly mistaken.[27] I am inclined to agree with their critique, but that is beside the point. The right not to be punished should be protected by the level of scrutiny positive law currently provides to these two rights—even if our best theory of political morality would not protect them at all. At the same time, I hope that the body of constitutional law governing these rights is not *too* implausible.[28] If we believe that the present approach to gender-based discrimination or commercial speech is roughly defensible, we will be hard pressed to explain why the right not to be punished should be entitled to any less protection. Whatever may be true of *political* expression, I see no basis for conceding that the right not to be punished is less significant than the right of *commercial* expression.[29] If the state needs a fairly powerful reason to infringe the latter right, it is difficult to see why a lesser standard of justification should be needed to infringe the former.

Over time and through the trial and error distinctive of the common law, courts have refined a test to determine the constitutionality of state actions that implicate those rights that are granted an intermediate level of protection. To assess a law that interferes with the right of commercial speech, for example, judges apply what has come to be known as the *Central Hudson* test.[30] To uphold a challenged regulation, courts must decide that the governmental interest in enacting the law is *substantial,* and if so, whether the law *directly advances* the government's objective and is no *more extensive than necessary* to achieve its purpose. I plan to

---

26. I make no effort to define commercial speech more precisely. See Nat Stern: "In Defense of the Imprecise Definition of Commercial Speech," 58 *Maryland Law Review* 89 (1999).

27. The best critique of the commercial speech doctrine—from which I borrow heavily—is by Shiner: *op. cit.,* note 25. Shiner argues that "commercial expression should not be protected at all, not that it should be protected albeit at a lower level." *Id.,* p.116.

28. Some justices contend that commercial speech is entitled to *more* protection than it is presently given—to the same degree of protection afforded to political speech. Justice Thomas, for example, would hold both kinds of speech to be equally valuable for purposes of constitutional analysis. See his dissent in *44 Liquormart Inc. v. Rhode Island,* 517 U.S. 484 (1996).

29. For present purposes, I ignore textualist arguments that allege that commercial speech is entitled to more protection *qua* speech than rights not explicitly mentioned in the Constitution.

30. *Central Hudson Gas & Electric Corp. v. Public Service Commn. of New York,* 447 U.S. 557 (1980).

borrow this formula as the cornerstone of a theory of criminalization to be applied to each and every criminal offense.[31] As this test will play a central role in my project, it is imperative to clarify its component parts. The following points are reasonably clear. When rights are granted an intermediate level of protection, the requirement that the governmental interest be *substantial* is greater than the requirement that it be rational but less than the requirement that it be compelling. Moreover, the requirement that the law *directly advance* the government's interest is greater than the requirement that the law be rationally related to that interest but less than the requirement that it be necessary to further that interest. Finally, the requirement that the law not be *more extensive than necessary* to achieve that interest is greater than the requirement that the law be a rational means to attain that interest but less than the requirement that it be narrowly tailored to further that interest. When intermediate scrutiny is applied to particular laws, the outcome is not all but foreordained by the test itself. Sometimes the state wins; sometimes it loses. Beyond these simple observations, however, the details become murky. As we will see when applying this test to specific instances of legislation, different interpretations of each prong may produce different outcomes.

Because of this difficulty and several others we will confront, scholars have become highly critical of the tiered scrutiny I borrow from constitutional law.[32] A few justices are equally dismissive.[33] Commentators warn that "the neat compartments of tiered scrutiny are beginning to collapse."[34] I hope that the many problems and uncertainties these critics note do not dash my ambitions. Despite widespread dissatisfaction from all points along the political spectrum, no plausible rival to tiered scrutiny is on the horizon, and courts and commentators have no choice but to take *some* principled approach to the hard cases that inevitably arise when state authority clashes with valuable rights. No theory of criminalization will yield definitive answers to every difficult case, and the theory I sketch here is no exception. I do not allege that my minimalist theory of criminalization is unproblematic or unambiguous. Obviously, it is neither. My more modest claim is that a theory adapted from a test of intermediate scrutiny, when conjoined with the internal constraints from chapter 2, provides better criteria of criminalization than any of the alternatives currently available, and is far superior to the approach actually taken at the present time. At the very least, the test of intermediate scrutiny raises the very questions that must be addressed before a criminal statute should be enacted. As we will see, competing theories fail to do so.[35]

31. Slight alterations are necessary to render *Central Hudson* applicable to penal legislation. Although irrelevant to the present inquiry, the test contains an earlier prong: commercial speech cannot involve unlawful activity or be false or misleading.
32. See the contributions in Stephen E. Gottlieb, ed.: *Public Values in Constitutional Law* (Ann Arbor: University of Michigan Press, 1993).
33. See, for example, the citations in Stephen E. Gottlieb: "Introduction: Overriding Public Values," in *id.*, pp.2–3. In particular, Justice Scalia describes intermediate scrutiny as a test with "no established criterion" that is applied "when it seems like a good idea to load the dice." *United States v. Virginia*, 518 U.S. 515, 568 (1996) (Scalia, J., dissenting).
34. Calvin Massey: "The New Formalism: Requiem for Tiered Scrutiny?" 6 *University of Pennsylvania Journal of Constitutional Law* 945, 946 (2004). Massey's remark is partly supported by his claim that recent Supreme Court decisions have "embraced the form of tiered scrutiny but snubbed its substance." *Id.*
35. See chapter 4.

Intuitively, it is plausible to suppose that this test roughly describes the general criteria that each criminal law should be made to satisfy. Governments should not infringe the right not to be punished without a substantial reason. Moreover, criminal statutes must directly advance the state's interest and should be no more extensive than necessary to achieve their objective. Unless these conditions are imposed on each criminal offense, the right not to be deliberately subjected to hard treatment and censure through state action will receive inadequate protection. Obviously, our current practice does not apply this test to existing criminal legislation. The failure to protect the right not to be punished by relatively stringent criteria such as those embodied in the foregoing test is the reason the United States suffers from rampant overcriminalization today. Thus I hope that most legal philosophers will initially sympathize with my contention that a test of intermediate scrutiny is suitable for deciding whether criminal statutes are justified. But any consensus I imagine to exist is likely to evaporate when the crucial components of this test are explicated. What do these criteria really mean, and how should they be applied to concrete examples? The devil, as we all have learned, is in the details. In what follows, I offer my own conjectures about how the many questions raised by this inquiry might be answered. But I am not overly apologetic about the fact that I present only a sketch of a theory. I hope that the inconclusive nature of my remarks is interpreted less as a failing of my project than as an indication of the enormous amount of scholarly work that remains to be done in constructing a theory of criminalization. Better answers can be expected to emerge as more and more commentators are encouraged to think long and hard about whether particular criminal laws pass this test. My primary goal is to construct an appropriate framework for the analysis of penal statutes.

One crucial difference between the application of intermediate scrutiny to commercial speech or gender-based discrimination and its application to criminal offenses should be stressed at the outset. This important dissimilarity consists in the political body that should be given the authority to decide whether the justificatory criteria are satisfied. Obviously, we can expect massive disagreement in applying this theory to particular disputes, so a great deal of practical significance depends on who is ultimately granted the responsibility to do so. Courts originally devised tests of intermediate scrutiny and retain the power to decide whether their requirements are met by laws that regulate commercial speech or discriminate on the basis of gender. I am reluctant to suppose, however, that courts should enjoy a comparable power when the right not to be punished is implicated.[36] Although I borrow my external principles of criminalization from constitutional law, I need not maintain that this theory is located in constitutional interpretation. Reflections about institutional competence support this position. Presumably, courts lack the resources and expertise of legislatures to decide many (but not all) of the issues that I believe must be resolved by applications of this

36. In the context of commercial speech, courts construe the First Amendment. In the context of gender-based discrimination, courts interpret the Equal Protection clause of the Fourteenth Amendment. But what part of the Constitution would courts purport to be interpreting when applying this test throughout the criminal arena? The best candidate would be the Due Process clause of the Fourteenth Amendment.

theory of criminalization: whether noncriminal approaches to given problems are less restrictive than criminal solutions, whether particular kinds of conduct merit condemnation, whether statutes serve important expressive functions, whether given coordination problems are important and require state action, and the like. Adversarial processes may be ill suited to make many of these determinations. Admittedly, courts purport to resolve many of these matters when states discriminate between genders or interfere with commercial speech. The limited success of their efforts, however, reinforces my suspicion about their institutional competence. Some of the difficulties in applying tests of intermediate scrutiny to particular disputes in constitutional law arise because courts have been expected to perform tasks at which they are not very proficient. I do not insist that courts be granted the authority to decide whether this test is satisfied by particular instances of criminal legislation and to strike those laws that fail.

Thus I direct this theory of criminalization to legislatures rather than to courts. Applications of this theory pose the questions that legislators must answer, individually and collectively, in order to safeguard the right not to be punished. This right is protected by imposing stringent criteria on justified criminal legislation—on penal laws that infringe rather than violate the right not to be punished. Addressing this theory to legislatures helps to correct a well-known imbalance in jurisprudence. Legal philosophers have been preoccupied with the judicial to the neglect of the legislative branch of government.[37] But an immediate question arises. What remedies are available if legislatures apply this theory incorrectly, implement it in bad faith, or simply ignore it altogether? The answer, regrettably, is that no legal remedies may be available to those citizens whose rights have been violated. Does this admission presuppose that the whole endeavor of defending a theory of criminalization is unlikely to achieve anything of practical significance in the real world?

Perhaps. It is worth pointing out, however, that most of the constraints on legal authority defended by commentators succumb to a similar fate. Consider, for example, the *neutrality* principle.[38] Many legal philosophers interpret liberal political theory to require that states remain neutral with respect to competing conceptions of the good.[39] Of course, others disagree.[40] To the best of my knowledge, however, no theorist who defends or attacks the neutrality constraint has presupposed that courts must be given the authority to apply it. What good, then, is this principle if legislatures fail to heed it and do not treat persons as neutrality demands? The answer, I submit, is that this principle functions as a powerful tool of criticism among scholars and citizens alike. If sound, the neutrality constraint

37. Excellent books about the judicial branch continue to appear. By contrast, little of philosophical significance examines the legislative process. For a prominent exception, see Jeremy Waldron: *Law and Disagreement* (Oxford: Clarendon Press, 1999).
38. My subsequent remarks about the neutrality principle could be made about the harm principle as well. Few theorists believe that courts should be given the authority to find laws unconstitutional because they do not proscribe harm. But see Claire Finkelstein: "Positivism and the Notion of an Offense," 88 *California Law Review* 335 (2000).
39. For example, see Jeremy Waldron: "Legislation and Moral Neutrality," in his *Liberal Rights: Collected Papers* (Cambridge: Cambridge University Press, 1993), p.151.
40. See George Sher: *Beyond Neutrality* (Cambridge: Cambridge University Press, 1997).

provides a principled basis to object to criminal statutes that exceed the bounds of legitimate state authority.[41] I propose that the external constraints in a theory of criminalization should play a similar role. Admittedly, legislatures in the United States have not tended to pay a great deal of attention to academic criticism in the arena of criminal justice.[42] As James Whitman notes, "to an extent unmatched elsewhere in the developed world, America allows fundamental policy choices to be made through the political process, denying a leading role to criminal justice professionals."[43] Perhaps little can be done to reverse this trend and persuade authorities to follow our advice. To have any prospects of success, however, legal philosophers first must have sound advice to give. I hope that the conjunction of the internal and external constraints represents major progress in developing a plausible theory of criminalization.

II: THE DEVIL IN THE DETAILS

I now turn attention to each of the external constraints in the test of criminalization itself. Nothing here will be the least bit simple or straightforward. It is not even obvious how to individuate the conditions in the criteria I have borrowed. Should it be interpreted to contain two, three, four, or perhaps even a greater number of separate components? In what follows, I suppose that applications of these conditions to penal legislation are best construed to involve three basic inquiries, each of which can be subdivided further, and some of which are interrelated.[44] First, the state must have a substantial interest in whatever objective the statute is designed to achieve. Second, the law must directly advance that interest. Third, the statute must be no more extensive than necessary to achieve its purpose. Although these conditions are presented in a particular sequence, I see no reason to assume that they must be implemented "stepwise." That is, we need not suppose that each criterion must be evaluated only if those preceding it are satisfied. Nonetheless, in this section I examine each of these constraints in the order in which I have presented them.

First, criminal legislation must aim toward a substantial state interest. On closer inspection, this initial prong of the test of criminalization can be seen to include three analytically distinct parts: Legislators must (1) identify a state interest, (2) determine its legitimacy, and (3) decide whether that interest is substantial. Obviously, no one can pretend that this first condition is satisfied (or breached) unless he is able to identify the state interest a given statute is intended to serve. What is meant by "the state interest"? I take this question to be closely related

41. See, for example, Douglas Husak: "Liberal Neutrality, Autonomy, and Drug Prohibitions," 29 *Philosophy and Public Affairs* 43 (2000).
42. George Fletcher is among those many commentators who urge that "policy makers in the field of criminal justice should pay more attention to academic criticism." See: "The Fall and Rise of Criminal Theory," 1 *Buffalo Criminal Law Review*," 275, 281 (1998).
43. James Q. Whitman: "A Plea Against Retributivism," 7 *Buffalo Criminal Law Review* 85, 93 (2003).
44. As I describe below, one helpful device to identify the real objective of legislation is to assess the degree of fit between various possible rationales and the conduct actually proscribed.

to an inquiry raised in chapter 2: What harm or evil does the statute proscribe? I noted that several disputes in the general part of criminal law—how to construe conditional intentions, or whether a number of defenses to liability are available, for example—cannot be resolved without answering this question. I also noted the difficulty of settling on a description of the harm or evil given offenses are intended to prohibit. Legislators who hope that these disputes will be resolved correctly in particular cases have good reason to articulate a rationale for the laws they create. Even so, some disputes will be intractable. But we should not generalize from hard cases to conclude that the whole enterprise of identifying statutory purposes is hopeless.

What exactly are we trying to find in our quest for the *ratio legis?* A powerful case can be made for focusing on the legislature's *actual* ends, its *stated* objectives, or its *possible* aims—or, perhaps, on some complex combination of each. The option that is finally chosen can make all the difference to whether a statute is justified. Many cases are easy. But in cases of uncertainty, how should we decide between these three possible alternatives? Theorists have struggled mightily—typically in the context of defending an account of statutory interpretation—to discover the point or objective of given laws. In fact, the volume of commentary on this issue dwarfs that on the topic of criminalization itself, and I cannot begin to do it justice here. For the most part, I endeavor to sidestep rather than to resolve this complex matter, because *any* respectable test of criminalization that applies more than a casual level of scrutiny to particular offenses must wrestle with the problem of how legislative purposes should be identified. No one should make too much of a difficulty that rival theories encounter as well. Moreover, as I continue to point out, much of the scholarly work in the general part of criminal law is futile if statutory objectives cannot be discerned. The consequences for all of criminal theory would be disastrous if the search for statutory purpose were abandoned. Exactly *how* purposes should be discovered is immensely controversial, but *that* statutes have purposes can scarcely be denied.[45]

Consider some disadvantages of each of the three options I have distinguished. Adopting the rationale (if any) legislatures offer at face value would invite subterfuge and deceit, so reliance on the *stated* objective of the statute is problematic. But employing the *possible* purposes would spare legislatures from bearing the burden of proof in defending the statutes they enact. Thus I prefer to take the *real* or *actual* end of legislation when applying a test of criminalization. Since my theory is addressed primarily to legislators, they are in a relatively privileged position to identify their true motives. Nonetheless, this alternative encounters many familiar difficulties, such as how to attribute a single purpose to a group of legislators.[46] In addition, I admit that my preferred option has peculiar implications. Two jurisdictions might enact an identical statute but differ only in the objective

---

45. "Negating the existence of this abstract and general purpose is like negating the legislation itself. Anyone seeking to reinforce the status of the legislative body and accord it its proper place in the constitutional structure should assume the existence of such purpose." Aharon Barak: *Purposive Interpretation in Law* (Princeton: Princeton University Press, 2005), pp.133–134.

46. See *id.*, pp.132–135.

the law is designed to serve. If the rationale is illegitimate in the first jurisdiction but legitimate in the second, one and the same law can be unjustified in the former but justified in the latter. Is this odd result a *reductio ad absurdum* of my proposal to focus on the actual end of legislation in applying a test of criminalization?[47] I hope not, but reasonable minds may differ in their replies.

Again, we should not exaggerate these difficulties or hold them to be fatal to attempts to implement a theory of criminalization. Any respectable effort to limit the criminal sanction must suppose that penal statutes are designed to proscribe a nontrivial harm or evil. It is not surprising, however, that judges have been loathe to attempt to divine the true purpose of given offenses. Courts have been reluctant to ascertain the real objective of a law, "even when the asserted government purpose seems quite clearly pretextual and the true purpose illegitimate."[48] Commentators must overcome this reticence if they hope to implement a theory of criminalization that places the burden of proof on those who favor state action that subjects persons to the hardship and condemnation inherent in punishment. Without minimizing the obstacles, I do not regard them as insuperable. As Bhagwat Ashutosh has noted:

> In contrast to the difficulty of locating and evaluating empirical evidence about means, information about legislative ends and purposes is often far more accessible. After all, it is not particularly difficult to make reasonable judgments about the motivations behind legislation in most cases. Statutory text and structure, legislative history, and an examination of political context provide strong and generally adequate tools with which to make these determinations. In fact, . . . evaluating legislative purposes may be what courts are *best* suited to, given their typical training and expertise.[49]

If Ashutosh is correct that courts can perform this job reasonably well, commentators might be able to do even better. At any rate, identifying the real purpose of a given statute is only the first of several areas where attempts to apply the internal and external constraints to particular offenses will prove enormously divisive.

Assuming the state objective has been correctly discerned—admittedly, a huge assumption—the next step is to decide whether that purpose is legitimate. This problem is also daunting—as much as any in political philosophy. Nothing less than a theory of the state can settle disputes about whether given objectives are legitimate. Not surprisingly, I have nothing quite so ambitious to offer. Any theory of the state is bound to be as controversial—and probably more so—as a theory of criminalization itself. Constitutional law offers only minimal assistance; in the vast majority of cases, the legitimacy of a governmental interest is taken for granted. Under our existing (but deficient) theory of criminalization, only the handful of offenses that have been found to lack a rational basis would fail this prong of our test. As we have seen, however, many of these decisions evoke heated

---

47. This difficulty emerges whenever the mental states of agents are included in a test to justify their actions or policies. For a discussion of this problem in the context of freedom of expression, see Larry Alexander: *Is There a Right of Freedom of Expression?* (New York: Cambridge University Press, 2005).
48. Bhagwat Ashutosh: "Purpose Scrutiny in Constitutional Analysis," 85 *California Law Review* 297, 307 (1997).
49. *Id.,* pp.322–323.

debate. In the absence of a theory of the state, some disagreements about whether particular statutes satisfy this first condition may remain unresolved.

The task at hand would be overwhelming unless we keep in mind that we do not require an exhaustive inventory of legitimate state interests but, rather, a catalogue of state interests that are permissibly pursued through the penal law. Our topic becomes more manageable by recalling the internal constraints all theories of criminalization must satisfy. In particular, the hard treatment and censure inherent in punishment may not be imposed unless conduct is wrongful, and the burden of proof should be placed on those who favor criminal liability. But even though these internal constraints help to narrow the inquiry, it needs to be narrowed still more. Few theorists believe the state has a legitimate interest in proscribing *all* wrongful conduct.[50] As Victor Tadros points out, the state lacks a legitimate interest in proscribing even some of those instances of wrongful conduct that exhibit a disregard for others. A person acts wrongfully when he forgets his spouse's birthday or betrays the trust of a friend, for example, but presumably does not become eligible for state punishment.[51] Although nearly every commentator will agree with these judgments, it is much harder to explain the basis of their confidence. The most plausible explanation, I think, reveals that the desert constraint—the requirement that punishment must be deserved—is not simply redundant with the wrongfulness constraint—the requirement that punishment may be imposed only for conduct that is wrongful. The challenge is to specify the *kind* of wrongs the state has an interest in proscribing—that is, the kind of wrongs that render wrongdoers deserving of state punishment. Because punishments are imposed in a public forum *in the name of the state*, criminal conduct must be regarded as a *public* wrong—not in the sense that it is a wrong done *to* the public but rather that it is a wrong that is the *proper concern* of the public.[52] Wrongs such as the foregoing are *not* the proper concern of the public; *private* wrongs, however identified, are not candidates for deserved punishment and thus for criminalization.[53]

How might we distinguish those wrongs that are the proper concern of the public from those that are not? Again, few topics have evoked as much controversy among political philosophers, and I cannot hope to say much that is helpful here. I believe it is misguided to suppose we might generate a list of specific behaviors that are inherently private, immune for all time from state punishment. Changes in social circumstances can shift the boundary between the public and private spheres. At the present time, for example, Western countries lack a legitimate interest in restricting decisions to procreate. But we should not conclude that this matter must always remain purely private. It is possible to imagine a time and place in which overpopulation is a pressing problem and decisions

---

50. Legal moralists constitute the likely exception. See chapter 4, section III.
51. Victor Tadros: *Criminal Responsibility* (Oxford: Oxford University Press, 2005), p.83.
52. See S. E. Marshall and R. A. Duff: "Criminalization and Sharing Wrongs," XI *Canadian Journal of Law & Jurisprudence* 7 (1998).
53. The need to give reasons to believe that punishments should be imposed by the *state* is a recurrent theme in the work of Jeffrie G. Murphy. For example, see: "Retributivism, Moral Education, and the Liberal State," 4 *Criminal Justice Ethics* 3 (1985).

about whether or how many children to produce would become a proper concern of the public.[54]

Some theorists have argued that wrongs to individual victims become matters of public concern when they cause social volatility[55] or erode the bonds of trust in society.[56] I submit that a better way to draw the elusive line between public and private wrongs at a given time and place is by trying to determine whether the individual victim or the community should control the decision to initiate and pursue a complaint. If a dispute is purely private, the individual who is wronged should retain the power to decide whether the wrongdoer must be made to respond.[57] The prerogative to forgive and forget is retained by the victim. It is not quite right to say that private wrongs are "not my business;" it may be true that all wrongs are everybody's business in the sense that each of us has a reason to prefer that they not occur. But redress is another matter entirely. A theory of responsibility generally, and a theory of criminal responsibility in particular, must be *relational* in specifying the person or body *to whom* we are responsible.[58] The person or body to whom we are responsible has standing to call us to account for our failure to discharge our responsibilities. As S. E. Marshall and Antony Duff point out, "a 'criminal' model puts the community (the state) in charge. The case is investigated by the police; the charge is brought by Regina, the People or the State; whether it is brought, and how far it proceeds, is up to the prosecuting authority; it is not for the victim to decide whether any decision it produces is enforced."[59]

Of course, this device to distinguish public from private wrongs requires a principled basis to decide whether to place the individual victim or the community in charge of pursuing a given complaint. Marshall and Duff suggest that some wrongs done to individual members of a community should also be understood as wrongs done to the community itself, a community defined by shared values and interests.[60] Clearly, the whole community has a stake in reducing violence, even when violence involves domestic partners behind closed doors.[61] Thus we should determine whether the state has a legitimate interest in resorting to the penal sanction by asking whether given wrongs are done not only to individual victims but also

54. For a similar observation in the context of distinguishing self-regarding from other-regarding conduct, see the discussion of "garrison thresholds" in Joel Feinberg: *Harm to Self* (Oxford: Oxford University Press, 1986), pp.21–23.

55. See Lawrence C. Becker: "Criminal Attempts and the Theory of the Law of Crimes," 3 *Philosophy and Public Affairs* 262 (1974).

56. See Susan Dimock: "Retributivism and Trust," 16 *Law and Philosophy* 27 (1997).

57. I do not suppose that all wrongful conduct must wrong individual victims. Wrongful conduct that does not wrong an identifiable victim creates special problems for the public/private distinction and thus for a theory of criminalization. See the discussion in Derek Parfit: *Reasons and Persons* (Oxford: Oxford University Press, 1984).

58. See R. A. Duff: "Criminal Responsibility, Municipal and International" (forthcoming).

59. *Op. cit.*, note 52, p.15. Marshall and Duff immediately add that "in practice, it might be the case that wrongdoing is investigated only if the victim first complains to the police." Still, the state retains the authority to initiate and pursue criminal proceedings.

60. *Id.*, p.21.

61. See Victor Tadros: "The Distinctiveness of Domestic Abuse: A Freedom-Based Account," in Stuart Green and R. A. Duff, eds.: *Defining Crimes: Essays on the Special Part of Criminal Law* (Oxford: Oxford University Press, 2005), p.119.

to the shared values and interests of communities. Many political philosophers—especially those in the liberal tradition—are likely to be uncomfortable about an invitation to incorporate the values and interests of communities into a theory of criminalization.[62] As far as I can see, however, penal theorists have no real choice. Unless some wrongs are done not only to individual victims but also to the community at large, we will be hard pressed to explain why the *state* has a legitimate interest in responding with the hardship and censure inherent in punishment.

Marshall and Duff's insights might be applied to the following example. As far as I am aware, no theorist has called for the criminalization of all torts or breaches of contract. The desire to preserve *some* line between the criminal and civil law is so entrenched that this divide might be taken as a datum for which all theories of criminalization must account. What explains this remarkable consensus? The answer cannot be that civil defendants behave permissibly. Breaches of the promises inherent in contracts, for example, are among the paradigm examples of wrongful conduct. Nor can the answer be that the seriousness of civil wrongs is insufficient to merit the hard treatment and condemnation of the penal sanction. Some wrongs that are and ought to be civil involve as much culpability and cause as much harm as many wrongs that are and ought to be criminal. Why, then, do many of those who commit civil wrongs not deserve state punishment? What is needed is a reason to believe that, at the present time, individuals who are wronged should retain the sole power to decide whether to initiate proceedings against tortfeasors and those who breach their agreements. The state should not intervene if an individual who suffers a loss through a tort or breach of contract elects not to pursue a civil remedy. Applications of this test will not reveal an immutable contrast between criminal and civil wrongs. One could well imagine that some torts or breaches of contract (that are not also crimes at the present time) could eventually become wrongs to the shared values and interests of the community.

Once the state interest has been identified and found to be legitimate, the final stage in the first part of our test of intermediate scrutiny is to assess whether that interest is substantial. Of course, there is nothing magical about this word; the point is that valuable rights may be infringed only to further state interests of special significance.[63] At this point the divergence between the internal and external constraints in a theory of criminalization becomes apparent. It is not enough that the statute is designed to proscribe a nontrivial harm or evil; the state must have a substantial interest in combating this harm or evil. A theory of the state—which I have not tried to produce—requires supplementary principles to help resolve debates about whether a given legitimate state interest qualifies as substantial.

---

62. The general worry is that the communities might be intolerant. In a diverse and pluralistic political society, however, the shared values of communities are more likely to produce a minimalist criminal law. Moreover, a requirement that criminal conduct must involve a wrong that concerns the community is only a necessary condition in a theory of criminalization. Much of the unease about social intolerance is put to rest by the development of a "liberal communitarian" approach in R. A. Duff: *Punishment, Communication, and Community* (Oxford: Oxford University Press, 2001).

63. See Nicola Lacey: *State Punishment* (London: Routledge, 1988), p.112.

Clearly, these matters will generate further dispute, and constitutional analysis is of limited help here as well.[64] As Ashutosh has noted, "the Court's analysis of 'government interests,' and in particular what constitutes a compelling or important interest, is almost entirely undeveloped."[65] Criminal theorists must try to do better. This task describes yet another research project that must be undertaken by serious attempts to develop the details of a theory of criminalization.

Unless the requirement of a substantial state interest is wholly redundant with that of a legitimate state interest, it follows that some interests, although legitimately pursued by the state, are not sufficiently important to warrant infringements of the right not to be punished. Even though this point is patently obvious, it is crucial for purposes of implementing a theory of criminalization. A given interest may not rise to the level needed to justify criminal sanctions, even though the state would be permitted to resort to noncriminal means to discourage behaviors that implicate it. This constraint gives us further reason not to punish private wrongs. Even if we concede that the state has a legitimate interest in proscribing *all* wrongs, it lacks a substantial interest in proscribing those wrongs that are private. Later I speculate that *paternalistic* laws—those designed to protect persons from the negative consequences of their own behavior—are another category of offense that serves legitimate but not substantial state purposes. Despite inevitable controversy about particular examples, however, the general point is clear: The criminal law is special; requiring a substantial state interest for particular statutes is an appropriate way to mark what is special about it.

How might we begin to decide whether given legitimate governmental interests are substantial?[66] Instead of defending a theory of the state, I can only comment on the significance of a few candidates. Most obviously, the prevention of physical harm will qualify as compelling and, *a fortiori,* as substantial. Only anarchists would deny that a central function of the state is to protect persons from violence. I assume that many economic harms are clear examples as well. Thus the criminal law should proscribe forced transfers of property rights, even if we believe these rights to be conventional rather than natural. Of course, hard or borderline cases within these categories are familiar to legal philosophers.[67]

Preventing physical and economic harm is hardly the only important state objective. Securing public goods is among the least controversial state function. In economic theory, public goods have two essential properties. They are

64. See Stephen E. Gottlieb: "Compelling Governmental Interests: An Essential But Unanalyzed Term in Constitutional Adjudication," 68 *Boston University Law Review* 917 (1988).

65. Ashutosh: *op. cit.,* note 48, p.308.

66. One promising strategy is to examine attempts by foreign states to decide comparable issues. This methodology would require a better grasp of comparative law than contemporary theorists tend to possess. It is clear, for example, that section 7 of the Canadian Charter of Rights and Freedoms, which provides for "the right nor to be deprived [of liberty] except in accord with principles of fundamental justice," has produced more in the way of substantive restrictions on criminalization than anything in the United States Constitution. In general, see Don Stuart: *Charter Justice in Canadian Criminal Law* (Toronto: Carswell, 4th ed., 2006). See also the discussion of the Canadian case of *Regina v. Oakes* (1986) 26 DLR (4th) 200, in Shiner: *op. cit.,* note 25, pp.70–72.

67. See the discussion of "hard cases for the harm principle" in Joel Feinberg: *Harm to Others* (New York: Oxford University Press, 1984), pp.65–104.

nonrival—the amount consumed by one person does not limit the availability of the good to others—and they are *inexcludable*—if the good is provided to some, it becomes available to all and no one may effectively be prevented from enjoying it.[68] Political philosophers disagree about what public goods are sufficiently important to be provided by the state. Examples typically include roads, air traffic control, a postal system, public health, environmental protection, and a host of others. But even if theorists could agree about which items belong on this list, they still would disagree about the quantity and quality of the public good the government should produce. Although the state may have an uncontested interest in supplying a given public good, it may lack a substantial interest in ensuring that it exceeds a minimum threshold. Ongoing controversies about the appropriate level of environmental protection, for example, are not likely to be resolved anytime soon. In any event, persons who wrongfully interfere with state efforts to provide public goods are excellent candidates for deserved punishment.

Further dispute will surround the use of the criminal law to enforce solutions to coordination (or collective action) problems.[69] Recall that persons have a coordination problem "where each must choose between exclusively alternative courses of action, the directly consequentialist returns of which each depend on both his own choices and those of others."[70] The rule in the United States requiring motorists to drive on the right side of the road is a paradigm example of a solution to a coordination problem. When such solutions exist, each motorist increases his utility by driving on whatever side is required, and (almost) none could do better (and in fact would do worse) by driving in the opposite direction. Under what circumstances do persons behave *wrongfully* when they fail to comply with a state solution to a coordination problem? I have addressed this question in my treatment of *malum prohibitum* offenses.[71] Whether or not my arguments are persuasive, I assume that few commentators would contest the justifiability of criminal laws to ensure that persons respect solutions to at least some coordination problems.

To my mind, however, the most challenging issue that arises in applying the first condition of our test of criminalization to penal legislation is whether and to what extent the state has legitimate and even substantial interests that do not directly involve prevention. Each of the foregoing examples of legitimate state interests involves efforts to reduce the incidence of the conduct proscribed. As I have indicated, however, Joel Feinberg was perhaps the first to argue—persuasively, I think—that the criminal law does not exist solely to decrease the amount of criminal behavior; it also has an *expressive* function.[72] An important objective of the criminal law is to convey both to the offender and to the community the wrongfulness of his conduct. This objective persists even if no one's behavior is changed

68. See Maurice Peston: *Public Goods and the Public Sector* (London: Macmillan, 1972).
69. For the classic account of how the need to solve coordination problems and promote collective goods provides a general justification for legal authority, see John Finnis: *Natural Law and Natural Rights* (Oxford: Clarendon Press, 1980).
70. Leslie Green: "Law, Co-ordination, and the Common Good," 3 *Oxford Journal of Legal Studies* 299, 301 (1983).
71. See chapter 2, section IV.
72. Joel Feinberg: "The Expressive Function of Punishment," in his *Doing and Deserving* (Princeton: Princeton University Press, 1970), p.95.

as a result of the expression. To be sure, theorists have challenged Feinberg's views about exactly what it is that punishment expresses, how the expressive and hard treatment components cohere in a single rationale of punishment,[73] and whether social conditions in the United States are conducive to understanding expressivist messages.[74] For present purposes, however, the central question is not only whether the state's expressive interests (however explicated) are legitimate but also whether to regard them as substantial. Reasonable minds may concur about whether these interests exist but differ about whether their importance rises to the level needed to justify infringements of the right not to be punished. If we agree that these expressive functions are sufficiently important, the state has good reason to retain all those crimes that serve it. The significance of this conclusion can scarcely be exaggerated in developing a theory of criminalization.

As a matter of positive law, constitutional scholars may regard these questions as having been resolved by the leading case of *Lawrence v. Texas*.[75] At issue was the validity of a Texas statute criminalizing "deviate sexual intercourse" between two people of the same sex. The Supreme Court found the statute unconstitutional, despite denying that it violated rights sufficiently important to attract more than the minimal level of rational scrutiny. The state interest in support of the statute— "society's belief that certain forms of sexual behavior are 'immoral and unacceptable'"—was said to be illegitimate.[76] I do not insist, of course, that commentators who implement the theory of criminalization I defend must believe that *Lawrence* was decided correctly. But many theorists attracted to expressivist rationales for criminal statutes are likely to sympathize with the result in *Lawrence*. The basis for distinguishing legitimate from illegitimate moralistic expressions is easy to articulate but difficult to apply. Mere *allegations* of immorality, unsupported by argument or evidence, should not allow the state to infringe the right not to be punished. Something more than bald assertion is needed to give the state a legitimate (let alone substantial) interest in using the criminal law for expressivist purposes. Perhaps the most astounding feature of the dissenting opinions in *Lawrence* is the absence of a single reason to believe that homosexual sodomy is immoral. Allegations of immorality do not become more credible just because they are bolstered by historical data or surveys of public opinion. Without supporting argument, we cannot be sure that what is expressed is a moral judgment rather than the collective prejudice of the community. This controversy is reminiscent of the Hart/Devlin debate we have already encountered.[77] Much of the disagreement about the justifiability of the statute in *Lawrence* can be attributed to a difference of opinion about whether "deviate sexual intercourse" is indeed wrongful.[78] We cannot hope to make any progress

73. See the exchange between R. A. Duff: "Punishment, Communication, and Community," and Andrew von Hirsch: "Punishment, Penance and the State," in Matt Matravers, ed.: *Punishment and Political Theory* (Oxford: Hart Pub. Co., 1999), p.48 and p.69.
74. See Toni M. Massaro: "Shame, Culture, and American Criminal Law," 89 *Michigan Law Review* 1880 (1991).
75. *Op. cit.*, note 17.
76. *Id.*
77. See chapter 2, section I.
78. See Adil Ahmad Haque: "Lawrence v. Texas and the Limits of the Criminal Law," 42 *Harvard Civil Rights—Civil Liberties Law Review* 1 (2007).

in resolving this controversy unless reasons pro and con are placed on the table. If we demand reasoning rather than unsubstantiated assertion, we might be able to retain expressivist rationales for criminalization without repudiating the result in *Lawrence*.

Contrast proscriptions of deviate sexual intercourse with the wave of hate-crime legislation that recently swept over jurisdictions throughout the United States. Hate-crime statutes overlap with other offenses; they redefine conduct that is already criminal by creating a new offense or an aggravated form of an existing offense. It is unlikely that these statutes will prove to be more effective in deterring the conduct proscribed. Much of the rationale for recriminalizing what was already prohibited is to allow the state to adopt an unequivocal stance on the wrongfulness of violence motivated by racial, religious, or gender bias. As one commentator observes, "the fierce political controversy over this issue seems to me almost entirely about the importance of criminal law as a definer of moral values."[79] If expressive functions are sufficiently important, and arguments can be produced to show why crimes motivated by hatred are worse than those motivated by other emotions such as greed or jealousy, these laws are likely to satisfy the first prong of our test of criminalization.[80] Of course, only a few overlapping offenses can be salvaged in this way. The offense of damaging library materials, for example, is simply not comparable. In light of our history of discrimination and our commitment to equality, it is plausible to suppose that overlapping hate crimes are defensible for reasons that simply do not apply to the overlapping offense of defacing a library book.

We might better appreciate the difficulties in resolving some of these problems by examining particular controversies involving commercial speech—the context in which the *Central Hudson* test of intermediate scrutiny was originally developed. Not surprisingly, courts have struggled in attempting to decide whether a given state objective is substantial when statutes implicate the right of commercial speech. According to the exhaustive survey undertaken by Roger Shiner, the government interest in regulating commercial speech has been deemed insubstantial exactly seven times.[81] In five of these cases, however, the Court did not allow states to ban advertisements because it did not agree that the advertisements in question were false or misleading. Only two cases remain. In the first, the proposed interest in shielding recipients from materials likely to be regarded as offensive was held to be insubstantial.[82] In the second, the Court found the state lacked a substantial interest in facilitating restrictions on alcohol consumption by adults.[83] But the Court employed *ad hoc* reasoning rather than careful analysis to support its conclusion that these interests were not substantial.

---

79. Gerald E. Lynch: "Towards a Model Penal Code, Second (Federal?): The Challenge of the Special Part," 2 *Buffalo Criminal Law Review* 297, 332 (1998).
80. For a skeptical assessment of whether these arguments can be produced, see James B. Jacobs and Kimberly Potter: *Hate Crimes: Criminal Law & Identity Politics* (New York: Oxford University Press, 1998), p.33.
81. Shiner: *op. cit.*, note 25, p.252.
82. *Bolger v. Youngs Drug Products Corp.*, 464 U.S. 60, 71 (1983).
83. *Rubin v. Coors Brewing Co.*, 115 S. Ct. 1585 (1995). Later, however, the Court accepted as substantial the state interest in regulating gambling. See *Greater New Orleans Broadcasting Assn. Inc. v. United States*, 119 S. Ct. 1923 (1999).

Perhaps no meaningful generalization can be derived from the latter two cases. Still, it is tempting to infer that paternalistic penal interferences—those designed to protect individuals from the negative consequences of their own voluntary choices—are deemed insubstantial. The foregoing cases suggest that the state lacks a substantial interest in prohibiting commercial speech (that is neither false nor misleading) on the ground that persons might be worse off because of the information they would receive. This train of thought provides an intriguing means to resist paternalistic legislation—as many legal philosophers are wont to do. Consider the hostility toward paternalism displayed by Joel Feinberg, for example. In performing the balancing needed to decide whether particular statutes are justified, Feinberg insists that paternalistic rationales should have no weight on the scales at all.[84] Apparently, the fact that mandatory seat belts would prevent devastating injuries to thousands of drivers who do not wish to go through windshields counts for absolutely nothing in deciding whether to enact such legislation. Expressed in the terminology I adopt here, Feinberg denies that the state has an interest in the objectives served by paternalistic laws. This position is counterintuitive. Even if paternalistic rationales ultimately are outweighed by countervailing considerations, how can they be thought to lack weight in the first place?[85] Applications of a test of intermediate scrutiny to paternalistic penal laws suggest a more plausible approach. We need not discredit the goals of criminal paternalism altogether to suppose that the state lacks a substantial interest in protecting adults from the negative consequences of their voluntary choices. We might concede that the state has a legitimate interest in enacting paternalistic legislation but deny that this interest has sufficient weight to justify inflictions of penal sanctions. This conclusion would be important, because at least some instances of criminal legislation appear to be supported by a paternalistic rationale.[86] In any event, as we soon will see, cases of criminal paternalism probably fail additional conditions that a minimalist theory of criminalization should include.

We might make further progress in deciding which state interests are substantial by critically examining those cases involving commercial speech in which the Court *has* found this standard to be met. Most informative are those cases that include a thoughtful dissent, as the different approaches taken by each side of a divided court may help to clarify how we should construe the first condition in our test of criminalization. One such case—which I discuss in some detail—is *Posadas*.[87] The facts of *Posadas* are straightforward. Even though casinos and other forms of gambling were permitted in Puerto Rico, a statute banned all advertising of casino gambling to the Puerto Rican public while allowing advertising aimed at tourists. A local casino challenged the constitutionality of the selective prohibition. The Supreme Court upheld the statute, allegedly applying the *Central*

84. Feinberg: *op. cit.*, note 54, pp.25–26.

85 See the challenge to Feinberg's approach posed in Russ Shafer-Landau: "Liberalism and Paternalism," 11 *Legal Theory* 169 (2005).

86 See Douglas Husak: "Legal Paternalism," in Hugh LaFollette, ed.: *Oxford Handbook of Practical Ethics* (Oxford: Clarendon Press, 2002), p.387.

87. *Posadas de Puerto Rico Associates dba Condado Holiday Inn v. Tourism Co. of Puerto Rico et al.*, 478 U.S. 328 (1986).

Hudson test. Of particular relevance is the Court's reasoning (or lack thereof) about whether the law promotes a substantial state interest.

Obviously, the Court's analysis could not get off the ground unless it was able to identify the purpose of the statute. We have encountered this problem repeatedly. Different descriptions of this interest can lead to different judgments about whether it is substantial. Clearly, the state's immediate objective was to reduce the incidence of casino gambling among Puerto Rican residents. But why should the state care about whether its residents gamble in casinos if it is unwilling to ban casinos altogether? The majority in *Posadas* answered this crucial question by speculating that the legislature must have believed that "[excessive] casino gambling among local residents...would produce serious harmful effects on the health, safety and welfare of the Puerto Rican citizens, such as the disruption of moral and cultural patterns, the increase in local crime, the fostering of prostitution, the development of corruption, and the infiltration of organized crime."[88] If this description of the statutory objective were accurate, no one would dispute the Court's subsequent determination that "the Puerto Rico Legislature's interest in the health, safety, and welfare of its citizens constitutes a 'substantial' governmental interest."[89]

What is noteworthy about the majority opinion in *Posadas* is the Court's deference to what it imagined to be the objectives of the Puerto Rican legislature. Justice Brennan, in dissent, was prepared to question whether the majority was correct to infer that the legislature believed that excessive casino gambling among local residents would produce the foregoing harms.[90] After all, he reasoned, no *evidence* indicated that the Puerto Rico legislature thought that serious harms would result if residents were allowed to gamble in casinos. Indeed, he suggested, the evidence indicated exactly the opposite. Puerto Rico had legalized casinos and permitted its residents to patronize them. Thus, he continued, the legislature could not have supposed the "serious harmful effects" mentioned by the majority would occur if its residents had been allowed to gamble there. Brennan then proposed an alternative hypothesis about the real statutory objective. "It is surely not farfetched to suppose that the legislature chose to restrict casino advertising not because of the 'evils' of casino gambling, but because it preferred that Puerto Ricans spend their gambling dollars on the Puerto Rico lottery."[91] Even if this objective is legitimate, can it be sufficiently substantial to warrant the infringement of rights as valuable as those implicated by criminal legislation? In light of the legislature's determination that serious harm would not result if residents were permitted to gamble in casinos, Brennan could not fathom how Puerto Rico's interest in banning local advertising could possibly be characterized as substantial.

How might one decide who is correct about the real statutory objective in hard cases like *Posadas*? One way to proceed is by considering a subsequent prong of intermediate scrutiny: the degree of "fit" between the legislature's ends and the

---

88. *Id.*, p.341.
89. *Id.* The Court cited *Renton v. Playtime Theatres, Inc.*, 475 U.S. 41, 54 (1986), in which it found cities to have a substantial interest in "preserving the quality of life in the community at large."
90. *Id.*, p.352 (Brennan, J., dissenting).
91. *Id.*, pp.353–354.

means it chooses to accomplish them. A law will survive only if it is no more extensive than necessary to achieve the government's purpose. I say more about this condition later. At this time, I simply point out that we have reason to suspect that the real objective of the legislature has not been identified correctly when the fit between means and ends is poor. In *Posadas,* the Court noted that types of gambling other than in casinos—such as horse racing, cockfighting, and the lottery—were lawful to advertise to local residents. The Court responded to this peculiar fact by admitting that the aim of the legislature could not have been to reduce the demand for *all* games of chance but only to reduce the demand for casino gambling in particular. But why the disparity? Horse racing, cockfighting, and the lottery were said to be "traditionally part of the Puerto Rican's roots," so the Court speculated that the legislature must have found the risks of casino gambling to be "significantly greater than those associated with the more traditional kinds of gambling."[92] According to Brennan, however, no evidence showed that casinos posed a different degree of risk than other types of gambling. Moreover, it is dubious that measures to reduce the patronage of casinos among local residents would directly advance Puerto Rico's interest in controlling the "serious harmful effects" alleged to be peculiar to casinos. In particular, it is unclear how banning casino advertising to local residents would alleviate prostitution, the incidence of corruption, or the growth of organized crime. Because Puerto Rico actively promoted its casinos to tourists, these problems were likely to persist whether or not its residents were encouraged to gamble there. In short, Brennan would not simply allow the Court to speculate about the possible reasons that might have led the government to restrict commercial speech. Because he believed the government must bear the burden of justifying the challenged regulation, it needed to identify its real interests and prove them to be substantial. In *Posadas,* Brennan concluded that the state had failed to meet this challenge.

How much can we learn from *Posadas* about how to apply a theory of criminalization? The majority opinion contains more conjecture and bald assertion than evidence and argument about whether the state has a substantial interest in enacting a statute that implicates an important right.[93] Not surprisingly, I believe Brennan's approach is preferable. A test of intermediate scrutiny should not allow courts and commentators to invent possible rationales to legitimize statutes. A minimalist theory of criminalization places the burden on the state to defend penal legislation. We must do our best to identify the real objective of the legislature, assessing the accuracy of our description by examining the degree of fit between means and ends. Only then can we determine whether this interest is sufficiently important to qualify as substantial and thus capable of overriding the right not to be punished. Clearly, the judgments required to implement this test are extraordinarily controversial. Because the state presently recognizes almost no limits on its authority to impose penal sanctions, legal philosophers have had little

92. *Id.,* p.343.
93. Thus Shiner concludes that "*Posadas*...marked the low point of the Court's standard for constitutional protection of commercial speech." *Op. cit.,* note 25, pp.57–58.

occasion to address these matters in the criminal arena. Commentators can expect to flounder until they gain more experience applying a theory of criminalization.

Whether or not we agree that a challenged statute serves a substantial state interest, the *second* component of our test of intermediate scrutiny requires a determination of whether the law directly advances that interest. Here we move from the *what* of legislation to the *how*. To make this transition, we need empirical evidence rather than unsupported speculation (as illustrated in *Posadas*) that the legislative purpose will actually be served. It is hard to think of a single innovation that would have a more profound impact on the phenomenon of overcriminalization. At the present time, persons may be subjected to hard treatment and censure, despite the complete lack of evidence that the statute in question will attain its objective. As Paul Robinson and Michael Cahill point out, "when a new and unnecessary specific offense, such as 'library theft,' is proposed, the issue becomes a referendum on whether legislators care about public libraries, not on whether the proposed legislation will actually do anything to combat the problem of theft."[94] A government should be especially resistant to *criminal* statutes with no realistic prospects of attaining their goals. Penal laws implicate rights. I have not insisted that rights may never be infringed for consequentialist reasons. But surely consequentialist considerations allow rights to be infringed only when we have good reason to believe that the statute in question actually will succeed in furthering its objective.

Although this condition may seem trivial, it jeopardizes an enormous amount of criminal legislation. In particular, a requirement to provide empirical support cannot be met by facile allegations that a statute is justified simply because it will deter. Even without contesting the judgment that the state has a substantial interest in preventing whatever conduct has been proscribed, some reason must be given to believe that the statute in question will actually do so. In a great many cases, social scientists have demonstrated that the conditions under which statutes achieve marginal deterrence simply do not exist. Paul Robinson and John Darley describe three assumptions that must be satisfied before the enactment of a particular rule can be expected to change behavior.[95] First, potential offenders must be aware of the rule, either directly or indirectly. Second, their knowledge must be able to influence their behavior at the moment decisions are made. Third, they must believe that the perceived costs outweigh the perceived benefits of offending. Although generalizations about all of criminal law are perilous, Robinson and Darley contend that "the alleged path of influence from doctrine to behavioural response . . . faces so many hurdles and is so unlikely to clear them all that it will be the unusual instance in which the doctrine can ultimately influence conduct."[96] They conclude that "the

---

94. See Paul H. Robinson and Michael T. Cahill: "The Accelerating Degradation of American Criminal Codes," 56 *Hastings Law Journal* 633, 644–645 (2005).

95. Paul H. Robinson and John M. Darley: "Does Criminal Law Deter? A Behavioural Science Investigation," 24 *Oxford Journal of Legal Studies* 173 (2004). Admittedly, Robinson and Darley are more interested in criminal law *doctrine*—like the rules governing whether persons may use deadly force in self-defense. I believe, however, that their analysis can be extended to criminal statutes.

96. *Id.*, p.174

standard use of deterrence analysis to formulate criminal law doctrine seems wildly misguided."[97]

A bit of elaboration is helpful. Criminologists have found that few potential offenders are aware of more than the broadest outline of how the majority of statutes pertain to their conduct. The experience and gossip on which they tend to rely frequently leads to mistaken impressions. The extent of public misinformation about the availability of such defenses as insanity is nothing short of astounding, and repeat offenders do almost no better than first offenders in stating the law or in predicting the severity of sentences imposed for various crimes.[98] In addition, whatever accurate information potential criminals happen to possess is unlikely to influence their behavior. Psychological states such as anger, rage, the desire for revenge or retaliation, intoxication, and impulsiveness often swamp rational deliberation at the time the offense occurs.[99] The influence of peer pressure on many crimes further lowers the probability that offenders will bring relevant information to bear on their conduct. Finally, those few criminals who are sufficiently informed and rational have good reason to believe that crime pays; they believe they are unlikely to be caught, arrested, prosecuted, and convicted. David Anderson has found that "76 percent of active criminals and 89 percent of the most violent criminals either perceive no risk of apprehension or have no thought about the likely punishments for their crimes."[100] Their attitudes are warranted; only about 2% of all indictable offenses result in a conviction.[101] And social scientists have long recognized that uncertainties and lengthy delays in imposing punishments erode whatever deterrent effect penal sanctions might have had. In view of these unsurprising empirical findings, criminal theorists should be much more skeptical of allegations that a new statute will directly advance the state interest in deterring unlawful behavior.[102] This allegation borders on the preposterous when an overlapping offense simply adds to the quantum of punishment for which offenders would be eligible.[103] The same can be said of ancillary offenses, many of which involve technicalities dimly understood even by attorneys. The burden of proof should be placed on those who believe that greater numbers of crimes and more severe sanctions will be effective in preventing given kinds of conduct. Mere allegations of deterrence are insufficient to justify a criminal offense.

The need to produce empirical data about the effectiveness of criminal proscriptions might jeopardize the justifiability of some or even all drug

---

97. *Id.*, p.205.

98. See David Anderson: "The Deterrence Hypothesis and Picking Pockets at the Pickpockets's Hanging," 4 *American Law & Economic Review* 295 (2002).

99. See David P. Farrington: "Developmental Criminology and Risk-Focused Prevention," in Mark Maguire, Rod Morgan, and Robert Reiner, eds.: *Oxford Handbook of Criminology* (3rd ed., 2002), p.657.

100. *Op. cit.*, note 98, n4.

101. See Andrew Ashworth and Michael Redmayne: *The Criminal Process* (Oxford: Oxford University Press, 3rd ed., 2005), p.138.

102. Legal philosophers are familiar with evidence that questions whether the death penalty achieves marginal deterrence, but are less likely to extend their interest in empirical findings elsewhere throughout the substantive criminal law.

103. See John M. Darley: "On the Unlikely Prospects of Reducing Crime by Increasing the Severity of Prison Sentences," XIII *Law and Policy* 189 (2005).

prohibitions—my favorite example of overcriminalization in the United States today. Certainly the myriad overlapping and ancillary drug offenses are unlikely to satisfy this criterion. Can anyone seriously believe that each of the several charges typically brought against defendants such as Rodriguez accomplish more and more deterrence?[104] But the difficulties run deeper. As I endeavor to show, an empirical requirement in a test of criminalization may undermine the *entire* regime of drug prohibitions. As many commentators have argued, drug prohibitions may cause more crime, violence, and overall disutility than drug use itself.[105] No one should concede that a given statute directly advances the state's interest in deterrence if the prohibition is counterproductive and actually makes matters worse.

To illustrate my concerns, let us assume that deterrence is the objective of drug prohibitions. For three distinct reasons, drug proscriptions may fail to achieve this goal and thus will not satisfy the second prong of our test of intermediate scrutiny.[106] First, *substitution effects* create doubts about whether these laws are effective. Suppose that the state proscribes drug A, and threats of punishment succeed in reducing its use. It is hard to see how this conclusion would demonstrate that the statute directly advances a substantial state interest if many of those persons deterred from consuming A simply switch to an even more dangerous drug B. The substitution effects of drug prohibitions are largely unknown.[107] But several commentators have argued that the development and popularity of hazardous substances like PCP and crack would not have occurred but for the criminalization of less toxic drugs.[108] In short, one must always examine substitution effects before any prohibition regime is proclaimed to be successful. The failure to take these effects into account in applying a theory of criminalization is comparable to and no less problematic than the failure to take opportunity costs into account in applying a theory of economics. At the very least, substitution effects complicate our understanding of what it means for a given law to directly advance its objective.

Two additional hypotheses explain why prohibitions might not deter the incidence of illicit drug use. Consider the *forbidden fruit phenomenon*. Many individuals—most notably adolescents—are known to be attracted to a type of conduct precisely *because* it is banned.[109] These individuals are more likely to engage in given

104. See chapter 1, section IV.
105. See Robert MacCoun and Peter Reuter: *Drug War Heresies* (Cambridge: Cambridge University Press, 2001).
106. At least one critic of drug prohibitions predicts a net *decrease* in use after decriminalization. See David Boaz: "The Consequences of Prohibition," in David Boaz, ed.: *The Crisis in Drug Prohibition* (Washington, D.C.: Cato Institute, 1990), p.1.
107. Prohibition almost certainly has led some persons to prefer licit to illicit drugs, and to abuse prescription medications. These preferences may not be defensible on harm-reduction grounds. According to one commentator, "one of the silver linings on the black cloud of greater drug use under different legalization regimes is the prospect that less dangerous drugs would drive out the more dangerous ones." Ethan Nadelmann: "Thinking Seriously about Alternatives to Drug Prohibition," in Jefferson Fish, ed.: *How to Legalize Drugs* (Northvale, N.J.: Jason Aronson, 1998), pp.578, 590.
108. See, for example, Randy E. Barnett: "Curing the Drug-Law Addiction: The Harmful Side Effects of Legal Prohibition," in Jeffrey Schaler, ed.: *Drugs: Should We Legalize, Decriminalize, or Deregulate?* (Amherst, N.Y.: Prometheus Books, 1998), p.155.
109. Perhaps this phenomenon is best confirmed in ratings for sexual content and violence in television and film. See Brad J. Bushman and Angela D. Stack: "Forbidden Fruit Versus Tainted Fruit: Effects of Warning Labels on Attraction to Television Violence," 2 *Journal of Experimental Psychology* 207 (1996).

behaviors that have been proscribed. Although all drug policy experts acknowledge the importance of the forbidden fruit phenomenon in explaining the prevalence of drug use, its true extent is unknown.[110] Still, its role is probably significant. Social scientists have vividly described how social norms motivate people to engage in risky conduct.[111] The decision to smoke a cigarette or not to buckle a seat belt is less a function of the utility of these behaviors than of their impact on reputations.[112] Because reputations are altered by the legal status of the conduct in question, drug use is almost certainly subject to a substantial forbidden fruit effect. Suppose, then, that the forbidden fruit phenomenon were sufficiently extensive to increase the incidence of drug use as much or more than threats of punishment reduce it. Unless the offense of drug use and possession has important expressive functions, this supposition would undercut the justification for punitive sanctions in a theory of criminalization that includes the second prong of an intermediate scrutiny test.

A final mechanism explains how the incidence of drug use might be unchanged even though punishments no longer were imposed. The majority of drug users quit voluntarily after a relatively brief period of experimentation—typically, within about five years of initial use.[113] But millions have been arrested and convicted, and punishment itself can raise the probability of subsequent deviance by exacerbating criminogenic tendencies in the long run. Although sentences for drug offenses are severe, no one seriously proposes to keep users behind bars indefinitely.[114] Because of their criminal records, drug offenders who have been incarcerated are less likely to find housing or employment, to reestablish ties with families, or to regain their self-esteem.[115] As a result, they are at greater risk to resume their use of drugs. If the increase due to punishment were equal to or greater than the decrease due to deterrence, criminal sanctions would actually bring about more rather than less drug use.[116] In combination, these three factors may show drug proscriptions to be ineffective and perhaps even counterproductive. This conclusion is plausible, as threats of punishment are not especially effective in deterring drug consumption.[117] Only an honest empirical assessment can establish whether this conclusion

110. "The drug research literature has no systematic research on the forbidden fruit hypothesis." MacCoun and Reuter: *op. cit.*, note 105, p.89.

111. See Elijah Anderson: *Streetwise: Race, Class, and Change in an Urban Community* (Chicago: University of Chicago Press, 1990).

112 See Cass Sunstein: "On the Expressive Function of Law," 144 *University of Pennsylvania Law Review* 2021 (1996).

113. See MacCoun and Reuter: *op. cit.*, note 105, p.16.

114. The Constitution, however, creates no barriers to life imprisonment without parole for drug possession. See *Harmelin v. Michigan*, 501 U.S. 957 (1991).

115. The probability of many of these results is increased by the collateral consequences of drug convictions. See Nora V. Demleitner: "'Collateral Damage': No Re-Entry for Drug Offenders," 47 *Villanova Law Review* 1027 (2002).

116. In addition, the infliction of severe punishments to deter drug use may undermine stability by exacerbating the precursors to social disruption, thereby increasing crime and drug use in the long run. See Tracy Meares: "Social Organization and Drug Law Enforcement," 35 *American Criminal Law Review* 191 (1999).

117. See, for example, Jeffrey Fagan: "Do Criminal Sanctions Deter Drug Offenders?" in Doris MacKenzie and Craig Uchida, eds.: *Drugs and Criminal Justice: Evaluating Public Policy Initiatives* (Thousand Oaks: Sage Publications, 1994), p.188. More specifically, the 11 states in the United States that have "decriminalized" marijuana—treating small amounts of possession as a minor offense subject to a fine rather than arrest or jail—have no greater rates of marijuana use than states in which users are subject to arrest and jail. See 12:2 *Marijuana Policy Report* 4 (2006).

is correct. Needless to say, the hysteria and hyperbole of the drug war have not facilitated a good-faith evaluation of existing policy.

As I have indicated, however, an objective of many criminal laws—and of drug prohibitions in particular—is expressive rather than preventive. If expressive functions are sufficiently important to satisfy the first condition in our theory of criminalization, the lack of deterrence may be beside the point. But *can* the justifiability of the offense of illicit drug possession be salvaged on expressivist grounds? This issue is one of the most hotly contested points of debate between contemporary prohibitionists and their critics. Admittedly, a number of commentators strongly denounce drug use in *moral* terms, employing expressivist rhetoric to explain the differential treatment of licit and illicit drugs within our criminal justice system. Consider, for example, the opinion advanced by James Q. Wilson:

> If we believe—as I do—that dependency on certain mind-altering drugs is a moral issue and that their illegality rests in part on their immorality, then legalizing them undercuts, if it does not eliminate altogether, the moral message. That message is at the root of the distinction between nicotine and cocaine. Both are highly addictive; both have harmful physical effects. But we treat the two drugs differently, not simply because nicotine is so widely used to be beyond the reach of effective prohibition, but because its use does not destroy the user's essential humanity. Tobacco shortens one's life, cocaine debases it. Nicotine alters one's habits, cocaine alters one's soul.[118]

William Bennett and Barry McCaffrey, the country's most prominent former drug czars, concur.[119] Public opinion appears to support their views. Roughly two-thirds of Americans agree that illicit drug use is morally wrong. Sixty-four percent say that marijuana use is morally wrong, and 76% report that they would continue to oppose the legalization of cocaine and heroin, even if they could be guaranteed that it would lead to less crime.[120]

Laws that serve expressive functions may seem immune from the need for empirical confirmation mandated by our theory of criminalization. No one who proposes to ban flag burning, for example, really believes that a statute is needed to deter. Few residents of the United States burn flags at the present time, although it is safe to predict that the enactment of a new offense would actually increase the proscribed behavior. Like a hate crime, this statute could be justified only on the ground that it expresses the state's moral aversion to the destruction of venerated national symbols. Even expressivist defenses of given statutes, however, require empirical support. Consider the most popular objection to fundamental reform of our drug policy: It would "send the wrong message."[121] Although this objection

---

118. James Q. Wilson: "Against the Legalization of Drugs," 89 *Commentary* 21, 26 (1990). More recently, Wilson claims that nicotine addiction is unlike cocaine addiction in that the former "may hurt the body" while the latter "degrades the spirit." See James Q. Wilson: *The Moral Sense* (New York: Free Press, 1993), p.94.

119. William Bennett: "The Plea to Legalize Drugs Is a Siren Call to Surrender," in Michael Lyman and Gary Potter, eds.: *Drugs in Society* (Cincinnati: Anderson Pub. Co., 1991), p.339.

120. See the several surveys described in Robert J. Blendon and John T. Young: "The Public and the War on Illicit Drugs," 279 *Journal of the American Medical Association* 140–141 (1998).

121. Two commentators describe this as "the most frequent objection to harm reduction" reforms. See MacCoun and Reuter: *op. cit.*, note 105, p.388.

is rarely developed in detail, I interpret it to say that illicit drug use must remain criminal in order to express the moral disapproval of the state. Many commentators suppose that the failure to retain criminal sanctions would indicate that drug use is condoned. But is this supposition true? How do we know? What is important is not only the message legislators intend to convey but also the content of the message citizens actually receive.[122] Perhaps the imposition of criminal penalties for users of popular drugs like marijuana conveys hypocrisy rather than disapprobation. No serious research has tried to identify how citizens actually construe the message received by existing drug laws, or how the content of this message would be altered by various reforms.[123] If we include an empirical component in our test of criminalization, we must not allow conjecture about expressive functions to substitute for evidence—assuming, of course, that the conveyance of messages represents a substantial state objective in the first place.

Moreover, many critics emphatically reject the expressivist defense of drug proscriptions endorsed by the aforementioned commentators. Some argue that drug use is protected by a moral right[124] while others add that support for this right can be found in the Constitution.[125] A great many reformers prefer to understand drug abuse as a *medical* problem.[126] Presumably, little or no moral stigma attaches to conditions that require medical treatment. Still others who refrain from moralistic condemnation reject disease models of use and addiction.[127] These disagreements are important. If we really aspire to contract the size and scope of the criminal law by changing our drug policy, the more obvious route is to question whether drug use is wrongful and merits the censure inherent in punishment. If no condemnation is warranted, we do not need the external principles in a theory of criminalization to undermine the justifiability of these laws. The internal constraints introduced in chapter 2 do the job more simply and with less controversy. But how should we decide who is correct about the moral status of drug use? This disagreement seems intractable.[128] The challenge for criminal theorists is to decide what to do in the face of these disagreements rather than to determine what to do in the unlikely event that these disagreements are finally resolved.[129] Clearly, we owe a reply to those commentators who insist that illicit drug use is wrongful. One

---

122. Thus Duff prefers to construe these theories as *communicative* rather than as *expressive*. See *op. cit.*, note 62, pp.27–30.

123. "In the absence of [empirical] evidence, the rhetorical hypothesis that harm reduction conveys approval of drug use is largely speculative." See MacCoun and Reuter: *op. cit.*, note 105, p.391.

124. See Douglas Husak: *Drugs and Rights* (Cambridge: Cambridge University Press, 1992).

125. See David Richards: *Sex, Drugs, Death, and the Law: An Essay on Human Rights and Overcriminalization* (Totowa, N.J.: Rowman & Littlefield, 1982); and Robert W. Sweet and Edward A. Harris: "Moral and Constitutional Considerations in Support of the Decriminalization of Drugs," in Fish: *op. cit.*, note 107, p.430.

126. See Alan Leshner: "Addiction Is a Brain Disease, and It Matters," 278 *Science* 45 (1997).

127. See Gene M. Heyman: "Is Addiction a Chronic, Relapsing Disease?" in Philip B. Heyman and William N. Brownsberger, eds.: *Drug Addiction and Drug Policy* (Cambridge: Harvard University Press, 2001), p.81; and Jacob Sullum: *Saying Yes: In Defense of Drug Use* (New York: Tarcher/Putnam, 2003).

128. Research suggests that such disagreements are surprisingly infrequent in the criminal arena—at least about the relative seriousness of different crimes. See Marvin E. Wolfgang and Neil Alan Weiner, eds.: *Criminal Violence* (Beverly Hills: Sage, 1982).

129. For further thoughts on this topic, see Waldron: *op. cit.*, note 24.

would *like* to respond to their *arguments*. Unfortunately, arguments for the alleged immorality of drug use almost never are produced; this judgment is typically put forward as a kind of brute moral fact or incontrovertible moral intuition. In the absence of an argument in favor of this judgment, it is hard to know how a reply should be structured. We are in the same position as those who question whether a proscription of deviate sexual intercourse expresses a moral message or is a mere prejudice dressed in moral garb. When commentators do not *defend* their views, such conflicts are nearly impossible to resolve.

Drug offenses are not the only crimes jeopardized by a requirement that penal sanctions must not be counterproductive. This constraint threatens to undermine all criminal paternalism. Paternalistic rationales seldom justify the enactment of a criminal law for a straightforward reason. The punishment for violating a criminal law is almost always more detrimental to an offender than is the harm that he causes or risks to himself by engaging in the proscribed behavior.[130] A requirement that laws have some potential to attain their objectives—in this case, to benefit the very person whose conduct is prohibited—would seemingly preclude criminal paternalism altogether. The following example helps to explain my reservations about paternalism as a rationale for penal legislation. Imagine that some activity—boxing, for example—risks substantial injuries to persons who engage in it. Suppose also that some persons are foolishly inclined to perform this activity, perhaps because it is exciting, euphoric, or profitable. Why not protect these persons by enacting a criminal statute to punish boxers?[131] My answer has already been given. A criminal law merely proscribes behavior but cannot always prevent it. In a world of perfect compliance, no instances of the proscribed activity would occur. Perfect deterrence, of course, is unattainable. The threat of criminal punishment may succeed in reducing the incidence of the activity, but many persons will persist in boxing, whatever the law may say. Suppose that Rocky is one such person. What should be done to him if he is detected? Presumably, Rocky becomes subject to punishment, unless the state does not mean what it says in classifying the conduct as criminal.

How might Rocky's punishment be justified? Two answers might be given. First, criminal sanctions might deter others from following his foolish example. For this outcome to occur, the certainty, proximity, and severity of the sentence must be sufficient to increase compliance. As I have indicated, these conditions seldom obtain, and they are even less likely to be satisfied in cases of criminal paternalism. Behavior between consenting adults is more difficult to detect than crimes that produce an unwilling victim. Only a punishment disproportionate to the seriousness of the offense could be expected to dissuade others. Moreover, punishing Rocky in order to increase general deterrence can hardly be thought to promote the interests of Rocky himself. That is, the state does not treat *Rocky* paternalistically when he is punished to deter

---

130. See Michael Bayles: "Criminal Paternalism," in J. Roland Pennock and John W. Chapman, eds.: *Nomos XV: The Limits of Law* (New York: Lieber-Atherton, 1974), p.174.

131. See Nicholas Dixon: "Boxing, Paternalism, and Legal Moralism," 27 *Social Theory and Practice* 323 (2001).

others. If the law purports to treat Rocky paternalistically, punishment must be thought to be in *his* interest—which provides the second possible answer to the question of how his punishment might be justified. This second answer, however, is even more implausible. How can punishing Rocky promote his interests? At best, Rocky is a member of a class of persons treated paternalistically. But is Rocky himself really better off when punished than when free to box? The answer probably depends on further details about his sentence. A small monetary fine would not be especially detrimental to Rocky's welfare. If the threat of further fines induces him to stop boxing, the law will have succeeded in protecting him. The difficulty, of course, is that small fines are unlikely to discourage him, and he may continue to box even though he pays them. Suppose, then, that Rocky is imprisoned. This mode of punishment has (perhaps!) a greater probability of successfully deterring him from boxing. But it is hard to believe that imprisonment is really in Rocky's interest. Can a legislator seriously maintain that Rocky is better off not boxing in jail than boxing out of jail? If the answer to this question is negative, Rocky's punishment cannot be justified paternalistically.

Only rarely can the foregoing kind of question be answered affirmatively. Almost no conduct that sane adults are voluntarily inclined to perform is so destructive of their welfare that they are better off in jail than free to continue to engage in it. Perhaps a few counterexamples to this generalization can be found. Consider a promoter who offers large sums of money to induce persons to engage in gladiatorial contests to the death.[132] I concede that the well-being of potential combatants would probably be enhanced by a punishment sufficiently severe to deter them. Few examples in the real world, however, are analogous. Because the second prong of intermediate scrutiny holds a law to be unjustified when the "cure" is worse than the "disease," legislators should be extremely reluctant to back paternalistic laws with criminal sanctions.

This basis for objecting to criminal paternalism illustrates one of the few occasions in which it seems to be important to be conceptually clear about how criminal sanctions can be justified notwithstanding the existence of a right not to be punished. Recall that punishments might be justified on at least two grounds: because they *cancel* or because they *override* the right not to be punished.[133] In most contexts, this distinction is immaterial. The cogency of my latest reservation about criminal paternalism, however, may require the right not to be punished to be overridden rather than canceled. If that right were canceled and thus ceased to exist, the deprivations and stigma endured by offenders simply would not count in a balancing that purports to decide how the enforcement of a given law affects the well-being of offenders. Because I believe that these effects *should* be weighed in the balance, any losses persons may deserve by violating paternalistic statutes must be offset by greater gains if the laws are to be justified *qua* paternalism. I claim

---

132. This example looms large in the thought of Joel Feinberg: *Harmless Wrongdoing* (New York: Oxford University Press, 1988), pp.328–331.
133. See chapter 2, section II.

that this condition will almost never be satisfied; enforcing these laws will seldom promote the interests of the very persons who are punished for breaching them.[134] Nor will proportionate punishments be likely to deter them from engaging in the proscribed conduct in the first place.

Since criminal paternalism is so rarely justified, few of the interesting questions about legal paternalism are about the criminal law. Instead, they are questions about other domains of law.[135] Sometimes, paternalistic rationales for laws cause little dispute. For example, health and safety regulations may require that water contain fluoride. States can sponsor advertisements to discourage unhealthy behaviors such as excessive alcohol use. These sorts of regulations are not enforced through criminal penalties, and only occasionally do they give rise to objections from philosophers who purport to dislike legal paternalism. The reluctance of these philosophers to complain about such examples probably indicates that they are less opposed to legal paternalism per se than to legal paternalism enforced by penal sanctions. In my view, these noncriminal modes of law are more easily justified because they do not implicate a valuable right: the right not to be punished.

Even if I am mistaken about both drug offenses and paternalism, I contend that *all* criminal statutes—even those designed to promote expressive functions—must withstand empirical scrutiny. The crucial practical problem, I think, is not whether empirical evidence should be required to justify criminal laws but to specify how persuasive this empirical evidence must be in order to satisfy the second prong of our test. A disagreement about this matter has divided the Court in its decisions about commercial speech,[136] and clearly it would divide commentators when criminal statutes are assessed. Cursory amounts of data are likely to be selective and self-serving, while more methodologically sophisticated studies may overwhelm the competence of those who are charged to evaluate them.[137] Nonetheless, it is eminently sensible to demand more than a mere rational basis for believing that the law *might* produce its intended benefits. No one should allow the right not to be punished to be overridden by efforts to attain a goal when there is little reason to suppose these efforts would be effective.

I turn finally to the *third* and last external constraint in our test of criminalization, which requires the state to show that the challenged offense is no more extensive than necessary to achieve its objective. To apply this condition, legislators

---

134. Other questions about the justifiability of criminal paternalism can be raised. For example, do persons really *deserve* punishment for failing to take proper care of themselves? This question illustrates one of the unresolved perplexities in trying to reconcile paternalistic coercion with a theory of criminalization.

135. The famous issue posed by John Stuart Mill and discussed by a host of subsequent philosophers—whether persons should be free to permanently abdicate their freedom by voluntarily becoming slaves—is best construed not as a question about the scope of the criminal law, but rather as a question about the limits of freedom of contract. Suppose that Sue agrees to become Jane's permanent slave. Courts have no reason to become involved as long as Sue remains content to honor her agreement; no law prevents persons from entering into a *de facto* arrangement of slavery. But how should the law respond if Sue changes her mind and Jane seeks to enforce their agreement? In such an event, courts would declare the agreement unconscionable and unenforceable on grounds of public policy—presumably for paternalistic reasons. No one becomes subject to punishment; the criminal law need not become involved.

136. See *Florida Bar v. Went For It Inc.*, 515 U.S. 618 (1995).

137. In this context, Shiner observes that "courts are far more likely to fudge the application of such a high-level test than invariably to find against every government that fails to meet it." *Op. cit.*, note 25, p.58.

must be prepared to entertain and evaluate alternative means to attain the statutory purpose. Strictly speaking, the challenged law need not be *necessary* to achieve its goal. All that is required is that no alternative that is equally effective be less extensive than the statute in question. Applying this condition throughout the corpus of penal laws would open up an entirely new area of investigation. Deciding whether and under what circumstances various options (both criminal and noncriminal) would be as effective but less extensive than a challenged offense would again necessitate research that criminal theorists have seldom recognized the need to undertake.[138]

In requiring that no alternative that is equally effective be less extensive than the statute in question, this final prong of intermediate scrutiny imposes a presumption against *overinclusive* criminal laws. As the concept of overinclusion will be central to my discussion, a definition of this term will be helpful. Judgments that a statute is overinclusive (or underinclusive, for that matter) are necessarily relative to the law's objective. An offense is overinclusive when its justificatory rationale applies to some but not all of the conduct it proscribes; it is underinclusive when its justificatory rationale applies to more conduct than it proscribes.[139] In other words, it is possible to cause (or risk) the harm or evil an underinclusive law is designed to proscribe without actually breaking that law, and it is possible to break an overinclusive law without actually causing (or risking) the harm or evil that law is designed to proscribe. Neither overinclusion nor underinclusion is regarded as problematic under the rational basis test, which presently functions as the operative theory of criminalization in the United States. Under contemporary constitutional law, a statute may be justified even though it proscribes some instances of conduct that do not bring about the harm or evil the statute is intended to prevent. Thus a presumption against overinclusive penal legislation is extraordinarily important in a theory of criminalization, and has enormous potential to contract the size and scope of the criminal law. As I describe in greater detail later, offenses of risk prevention (and proscriptions of drugs and guns in particular) are especially vulnerable to problems of overinclusion. Hence I postpone a more detailed examination of this condition until I discuss this kind of statute.[140]

Overinclusive legislation becomes more objectionable when valuable rights are implicated. For example, a law to prevent minors from accessing obscene depictions on the Internet is worrisome largely because it burdens the First Amendment rights of adults—even though the state may have a compelling interest in protecting children from the evils of pornography.[141] If I am correct that the right

138. Perhaps this dearth of research is due to the fact that criminal theorists tend to be legal philosophers who are unskilled in empirical methodology. In any event, "there has never been a thoroughgoing examination [in the United Kingdom] of . . . whether some form of non-criminal enforcement could be devised to deal effectively with [given kinds of offences]." Andrew Ashworth: *Principles of Criminal Law* (Oxford: Clarendon Press, 4th ed., 2003), p.50. The same observation applies to the United States.
139. For the classic account of overinclusion and underinclusion, see Fredrick Schauer: *Playing by the Rules* (Oxford: Clarendon Press, 1991), pp.31–34.
140. See section III.
141. For example, see *Reno v. A.C.L.U.*, 521 U.S. 844 (1997).

not to be punished is valuable, it is plausible to recognize a presumption against overinclusive legislation throughout the whole of the substantive criminal law. But why does this final prong of our test impose only a *presumption* rather than an outright ban on the justifiability of overinclusive criminal legislation? Surely a blanket prohibition of overinclusive criminal laws would better advance a minimalist agenda.

My answer is that there *may* be good reason to prefer one statute to another—it might be more effective in attaining its purpose—even if the former is overinclusive and the latter is not. In other words, overinclusion may be impossible to eradicate if the objective of the law is to be achieved. To illustrate why overinclusive statutes might be justifiable notwithstanding the presumption against them, consider moving-vehicle offenses. Virtually all moving-vehicle offenses, I assume, are designed to reduce the probability of a crash. Clearly, however, a driver can commit the offense of crossing over the median line on a curved highway, for example, without increasing the likelihood that a crash will occur. This possibility arises for at least two reasons, only one of which raises normative difficulties for the justifiability of the offense. First, no other car may happen to be approaching in the opposite direction, even though the driver is unaware of this fact. If our driver has the road to himself, his unlawful driving can hardly create a substantial risk of harm to others. I call these cases of *epistemic fortune*. Liability is appropriate in such cases, because these drivers are culpable and behave wrongly; their actions display the same kind of disregard for the safety of others that is shown by drivers who lack epistemic fortune. But a driver may commit this offense without increasing the probability of a crash for a second reason. When this reason obtains, liability will prove more difficult to justify. A particular defendant may have very good reason to believe—in fact, he may *know*—that another car is not approaching in the opposite direction. The driver may have had a clear view of the highway for miles ahead before reaching the turn where his vision became obstructed. In such a case, our driver is not simply fortunate that another car is not approaching; he knew his conduct would not cause a crash. I call these cases of *epistemic privilege*. It is facetious to allege that epistemically privileged drivers exhibit the same disregard for safety as those who are epistemically fortunate. As far as I can see, these drivers demonstrate no less regard for others—and they are no more arrogant—than those who obey the law. If I am correct, the challenge for a theory of criminalization is to decide whether and for what reason criminal liability may be imposed on epistemically privileged defendants who commit these offenses.

The following argument suggests why liability may be imposed on the epistemically privileged and the epistemically fortunate alike. We simply have no reliable method to distinguish epistemically privileged from epistemically fortunate drivers who cross the median line on a curved highway. To reduce the number of crashes—a substantial state objective—we have little alternative but to draft a statute that punishes both classes of persons. After all, our theory of criminalization does not preclude overinclusive criminal laws altogether but only those criminal laws that are more extensive than necessary. Minimalists would prefer a statute that spares the epistemically privileged while punishing the epistemically fortunate. Unless someone can suggest how such a statute could be drafted and enforced, however, the state has no realistic choice but to enact an overinclusive offense. If this argument is sound, our theory of criminalization will allow over-inclusive statutes under these limited conditions. It may be preferable to tolerate these laws when substantial state objectives (such as the reduction of crashes) can-not be attained otherwise. Nonetheless, this result is unfortunate and should be tolerated reluctantly—even if it is a practical necessity.

I suspect that relatively few statutes will overcome the presumption against overinclusion; often it is possible to draft and enforce a law that furthers its objec-tive without subjecting so many persons to liability. Victor Tadros offers a clear example of an offense that can easily be made less inclusive.[142] A Scottish statute provides that "any person who, without lawful authority to be there, is found in or on a building or other premises . . . so that, in all the circumstances, it may reasonably be inferred that he intended to commit theft there shall be guilty of an offense."[143] Tadros asks us to imagine a defendant—call him Smith—whose behavior creates a reasonable inference of an intention to steal, but who subse-quently provides conclusive evidence that he lacked this intention. No one could believe that the purpose of this statute would be furthered by punishing Smith. Thus the statute is overinclusive. Moreover, Smith is epistemically privileged in knowing he did not have an intention to steal at the time he was apprehended. Our theory of criminalization holds this statute to be unjustified unless a more narrowly tailored law could not be written without undermining the substantial state interest in preventing theft. In this case (and most others), a better statute *can* be drafted. The offense could require an actual intention to steal. Evidence of this culpable intention is more readily available than in the case of the driver who claims epistemic privilege when in fact he was merely fortunate.

Although a presumption against overinclusive criminal legislation is entailed by the external constraints in our theory of criminalization, it may also be derived from the internal constraints I described in chapter 2. Overinclusive statutes fre-quently impose more punishment than is necessary to achieve their objectives. The residue of unnecessary punishment is hard to justify because desert is personal; no one deserves criminal sanctions simply because state purposes are furthered by drafting and enforcing statutes that subject him to liability. The hardship and stigma inherent in punishment must be justified for each and every person on whom they are imposed. As Henry Hart stressed decades ago, legislatures must be "able to say in good conscience in each instance in which a criminal sanction is imposed for a violation of law that the violation was blameworthy and, hence, deserving of the moral condemnation of the community."[144] Thus the presump-tion against overinclusive legislation is rebutted only when these substantial state objectives cannot otherwise be achieved. Although I believe such cases will be fairly unusual, reasonable minds will differ about whether the presumption against overinclusive criminal legislation is rebutted in particular circumstances. Once

---

142. Victor Tadros: "Politics and the Presumption of Innocence," 1 *Criminal Law and Philosophy* 193 (2007).
143. Civic Government (Scotland) Act 1982, s.57.
144. Henry Hart: "The Aims of the Criminal Law," 23 *Law & Contemporary Problems* 401, 412 (1958).

again, applications of this theory of criminalization are difficult and controversial. However these issues are resolved, all cases in which the presumption has been overcome are occasions for regret. The state should keep trying to find a means to accomplish its ends with a less extensive law.

In any event, the final prong of our test does not create a similar presumption against criminal laws that are *underinclusive*. To be justified, one might suppose that a criminal law should apply uniformly to each instance of conduct the state has the same reason to proscribe. Ideally, the government should treat persons as equals in protecting the right not to be punished; it should not subject some to hardship and stigma while sparing others if it has an equally good basis to punish both. For example, a statute prohibiting one substance because of its addictive properties is underinclusive unless other substances with comparable addictive properties are prohibited as well—assuming, of course, that other factors do not justify the disparate treatment of the two substances.[145] Strict scrutiny may preclude underinclusive criminal legislation, but the test of intermediate scrutiny I propose to incorporate into a theory of criminalization is more permissive.[146] States should be allowed to combat problems one step at a time, and commentators should be far less worried about too little punishment than about too much.

Underinclusive statutes are not altogether unproblematic in our theory of criminalization. Significantly, however, the test of intermediate scrutiny raises inquiries about underinclusive and overinclusive penal legislation at different analytical points. Questions about overinclusion pose the issue whether the statute is more extensive than necessary to achieve its objective. Perhaps the substantial state interest could have been attained by imposing less punishment, or by not imposing punishment at all. As the discussion of *Posadas* suggests, however, concerns about underinclusion arise at an earlier stage of our inquiry. Questions about underinclusion help to ensure that the state really is aiming toward the objective it alleges to be promoting. For example, a statute prohibiting the ritualistic animal sacrifice of Santerians is probably not designed to prevent cruelty to animals, as a great deal of conduct that is equally cruel to animals is permitted.[147] But once we become confident we have identified the legislative objective correctly, underinclusive statutes will be much less objectionable than overinclusive statutes in our theory of criminalization.

Because this final prong of intermediate review should be construed only to create a presumption against overinclusive criminal legislation and does not entail that the challenged statute be necessary to achieve its objective, it is probably an exaggeration to say—along with a few prominent theorists—that the criminal law may be used only as a *last resort*.[148] Commentators should, of course, remain

---

145. See the unusual rationale for tolerating underinclusive drug offenses defended by George Sher: "On the Decriminalization of Drugs," 22 *Criminal Justice Ethics* 30 (2003).
146. Admittedly, courts have been skeptical of underinclusive statutes in the context of commercial speech. See, for example, *City of Cincinnati v. Discovery Network, Inc., et al.*, 507 U.S. 410 (1993). One commentator points out that "more protection [is] offered to commercial speech than *Central Hudson* seems to require." See Note: "Making Sense of Hybrid Speech: A New Model for Commercial Speech and Expressive Conduct," 118 *Harvard Law Review* 2836, 2853 (2005).
147. See *Church of the Lukumi Babalu Aye v. City of Hialeah*, 508 U.S. 520 (1993).
148. "It is often—in fact, very often—claimed that criminalization is the legislator's *ultima ratio*." Nils Jareborg: "Criminalization as Last Resort (*Ultima Ratio*)," 2 *Ohio State Journal of Criminal Law* 521, 523 (2005).

mindful of the many nonlegal and noncriminal means to secure compliance with norms.[149] Clearly, however, the theory of criminalization sketched here does not require the state to conduct a series of experiments in which alternative strategies to attain its objective are implemented and found to be deficient. Perhaps alternatives must literally be exhausted before a state is permitted to go to *war*, but not before a state is permitted to enact an offense.[150] Moreover, although the details of a last-resort principle seldom are provided, the requirement is typically construed to suggest that alternative means of *crime reduction* be exhausted before penal sanctions may be employed.[151] If a given law has important expressive functions, however, the fact that other measures may be more effective in preventing the proscribed conduct will not be decisive.[152] A statute with important expressive purposes may pass our theory of criminalization, even if an alternative that is less extensive does as well or better in deterring crime. At the very least, however, this final condition of our test requires that alternatives to given laws be identified and assessed. Thus it functions as an important tool in combating the problem of overcriminalization—as I illustrate below.

The foregoing discussion demonstrates the enormous uncertainty and complexity in applying intermediate levels of scrutiny to legislation, criminal or otherwise. To be justified, criminal laws must satisfy the external constraints I have described. An offense must aim toward a substantial state objective, directly advance that interest, and be no more extensive than necessary to achieve its purpose. As I have indicated, each of the three prongs of this test creates its own interpretive difficulties. Are these problems so formidable that the theory of criminalization is impossible to implement? Can the several requirements be manipulated to justify any result legislatures might prefer? I think not. In fact, I anticipate surprisingly few disagreements in applying this test to many of the offenses in two of the three categories of relatively new crime I distinguished in chapter 1. The myriad overlapping offenses in our criminal code present the easiest case. The fact that other statutes already proscribe the defendant's conduct seems to show that overlapping laws are more extensive than necessary to achieve whatever substantial objective the state may have. Although each statute may appear to be justifiable when considered independently, the last prong of our test requires an evaluation of different strategies for achieving the legislative purpose. One plausible alternative is to reduce the incidence of overlapping offenses. In the current climate of overcriminalization, this solution would undermine incentives to plea-bargain. But if a minimalist theory of criminalization were implemented, the state would have less need to encourage these bargains in the first place. Thus I conclude that offenses that overlap with existing crimes will have an uphill climb to satisfy our test of criminalization.

149. For a nice discussion, see Mark R. Reiff: *Punishment, Compensation, and Law* (Cambridge: Cambridge University Press, 2005), especially chap. 1.
150. But see the critical discussion of a last-resort principle in just war theory provided by Michael Walzer: *Arguing About War* (New Haven: Yale University Press, 2004), p.160.
151. See, for example, Jonathan Schonsheck: *On Criminalization* (Dordrecht: Kluwer Academic Publishers, 1994), especially p.68.
152. See Douglas Husak: "The Criminal Law as Last Resort," 24 *Oxford Journal of Legal Studies* 207 (2004).

Much the same verdict pertains to ancillary offenses. Although the state may have a legitimate interest in gathering information and prohibiting "aid-like" conduct subsequent to a criminal offense, can these interests be sufficiently important to warrant infringements of the right not to be punished? A less intrusive means to accomplish this objective is to prosecute persons for the behavior the state really wants to prevent—the conduct for which the ancillary offense is ancillary. Is this task really so hard to accomplish? I do not insist that each and every one of these two kinds of offense must inevitably fail to withstand intermediate scrutiny. In particular, as we have seen, some of these crimes may serve expressive functions—if, indeed, expressive functions promote substantial state interests. Still, the burden of proof lies squarely on those who contend these laws to be justified. As far as I can see, only crimes of risk prevention—to which I now turn—are likely candidates to survive applications of this test.

I have only begun the extraordinarily difficult task of constructing and defending a theory of criminalization. Despite the several problems I have noted, I maintain that this sketch of a theory is vastly superior both to existing practice and to any of the alternatives I assess in chapter 4. I repeat, however, that these constraints will be hard to implement. Perhaps I have misapplied them myself; commentators are encouraged to improve upon my efforts. As we have seen, the *Central Hudson* test has proved difficult to apply to laws that regulate commercial speech, and the task of implementing the external constraints throughout the entire substantive criminal law will generate even more controversy. The devil, as I have said, is in the details. But I do not construe this admission as an *objection* to this theory, and certainly not as a *fatal* objection. At the present time, we lack a framework for assessing penal statutes, and far greater debate *should* surround the enactment of criminal laws. My own possible misapplications of this theory should not be confused with defects in the theory itself. We should all agree that the state needs excellent reasons to deprive persons of the right not to be subjected to the hard treatment and censure inherent in punishment. The test of criminalization I have proposed raises the very questions that must be addressed and answered before the government should be allowed to resort to the penal sanction.

III: CRIMES OF RISK PREVENTION

Unless they serve important expressive functions, I suspect that few overlapping or ancillary offenses will survive applications of the theory of criminalization I have borrowed from constitutional thought. Of the three categories of relatively new offense that have contributed most to the problem of overcriminalization, crimes of risk prevention (or risk creation) are the most likely to emerge unscathed. Indeed, a great many of these crimes *do* involve legitimate impositions of the penal sanction. The criminal law is appropriately employed not only to reduce harm but also to reduce the *risk* of harm. But when? Theorists have made disappointingly little progress in answering this question. The test of criminalization I have defended in sections I and II provide the basis for an answer. To satisfy this test, the government must have a substantial interest in enacting a criminal prohibition, the statute must directly advance the government's objective, and the law must be no more extensive than necessary to achieve its purpose. Applications of these criteria to offenses of risk prevention raise issues sufficiently complex to merit separate treatment. Regrettably, this separate treatment is probably as abstract and difficult as any topic in a theory of criminalization.

Because offenses of risk prevention are *inchoate* offenses, it is important to begin by clarifying the distinction between inchoate and consummate crimes. Commentators do not agree about how to draw this basic distinction.[153] I understand an offense to be consummate if it proscribes conduct that is harmful on each and every occasion in which it is performed.[154] More precisely, each act-token of an act-type proscribed by a consummate offense produces a harm or evil.[155] It is not surprising that most of the principles venerated by criminal theorists have been developed with consummate offenses in mind. Core crimes—arson, rape, murder, and the like—are examples of consummate offenses. Each commission of these crimes violates the rights of others and thus causes them harm.[156] Not all offenses, however, are comparable. An offense is inchoate if it proscribes conduct that does *not* cause harm on each and every occasion in which it is performed. More precisely, some act-tokens of the act-type proscribed by an inchoate offense do not produce a harm or evil. Even though these statutes are not designed to reduce the occurrence of harm itself, there is something almost as bad they *are* designed to reduce: a *risk* of harm that might materialize.[157] Let us define an *ultimate* harm as the harm risked by a given inchoate offense. Persons who commit inchoate offenses risk but need not cause an ultimate harm; these crimes are designed to reduce the risk that an ultimate harm will occur.

If this way to understand the contrast between consummate and inchoate offenses is sound, success in sorting particular statutes into one category or the other depends on our ability to decide whether given offenses proscribe an ultimate harm or the mere risk of an ultimate harm. As George Fletcher rightfully claims, we cannot draw this distinction without a catalogue of ultimate harms the law seeks to prevent.[158] A few of his examples illustrate the perils of categorization. Consider proscriptions of vagrancy or the dissemination of

---

153. Although few commentators address the issue specifically, rival accounts of the distinction between inchoate and consummate offenses can be found. See, for example, Joshua Dressler: *Understanding Criminal Law* (New York: Matthew Bender & Co., 4th ed., 2005), p.405.

154. It may be preferable to use the phrase "harm or evil." To avoid repetition, however, I sometimes drop the "or evil" locution.

155. A *net* balance of harm need not occur, however, when persons are *justified* in committing an offense. For present purposes, I ignore the complication that justifications pose to my claims.

156. Some theorists maintain that a few instances of core offenses like rape and burglary are harmless. See, for example, John Gardner and Steven Shute: "The Wrongness of Rape," in Jeremy Horder, ed.: *Oxford Essays in Jurisprudence* (Oxford: Oxford University Press, 4th Series, 2000), p.193; and Arthur Ripstein: "Beyond the Harm Principle," 34 *Philosophy & Public Affairs* 215 (2006). Significantly, neither author indicates exactly what harm *is* such that they believe the acts they describe are harmless. Ripstein, for example, appeals to an "ordinary understanding of harm." *Id.*, p.218.

157. Some commentators construe conduct that risks harm as harmful. See Claire Finkelstein: "Is Risk a Harm?" 151 *University of Pennsylvania Law Review* 963 (2003).

158. George Fletcher: *Rethinking Criminal Law* (Boston: Little, Brown & Co., 1978), p.133.

obscene materials. Are these behaviors harmful per se, or are they punished to decrease the probability that subsequent harms will occur?[159] Without a means to identify harms, these questions—like countless others raised by a theory of criminalization—cannot be answered.

The three most familiar examples of offenses of risk prevention are attempt, solicitation, and conspiracy. Clearly, these inchoate crimes are designed to reduce the risk of ultimate harms. Suppose we lived in a possible world in which human effort were so inefficacious and futile that an attempt to kill, for example, did not increase the probability that anyone would actually die. In this (barely imaginable) world, the state would have no reason to proscribe attempts. Obviously, that world is unlike the actual world. We inhabit a place where persons who commit inchoate offenses increase the likelihood that ultimate harms will occur.[160]

All jurisdictions go far beyond the well-known triad of attempt, solicitation, and conspiracy to enact an enormous number of additional inchoate crimes. Virtually all commentators agree that many of these offenses are justified, and I concur in their judgment.[161] Allowing offenses of risk prevention into our criminal law, however, has the potential to expand the scope of state authority exponentially. Several (actual and possible) offenses that seemingly are incompatible with a minimalist theory of criminalization might appear to be justified if construed to reduce the risk of harm rather than harm itself. Imagine a criminal law I assume nearly everyone would regard as unjustified: a statute punishing persons who drop out of high school prior to graduation. No one should pretend the conduct proscribed is harmful per se; clearly, the act of dropping out of school need harm no one at all, including the perpetrator himself. Nonetheless, students who fail to graduate from high school increase the *risk* of subsequent harm; *ceteris paribus,* they are more likely to be represented in populations of offenders who victimize others. Why, then, is this imaginary offense so clearly unjustifiable? My central ambition in this section is to provide a framework within which such questions can be answered. In the course of distinguishing between different kinds of inchoate offense, I defend and apply four distinct principles to limit the authority of the state to punish persons who engage in conduct that creates the risk of harm rather than harm itself.

The first two principles are clear and need little elaboration. I call the first the *substantial risk* requirement. Recall that the test of criminalization requires criminal laws to promote a *substantial* state interest. Because the prevention of trivial harms cannot justify state infringements of the right not to be punished, it is apparent that the prevention of trivial risks provides even less of a rationale. Virtually all behavior involves *some* level of risk; criminal liability to prevent insubstantial risks would threaten to punish all human activity. Thus a theory of criminalization

159. *Id.,* pp.132–133.
160. The possible world I describe resembles the actual world only when attempts are factually impossible. I ignore the difficult problems that impossible attempts pose for a theory of criminalization. For a discussion of these complexities, see R. A. Duff: *Criminal Attempts* (Oxford: Clarendon Press, 1996).
161. For a rare dissent, see Randy E. Barnett: "Restitution: A New Paradigm of Criminal Justice," in Randy Barnett and John Hagel III, eds.: *Assessing the Criminal* (Cambridge: Ballinger Pub. Co., 1977), p.349.

should preclude offenses of risk prevention unless they are designed to reduce a substantial risk.[162] Indeed, this requirement is explicitly included in many statutory definitions of recklessness and negligence. According to the Model Penal Code, a person cannot be reckless or negligent unless he disregards a substantial risk.[163] Liability to prevent an insubstantial risk would punish individuals who are even less culpable than those who are negligent, and codes should rarely if ever impose liability on persons with so little culpability.

Second, the test of intermediate scrutiny requires criminal statutes to directly advance the government's interest. When applied to inchoate offenses, this requirement entails that the proscription in question must actually decrease the likelihood that the ultimate harm will occur. I call this second principle the *prevention* requirement. If enacting the inchoate offense did not make the incidence of the ultimate harm less probable, the state interest in preventing that harm could hardly justify the proscription. No one should favor juvenile curfew laws, for example, unless they actually help to reduce juvenile crime.[164] I take the need for both the substantial risk and the prevention requirements to be obvious, even though their application to particular cases may be contested. No one would fail to include these principles in a theory of criminalization that pertains to offenses of risk prevention. As we will see, however, it is far less clear that these conditions are satisfied by all of the crimes of risk prevention that clutter our criminal codes today.

A few distinctions are helpful before introducing the remaining two principles. As I have indicated, R. A. Duff has made the most thoughtful efforts both to catalogue the various kinds of offense of risk prevention (or what he calls endangerment offenses) as well as to describe the principles that might justify them.[165] I focus my attention here on what I take to be his two most important contrasts: direct and indirect offenses of risk prevention and explicit and implicit offenses of risk prevention. According to Duff, an offense to prevent risk is direct "if the relevant harm would ensue from the criminalized conduct without any intervening wrongful human action"; it is indirect "if the harm would ensue only given further, wrongful actions by the agent or by others."[166] Tossing bricks from the roof of a building onto a crowded street would be an example of direct endangerment, whereas selling a gun to a felon would be an example of indirect endangerment, as harm in the latter case would ensue only if the gun were misused. Offenses to prevent risk are explicit "when their commission requires the actual creation of the

162. Notice that "substantial" does double duty in a theory of inchoate criminal legislation. First, the state must aim toward a substantial state interest in enacting the offense. Next, the proscribed conduct must prevent a substantial risk that a harm will occur.

163. See Model Penal Code, §2.02(b). Despite the plain language of this statute, some commentators do not believe that the requirement that a risk be substantial is independent of the requirement that a risk be unjustifiable. See Larry Alexander: "Insufficient Concern: A Unified Conception of Criminal Culpability," 88 *California Law Review* 931, 934 (2000).

164. For a discussion of juvenile curfew laws, and skepticism about whether they are effective, see Toni L. Conner: "Juvenile Curfews: Political Pandering at the Expense of a Fundamental Right," 109 *West Virginia Law Review* 459 (2007).

165. R. A. Duff: "Criminalizing Endangerment," in Green and Duff: *op. cit.*, note 61, p.43.

166. *Id.*, p.62.

relevant risk—a risk specified in the offence definition"; they are implicit "if their definition does not specify the relevant risk (the risk that grounds their criminalization), so that they can be committed without creating the risk."[167] Duff lists dangerous driving as an example of an explicit endangerment offense and drug possession as an example of an offense of implicit risk prevention. Clearly, each of these offenses is inchoate because a person can (and typically does) commit them without harming anyone—even himself.

I begin with Duff's second distinction—between implicit and explicit offenses of risk prevention. This contrast depends on whether or not a defendant can commit the offense without actually creating the relevant risk. Dangerous driving is Duff's example of an explicit offense of risk prevention, presumably because no one can drive in the way the statute proscribes—dangerously—without creating a risk. Notice, however, that no one can "stand dangerously," "breathe dangerously" or "smile dangerously" without creating a risk; in the absence of a risk, these activities would not be dangerous. Even though the inclusion of such adverbs transforms the statute into an instance of explicit risk prevention as Duff defines it, these offenses do not inform us of *what* harm is risked. Thus I propose what I hope to be a more illuminating contrast that is closely related but not identical to Duff's. Henceforth I call an offense of risk prevention explicit when it specifically identifies the ultimate harm to be prevented. Implicit offenses of risk prevention, by contrast, are those inchoate crimes that do not mention the ultimate harm to be prevented. With this distinction in mind, return to Duff's example of dangerous driving. Although his definition categorizes this offense as an instance of explicit risk prevention, my alternative account categorizes it as an instance of implicit risk prevention. The reason is simple. We cannot decide whether someone can drive dangerously without creating the relevant risk unless we know *what* risk is created when someone engages in the proscribed activity. Because the statute itself does not identify the ultimate harm that is risked, I categorize this offense as an instance of implicit risk prevention. This classification is easy to miss because the ultimate harm to be reduced by the offense of dangerous driving is patently obvious: This offense is designed to reduce the risk that drivers will cause a crash resulting in personal injury and/or property damage. Still, the fact that the nature of the ultimate harm to be prevented is beyond dispute does not transform this statute into an instance of explicit risk prevention, as the statute itself does not mention this ultimate harm.

When fully specified, the most familiar examples of inchoate offenses *do* include a specific reference to the ultimate harm to be reduced and thus are instances of crimes of explicit risk prevention. Consider again the three most well-known inchoate offenses: attempt, solicitation, and conspiracy. Clearly, attempts per se are not crimes; attempts are criminal only when what is attempted is itself a crime. The particular crime attempted must be specified in the indictment and generally refers to the ultimate harm to be reduced by the inchoate offense.[168] The same is true of the inchoate offenses of solicitation and conspiracy. No one should

---

167. *Id.*, p.59.
168. I say *generally* rather than always, as the crime attempted may be inchoate as well and thus need not describe the ultimate harm the offense is designed to prevent. Attempted burglary is one such example. Henceforth I ignore

be punished for conspiring to do something (or soliciting something) unless the something he conspires to do (or solicits) is a crime.[169]

Although the fully specified inchoate offenses of attempt, solicitation, and conspiracy are crimes of explicit risk prevention, the vast majority of new offenses of risk prevention that contribute to the problem of overcriminalization are examples of crimes of implicit risk prevention. They fail to mention the ultimate harm to be reduced by the inchoate offense. Applying our test to these offenses will prove to be a nightmare. As we have seen, the first (and most recurrent) of several difficulties in applying a theory of criminalization to a given offense is to understand why the legislature enacted it. In the case of offenses of explicit risk prevention, such as attempted murder, this first problem has a straightforward solution. The legislative interest in proscribing attempted murder is to reduce the commission of murders—as substantial an interest as might be found. Nor is this first problem difficult when the state has an obvious reason to enact an offense of implicit risk prevention, as in the case of dangerous driving. Everyone concedes the state has a substantial interest in reducing the incidence of crashes caused by persons who drive dangerously. But this problem will prove formidable with that class of offenses of implicit risk prevention in which the legislative interest is *not* so obvious. If we do not know the nature of the ultimate harm these offenses are designed to prevent, it goes without saying that we cannot apply any of the three prongs of our test. We cannot determine whether the state has a substantial interest in creating the offense, whether the law directly advances the government's objective, or whether the statute is more extensive than necessary to achieve its purpose. In short, our test of criminalization will not get off the ground.

These difficulties are not merely speculative. Return to the offense of drug possession—the most frequently enforced offense in federal law today. In discussing the strict liability drug homicide statute upheld in *Rodriguez,* I promised to indicate why the crime of drug possession represents a dubious imposition of the penal sanction.[170] Although I have already questioned the entire regime of drug proscriptions, it is time to redeem my pledge in more detail. The proscription of drug possession is an inchoate offense. No harm inevitably occurs on each occasion in which this offense is committed. A world in which cocaine is possessed need contain no more harm than a world in which cocaine did not exist at all. Presumably, illicit drugs are illegal to possess because possession increases the probability that an ultimate harm will result. The *nature* of this ultimate harm, however, is not identified by the statute itself. Thus this proscription is an example of an offense of implicit risk prevention. It is tempting to suppose that the ultimate harm to be prevented by this statute is the *use* of drugs. After all, no harm would occur if drugs were possessed but never used. Still, use cannot be the

---

this complication. See the discussion in Jeremy Horder: "Crimes of Ulterior Intent," in A. P. Simester and A. T. H. Smith, eds.: *Harm and Culpability* (Oxford: Clarendon Press, 1996), p.153.

169. As a matter of positive law, doctrines of conspiracy that reject this principle have been "strongly criticized by commentators as violative of the principle of legality." At common law, conspiracy requires an agreement to commit an unlawful act, but "unlawful" may be broader than "criminal." See Dressler: *op. cit.*, note 153, p.465.

170. See chapter 1, section IV.

ultimate harm the offense of possession is designed to reduce, because use is no more an ultimate harm than possession. In other words, the offense of drug use also is inchoate, designed to reduce a subsequent harm that is risked when drugs are consumed.[171] Again, however, the nature of this ultimate harm remains unidentified—and, quite frankly, is mysterious. As a result of this uncertainty, applications of our test to the most frequently enforced offense in federal law involve enormous conjecture and guesswork. This predicament should not be tolerated in a minimalist theory of criminalization that places the burden of proof on those who favor penal liability.

Of course, Rodriguez himself was caught not only possessing an illicit drug but also distributing it. Jurisdictions regard this crime as more serious than the separate crime of possession.[172] For present purposes, the important point is that all of the foregoing claims about the offense of drug possession apply with equal force to the offense of distribution. That is, drug distribution is also an inchoate offense of implicit risk prevention; no harm inevitably occurs when this offense is committed.[173] A world in which cocaine is distributed need contain no more harm than a world in which cocaine did not exist at all. Presumably, drugs are illegal to distribute because distribution increases the likelihood that an ultimate harm will result.[174] Again, this ultimate harm cannot be possession or use; its nature is unidentified. It will prove convenient to give a name to the ultimate harm the offenses of drug possession, use, and distribution are designed to proscribe. To avoid question-begging, I refer to this elusive harm as *harm X*.[175]

What practical role does the contrast between explicit and implicit offenses of risk prevention play in a theory of criminalization? The answer to this question invokes the third constraint to be included in that part of a theory of criminalization that pertains to inchoate offenses. I call this condition the *consummate harm* requirement. According to this principle, the state may not proscribe conduct to

171. More precisely, an offense of drug use *would* be an inchoate offense if it existed. In fact, relatively few states—approximately a dozen—proscribe illicit drug use per se.
172. For a discussion of the distinctive character of drug distribution, see Peter Alldridge: "Dealing with Drug Dealing," in Simester and Smith, eds.: *op. cit.*, note 168, p.239.
173. A few other commentators recognize this offense as inchoate. For example, see Paul Robinson: *Structure and Function in Criminal Law* (Oxford: Oxford University Press, 1997), pp.63–64.
174. Although the offense of drug distribution resembles the offense of drug possession inasmuch as both are inchoate, it is important to notice that many other offenses of distribution—those not involving contraband—are dissimilar. Property rights are routinely violated by the act of distributing stolen goods, for example. Many legal theorists construe property rights as *bundles*—general rights encompassing more specific rights over what is owned. These more particular rights—the "sticks" in the "bundle"—include the right to possess, alienate, and exclude. When someone steals my car and sells it to another, my rights are violated not only by the initial theft but also by the subsequent sale, as no one has the right to sell my car without my consent. Thus someone who commits the offense of distributing stolen property violates the rights of the property owner. Wrongful violations of rights qualify as harms. If this analysis is correct, an offense of distribution need not be inchoate; it may not be designed to reduce the likelihood of an ultimate harm, but might proscribe conduct that is harmful in and of itself. The offense of distributing illicit drugs is different in this respect. Because this act does not violate property rights (or, indeed, any rights at all), no one need be harmed by it in the way I am harmed when my stolen car is sold. The act of cocaine distribution from Rodriguez to Hendricks and Bennett was harmless; it is proscribed because it increases the risk of an unidentified ultimate harm.
175. In using the singular rather than the plural, I do not mean to suggest that there can be only *one* ultimate harm these offenses are designed to prevent.

reduce the risk of a given harm unless the state would be permitted to proscribe conduct that intentionally and directly causes that same harm. In other words, no theory of criminalization should justify an inchoate offense prohibiting an act that creates the risk of an undesirable state of affairs unless a consummate offense prohibiting an act that intentionally and directly causes that very state of affairs would also be justified. The truth of the consummate harm requirement is generally taken for granted when inchoate offenses are explicit. In such cases, the state of affairs to be prevented is specifically identified. Unless this state of affairs is a harm that should be criminalized when brought about directly and intentionally, liability for an inchoate offense would not be contemplated. As I have indicated, for example, liability for attempt presupposes that what is attempted is a crime; persons who attempt to perform an act that is not a crime simply have not committed a criminal attempt. If the crime attempted is precluded by a theory of the penal sanction, no one would propose to retain a separate offense of attempting to commit that crime. When inchoate offenses are implicit, however, the consummate criminal harm requirement may escape our notice. Without knowing what ultimate harm these inchoate offenses are designed to reduce, we can easily lose sight of the consummate harm requirement.

The rationale for the consummate harm requirement is straightforward. It cannot be worse to risk bringing about an undesirable state of affairs than to engage in conduct that deliberately and directly brings about that same state of affairs. In any hierarchy of culpable states, recklessness is less culpable than intention (or purpose). If the act of intentionally and directly causing a result should not be criminalized, the state cannot be justified in enacting an inchoate offense to prevent persons from merely creating a risk of that result. For example, as the act of intentionally failing to save money neither is nor ought to be a criminal offense, an inchoate offense designed to prevent persons from engaging in conduct that increases the risk that they will fail to save money would be incompatible with the consummate harm requirement and thus precluded by our theory of criminalization.

Because (*ex hypothesi*) we may not know what consummate harm the statute is designed to prevent, we cannot be certain whether a given offense of implicit risk prevention satisfies the consummate harm requirement. The most we can conclude is that some purported rationales for these laws are incompatible with this principle. To illustrate, return to the crime of drug possession, an offense of implicit risk prevention designed to reduce the probability of (what I have called) harm X. No one should be confident about his ability to identify harm X. Many candidates have been proposed. If we hope to specify harm X correctly, we have little alternative but to rely on the opinions of commentators who defend this law.[176] Consider, for example, the judgment of Daniel Lungren, former Attorney General of California. He protests against "legalizing drugs" by predicting that repeal of these proscriptions would increase "homelessness,

---

176. I survey four of the most plausible candidates about the identity of harm X in Douglas Husak: *Legalize This!* (London: Verso, 2002).

unemployment, welfare, lost productivity, disability payments, school dropouts, lawsuits, medical care costs, chronic mental illness, accidents, crime, child abuse, and child neglect."[177] Each of these alleged consequences of drug use is a possible specification of harm X.

I am skeptical that many of these rationales for drug prohibition would survive intermediate scrutiny. Consider the compatibility of these allegations with the prevention requirement. Do proscriptions of illicit drug use really decrease the risk of each of the social maladies Lungren mentions? Generalizations are perilous, but empirical evidence for these claims seldom is provided.[178] Does illicit drug use really cause greater amounts of crime, for example? Many criminologists think not. Even James Q. Wilson—a steadfast opponent of drug decriminalization—admits that drug prohibitions probably cause more crime than drug use. He contends: "It is not clear that enforcing the laws against drug use would reduce crime. On the contrary, crime may be caused by such enforcement."[179] Other researchers claim that, once we control for other variables, smokers of marijuana actually are less likely than nonsmokers to commit further crimes.[180] Drug proscriptions would become imperiled if we impose a higher standard of justification on criminal offenses than current law requires and insist that purported rationales for punishment rest on a solid empirical foundation.

Let us suppose, however, that Lungren is correct that the failure to punish illicit drug possession would lead to each of the undesirable states of affairs he mentions. Even so, most of his allegations fail to provide a viable defense of the statute. We may well wonder whether the state has a substantial interest in alleviating each of the ills Lungren recites. Some of his rationales are unabashedly paternalistic—designed to protect drug users from the negative consequences of their own actions—and I have already provided two reasons to doubt that criminal paternalism is justified: The state may lack a substantial interest in protecting adults from their own proclivities, and the cure of punishment is likely to be worse than the disease it is designed to treat. But the consummate harm requirement provides an even better reason to conclude that much of Lungren's argument is unpersuasive. We are not justified in proscribing drug possession because drug use leads to lost productivity, for example, as conduct that deliberately and directly causes lost productivity neither is nor ought to be criminalized. Because no one proposes to prohibit acts that make workers less productive—such as deliberately quitting one's job and becoming unemployed—it follows that conduct that merely increases the risk of becoming less productive should not be a crime. Proscribing

177. Daniel Lungren: "Legalization Would Be a Mistake," in Timothy Lynch, ed.: *After Prohibition* (Washington, D.C.: Cato Institute, 2000), pp.179, 180–181.
178. Some longitudinal studies suggest that, as a class, moderate users of illicit drugs are more psychologically well-adjusted than abstainers. See, for example, Jonathan Shedler and Jack Block: "Adolescent Drug Use and Psychological Health," 45 *American Psychologist* 612 (1990).
179. James Q. Wilson: "Drugs and Crime," in Michael Tonry and James Q. Wilson, eds.: *Drugs and Crime* (Chicago: University of Chicago Press, 1990), p.522.
180. See the references in Lynn Zimmer and John Morgan: *Marijuana Myths, Marijuana Facts* (New York: Lindesmith Center, 1997), p.90.

conduct that causes the risk of an undesirable outcome while failing to proscribe conduct that directly and deliberately brings about that very outcome is incompatible with a principle in that part of a theory of criminalization that pertains to inchoate offenses.

Do the foregoing considerations show that the offense of drug possession—an offense of implicit risk prevention—cannot be justified by a theory of criminalization that includes the consummate harm requirement? Of course not. The latter requirement merely constrains what can count as an acceptable rationale for an offense of risk prevention. Perhaps other rationales for the crime of drug possession *do* satisfy the consummate harm requirement. Lungren himself lists some more promising candidates for harm X; he alleges, *inter alia,* that illicit drug use increases child abuse. I concede that this rationale for drug proscriptions satisfies the consummate harm requirement. After all, conduct that deliberately and directly abuses children is and ought to be criminalized.

But we have not yet completed that part of a theory of criminalization that pertains to offenses of risk prevention. A fourth principle, which I ultimately call the *culpability* constraint, is needed as well. The final prong of our test rejects criminal laws that are more extensive than necessary to achieve their objectives. As we have seen, this condition imposes a presumption against overinclusive criminal legislation—a presumption that jeopardizes a great many offenses of risk prevention. Recall that a statute is overinclusive when its justificatory rationale applies to some but not all of the conduct proscribed. Because the purpose of an inchoate offense is to reduce the probability of an ultimate harm, a given offense of risk prevention is overinclusive when a defendant can breach it *without* increasing the likelihood of that harm. How can a theory of criminalization allow such a person to be punished?[181] In my earlier discussion of moving-vehicles offenses, I conceded that an overinclusive statute might be justified because of the practical difficulties of separating the epistemically fortunate from the epistemically privileged. I admitted that we must regrettably tolerate overinclusive laws when substantial state objectives cannot be attained in their absence. Might this concession salvage the offense of drug possession? Unfortunately, no simple answer can be given. In light of the uncertain nature of harm X, no one can hope to demonstrate that epistemically privileged persons can or cannot be distinguished from those who are merely fortunate. In other words, it is nearly impossible to show that a drug proscription is more extensive than necessary to achieve its purpose. Once again, the most that can be accomplished is to identify a few plausible candidates for the ultimate harm X that this offense is designed to reduce, show how epistemically privileged persons can commit the offense without increasing the probability that X will occur, and propose a statute that is less extensive to reduce X. At that point, allocations of the burden of proof would play an important role. Those who defend the justifiability of the offense of drug possession must offer a different specification of the ultimate harm X, show that epistemically privileged persons

181. For earlier thoughts, see Douglas Husak: "Reasonable Risk Creation and Overinclusive Legislation," 1 *Buffalo Criminal Law Review* (1998), p.599. My current view is that a theory of criminalization should contain a strong but rebuttable presumption rather than an outright ban on overinclusive criminal legislation.

cannot commit this offense without increasing the probability that X will occur, or argue that a statute could not be drafted or enforced that would punish the epistemically fortunate while sparing the epistemically privileged. I am dubious that persons who endorse drug prohibitions will be able to meet this challenge. But we cannot know until we try; the test of criminalization operative in law today is so uncritical that the questions I raise are seldom addressed.

To support my suspicions, return to Lungren's several attempts to specify what I have called harm X. Recall his allegation that illicit drug use increases child abuse. I admitted that this rationale for drug proscriptions satisfies the consummate harm requirement. Suppose it satisfies the substantial risk constraint and the prevention constraint as well. Even so, Lungren's rationale fails to show that existing drug proscriptions are no more extensive than necessary to accomplish their objective. After all, the overwhelming majority of adults can and do use drugs without increasing the risk that a child will be abused. Therefore, this statute is overinclusive and presumptively unjustified. Some persons who use drugs without increasing the risk of child abuse are epistemically fortunate, whereas others are epistemically privileged. Thus far, this example parallels that of moving-vehicle offenses. At this point, however, the examples diverge, and the divergence is crucial for purposes of justification. I claim that the epistemically privileged class of drug users who do not increase the risk of child abuse is easily distinguished from the class of drug users who are merely fortunate. Moreover, it would be simple to draft a statute to reduce the likelihood that drug users would abuse children that did not simultaneously punish the epistemically privileged. A preferable statute, I submit, would prohibit drug use only among parents with children of a given age. Adults without children, or adults whose children were fully grown, would not be prohibited from using drugs. A statute punishing all drug users because some drug users increase the risk of child abuse, when the two classes of users are easily distinguished, is more extensive than necessary to accomplish Lungren's objective. This statute is overinclusive, and the presumption against overinclusive legislation is not rebutted. Unless other reasons show the more narrow statute to be inferior to the overinclusive prohibition Lungren favors, I conclude that this particular specification of harm X does not justify a broad proscription of drug use in a theory of criminalization that accepts the external constraints I have described. Perhaps some other specification of harm X will justify a general proscription of drug use; I cannot be expected to rebut every possible rationale before we are entitled to reject the offense as unjustified. The burden of proof should be placed on those who favor the categorical prohibition.

It is apparent that a great deal of guesswork is needed to show that given offenses of implicit risk prevention—like drug proscriptions—fail our test of criminalization. Still, it is clear that many overlapping and/or ancillary drug offenses are almost certainly overinclusive, with little need for conjecture. Earlier, I discussed the strict liability element in statutes prohibiting drug possession or distribution in proximity to a school zone.[182] Although the proscribed acts may

182. See chapter 2, section I

seem especially culpable and important to deter, almost none of the cases in which this charge is brought involve sales of drugs to minors.[183] These statutes have been construed so broadly that virtually all drug offenses in urban areas fall within their parameters.[184] It is nearly impossible to find a place in a municipality that is *not* within 1,000 feet of a school zone. Federal law in particular ensures this result. It originally prohibited drug distribution near a "schoolyard," but was subsequently amended to include public housing projects, public or private youth centers, public swimming pools, or video arcades.[185] Recall that a defendant was convicted of this offense even though she distributed drugs within a prison that happened to be near a school.[186] The risk that schoolchildren will use drugs is not increased in this kind of situation. It is difficult to imagine that schoolchildren would break into prison to procure drugs.

As I have emphasized, a presumption against overinclusive criminal laws would jeopardize any number of penal statutes; drug prohibitions hardly are unique. To further support my claim, I propose to briefly consider the regime of gun control.[187] Guns and drugs are generally thought to be among the most dangerous instrumentalities in the United States today. Unlike our system of drug control, however, which seeks to ban the distribution and possession of many given substances altogether, the primary goal of gun control policy is to "[keep] firearms out of the hands of dangerous and irresponsible persons."[188] In other words, the central objective is to prevent members of ineligible groups from owning guns. The list of persons prohibited from owning guns has grown over time. The first important federal gun laws—the National Firearms Act of 1934 and the Federal Firearms Act of 1938—prohibited the transfer of firearms to fugitives or to persons convicted or under indictment for a violent crime. The Gun Control Act of 1968, the Firearms Owners' Protection Act of 1986, and the Brady Handgun Violence Prevention Act of 1993 expanded this list by adding all felons, minors, illegal aliens, illicit drug users, adjudicated mental incompetents, persons dishonorably discharged from the military, anyone who renounces his citizenship, and those under a restraining order for domestic violence.[189] Countless ancillary regulations are designed to enhance the effectiveness of this general strategy—to help ensure that ineligible persons do not manage to obtain firearms. The Gun Control Act of 1968 required purchasers to testify to their eligibility but did not make licensed dealers verify the accuracy of the information they were given. The Brady law required licensees to delay the sale until they

---

183. See New Jersey Commission to Review Criminal Sentencing: *Report on New Jersey's Drug-Free Zone Crimes and Proposal for Reform* (December 2005), pp.9–10.

184. See Richard Singer: "The Model Penal Code and Three Two (Possibly Only One) Way Courts Avoid Mens Rea," 4 *Buffalo Criminal Law Review* 139, 195–206 (2000).

185. 21 U.S.C. §860 (2004).

186. *New Jersey v. Ogar*, 551 A.2d 1037 (1989).

187. For earlier thoughts, see Douglas Husak: "Guns and Drugs: Case Studies on the Principled Limits of the Criminal Sanction," 23 *Law and Philosophy* 437 (2004).

188. James B. Jacobs and Kimberly A. Potter: "Keeping Guns Out of the 'Wrong' Hands: The Brady Law and the Limits of Regulation," 86 *Journal of Criminal Law and Criminology* 93 (1995).

189. See the complete list in 18 U.S.C. §922 (2001).

could conduct a background check on prospective handgun buyers.[190] But no one believes that these ancillary provisions are more than marginally effective in achieving their goal of keeping guns out of the wrong hands. The state has made it somewhat more difficult, time consuming, and expensive for dangerous individuals to acquire guns. Still, the system is easily circumvented; the Brady Act does not prevent "straw purchases" by which disqualified persons enlist a friend or relative to buy a gun for them. Moreover, ineligible buyers can easily purchase a firearm from a seller who is not a federal licensee. Subsequent legislative initiatives have sought to extend the scope of background checks under the Brady law to firearms not bought from federal licensees. Several commentators agree that "the top priority for gun policy is to close the gaping loophole in the current regulatory system, which exempts private sales of used guns from the background-check requirements imposed on licensed gun dealers."[191]

For present purposes, the most important point is that our present strategy seeks to minimize the risk of violence by trying to keep guns out of the hands of dangerous persons. But no efforts are made to ensure that given individuals are indeed dangerous before they are barred from owning guns. Instead, persons are disqualified on actuarial grounds—that is, because of their membership in designated groups. The difficulty with this policy is apparent. Most (and perhaps all) of the disqualified groups contain significant numbers of members who are not dangerous, and whose gun ownership would not create a substantial risk of harm—at least, no greater risk than that of the average person.[192] If I am correct, it follows that our current system of gun control is overinclusive.

Consider three examples. The Brady law bars all felons from owning guns, no matter what their felony or how long ago it occurred.[193] It is highly unlikely, however, that an elderly man who was convicted of insider trading 20 years earlier poses a greater risk of harm by owning a gun than the average person. In addition, users of controlled substances are ineligible to possess guns. Where is the evidence that consumers of each illicit drug, such as marijuana, are more likely to misuse firearms? Finally, illegal aliens are prohibited from owning guns. No evidence indicates that illegal aliens pose a greater risk of harm of gun violence than the average person. In any event, it is clear that significant numbers of illegal aliens pose no appreciable risk of harm at all. Hence each of these three exclusions is overbroad.[194] The fact that our current strategy of gun control is overinclusive will not disturb those citizens who are convinced that we need more rather than

190. Mandatory background checks required under the Brady law were held unconstitutional in *Printz v. United States*, 521 U.S. 898 (1997). However, all the states covered by Brady—those that did not already provide for background checks as a matter of state law—agreed to implement the background checks voluntarily.
191. Philip J. Cook and Jens Ludwig: *Gun Violence: The Real Costs* (New York: Oxford University Press, 2000), p.12.
192. It is noteworthy that the California Supreme Court has held that the carrying of a concealed weapon by an ex-felon, though felonious, is not a felony inherently dangerous to human life that triggers applications of the felony-murder rule. See *People v. Satchell*, 489 P.2d 1361 (1972).
193. Federal law authorizes the removal of this "firearms disability" for felons with an adequate "record and reputation," but no applications to allow gun ownership have been approved under this provision since 1992.
194. Of course, felons lose other rights as well, such as the right to vote. But it is hard to see how this policy would survive if subjected to a heightened level of scrutiny. As one commentator has noted, "there are so many

less gun control in our country today. Felons, drug users, or illegal aliens who
are punished for unlawful gun possession are unlikely to attract much sympathy
from the public. Nonetheless, overinclusion *should* be a grave concern; our theory
of criminalization creates a presumption against such legislation by condemning
statutes that are more broad than necessary to accomplish their purposes. Later
I suggest how a less inclusive statute could be drafted without undermining the
important objective of reducing gun violence.

Many commentators respond to this difficulty by contending that our current
system of gun control is too selective.[195] Perhaps a better idea is to ban the possession and distribution of guns altogether. In other words, our regime of gun
control should mimic that of drug control. This proposal, however, would only
compound the problem of overinclusion. If the injustice caused by overinclusion infects our current strategy of trying to keep guns out of the wrong hands,
it would certainly plague a more sweeping proposal to prohibit gun ownership
altogether. First, notice how wide the net of criminality would need to be cast
if guns were to become contraband, illegal for anyone to possess. This proposal
would instantly transform tens of millions of law-abiding Americans into criminals. Although no one knows the exact figure, approximately 250 million guns
are in private hands throughout the United States. Perhaps 100 million of these
are handguns. Roughly 40% of households report owning at least one gun; about
26% own a handgun. Relatively few of these owners create a substantial risk of
harm. Gary Kleck observes "that if gun restrictions were indiscriminately aimed
at reducing gun availability in the general population rather than just some high-
risk subsets of it, for every gun seized (or kept out of civilian hands) that would
eventually be involved in a crime, perhaps about 100 'noncriminal' guns would
have to be seized, with the ratio probably in excess of 50 even if the effort focused
solely on handguns."[196] Suppose, then, the state were to concentrate on "Satur-
day Night Specials"—the type of gun preferred by criminals. One problem with
this idea involves the substitution effects I mentioned in the context of drug
policy: Criminals may simply substitute more lethal firearms for those that are
banned.[197] But a more fundamental difficulty is that only 1% to 2% of these guns
would ever be used in a violent crime.[198] These statistics should alarm those who
are worried about the twin problems of too many criminal laws and too much
punishment. Criminal law minimalists should not be enthusiastic about a plan
to transform 50 or more people into offenders in order to prevent a crime that
one of them may commit. The number of criminals—already swelled by drug

constitutional arguments against the disenfranchisement of felons that one can only wonder at the survival of the
practice." George P. Fletcher: "Disenfranchisement as Punishment: Reflections on the Racial Uses of Infamia," 46
UCLA Law Review 1895, 1903 (1999).
195. Former Senator Chafee of Rhode Island would ban the manufacture, sale, and home possession of handguns within the United States. See also Nicholas Dixon: "Why We Should Ban Handguns in the United States,"
12 *St. Louis University Public Law Review* (1993), p.243; and Deborah Prothrow-Stith and Michaele Weissman:
Deadly Consequences (New York: Harper-Collins, 1991).
196. See Gary Kleck: *Targeting Guns: Firearms and Their Control* (New York: Aldine De Gruyter, 1997), p.9.
197. *Id.*, pp.114–117.
198. Kleck indicates that this is the most realistic estimate in *id*, p.131.

prohibitions—would rise exponentially to include the vast population of individuals whose conduct would suddenly be proscribed.

Of course, overinclusion is not always fatal in our theory of criminalization. As Kleck points out, however, groups with the highest rates of gun ownership tend to have the lowest rates of violence. They include residents in rural areas, those with higher incomes, whites, middle-age and older individuals, and married couples. Conversely, groups with the lowest rates of gun ownership tend to have the highest rates of violence. They include urbanites, the poor, blacks and Hispanics, the young, and unmarried individuals. Gender provides the only consistent exception to this pattern; men are more likely both to be violent and to own guns.[199] But the central point remains: Whatever may be true of a violent minority, the demographic characteristics of gun owners indicate that few pose a substantial risk of harm. The rationale for gun prohibition simply does not apply to most of them. Unless a more narrow statute simply cannot be drafted without undermining the objective these laws are designed to serve, a minimalist theory of criminalization must reject categorical schemes of gun proscriptions. In case this conclusion sounds too pessimistic, I repeat that nothing I have said forecloses strategies that do not involve punishment to reduce the availability of guns as well as the incidence of gun violence. The penal law is special; noncriminal devices to achieve important state objectives may be justifiable even though criminal statutes are not.

If the foregoing arguments are sound, many implicit offenses of risk prevention—like the (real) crime of drug possession and the (imaginary) crime of gun possession—are almost certainly overinclusive and presumptively unjustified. A small handful of these offenses are exceptions. The offense of driving on the wrong side of the road, for example, specifies a *malum in se* and solves a coordination problem. This offense is not overinclusive, as deviations from the solution to the coordination problem almost always pose a danger. Exceptions aside, how might the substantive criminal law be reformed to avoid overinclusion?[200] I will briefly sketch some of the several possible approaches that might be taken. First, one might ensure that the very individuals whose conduct is proscribed are those who pose elevated risks of harm. An ideal criminal code would not allow a person to be punished for creating a risk of harm in the absence of good reason to believe he posed that very risk. Although the individualized tests required to implement this solution would often be cumbersome, the resulting scheme would not be overinclusive. A second approach would require offenses to include a term to ensure that a substantial risk of harm is created by the conduct proscribed.[201] "Unreasonable" or "dangerous" are possible candidates. The offense of dangerous

---

199. *Id.*, pp.21–22.
200. Frederick Schauer contends that "*all* rules are either actually or potentially under- and over-inclusive." See *op. cit.*, note 139, pp.32–33, n.23 (emphasis in original). If Schauer is correct, underinclusion and overinclusion may be inevitable as long as law is composed of rules. In any event, none of the rationales Schauer examines in favor of adopting overinclusive and underinclusive rules—fairness, reliance, efficiency, risk aversion or separation of powers—provides any reason to reject a presumption against overinclusive *criminal* statutes.
201. See Duff: *op. cit.*, note 165, p.62.

driving, for example, is not overinclusive. Defendants can hardly complain that their acts of dangerous driving do not create a substantial risk. No theory of criminalization should oppose the enactment of an offense of using a gun or drug unreasonably, for example.[202]

In what follows, however, I briefly defend yet a third solution.[203] My preferred approach is to enact only those offenses of risk prevention that require defendants to act culpably with respect to the ultimate harm to be prevented. The criminal law employs this device when imposing liability for the well-known inchoate offenses of attempt, solicitation, and conspiracy. A person should not be guilty of attempting to commit a crime, for example, unless he *intends* to commit that crime.[204] Even though many of these defendants will not succeed in causing harm, there is good reason to think that each of them deserves to be punished. A person who intends to commit a crime—and performs an overt act that constitutes an attempt to do so—clearly acts wrongfully and deserves hardship and censure. Existing law does not require an intention to bring about the ultimate harm when persons commit offenses of implicit risk prevention. Remarkably, defendants need act with no culpability whatever with respect to the harm to be prevented. One might even say that offenses of implicit risk prevention impose a covert kind of strict liability with respect to the ultimate harm. Existing drug offenses, for example, punish individuals who act with no culpability at all—not even negligence—for harm X.[205] Persons can and do, for example, incur liability for their use and possession of illicit drugs, despite having no culpability with respect to any of the harms Lundgren mentions. This injustice is easily remedied. Commentators should be less critical of a statute imposing criminal liability for drug possession if persons could not be punished unless they intended to cause, knew they would cause, or were reckless about causing an ultimate harm by their use of drugs. Even a requirement of negligence with respect to the ultimate harm X would represent a quantum leap in the justice of our drug policy.

This strategy to distinguish justified from unjustified inchoate offenses implements the fourth and final constraint that should be included in that part of a theory of criminalization that pertains to offenses of risk prevention: a principle I call the *culpability* requirement. This principle withholds liability from persons who create a risk of harm unless they have some degree of culpability for the ultimate harm risked. It is not enough that the performance of the proscribed conduct just happens to make the occurrence of the ultimate harm more likely. Lighting a match in proximity to a haystack, for example, increases the probability of a fire,

202. Some commentators caution that such solutions "would burden liberty more than a more broadly crafted law" because it would give too much discretion to law enforcement officials. See Arthur Ripstein: "Prohibition and Preemption," 5 *Legal Theory* 235, 259 (1999).
203. Additional solutions might exist. For example, the state could allow a *defense* when defendants commit the offense under circumstances in which they do not increase the risk of the ultimate harm to be prevented. But allowing defenses is a poor substitute for dealing with the problems caused by crimes that should not have been enacted in the first place.
204. See Duff: *op. cit.*, note 165, p.5.
205. Moreover, the offense of drug possession is supplemented by overlapping and ancillary offenses that are even *more* overinclusive—like the offense of possessing drug paraphernalia.

but penal liability for this behavior is not justified on this basis alone. Persons who perform the proscribed act (e.g., lighting the match) should not be punished unless they are culpable for the ultimate harm (e.g., the fire) to be prevented. Reasonable minds may differ about exactly *how* culpable offenders must be in order for penal liability to be justified. Few criminal codes punish persons for the inchoate offenses of attempt, solicitation, or conspiracy unless they perform an overt act with the *intention* to bring about an ultimate harm. But suppose knowledge replaced purpose as the degree of culpability needed for liability for these offenses. As a result, a defendant would be guilty of solicitation, for example, by performing an act he knew would encourage the commission of a crime, even though he did not perform his act with that objective in mind. Or suppose that recklessness sufficed as the level of culpability needed to impose liability for inchoate offenses. As a result, a defendant would be guilty of solicitation by consciously disregarding the substantial and unjustifiable risk that his act would encourage the commission of a crime. As far as I am aware, no commentator has suggested that liability for an inchoate offense would be justified unless defendants are at least reckless with respect to the ultimate harm risked.[206] As I have indicated, however, even a culpability requirement of negligence for offenses of risk prevention would be a major innovation in the substantive criminal law.

The implementation of the culpability requirement would solve many of the problems associated with Duff's remaining category of offenses of risk prevention: those he calls indirect. Recall that offenses of risk prevention are direct "if the relevant harm would ensue from the criminalized conduct without any intervening wrongful human action"; they are indirect "if the harm would ensue only given further, wrongful actions by the agent or by others."[207] Causing an explosion that endangers life is a direct endangerment offense, whereas carrying a weapon in public is an example of an indirect endangerment offense. Although Duff himself is reluctant to generalize about the justifiability of these kinds of offense,[208] many commentators sensibly resist the criminalization of otherwise lawful behavior simply because third parties might take advantage of the opportunity to commit a crime.[209] The culpability requirement ensures that such conduct will not be criminalized unless the defendant himself is culpable with respect to the ultimate harm to be prevented—in this case, that third parties commit a crime. The very same analysis applies to cases in which the harm would not occur without further wrongful acts by the agent himself. Persons should not be punished for a prior act that is harmless unless they are at least negligent about whether it will lead them to commit a subsequent act that would cause an ultimate harm.[210]

---

206. See Glanville Williams: "The Problem of Reckless Attempts," *Criminal Law Review* 365 (1983).
207. Duff: *op. cit.*, note 165, p.62.
208. *Id.*, p.64.
209. See Andrew von Hirsch: "Extending the Harm Principle: 'Remote' Harms and Fair Imputation," in Simester and Smith: *op. cit.*, note 168, p.259.
210. Cases of intoxication present this issue most starkly. But the most celebrated case that applies this principle, interpreting a statute precluding the negligent operation of a vehicle resulting in death, is *People v. Decina*, 138 N.E.2d 799 (1956). Although the defendant was not acting culpably at the time he caused death—indeed, he was undergoing an epileptic seizure and thus was not acting at all—Decina's liability was based on his prior culpable act of failing to take medication that would have prevented the accident.

A corollary of the culpability requirement is worth noting. Our test of intermediate scrutiny precludes criminal statutes that are more extensive than necessary to
achieve their objectives. But many existing inchoate offenses not only punish individuals who act without culpability with respect to the ultimate harm to be prevented, they also impose liability on persons who have taken effective precautions
to *minimize* the probability that harm will occur. These persons should not be
punished if they are epistemically privileged and easily identified. If given chemi-
cals are dangerous only when stored improperly, for example, a statute should not
proscribe their possession *simpliciter*. An unqualified prohibition is more extensive
than necessary to achieve its objective, and must be narrowed by the insertion of
an appropriate "unless" clause. More abstractly, when given measures succeed in
reducing the probability of harm below whatever level is deemed to be substantial, an offense of risk prevention is unjustifiably overinclusive if it punishes those
epistemically privileged persons who adopt such measures. What could be the
justification for punishing all individuals, simply because a subset has failed to
take proper precautions? If possible, criminal statutes should be drafted to impose
liability only on those persons whose conduct creates the relevant risk, and the
relevant risk is not created by those who adopt effective measures to reduce it.

In this section I have sought to defend four constraints that should be included
in a theory of criminalization designed to limit the proliferation of offenses of
risk prevention. First, the substantial risk requirement: These offenses are justified only if they are designed to reduce a substantial risk. Second, the prevention
requirement: The proscription in question is justified only if it actually decreases
the likelihood of the ultimate harm. Third, the consummate harm requirement:
An offense to prevent the risk of harm is justified only when a statute proscribing
conduct that deliberately and directly causes that very harm would be justified as
well. Fourth, the culpability requirement: An offense designed to reduce the risk
of an ultimate harm is justified only when defendants act culpably with respect
to the ultimate harm risked. The latter two constraints are more complex than
their two predecessors, requiring more elaboration. With just a bit of ingenuity,
I believe that each of these four principles can be derived from the more general
theory of criminalization I have borrowed from a constitutional test of intermediate scrutiny. These constraints allow the state to further the general goal of inchoate offenses such as attempt, solicitation, and conspiracy: to punish risky conduct
before harm occurs and thereby to reduce the occurrence of harm. Like everything
else about this theory of criminalization, these principles will be difficult to interpret and apply to particular cases. I have not tried to downplay these problems;
they are painfully evident in my discussions of drug and gun control. But criminal
law minimalists actually may take comfort from the extent of these difficulties.
Because the burden to justify penal laws should be allocated to the state, any problems in applying these four principles will help to retard the growth in the number
of offenses of risk prevention.

My theory of criminalization—or, rather, my sketch of a theory—is now complete. This theory consists in the conjunction of the four internal constraints
introduced in chapter 2 and the three external constraints defended here. I have
identified a total of seven distinct but overlapping constraints and developed a

number of arguments about why we should accept them. The most pressing challenge that remains, of course, is to provide substantive content for each of these principles. This is the task of a lifetime—indeed, of many lifetimes. Commentators will succeed only if they collaborate in deciding how these constraints should be construed and applied to particular cases. Their efforts will help to realize the minimalist aspirations we all should share: a contraction in the size and scope of the criminal law and the infliction of state punishment. Although an incredible amount of hard work remains to be done, even my sketch of a theory should be deemed a major advance if it improves on competing accounts of criminalization. My final task is to show that my theory meets this standard.

4

Alternative Theories of Criminalization

No one should dispute that the United States suffers from lots of punishment and lots of criminal law, and that these phenomena are related in ways that are obvious and not so obvious. I contend that enormous injustice results because we have *too* much punishment and criminal law. Although these claims are supported by intuitions that are widely shared, a normative theory of criminalization is needed to reinforce them. I have defended such a theory in the previous two chapters. This theory has many component parts, containing a number of overlapping yet distinct constraints that limit the authority of the state to impose penal liability. I have argued that some of these constraints are internal to the criminal law itself, while others derive from a more controversial political view about the conditions under which important rights—like the right not to be punished—may be infringed. Implementing this theory would advance a minimalist agenda by reducing the numbers of persons punished, the severity of their punishments, as well as the reach of the penal sanction generally.

The *extent* of this reduction in the size and scope of the criminal law is hard to anticipate, as little has been done to provide content to the internal and external constraints. We lack detailed accounts of harm, wrongfulness, and desert, for example, and have noted several difficulties applying a test of intermediate scrutiny to actual cases. In addition to the problems of which I am aware, legal philosophers are bound to find further shortcomings in the theory of criminalization I have sketched. Still, I trust that commentators will not exaggerate the significance of these difficulties. Uncertainties notwithstanding, I have offered numerous illustrations of how the application of this theory would help to combat the phenomenon of overcriminalization. Because rights are implicated by all penal legislation and the burden of proof in defending criminal statutes should be allocated to the state, I am confident that many of the new kinds of offense I have described will prove impossible to justify.

Despite the many complex issues my theory leaves unresolved, it is clear that the United States does not implement a better theory of criminalization at the present time. No one is prepared to argue that the exponential growth of criminal law and punishment conforms to any set of principles that should be dignified by the name of a *theory*. As William Stuntz observes, "American criminal law's historical development has borne no relation to any plausible normative theory—unless "more" counts as a normative theory."[1] I have argued that our current theory of

---

1. William J. Stuntz: "The Pathological Politics of Criminal Law," *100 Michigan Law Review* 505, 508 (2001).

criminalization—or what passes for such a theory—is woefully deficient. Constitutional law is far too permissive toward criminal statutes and has brought about the predicament of overcriminalization from which we now suffer. And I protest strongly against one possible response that might be made to the uncertainties that arise both in contemporary constitutional law and in my minimalist theory. According to this response, we should reject *both* approaches and muddle along as best we can without a set of principles that comprise a theory. This response, I fear, is a recipe for disaster and will only perpetuate the status quo. In this context, we should invoke the adage "it takes a theory to beat a theory." Commentators should accept my account unless and until they can produce a competitor that is superior to it.

Does any such competitor exist? This is the general question to which I turn in this final chapter. In what follows, I describe and critically examine what I take to be three distinct approaches to criminalization that legal philosophers have constructed: economic analysis, utilitarianism, and legal moralism.[2] Each of these accounts has spawned a massive literature, and I do not pretend to subject any to a thorough critique. My remarks are relatively brief. It is a truism that theories are easier to attack than to defend, and each of the views I discuss here has been attacked on countless occasions. Time and space are better used, I believe, to explicate and support my own theory than to discredit its rivals. I hope to say enough to reveal the inadequacies of these alternatives, although each is sufficiently resilient to offer a reply to many of my objections. At some point, however, these replies become more clever than convincing, and my ambition is to inflict enough damage to support my judgment that a new approach to criminalization is needed.

Despite the topic of this chapter, I confess to some misgivings as to whether there really *are* competitive theories about the scope and limits of the penal sanction. As I have indicated, with the possible exception of Jeremy Bentham, no prominent legal philosopher—living or dead—is closely associated with a theory of criminalization. Each of the alternatives I discuss suffers from a common shortcoming: It is too simple, containing too few resources to show why given impositions of the penal sanction are unjustified. Two of these views—economic analysis and utilitarianism—purport to derive implications for criminalization from more comprehensive normative theories and thus fail to capture what is special or distinctive about criminal liability. Legal moralism—the last alternative—is best construed as a partial theory, embellishing a single constraint that cannot function as a general account of criminalization. I focus on how these views differ from mine, and emphasize how my theory emerges better by comparison—even though it too is problematic. But if the deficiencies in these alternatives are as glaring as I conclude, we should be more willing to tolerate difficulties with the view I have defended. I encourage commentators to improve this theory rather than to reject it outright and thereby acquiesce in our current plight of overcriminalization.

---

2. I do not pretend that no other accounts of criminalization might be constructed. It is somewhat surprising, for example, that no detailed contractarian theory of the limits of the criminal law has been defended.

I also confess to some misgivings about my choice of *when* to discuss these three alternatives. Rival theories could be examined before or after my preferred account is introduced. If these alternatives were examined *before* I presented my theory, I would have delayed the exposition of my most original ideas. But a discussion of these alternatives *after* my theory has been presented threatens to be anticlimactic. I have decided to take the latter risk rather than the former.

I: LAW AND ECONOMICS

I choose an unusual place to begin my survey of alternative theories of criminalization: the economic analysis of law. No jurisprudential movement in the past half century has stimulated more legal reform in the United States than that of law and economics, yielding monumental insights in civil law. Nonetheless, I describe my starting point as unusual for a simple reason: This school of thought has made almost no contributions in the criminal domain. Commentators in this tradition have made progress describing optimal expenditures on law enforcement and characterizing levels of punishment that maximize deterrence. Their positions on these matters are presented in algebraic formulae that exceed the competence of most legal philosophers.[3] When we turn to matters of criminalization, however, the significance of this movement has been far less impressive.[4] Dropping all pretense of mathematical precision, many law and economics scholars candidly admit that "there is no simple, overarching definition of criminal acts."[5] Still, a few theorists have advanced general principles that purport to govern the imposition of criminal sanctions.[6] In what follows, I focus largely on the views of Richard Posner—the school's most eloquent spokesperson—in order to assess the strengths and weaknesses of the economic approach to criminalization generally.[7] Although the economic analysis of law has progressed substantially from the time of Posner's important contribution, relatively little additional work on the implications of economic analysis for the substantive criminal law has been produced.[8]

Why begin with a view that has won so few adherents? I suggest three reasons. First, economic analysts are thought to *have* a theory of criminalization. If the rivals to my theory are as few as I believe, this fact alone makes their account worth examining. I will try to show, however, that their central claims are riddled with so many qualifications of uncertain scope that we should be reluctant to concede

---

3. See Steven Shavell: *Foundations of Economic Analysis of Law* (Cambridge: Belknap Press of Harvard University Press, 2004), pp.473–539.

4. George Fletcher claims that leading scholars in the law and economics movement "have nothing to say about substantive criminal law." George P. Fletcher: *The Grammar of Criminal Law: American, European, International* (New York: Oxford University Press, 2007), p.59 n140.

5. Shavell: *op. cit.,* note 3, p.540.

6. Perhaps the first such attempt among contemporary economic theorists is Gary Becker: "Crime and Punishment: An Economic Approach," 76 *Journal of Political Economy* 169 (1968).

7. Ricahrd A. Posner: "An Economic Theory of the Criminal Law," 85 *Columbia Law Review* 1193 (1985).

8. A subsequent commentator in the same tradition describes Posner's contribution as "the only article, of which I am aware, that offers a positive economic theory of the substantive criminal law." Keith N. Hylton: "The Theory of Penalties and the Economics of Criminal Law," 1:2 *Review of Law and Economics* 1 (2005).

that economic analysis really qualifies as a genuine competitor to my theory. If my approach should be described as a sketch, economic analysis must be characterized as a scribble. Second, we should try to understand the widespread appeal of economic models generally. Many commentators seem attracted to economic analysis because they are averse to the apparent evaluation of law by reference to norms of morality. Thus they are tempted to try to construct a rationale for the criminal law on some other foundation. This motivation should be addressed—and discredited. Finally, one of the most intriguing parts of the economic analysis of crime is difficult to refute without adopting some of the more controversial features of my theory. In particular, we will be hard-pressed to reject the economic perspective on why we need punitive sanctions at all without conceding that the criminal law serves an important expressive function. If I am correct, the most compelling objection to economic analysis helps to bolster my account. In any event, philosophers of criminal law have much to learn from the failure of the economic analysis of crime.

In his seminal article, Posner begins by claiming that "the substantive doctrines of the criminal law . . . can be given an economic meaning and can indeed be shown to promote efficiency."[9] His general ambition, in other words, is to "derive the basic criminal prohibitions from the concept of efficiency."[10] Specifically, Posner alleges that "the major function of criminal law in a capitalist society is to prevent people from bypassing the system of voluntary, compensated exchange—the 'market,' explicit or implicit—in situations where . . . the market is a more efficient method of allocating resources than forced exchange."[11] *Efficiency*—the ultimate objective of law—is a technical term of art, equivalent in economic analysis to wealth maximization.[12] According to Posner, the particular distribution of resources that maximizes wealth places all goods in the hands of persons who value them most. One individual values a resource more than another if he is willing to pay more for it in money (or its equivalent). Therefore, Posner concludes, "the market is, virtually by definition, the most efficient method of allocating resources."[13] What is and ought to be forbidden, he concludes, "is a class of inefficient acts"—acts that fail to maximize wealth.[14]

After advancing this bold thesis, however, Posner immediately qualifies it in several respects. Most notably, he continues: "I certainly do not want to be understood, however, as arguing that every rule of the criminal law is efficient, or that efficiency is or ought to be the only social value considered by legislators and courts in creating and interpreting the rules of the criminal law."[15] Unfortunately, Posner does not elaborate on this important qualification. What values other than

---

9. *Op. cit.*, note 7, p.1194.
10. *Id.*, p.1195.
11. *Id.*
12. It is an open question whether efficiency maximizes utility, welfare, or any subjective state. Thus economic analysis is distinct from utilitarianism. See *id.*, p.1196 n.9.
13. *Id.*, p.1195.
14. *Id.*
15. *Id.*, pp.1194–1195. He later concludes that "*most* of the distinctive doctrines of the criminal law can be explained as if the objective of that law were to promote economic efficiency." *Id.*, p.1195 (emphasis added).

efficiency should the criminal law promote, how should they be identified and defended, and when should these values outweigh considerations of efficiency when they conflict? Posner does not try to answer these crucial questions, so his first qualification threatens to swallow his general rule. If these other values are numerous and supplant efficiency in a broad range of cases, we are left with the uninteresting claim that economic considerations should play an unspecified role in decisions about criminalization.

This qualification aside, Posner contends that his account "provides a straight-forward economic rationale for forbidding theft and other acquisitive crimes."[16] Theft is proscribed because it is a form of *market bypassing* that cannot possibly improve the allocation of resources. If I covet my neighbor's car, for example, it is more efficient to require me to negotiate and agree on a price than to allow me to take it and be made by a court to pay whatever the judge decides it is worth. Inefficient acts must be prevented, and simply requiring *ex post* compensation would fail to do so. If market bypassers merely were ordered to compensate victims for the losses they inflict, they would be indifferent between the option of buying goods *ex ante* on the market or taking these goods and paying their market price *ex post*. In the jargon of Guido Calabresi and Douglas Melamed, persons would lack an incentive to respect the distinction between property and liability rules—a distinction grounded in considerations of efficiency.[17] In addition, of course, compensation need not be paid until some time after the thief has enjoyed the free use of the property. Even more important, the probability of detection is less than one, so a great many perpetrators would not be required to pay compensation at all. To prevent persons from taking goods (even if they are caught and made to compensate owners *ex post*), the amount of damages must be greater than the market value of the loss inflicted. What is sometimes called a "kicker" is added to the damages to be paid by the defendant in order to induce him to engage in consensual transactions. For these reasons, "it is inefficient to allow pure coercive transfers of wealth."[18]

It is hard to say whether this economic account should be construed to preserve any of the internal constraints I argued that a respectable theory of criminalization must include. Perhaps inefficient acts *could* be described as wrongful, and market bypassing *might* be characterized as the ultimate harm or evil that criminal offenses should seek to prevent. But how can this theory possibly explain the desert constraint: the requirement that punishments be deserved? I have stressed that a sensible theory of desert will include a principle of proportionality—a principle that makes the severity of the punishment sensitive to the seriousness of the crime. The seriousness of the crime, in turn, is partly a function of the culpability of the offender.[19] How can economic theories hope to justify the extraordinary

16. *Id.*, p.1196.
17. See Guido Calabresi and A. Douglas Melamed: "Property Rules, Liability Rules, and Inalienability: One View of the Cathedral," 85 *Harvard Law Review* 1089 (1972).
18. *Op. cit.*, note 7, p.1196.
19. See Andrew von Hirsch and Nils Jareborg: "Gauging Criminal Harm: A Living-Standard Analysis," 11 *Oxford Journal of Legal Studies* 1 (1991).

significance the criminal law attaches to culpability in its theory of desert?[20] The question is not only whether inefficient acts should be punished, but also how severely to punish them. Existing codes tend to sentence persons with increasing severity when they commit criminal acts negligently, recklessly, knowingly, or purposely.[21] Admittedly, many theorists have argued that the culpability structure of criminal codes should be fundamentally rethought. Perhaps the criminal law should increase[22] or decrease[23] the number of culpable states to be countenanced. But the question remains: Why impose a more severe sentence when a given defendant behaves more culpably than another? Why does everyone agree, for example, that murderers typically deserve a longer sentence than defendants who commit manslaughter, who in turn should be punished more harshly than those who are guilty of negligent homicide? Even if economic analysis can offer a plausible account of why the criminal law should care about culpability in the first place,[24] it fails to explain why the criminal law should care about culpability in the way that it does: through its commitment to proportionality in ensuring that the severity of punishment is deserved.[25] This problem, I think, is all but fatal to an economic analysis of the criminal law.

In what follows, however, I propose to set aside considerations of culpability in order to examine further difficulties with Posner's account of criminalization generally and of theft in particular. These problems are instructive, as economic models are almost certain to fail elsewhere if they are inadequate to explain property offenses. For three reasons, the economic rationale for preventing theft is not nearly as straightforward as Posner claims. First, it is not clear that this rationale explains why the state should proscribe coerced transfers of property when the thief values the stolen item more than its owner. Why can't some thefts be efficient? The standard explanation is that various "secondary costs"—in particular, the costs of security and of avoiding victimization—justify a blanket prohibition of theft.[26] This reply, however, is an *ipse dixit*; it is simply an article of faith that thefts must be inefficient when these secondary costs are included in the calculations. Second, it is worth noting that Posner confines the scope of economic analysis to capitalist societies. This restriction is necessary, because no one could believe that the function of the criminal law is to protect markets in states where no markets exist. Clearly, however, socialist societies have and need criminal law

---

20. See the discussion in Kenneth Simons: "Rethinking Mental States," 72 *Boston University Law Review* 463, 503–515 (1992).

21. See Douglas Husak: "The Serial View of Criminal Law Defenses," 3 *Criminal Law Forum* 369 (1992).

22. See Alan C. Michaels: "Acceptance: The Missing Mental State," 71 *Southern California Law Review* 953 (1998).

23. See Larry Alexander: "Insufficient Concern: A Unified Conception of Criminal Culpability," 88 *California Law Review* 931 (2000).

24. See Jeffrey S. Parker: "The Economics of Mens Rea," 79 *Virginia Law Review* 741 (1993).

25. One commentator purports to defend economic analysis by concluding that "the doctrine of criminal intent is, on its own, an empty concept. Its key function is to serve as a label used to distinguish conduct that falls in the always-socially-undesirable or market-bypassing categories from conduct that is potentially socially desirable." See Hylton: *Op. cit.*, note 8, p.9.

26. See Richard L. Hasen and Richard H. McAdams: "The Surprisingly Complex Case against Theft," 17 *International Review of Law and Economics*," 367 (1997).

too. The task of justifying infringements of the right not to be punished is no less
onerous when economic activity is controlled by the state; one would expect the
structure of this justification to be relatively similar in countries where the means
of production are publicly owned. Although social and cultural variables will alter
the shape of the substantive criminal law in different times and places, I strongly
doubt that the basic principles of criminalization will differ radically depending
on the fundamentals of political economy. Finally, Posner himself acknowledges
yet another "important qualification" to his position. He concedes that coercive
transfers of wealth are inefficient only when they are *pure*. A transfer of wealth is
pure, he alleges, when it is "not an incident of a productive act."[27] New technolo-
gies like cellular phones "also cause all sorts of wealth transfers that are involuntary
from the standpoint of the losers,"[28] but Posner supposes that these inventions
increase rather than decrease wealth. But why does this vague definition not also
apply, for example, to new devices that can be used to pick locks or steal copy-
righted materials? Without a substantive account of when transfers are pure or
impure, it is hard to decide whether his rationale for proscribing coerced transfers
of wealth is illuminating.[29]

Of course, the most obvious difficulty with Posner's account of criminalization
is not its application to property offenses but its extension to crimes of violence
that do not involve transfers of wealth in any obvious sense. When Smith bat-
ters Jones because of jealousy or hatred, for example, how can his behavior be
construed as a form of market bypassing? Posner replies that "crimes of passion
often bypass implicit markets."[30] Again, we encounter the curious qualifier "often."
More fundamentally, however, commentators have been left to puzzle about the
nature of the "implicit market" that is allegedly "bypassed" when criminals deliberately kill or rape one another—and about whether the existence of this implicit
market could possibly account for why acts of murder and rape are and ought to
be proscribed.[31]

If these several problems are so glaring, why bother to pay attention to economic
analysis in a survey of theories of criminalization? After all, this jurisprudential
school has almost no adherents among contemporary philosophers of criminal
law. My answer is that the law and economics movement deserves credit for raising the central but frequently neglected question of why we should have a criminal law at all. When one person deliberately harms another—as in cases of core
criminality—why not simply rely on the remedies available in civil law? Typically,
tortfeasors are required to compensate victims for the losses they cause, and the
advantages of treating criminals similarly are evident. In principle, we would not
have to struggle with the question of how to override the right not to be punished

27. *Op. cit.*, note 7, p.1196.
28. *Id.*
29. See Alvin K. Klevorick: "On the Economic Theory of Crime," in J. Roland Pennock and John W. Chapman,
eds.: *Criminal Justice: Nomos XXVII* (1985), p.289.
30. *Op. cit.*, note 7, p.1197.
31. As one commentator observes, "once one thinks of the world in terms of transactions, it is not surprising to find
that one's explanation of the criminal law would be given in terms of transactions. The problem comes in the initial
formulation." Jules Coleman: "Crimes and Transactions," 88 *California Law Review* 921, 925 (2000).

if no punishments had to be inflicted. In practice, hundreds of billions of dollars would be saved if the state could avoid impositions of penal sanctions. If we are clear about the conditions in which tort remedies are adequate or inadequate, we may come to identify the conditions under which criminal punishment is justified or unjustified. If tort remedies prove suitable in a wide range of cases, economic theory—more clearly than the two competitive accounts I canvass below—has an enormous potential to curb overcriminalization.

Commentators disagree about the conditions under which compensatory mechanisms may replace punishment. Different answers to this question suggest distinct limitations on the scope of the criminal sanction. One type of answer seeks to specify the *kinds* of loss for which the criminal sanction is uniquely appropriate. In particular, the losses caused by crimes might be *noncompensable*. When compensation is impossible or necessarily inadequate, tort remedies cannot substitute for punishment.[32] Some noncompensable losses are inflicted when crimes lack identifiable victims. Treason, counterfeiting, and corruption among public officials are prominent examples. Homicide causes the most obvious noncompensable loss when victims are easily identified, and thus is a clear candidate for criminal prohibitions. A surprising number of losses may turn out to be noncompensable if we expand our horizon beyond identifiable victims and include the impact of criminality on third parties. A system that permitted assaults if compensation were paid *ex post* might give rise to general fear and anxiety throughout the population. It is hard to imagine how third parties could be compensated for *these* losses. According to this train of thought, conduct should be criminalized when the failure to punish it would spread fear and anxiety throughout society, even if individuals knew they would be fully compensated if they were victimized.[33] This answer, however, threatens to expand the criminal sanction too broadly, dashing the hope that economic analysis could effectively combat the phenomenon of overcriminalization. Many of the losses caused by tort give rise to enormous trepidation among potential victims. Any reasonable passenger in a vehicle should be worried about the risk of a crash, but no one concludes that automobile accidents should be transformed from a tort to a criminal offense. The contrast between conduct that does or does not cause fear and anxiety throughout society maps poorly onto the contrast between conduct that should or should not be criminalized. More generally, no theory of noncompensable losses appears to provide a plausible account of when penal sanctions are justified.

Posner himself provides a very different reason why monetary penalties generally are insufficient. The sad but uncontestable fact is that the great majority of persons who inflict losses on others lack sufficient wealth to fully compensate their victims.[34] As a result, few victims would receive compensation. Impecunious defendants might be forced to labor to pay their debts, but this option encounters

---

32. See the discussion of the inadequacy of compensation in Mark R. Reiff: *Punishment, Compensation, and Law* (Cambridge: Cambridge University Press, 2005), pp.102–108.
33. See Robert Nozick: *Anarchy, State, and Utopia* (New York: Basic Books, 1974), p.69.
34. See the statistics about the rate of poverty among arrestees in Shavell: *op. cit.*, note 3, p.544.

both practical and principled difficulties. In Posner's view, criminal sanctions thus are reserved for "cases where the tort remedy bumps up against a solvency limitation. This means that the criminal law is designed primarily for the nonaffluent; the affluent are kept in line, for the most part, by tort law."[35] Of course, many tortfeasors have modest resources as well, but this problem is mollified by third-party insurance. Despite the availability of insurance for tort liability, no one would allow criminals to buy insurance against the risk of performing conduct the state would prefer to prohibit. A world in which "crime insurance" could be purchased would be counterproductive, giving rise to "acute moral hazard." More crimes would take place in this world than if crime insurance were banned.[36] Because many criminals are unable to afford compensation and cannot rely on insurance, nonmonetary sanctions are required to induce compliance. Thus, the state has little recourse but to resort to criminal liability and punishment.

Most criminal theorists scoff at Posner's account. But exactly what is wrong with it? Suppose (contrary to fact) that culpable wrongdoers who were rational *had* sufficient wealth to be deterred by the need to compensate their victims *ex post*. Surely economic analysts are correct to insist that civil liability should be the preferred default position. A minimalist theory of criminalization—including the theory I have sketched in the previous two chapters—precludes punitive sanctions when a less extensive alternative is available. If the necessary "kicker" is added and a particular defendant has the means to compensate, why are monetary penalties an inappropriate response to serious crime? I believe it is hard to refute Posner's account without adopting one of the more controversial components of my theory: the claim that the criminal law has an expressive function. How could mere compensation possibly convey the stigma inherent in criminal punishment? If the state has a substantial interest in expressing condemnation, it is hard to see how a nonpunitive response to core criminality could be adequate.

Let me expand on this idea by returning to the question whether economic analysis preserves the internal constraints in a theory of criminalization. Criminal conduct is wrongful, and the fact that the criminal law is centrally concerned with wrongs as well as with harms or losses shows the folly of supposing that compensation could ever provide a complete substitute for criminal liability. Apart from its role as a deterrent, compensation is designed to place the victim in the position he occupied prior to the defendant's act. Some scholars say that compensation *annuls* the tort.[37] Whatever plausibility this claim may have in the context of civil law, it seems wholly misplaced in the criminal domain. In some sense, compensation might annul the *loss* caused by an act of theft, for example. But thieves are and ought to be subject to criminal liability not merely for causing a loss but for doing so wrongfully. How can a defendant hope to compensate for the *wrong* of theft as something over and above the material loss he has inflicted? The deliberate taking

35. Posner: *op. cit.*, note 7, pp.1204–1205.
36. *Id.*, p.1203.
37. This conception of corrective justice was defended (although subsequently modified) by Jules Coleman: "Tort Law and the Demands of Corrective Justice," 67 *Indiana Law Journal* 349 (1992).

of property and the inadvertent destruction of property are and ought to be distinguished.[38] Theft is a public wrong; it damages the shared values of communities. If so, how does placing the victim in the material position he occupied prior to the theft possibly annul the wrong? If this wrong is to be annulled, something in addition to compensation is required. If this something else is public condemnation—as seems plausible—economic theorists have not shown that the state may dispense with punishment even in an ideal world in which rational defendants possess sufficient resources to be deterred by the need to pay compensation. In short, economic analysis offers a deficient answer to the crucial question of when criminal liability and punishment would *not* be justified.

The foregoing considerations help to respond to the supposed appeal of economic theories. Many commentators are attracted to this mode of inquiry because they are averse to the apparent evaluation of law by reference to norms of morality. Moral norms have characteristics that make them ill-suited as a foundation for law. In particular, they are inherently uncertain and controversial.[39] Efficiency, by contrast, is alleged to be mathematically precise. But this motivation for embracing economic analysis is wholly misplaced. As I have indicated, the fundamental question a theory of criminalization must address is whether and under what conditions the state is justified in subjecting persons to punishment. This question poses a moral issue, and only a moral reply is capable of answering it. If economic analysis qualifies as a possible response, it must be interpreted to suggest that efficiency provides a moral justification for exposing persons to criminal sanctions.[40] Unless market bypassing were *wrongful*, however, it is unclear how the need to prevent it could produce punishments that are deserved. In other words, if efficiency does not provide a moral justification for infringing the right not to be punished, economic analysis does not merit serious consideration as a theory of criminalization. If I am correct, the fundamental issue about the limits of the penal law cannot be evaded by pretending that the economic analysis of crime avoids moral controversies. It simply offers a different moral answer to our original question.[41]

I conclude that economic analysis is inferior to my theory of criminalization. Among several other shortcomings I have recounted, it is so riddled with qualifications that it may not even qualify as a sketch of a theory. I suspect that Posner himself recognizes the weakness of his views about the criminal sanction. The final sentences of his article hardly brim with the confidence typically conveyed by a scholar persuaded by his own reasoning. Posner claims only to have shown that an economic analysis of the criminal law "is not [*sic*] weird as it sounds."[42] I am unconvinced that he succeeds in accomplishing even this modest objective.

---

38. See R. A. Duff: "Criminalizing Endangerment," in Stuart Green and R. A. Duff, eds.: *Defining Crimes: Essays on the Special Part of Criminal Law* (Oxford: Oxford University Press, 2005), p.43.
39. According to some economists, the problem with the retributive principle—that only those who have done wrong deserved to be punished—is that no one has succeeded in defining wrongdoing. See Louis Kaplow and Steven Shavell: *Fairness versus Welfare* (Cambridge: Harvard University Press, 2002), p.303.
40. "Typically, economists of law shy away from defending the normative attractiveness of efficiency." Jules Coleman: *The Practice of Principle* (Oxford: Oxford University Press, 2001), p.31.
41. See Ronald Dworkin: "Why Efficiency?" 8 *Hofstra Law Review* 563 (1980).
42. *Op. cit.*, note 7, p.1230.

II: UTILITARIANISM

No theory has exerted a greater influence on political and legal thought generally than utilitarianism. Countless varieties of utilitarianism have been contrasted, although I will make no effort to discuss them here. A critical examination of the several forms of utilitarianism that moral philosophers have constructed would require a volume of its own.[43] For simplicity, I suppose that utilitarians are consequentialists who contend that actions are right or institutions are justified when they maximize utility—that is, when they produce a greater amount of utility than any of their competitors. When applied to criminalization, I construe this theory to entail that the state is justified in enacting whatever set of proscriptions maximize utility.[44] I am aware that this account is cursory and that different utilitarian traditions will explicate it in different ways. One crucial respect in which this account is incomplete is that it omits a substantive description of the mysterious entity known as utility. If disutility is conceptualized as encompassing everything that might count against a proposal—including, say, its incompatibility with the constraints an adequate theory of criminalization should contain—*any* plausible theory would seemingly qualify as utilitarian.[45] I will try to evade this complication. Although given objections will be more forceful against some versions than others, I hope the following remarks are sufficient to undermine almost any theory of criminalization that is properly called utilitarian. At the very least, my comments should challenge philosophers to explain how their preferred version of utilitarianism is superior to my theory of criminalization.

Despite the extraordinary influence of utilitarianism generally, it is less clear that its impact has been comparable in the criminal domain. As far as I can determine, no living commentator has seriously attempted to implement a utilitarian agenda throughout the penal law. Prominent among the many reservations moral philosophers have expressed about utilitarianism is its incredibly rigorous demand of individual sacrifice for the good of others.[46] Persons seemingly are required to subordinate their own interests to improve the general welfare.[47] No criminal theorist can or should advocate a comparable level of sacrifice in the criminal law. Anglo-American commentators continue to struggle with the question whether

---

43. See, for example, the versions distinguished in—and the account ultimately defended by—Brad Hooker: *Ideal Code, Real World: A Rule-Consequential Theory of Morality* (Oxford: Oxford University Press, 2000).

44. Despite confusion among many commentators, a utilitarian theory of criminalization is importantly dissimilar from economic analysis. The latter seeks to prohibit inefficient acts of market bypassing no matter how much utility may be created by the transfer. See Posner: *op. cit.*, note 7, p.1195. They tend to resist utilitarian thinking for the simple reason that the "conventional limits of economics ... do not allow interpersonal comparisons of utilities." *Id.*, p.1197.

45. Theorists who construe utilitarianism this broadly are welcome to prepare a utilitarian defense of the internal and external constraints that comprise the theory of criminalization I have defended. I am not inclined to believe, however, that conformity with my theory will maximize anything other than justice.

46. See Bernard Williams: "A Critique of Utilitarianism," in J. J. C. Smart and Bernard Williams, eds.: *Utilitarianism: For and Against* (Cambridge: Cambridge University Press, 1973), p.77.

47. See Shelly Kagan: *The Limits of Morality* (Oxford: Clarendon Press, 1991). Of course, this supposed implication of utilitarianism is frequently contested. See, for example, Peter Railton: "Alienation, Consequentialism and the Demands of Morality," 13 *Philosophy and Public Affairs* 134 (1984).

any duties of Good Samaritanism should be mandated by the penal code.[48] Incorporating the level of sacrifice apparently called for by utilitarianism is not on anyone's short list of legal reforms.

Still, the impact of utilitarianism is significant. *Justifications* provide a context in which utilitarian thinking appears to have played a central role in criminal theory. I construe justifications as defenses that apply when a defendant acts permissibly, despite having committed a criminal offense.[49] A defendant is justified when he deliberately kills in self-defense, for example, even though his behavior satisfies each element of the crime of murder. How should we decide whether criminal conduct is justifiable? According to Paul Robinson, *all* justifications share a common structure: They obtain when the defendant's act produces a net balance of good over bad.[50] Clearly, this view of justifications is unabashedly utilitarian. If Robinson is correct, utilitarian reasoning explains a central feature of criminal liability. Even if particular offenses are not enacted for utilitarian reasons, utilitarianism would specify the conditions under which the commission of an offense is permissible and thus should not incur criminal liability or punishment.[51] Of course, one might well wonder why a theorist would be selective about utilitarianism. Why, that is, would utilitarianism be an attractive theory of justification if it were an unattractive theory of the offenses that need to be justified in the first place?

In any event, despite its apparent commitment to heroic demands of Good Samaritanism, utilitarianism has some potential to retard the growth of the penal law. Indeed, as we have seen, the two most prominent theorists who protested loudly against overcriminalization in the late 1960s were motivated largely by utilitarian concerns. Herbert Packer[52] and Sanford Kadish[53] cogently argued that criminal sanctions against private consensual behavior tend to be ineffective and counterproductive. No reasonable person could reject their modest negative thesis: Criminal laws are unjustified when they fail to further their objective or do more bad than good. Yet these theorists stopped short of endorsing a utilitarian theory of criminalization generally; they did not explicitly defend the parallel positive thesis that criminal laws are justified when they advance their aim and do more good than bad.[54] In other words, they did not suppose that a necessary condition for the justified imposition of criminal sanctions was also a sufficient condition. Both Packer and Kadish had good reason not to take this radical step,

---

48. See Michael Menlowe and Alexander McCall Smith, eds.: *The Duty to Rescue* (Hanover, Vt.: Dartmouth Pub. Group, 1993).

49. For further thoughts on the nature of justifications, see Douglas Husak: "On the Supposed Priority of Justification to Excuse," 24 *Law and Philosophy* 557 (2005).

50. Paul Robinson: 2 *Criminal Law Defenses* (St. Paul, Minn.: West Pub. Co., 1984), p.8.

51. For reasons to doubt the cogency of a utilitarian account of justifications, see Douglas Husak: "Justifications and the Criminal Liability of Accessories," 80 *Journal of Criminal Law and Criminology* 201 (1989).

52. Herbert Packer: *The Limits of the Criminal Sanction* (Stanford: Stanford University Press, 1968).

53. Sanford Kadish: "The Crisis of Overcriminalization," 374 *Annals of the American Academy of Political and Social Science* 157 (1967).

54. Both friends and foes of utilitarianism tend to contrast good with *harm*. In criminal theory, however, "harm" is best reserved as a technical term of legal art, and should not be equated with badness or disutility generally.

as Jeremy Bentham had embraced the latter view more than a century earlier.[55] In the history of criminal theory, no legal philosopher has explicated the details of a theory of criminalization and punishment more fully than Bentham. His (mostly) consistent adherence to the principle that criminal laws are justified when they produce more utility than disutility serves as the best historical illustration of a fully elaborated model of criminalization. Bentham's achievement represents not only the zenith of utilitarian thinking about the criminal law but also the peak of systematic reasoning about criminalization generally.

The very scope and breadth of Bentham's contribution has allowed subsequent legal philosophers to appreciate its strengths and weaknesses. Notwithstanding its considerable strengths, it is fair to say that its weaknesses are many. Almost no contemporary legal philosopher would endorse each of the principles Bentham used to determine whether and to what extent offenders should be punished for their conduct. For example, Bentham argued that the severity of punishments should "take into the account the profit not only of the *individual* offence to which the punishment is to be annexed, but also of such *other* offences of the *same sort* as the offender is likely to have already committed without detection."[56] This principle (among others) might have been penned by a philosopher intent on showing that a utilitarian theory of punishment yields a *reductio ad absurdum*.

In fact, the unpalatable implications of a utilitarian theory of punishment are even greater than those addressed by Bentham himself. Consider, for example, two kinds of punishment that only utilitarians could favor: collective and vicarious punishments. A punishment is *collective* when each member of a group is punished for an offense committed by a single member of that group. Collective punishments are routinely imposed in military training. When one soldier breaks a rule, the sergeant punishes *all* the soldiers in the platoon. A punishment is *vicarious* when one person is punished for an offense known to be committed by another. Vicarious punishments are typically used when an actual offender is difficult to apprehend or discourage but is intimately related to someone else who is easily targeted. When a parent breaks a rule, it may be more effective to punish his children. In the appropriate circumstances, no one should doubt that collective and vicarious punishments *work*; they can be fabulously successful in promoting utilitarian objectives such as deterrence. But these draconian practices are textbook examples of injustice despite their utilitarian rationale; they punish persons who are innocent of the offense and do not deserve hard treatment or censure.

I have defended a number of internal and external constraints a theory of criminalization should include. Utilitarians may manage to preserve a few of these constraints. They can easily explain why criminal sanctions should not be imposed unless they further their objective, for example. But the examples of collective and vicarious punishments illustrate a point that is widely acknowledged: utilitarians have tremendous difficulty accounting for the principle that punishments

---

55. Jeremy Bentham: *An Introduction to the Principles of Morals and Legislation* (London: Metheun, 1982).
56. *Id.*, p.170 (emphasis in original).

must be deserved.[57] In recent philosophical history, the most frequently cited and intuitively powerful counterexamples to utilitarianism involve situations in which innocent persons are punished for utilitarian gains. In the most well-known counterexample—henceforth described as the McCloskey counterexample—a vicious crime is committed that causes enormous anxiety in a community.[58] The real perpetrator cannot be caught, so an individual who is known by the authorities to be innocent is framed and sentenced. Good consequences supposedly ensue because the public is deceived into believing the person is guilty of the crime and deserving of his fate. When presented with the McCloskey counterexample, the majority of respondents deem it morally outrageous to punish a person the authorities know to be innocent, even to produce a significant gain in utility. Nearly all of us share the intuition that innocent persons have a right not to be punished—a right that utilitarian advantages do not outweigh.[59] Many features of the McCloskey counterexample might be (and have been) emphasized.[60] It is noteworthy, for example, that such counterexamples to a utilitarian theory of punishment always involve deception. Presumably, the explanation for this fact is that no citizen would openly tolerate punishment of those who do not deserve hard treatment and condemnation, even if he could be persuaded that utility would be maximized. This explanation reveals that the explicit pursuit of a utilitarian agenda would clearly be unjust if it disregarded the constraints that a theory of criminalization should be required to satisfy.[61]

The deficiencies in a utilitarian account of punishment are widely appreciated.[62] Contemporary moral philosophers are loathe to resort to utilitarian reasoning to identify whom to punish, or to what extent. In these matters, desert plays an indispensable role. When we turn to matters of criminalization, however, these difficulties are less likely to be acknowledged. Again, theorists are inclined to become selective utilitarians. For example, although A. P. Simester and G. R. Sullivan contend "it is retributivism which resolves who will be punished and how much punishment will be meted," they add "to be sure, utilitarianism is given

57. Moreover, utilitarians encounter insuperable problems justifying the principle of proportionality. See Andrew von Hirsch and Andrew Ashworth: *Proportionate Sentencing: Exploring the Principles* (Oxford: Oxford University Press, 2005).

58. See H. J. McCloskey: "A Non-Utilitarian Approach to Punishment," 8 *Inquiry* 249 (1965).

59. For a discussion of whether the realism of this objection poses a difficulty, see C. I. Ten: *Crime, Guilt, and Punishment* (Oxford: Clarendon Press, 1987), pp.18–32.

60. In particular, the McCloskey counterexample has been instrumental in motivating the transition to *rule-utilitarianism*. See John Rawls: "Two Concepts of Rules," 64 *Philosophical Review* 3 (1955). To my mind, the greatest difficulty in defending a rule-utilitarian solution to the problems I raise is to formulate the precise content of the rule(s) that should be followed. If these rules really maximize utility more than any alternative, they would be vulnerable to the same problems I discuss. Unfortunately, I cannot give rule-utilitarianism the attention it deserves.

61. This point is defended by Paul H. Robinson and Michael T. Cahill: *Law without Justice* (New York: Oxford University Press, 2006).

62. At least, *philosophers* appreciate these deficiencies. Nonphilosophers tend to afford a more central role to utilitarianism in their theorizing about punishment. See, for example, the significance of general deterrence in Christopher Slobogin: "The Civilization of the Criminal Law," 58 *Vanderbilt Law Review* 121 (2005). The fact that the normative difficulties with this theory are better understood by philosophers helps to explain why utilitarianism is comparatively healthy in related academic disciplines such as criminology and economics. Because philosophers themselves have had relatively little impact on the actual development of the criminal law, utilitarianism may have exerted more influence on the criminal justice system than philosophers would have preferred.

the task of determining which conduct should be punished."[63] But why should sympathies for utilitarianism be higher in the latter than in the former context? If utilitarianism fails as a theory of punishment, why should it succeed as a theory of criminalization? I suspect that part of the explanation for this disparity involves the extraordinary influence H. L. A. Hart exerted on legal philosophy generally and on criminal theory in particular. Hart famously argued in favor of a "mixed" justification of punishment by contending that utilitarian and retributive theories could be combined as coherent responses to different questions. Retributivism is a plausible answer to the questions "to whom may punishment be applied?" and "how severely may we punish?" while utilitarianism provides the best answer to "why are certain kinds of actions forbidden by law and so made crimes or offenses?"[64]

Despite the powerful appeal of Hart's suggestion, I believe that we should not attempt a complete divorce of questions about punishment from those involving criminalization.[65] I have repeatedly suggested that we cannot decide whether or to what extent persons should be punished without having a great deal of information about what they are punished *for*—information, that is, about the content of the penal law. Does the code that authorizes punishment respect the constraints I have argued a theory of criminalization must satisfy? If our statutes violate these constraints routinely, we may be better off without them. In other words, we can hardly decide whether to have an institution of punishment, or how to allocate punishments within that institution, without making at least some assumptions about the scope and limits of the penal sanction.[66] Indeed, I subsequently argue that the same objection believed to be decisive against a utilitarian theory of punishment—that it violates the rights of innocent persons by imposing unjustified punishments—is fatal to a utilitarian theory of criminalization as well.

The general approach to criminalization I have taken throughout this book posits a close conceptual connection between criminal law and punishment. If I am correct about this connection, one would anticipate that an objection to the utilitarian theory of punishment could be reformulated as an objection to the utilitarian theory of criminalization. This reformulation requires a slight alteration in the McCloskey counterexample. In the original case, a person—call her Jane—is unjustly punished. She is scapegoated for utilitarian gains even though she is known by the authorities to be innocent of a crime. Obviously, however, whether Jane is "innocent of a crime" depends on the content of the criminal law.

---

63. See A. P. Simester and G. R. Sullivan: *Criminal Law: Theory and Doctrine* (Oxford: Hart Pub. Co., 2000), p.21. To their credit, the third edition of this treatise contains an expanded treatment of criminalization. See Andrew Simester and G.R. Sullivan: *Criminal Law: Theory and Doctrine* (Oxford: Hart Pub. Co., 3rd ed., 2007).

64. H. L. A. Hart: *Punishment and Responsibility* (Oxford: Clarendon Press, 1968), pp.3, 6.

65. For a nice discussion of Hart's mixed theory of punishment, see Leo Zaibert: *Punishment and Retribution* (Burlington, Vt.: Ashgate Pub. Co., 2006), chaps. 1 and 5.

66. Hart himself ensures that punishment will not be imposed on persons known to be innocent of a crime by defining "central cases" of punishment as "for an offence against legal rules" and "for an actual or supposed offender for his offence." *Op. cit.*, note 64, pp.4–5. As a result, one of the most powerful reasons to doubt whether we should *have* an institution of punishment is set aside by the definition of what (a central case of) punishment *is*. For a discussion, see David Dolinko: "Some Thoughts about Retributivism," 101 *Ethics* 541 (1991).

Suppose a theorist purported to remedy this injustice by amending the penal code so that Jane no longer was innocent of a criminal offense. The content of the new crime of which she would be guilty would be (roughly) to be a person whose punishment would produce the greatest utility. Clearly, this imaginary crime would violate nearly every constraint on criminalization ever defended. No commentator would be taken seriously if he suggested that the enactment of this new offense would remedy the injustice to Jane. That is exactly my point. The same difficulty that led us to reject utilitarianism would persist, although it would have to be rephrased as an objection to a theory of criminalization rather than as an objection to a theory of punishment. In my modified example, the unjust violation of rights is not the punishment of a person who has not committed a crime. *Ex hypothesi*, Jane *is* guilty of an offense. Instead, the unjust violation of rights is the punishment of a person for a crime that should not exist, a crime that lies beyond the legitimate boundaries of the penal sanction. Unless our theory of criminalization contains the resources to prevent this imaginary offense from being enacted into law, we are left without a basis to articulate our powerful intuition that Jane is treated unjustly, in violation of her rights and contrary to her desert.

With a little ingenuity, I contend that any forceful objection to a theory of punishment can be reformulated as an objection to a theory of criminalization. To illustrate this point, consider the draconian kinds of practices I mentioned earlier: collective and vicarious punishments. Despite their utilitarian advantages, these practices violate principles of desert by punishing persons known to be innocent of a crime. Again, however, whether persons are "innocent of a crime" depends on the content of the substantive criminal law. Anyone who hopes to preserve the utilitarian benefits of these practices but is unwilling to punish the innocent could "solve" this problem simply by adding new offenses to our criminal code. He might proscribe (roughly) "being a member of a group when utilitarian advantages are gained by punishing all members of that group" and "being a person related to an offender in such a way that utilitarian advantages are gained by punishment." Innocence is magically transformed into guilt by a simple stroke of the legislative pen. Of course, no one would endorse these alleged solutions.[67] Anyone convinced of the injustice of collective and vicarious punishments would not be mollified by these additions to the criminal code, even though each of the persons punished would now be guilty of existing offenses. Crimes should not be enacted solely on utilitarian grounds if we are serious about safeguarding the rights of persons who do not deserve to be punished. Otherwise, even our best efforts to protect the innocent could easily be thwarted by the foregoing changes in the content of the substantive criminal law.

Although the foregoing examples of imaginary crimes are preposterous, less extreme illustrations actually can be found in positive law. Suppose the police get a tip that illicit drugs are being used inside a vacant building (or a car). They enter and find drugs on the floor, but none of the four people inside the building admits

---

67. See the illuminating treatment of guilt and innocence in R. A. Duff: *Trials and Punishments* (Cambridge: Cambridge University Press, 1986), pp.153–155.

his guilt. In this kind of situation, it may seem that no individual can or should be convicted of the offense of drug possession beyond a reasonable doubt. To protect the innocent, all four must be acquitted, despite the indisputable fact that one or more is guilty. The state, however, can easily circumvent this difficulty by imposing collective or vicarious punishments under a different name. The offense can be altered from actual possession to *constructive* possession, and the latter can be defined so that everyone in the building becomes guilty.[68] To mitigate the unfairness of this revision, this new crime might include a culpability requirement, so that no one could be convicted of constructive possession unless he knows of the drugs in the building. I assume that this change in the law is defensible on utilitarian grounds; the objective of deterrence is frustrated if no one in the building has an incentive to identify the perpetrator and everyone must be acquitted. Technically, no collective or vicarious punishments are imposed; everyone is punished only for his own offense, and not for the offense of anyone else. Yet it is hard to see why principled objections to collective and vicarious punishments would evaporate because of this statutory change. If we really believe that three of the persons in the original example are innocent and do not deserve to be punished, we would not abandon our objection if we were informed that the law had been revised to make each of them guilty. Much the same objection would persist; now we would complain that the *statute itself* is unjust. The statute is unjust because it disregards the constraints a theory of criminalization should be required to satisfy; it imposes penal liability on persons who do not deserve the hard treatment and censure inherent in punishment.

If the aforementioned argument is sound, it follows that utilitarianism is a defective theory of criminalization. Specifically, no one who rejects a utilitarian theory of punishment should accept a utilitarian theory of criminalization. Statutes acceptable to utilitarians are vulnerable to the same objection that is decisive against a utilitarian theory of punishment: They allow persons to be punished, despite their lack of desert. The injustice to the individuals who are punished can only be explained by appealing to the constraints a theory of criminalization should include. My theory respects these constraints; utilitarianism—at least as construed here—does not.

Although I believe the foregoing arguments suffice to discredit a utilitarian theory of criminalization, different kinds of considerations undermine this theory as well. Despite its supposed popularity, it is hard to know how to structure a real utilitarian analysis of whether a given kind of conduct should be punished. The details, again, would depend on the particular version of utilitarianism employed.[69] Still, one rarely encounters a sophisticated utilitarian analysis of *any*

---

68. The details of the law governing constructive possession vary from state to state. For an example from New Jersey, see *State v. Palacio*, 545 A.2d 764 (1988).

69. Many versions seem wildly implausible when applied to the criminal domain. Consider, for example, *preference* utilitarianism: the view that an action is right when it satisfies more preferences than any alternative action. Do proponents of this view really believe we should count (and weigh) preferences in deciding whether to proscribe a given kind of conduct? Can anyone seriously contend that we are justified in punishing someone for his behavior simply because more persons prefer that we do?

controversial issue.[70] Most commentators would agree that persons who commit core offenses like arson produce more disutility than disutility. But what about the act of consuming junk food? Or watching television? I do not deny that these sorts of inquiry are sensible. But is it really so clear that each of these activities *does* produce more good than bad? If not, why does no sensible utilitarian call for their proscription? Only a complex theory of criminalization—which includes the additional constraints I have defended—can deal with these topics adequately. When a utilitarian analysis appears to lead to counterintuitive positions on such issues, one immediately suspects that independent principles are used to resolve the problem and nonutilitarian factors infect the determinations.[71]

Whatever verdict a utilitarian should reach about these behaviors, the calculations are bound to change when punishment is added to the equation. In other words, even if watching television produces a net balance of disutility, the imposition of penal sanctions against this conduct may cause more bad than good. Utilitarians have not spoken with one voice about whether the benefits of crime or the disutility of the punishment inflicted on the offender should be balanced against the evils of crime and the social advantages of punishment when constructing a utilitarian analysis.[72] Should we really decide whether to proscribe sexual harassment, for example, by making an unbiased determination of whether the utility experienced by the perpetrators outweighs the disutility caused to the victims? Should our calculation include the disutility of the punishment suffered by the offenders?[73] On what possible basis can we *exclude* the utility gained by the perpetrator and/or the disutility of the punishment inflicted on the offender?[74] And how might we do so without begging the question? We cannot say that the fruits of criminal activities do not count in given utilitarian calculations without knowing what conduct is criminal—the very question we want our deliberations to answer. Attempts to solve this problem, I fear, are more likely to be ingenious than persuasive.[75]

This problem looms large when we return yet again to drug offenses—exhibit A in the case for overcriminalization. How should a consistent utilitarian decide whether to prohibit the consumption of drugs such as cocaine and alcohol?[76] Many

70. For a possible exception—that also illustrates many of the difficulties preparing a utilitarian analysis—see R. M. Hare: "What Is Wrong with Slavery," 8 *Philosophy & Public Affairs* 103 (1979).

71. See Dan Kahan: "The Secret Ambition of Deterrence," 119 *Harvard Law Review* 414 (1999).

72. See the discussion in Robert E. Goodin: *Utilitarianism as a Public Philosophy* (Cambridge: Cambridge University Press, 1995), chap. 9.

73. The disutility of punishment to offenders is taken into account in Deirdre Golash: *The Case against Punishment* (New York: New York University Press, 2005), pp.24–38.

74. John C. Harsanyi famously argues for the exclusion of "antisocial preferences" from the utilitarian calculus. See his "Morality and the Theory of Rational Behaviour," in Amartya Sen and Bernard Williams, eds.: *Utilitarianism and Beyond* (Cambridge: Cambridge University Press, 1983), p.39.

75. See the discussion in Dorsey D. Ellis: "An Economic Theory of Intentional Torts: A Comment," 3 *International Review of Law and Economics* 45 (1983).

76. Some commentators answer these questions with a level of confidence that is completely unwarranted. According to one theorist, for example, "cocaine, heroin, marijuana, alcohol, peyote, LSD, amphetamines, barbiturates, and tobacco are *very likely* to result in a *clear* preponderance of pain over pleasure in the long run for users and/or for others." Rem B. Edwards: "Why We Should Not Use Some Drugs for Pleasure," in Steven Luper-Foy and Curtis Brown, eds.: *Drugs, Morality, and the Law* (New York: Garland Pub. Co., 1994), p.183, 184 (emphasis added).

users enjoy these drugs—a lot. Presumably, their preferences and the ensuing utility must be included in an unbiased consequentialist calculation.[77] If these benefits are excluded, the case for criminalization has already been decided—on other grounds, of course. Moreover, if these benefits are uncounted, we have a precedent for disqualifying the utility of any number of additional behaviors known to create personal and social problems—like eating doughnuts or playing video games, for example. Obviously, *any* activity produces a net balance of disutility if its utility is excluded *ex ante*. Suppose, however, we somehow manage to determine that the consumption of given drugs produces a net balance of disutility. In deciding whether to proscribe these substances, is there reason to neglect the suffering of the literally millions of persons who will be punished for violating the law? Why is this latter factor routinely ignored when commentators assess our drug policy? I have no good answers to these important questions.

Of course, it would be naïve to suppose that these worries will persuade committed utilitarians to abandon their theory, or to openly supplement it with nonutilitarian constraints. Utilitarianism has proved remarkably resilient for centuries, and its proponents have developed many strategies to deal with objections and supposed counterexamples. But if the difficulties I have raised are cogent, a utilitarian account of criminalization is highly problematic and, I believe, inferior to the theory I have defended.

III: LEGAL MORALISM

Legal moralism is perhaps the most important theory of criminalization to rival the view I have defended here. Unlike economic analysis and utilitarianism, legal moralism is a view about the criminal law itself; it is not a more general normative theory that happens to have implications for criminalization. What exactly *is* legal moralism?[78] Different answers have been given, and no simple definition can hope to capture each of the many theories popularly regarded as versions of legal moralism.[79] In what follows, I focus attention on the particular account defended by Michael Moore, probably the most eminent philosopher of criminal law in the United States today. His monumental *Placing Blame* contains the most sophisticated explication and defense of legal moralism ever devised.[80]

---

77. "Indeed, the notion that the currently illicit drugs have benefits is almost completely ignored in the policy analytical literature on drug control." Robert J. MacGoun and Peter Reuter: *Drug War Heresies* (Cambridge: Cambridge University Press, 2001), p.70.

78. Joel Feinberg defines legal moralism as accepting the wrongfulness constraint but rejecting the requirement that criminal laws be designed to prevent harm or offense. "In the usual narrow sense," he writes, legal moralism is the view that "it can be morally legitimate to prohibit conduct on the ground that it is inherently immoral, even though it causes neither harm nor offense to the actor or to others." Joel Feinberg: *Harmless Wrongdoing* (New York: Oxford University Press, 1987), pp.xix–xx.

79. See Patrick Devlin: *The Enforcement of Morality* (Oxford: Oxford University Press, 1965). Lord Devlin is probably regarded as the most well-known legal moralist of the 20th century. But Devlin's views are better construed as consequentialist, because he believes that the preservation of morality through the criminal sanction is essential to protect society. See Douglas Husak: *Philosophy of Criminal Law* (Totowa, N.J.: Rowman & Allanheld, 1987), chapter 8.

80. Michael Moore: *Placing Blame* (Oxford: Clarendon Press, 1997).

Moore's formulation of legal moralism is simple—deceptively so. In essence, his view is that immorality (aptly characterized as culpable wrongdoing) is sufficient to justify the enactment of criminal laws and the punishment of persons who (inexcusably) violate them. To his credit, Moore understands the implications of a theory of punishment for a theory of criminalization. Thus, his description of legal moralism is intimately related to his account of retributivism, according to which "it is a sufficient reason for us to have punishment institutions (i.e., the criminal law)—and for us to use those institutions to mete out a particular punishment to a particular person on a particular occasion—that the person deserve to be punished."[81] Consequentialist considerations play no role in this determination; "the moral desert of an offender is a *sufficient* reason to punish him."[82] The corresponding theory of legislation holds that "all *and only* moral wrongs should be criminally prohibited."[83] In what follows, I critically evaluate legal moralism as so construed.[84] I point out its differences from the theory of criminalization I have sketched and argue that my account is preferable.

Before beginning, however, I need to emphasize two features of Moore's view that led me to characterize it as *deceptively* simple. The first involves the progressive theory of morality Moore believes the criminal law should enforce. Historically, legal moralists were obsessed with the proscription of so-called sexual vices such as obscenity, homosexuality, prostitution, and the like.[85] As a result, few legal moralists have favored reductions in the amount of criminal law or punishment.[86] Moore, however, is eager to disassociate himself from these traditional concerns; he contends, for example, that "morality is indifferent to sexual practices."[87] The second is Moore's claim that we should not construe too literally his thesis that immorality is sufficient for criminality.[88] Like any sensible theorist, Moore recognizes several grounds on which to limit the reach of the criminal sanction, even when immorality is involved. These grounds include legality, convenience, and epistemic modesty.[89] Perhaps most important, the criminal law should protect basic liberties from state interference; sometimes the goodness of allowing free choice outweighs the badness of leaving wrongful action unpunished.[90] Because of these restrictions, the particular kinds of conduct Moore ultimately would criminalize may not differ substantially from those proscribed by my minimalist

81. *Id.*, p.104.
82. *Id.*, p.88 (emphasis in original).
83. *Id.*, p.662 (emphasis in original). See also pp.646, 669.
84. For further thoughts, see Douglas N. Husak: "Retribution in Criminal Theory," 37 *San Diego Law Review* 959 (2000).
85. See Devlin: *op. cit.*, note 79.
86. See the accusations brought against retributivists in James Q. Whitman: "A Plea against Retributivism," 7 *Buffalo Criminal Law Review* 85 (2003).
87. *Op. cit.*, note 80, p.662.
88. Moore's clarification is that immorality suffices for criminality only "within the set of conditions constituting intelligible reasons to punish." *Id.*, p.173. For a critical discussion of whether this clarification is defensible, see Zaibert: *Op. cit.*, note 65, p.163.
89. *Id.*, p.68 and pp.661–665.
90. *Id.*, p.68 and pp.763–777.

theory.[91] Because Moore would not prohibit a great many of the behaviors traditional legal moralists have wanted to punish, he describes himself as a "liberal legal moralist."[92]

How should we assess this theory? Legal moralists typically accept the internal constraints I argued that any respectable theory of criminalization must include. In particular, criminal conduct must be wrongful and punishments must be deserved. Admittedly, legal moralists generally reject the principle that criminal liability requires harm.[93] Still, they need not reject the principle I have argued is internal to criminal law itself: the nontrivial harm or evil constraint. They may accept this latter constraint by supposing that criminal laws must be designed to proscribe *evil*, as something distinct from harm. If so, the wrongfulness and evil constraints probably become redundant; wrongful conduct just *is* conduct aimed at an evil. In any event, the most important difference between my own theory of criminalization and legal moralism is that the latter does not accept the external constraints I have argued a theory of criminalization should include—those I borrowed from a test of intermediate scrutiny in constitutional law. The right not to be punished should not be infringed in the absence of a substantial state interest, criminal statutes must directly advance that objective, and laws should be no more extensive than necessary to achieve their goal. Thus my arguments against legal moralism will not depend on the claim that harm need be caused or risked to justify penal liability. These arguments will enable us to appreciate the advantages of a complex theory that contains greater resources than legal moralism to resist objectionable impositions of the penal sanction.

Why believe that immorality is sufficient to justify criminal liability and punishment? In other words, why embrace legal moralism? Moore responds that the

91. See Moore's treatment of drug offenses in *id.*, pp.778–795.
92. *Id.*, p.661.
93. Moore's attack on the harm principle has two parts. First, he proposes three counterexamples—cases in which the legal moralist will criminalize but those who require harm will not: cruelty to animals, desecration of corpses, and destruction of species. Second, he alleges that the harm constraint is exclusionary. What, Moore asks, could possibly justify a decision not to extend the reach of the criminal sanction to some instances of culpable wrongdoing—those that do not cause harm? Why should the moral reasons that count elsewhere be deemed irrelevant when harm is not involved? In what follows, I try to respond briefly to both of these objections to the harm principle.
   I begin with a quick response to the three alleged counterexamples to the harm constraint. In the first place, theorists who accept the harm principle should refuse to be placed on the defensive; Moore's own theory is more vulnerable to counterexamples than its competitor. Still, we should address these alleged counterexamples directly. Moore's first and third cases do not raise insuperable difficulties. Cruelty to animals could be proscribed if a theorist holds that harm need not befall human beings in order to justify criminal penalties. Arguably, harm to nonhuman animals may count too. Acts that destroy a species might be proscribed under a similar rationale. The second alleged counterexample—desecration of corpses—may prove more difficult. I will not canvass the various replies that are available here. Perhaps the dead can be harmed, or the living have rights that survive their deaths. As a last resort, those who accept a harm principle may concede that criminal penalties are not justified in this case; statutes that protect corpses, when human sensibilities are unaffected, may be more a taboo than a defensible prohibition.
   The supposed theoretical difficulty Moore brings against the harm principle is even less persuasive. When harm is not caused, Moore asks why moral reasons become irrelevant as a basis for criminal legislation. What, he asks, could justify this exclusion? In fact, however, no exclusion is generated by the harm principle (or any other principle). On the complex theory I have defended here, several internal and external constraints need to be satisfied before conduct may be criminalized. By itself, wrongfulness is insufficient. If I am correct, wrongfulness and harm (or evil) are independently necessary (but not conjointly sufficient) for the legitimate imposition of criminal sanctions.

value of inflicting deserved punishments derives not from its consequences but solely from the value of implementing a principle of retributive justice. He writes, "punishing the guilty achieves something good—namely, justice—and . . . reference to any other good consequences is simply beside the point."[94] One way to motivate this view is to draw from parallel arguments in civil law. A rich and impressive philosophical literature reacts to the law and economics movement by construing tort liability as designed to implement a principle of corrective justice.[95] Surprisingly few theorists defend criminal liability along similar lines—as implementing a principle of retributive justice.[96]

For three reasons, I do not believe that the value of implementing a principle of retributive justice suffices to justify the enactment of criminal statutes that subject culpable wrongdoers to punishment. My first reason to reject the sufficiency thesis has already been discussed, and should not detain us further.[97] Some wrongs are private rather than public, and they do not merit a punitive state response. Admittedly, the line between public and private wrongs is exceedingly hard to draw, and legal moralists score points in pressing this difficulty. Unless the problem in drawing this line persuades us that the whole endeavor should be abandoned, however, wrongfulness cannot suffice for criminal liability and deserved punishment. Many egregious immoralities are not proscribed by the penal law, and no serious commentator favors their criminalization.[98] The reason we should not punish a breach of contract or a tort, for example, is not because these behaviors are not wrongful but because these wrongful behaviors are private.[99] As we have seen, Antony Duff has argued that a theory of criminal responsibility must be *relational* in specifying the person or body *to* whom we are responsible.[100] Only the person or body to whom we are responsible has standing to call us to account for our failure to discharge our moral responsibilities. When a wrong is private, redress should be at the option of the victim; his own voluntary decision not to pursue a complaint should be decisive.[101] Legal moralism obliterates the distinction between private and public wrongs. Without this distinction, even a liberal legal moralist will be forced to favor a bloated criminal code that makes our current predicament of overcriminalization pale by comparison.

94. *Id.,* p.111.

95. For a nice discussion, see Jules Coleman: *Risks and Wrongs* (Cambridge: Cambridge University Press, 1992). See also Ernest J. Weinrib: *The Idea of Private Law* (Cambridge: Harvard University Press, 1995).

96. But see David Wood: "Retributive and Corrective Justice, Criminal and Private Law," in Peter Wahlgren, ed: *Perspectives on Jurisprudence: Essays in Honor of Jes Bjarup* (Stockholm Law Faculty: 48 Scandinavian Studies in Law, 2004), p.541.

97. See chapter 3, section II.

98. See Leo Katz: "Villany and Felony: A Problem Concerning Criminalization," 6 *Buffalo Criminal Law Review* 451 (2003).

99. Significantly, civil wrongs also are harms. See John Kleinig: "Criminally Harming Others," 5 *Criminal Justice Ethics* 3 (1986).

100. See R. A. Duff: "Criminal Responsibility, Municipal and International" (forthcoming).

101. In the same vein, Duff suggests that legal moralists cannot make sense of jurisdictional or territorial restrictions on the scope of criminal liability. If all wrongdoing is the business of the state and provides a reason to criminalize, it would seem that England, for example, has a reason to punish under English law a German citizen who steals from a fellow German in Germany. The legal moralist position suggests that all instances of moral wrongdoing are the proper concern of every person and every state. See R. A. Duff: "Democratic Criminal Responsibility" (forthcoming).

Because it is speculative and plays no important role in my subsequent argument, I will be equally brief with my second challenge to the sufficiency thesis
of legal moralism. The value of implementing a principle of retributive justice
does not entail that justified punishments are intrinsically good or that we have
a reason to impose them. Ordinarily, of course, inflictions of a stigmatizing deprivation are intrinsically bad. The state (and everyone else) has a reason not to
impose them. When punishments are justified, however, they are not intrinsically
bad. It does not follow, of course, that they must be intrinsically good. The value
of implementing a principle of retributive justice may simply negate the reason
we typically have not to punish. We still may lack a reason in favor of inflicting
a justified punishment, as the state of affairs in which a justified punishment is
imposed may not be positively valuable. Something else may be needed to give us
a reason to punish—something other than the conclusion that a given punishment is not intrinsically bad.[102]

In what follows, I develop in greater detail my third and final reason to reject
the sufficiency thesis of legal moralism. This argument has two related but distinct
parts, each of which emphasizes the need to show why the *state* is the appropriate vehicle for imposing punishment. Legal moralists have struggled to explain
why the task of implementing a principle of retributive justice should fall to the
state.[103] I argue, first, that what culpable wrongdoers deserve may not be state
punishment, and, second, that when state punishment is justified, consequentialist
considerations play an indispensable role in its justification. My minimalist theory,
which includes consequentialist elements, contains the resources to explain why
punishment should be imposed by the state.

Moore's defense of the sufficiency thesis proceeds largely by appeals to intuitions. These intuitions, cultivated through well-known thought-experiments, are
designed to show that the state of affairs in which culpable wrongdoers are punished is superior to the state of affairs in which they are not punished—even
though no utilitarian objective is advanced. Legal moralists conclude that these
thought-experiments reveal respondents to hold retributive beliefs about the
rationale for criminal law and punishment, and demonstrate that consequentialism plays no role in their justification. Each example involves a person who commits a monstrous crime but whose punishment would not be justified according
to a utilitarian theory.[104] In other words, no good (beyond realizing a principle
of retributive justice) would be promoted by punishment. Although many distinguished philosophers report different intuitions about these cases,[105] I share
Moore's judgment that the state of affairs in which these individuals receive their
just deserts is preferable to the state of affairs in which they do not (even though

102. See Russell L. Christopher: "Deterring Retributivism: The Injustice of 'Just' Punishment," 96 *Northwestern University Law Review* 843 (2002).
103. Perhaps the contrast between retribution and vengeance requires that authority to punish be vested in the state. See Jeffrie G. Murphy: "The State's Interest in Retribution," 5 *Journal of Contemporary Legal Issues* 283 (1994).
104. The particular example Moore selects is *State v. Chaney*, 447 P.2d 441 (1970). Frequently, Moore presents examples in the first person, explaining what *he* would feel he deserved were he guilty of a serious crime. See *op. cit.*, note 80, p.145.
105. Moore describes and responds to many such philosophers in *id.*, pp.83–188.

the former may not be intrinsically good). I also concur with Moore about the crucial point that divides retributivists from consequentialists: our judgments about these respective states of affairs do not depend on utilitarian gains. Still, I will argue that these thought-experiments fail to establish what legal moralists claim and need: They do not show why the *state* is justified in punishing these culpable wrongdoers, or that consequentialism plays no role when state punishment *is* justified.

I contrast two cases to clarify what I believe these thought-experiments do and do not show. In case 1, a person clearly has engaged in culpable wrongdoing—even though his conduct happens not to be a crime. Consider David, who perpetrates a heinous wrong. For some reason, however—through a legislative oversight, or because no functioning legal system exists—David's conduct has not been proscribed. Thus, even on Moore's account, the state lacks the lawful authority to obtain the value of retributive justice. Suppose, however, that the outraged siblings of David's victim exact vengeance. They make him suffer a stigmatizing deprivation for his culpable wrongdoing—to the very same extent as would have been just had his act been criminal and his punishment been proportionate to his desert. State punishment has not been inflicted on David, although he has been made to suffer to the same degree as would have been appropriate if the state had punished him. I do not ask whether the siblings act permissibly. Almost certainly, they do not. Instead, my question is whether our retributive intuitions are satisfied. My own answer is affirmative.[106] If the objective of retributive justice is to give David his just deserts, I believe that this goal has been achieved.[107] State punishment, I conclude, is not the only possible means (even if it is the only permissible means) by which the demands of retributive justice might be obtained. The demands of retributive justice might be served even in situations in which the state lacks the lawful authority to punish the culpable wrongdoer.

In case 2, Linda commits the same act of culpable wrongdoing. No legislative oversight exists, however, and Linda's conduct has been duly criminalized prior to her offense. Before the state can arrest her, the siblings of her victim wreak their vengeance. Again, I am not interested to assess the conduct of the siblings. I ask: Do our retributive beliefs still allow the state to punish Linda, notwithstanding the fact that she already has been made to suffer to the appropriate degree for her crime? As in all these thought-experiments, we must assume that no good consequence will ensue from punishment. Should we continue to insist that state punishment is permitted? I think not. If I am correct, our retributive beliefs only allow culpable wrongdoers to suffer (or to receive a hardship or deprivation) for their culpable wrongdoing. These intuitions do not require that culpable wrongdoers be given their just deserts by being made to suffer through the imposition of state punishment. In other words, even when the state has the lawful authority to punish culpable wrongdoers, our retributive beliefs do not really show that *state punishment* is required.

---

106. For further discussion, see Douglas N. Husak: "Already Punished Enough," 18 *Philosophical Topics* 79 (1990).
107. Perhaps retribution makes additional demands. Some may object that retribution requires that culpable wrongdoers be made to answer in some appropriate way to those to whom they are responsible.

Let me clarify my position by guarding against a possible misunderstanding. In case 1, in which David's monstrous act happens not to be a crime, I am not simply maintaining that the principle of legality—which precludes punishment for conduct not previously defined as criminal—creates a barrier against punishment that overrides the reason in favor of punishment.[108] Both cases 1 and 2 are intended to challenge Moore's claim that *state punishment* is what culpable wrongdoers deserve. As an alternative, I propose that what culpable wrongdoers deserve is a stigmatizing deprivation or hardship. This difference may be blurred in the thought-experiments that legal moralists typically provide. We are invited to suppose that a culpable wrongdoer is not made to suffer for his crime unless he is punished by the state, and our intuitions recoil at this prospect. The point of my examples is to divorce state punishment from suffering by describing cases in which the latter is inflicted but the former is not. When a stigmatizing deprivation is imposed without state punishment, the retributive intuitions I share with Moore are satisfied and no longer allow punishment to be imposed.

In evaluating the thought-experiments presented by Moore, we tend to imagine that a culpable wrongdoer is not made to suffer for his crime unless he is punished because we assume that no body other than the state has the authority to treat David or Linda so horribly. I do not challenge this assumption. I do not condone the behavior of the vengeful siblings. My point is that devices other than state punishment can satisfy the demands of retributive justice. If we deny the authority to exact retribution in victims and confer a monopoly of punishment on the state (as we should), our reasons should not stem from the supposition that only state punishment can satisfy the demands of retributive justice. Our reasons to prefer the creation of an institution of state punishment to the imposition of private vengeance cannot be derived solely from the value of implementing a principle of retributive justice.

Another way to support my point invokes the elusive relationship of "fit" to which retributivists might appeal to explain the connection between crime and punishment. Just as there is something fitting or appropriate at reacting with disapproval at the sight of cruelty, we are encouraged to suppose that there is something fitting or appropriate about imposing state punishment on criminals. In reality, however, the fit we intuit does not really obtain between crime and punishment but, rather, between crime (as culpable wrongdoing) and a stigmatizing deprivation. We sometimes claim to intuit a fit between crime and punishment because we mistakenly suppose that the appropriate degree of punishment can only be produced by the state. Those who share the intuitions I reported should reject this supposition.

---

108. Can the principle of legality—*nullum poena sine lege*—be justified by a legal moralist? Suppose the state has neglected to criminalize an instance of culpable wrongdoing. Moore maintains that the state has a reason to punish such conduct, but the values that underlie the principle of legality provide a countervailing reason not to do so. According to Moore, the weight to be given to the principle of legality will nearly always override the competing principle that immorality should be punished. On a few occasions, Moore holds that the unfairness of punishing persons who have not violated an existing criminal law is outweighed by the enormity of the wrong that would go unpunished. His example of this phenomenon involves Nazi war criminals. *Op. cit.*, note 80, p.187. Why these values should be balanced in this way is not altogether clear.

Legal moralism is problematic because it offers no principled reason to believe that the *state* should punish persons who break its criminal laws.[109] If I am correct to conclude that our reasons to prefer state punishment to private vengeance cannot be derived solely from the value of implementing a principle of retributive justice, what *else* is required to justify criminal law and punishment? Why should citizens create an institution of criminal justice to do the work that can be done without the time, effort, and expense? Many possible answers might be given,[110] but my theory of criminalization provides a plausible solution. According to the external constraints my theory contains, the state must have a substantial interest before resorting to the criminal sanction, and the statute in question must directly advance that objective. The latter constraint is consequentialist; it looks forward rather than backward. Because the state must directly advance an important interest before it may employ penal sanctions, it is compelled to have good reasons to subject offenders to punishment. The solution to the problem of why the *state* has a legitimate interest in retribution is incorporated into the test of criminalization itself. Because legal moralists regard culpable wrongdoing as sufficient for criminal law and punishment, they lack the resources possessed by my theory to explain why the state should be in the business of dispensing criminal justice.

Unlike legal moralists, I do not believe that the institutions of criminal law and punishment can be justified solely as a means to implement a principle of retributive justice—even though I share the controversial intuition that the state of affairs in which culpable wrongdoers are punished is preferable to the state of affairs in which they are not. Consequentialist considerations must be included in the justification of criminal law and punishment. Moore has told only part of the story—indeed, a very important part. To complete the account, however, one must also show that the benefits of state punishment are worth its costs. Moore describes one of these benefits in impressive detail: Punishment is a means to implement retributive justice by giving culpable wrongdoers their just deserts. But what of the immense costs of punishment? I collectively refer to three of these costs as the *drawbacks* of punishment. As administered by the state rather than by a deity, citizens should be reluctant to create an institution of criminal justice because of these three drawbacks. First, the expense of our system of criminal justice is astronomical.[111] Our penal institutions cost huge sums of money that might be used to achieve any number of other valuable goods taxpayers might prefer: education, transportation, funding for the arts, and the like. Second, our system of punishment is susceptible to grave error. Despite the best of intentions,

---

109. Legal moralists might respond by saying that the best way to ensure that retributive justice will be done consistently is by giving states the sole authority to exact retribution. Even if true, this retort is vulnerable to my next objection: the value of achieving retributive justice seems insufficient to offset what I describe as the drawbacks of punishment.

110. For a noninstrumentalist defense of why only the state is permitted to punish, see Alon Harel: "Why Only the State May Punish: On the Vices of Privately-Inflicted Sanctions for Wrongdoing," *Cardozo Law Review* (forthcoming).

111. Although our criminal justice system incurs many additional costs, the expense of federal and state prisons in 2003 was over $185 billion. See U.S. Department of Justice: *Sourcebook of Criminal Justice Statistics*, table 1.1 (2003).

punishment is bound to be imposed incorrectly, at least occasionally.[112] Third, the power created by an institution of punishment is certain to be abused. Officials can and do exceed the limits of their authority, intentionally or inadvertently.[113] In combination, these three drawbacks render state punishment extraordinarily difficult to justify.[114]

Sensitivity to the drawbacks of punishment undermines the sufficiency thesis. Legal moralists seemingly suppose that their task is complete when they show that the punishment of culpable wrongdoers increases the amount of intrinsic value in the world, even though no gain in utility is produced when criminals receive their just deserts.[115] I understand why retributivists tend to dwell on this crucial point, inasmuch as consequentialists are unwilling to concede it. But this demonstration does not suffice to justify an institution of criminal law and punishment—even for legal moralists. They must show not only that giving culpable wrongdoers what they deserve is not intrinsically bad but that the *amount* of the value that punishment produces is sufficient to offset the drawbacks that inevitably result when an institution of criminal justice is created. Perhaps the value of realizing a principle of retributive justice would justify punishment in a possible world in which none of the foregoing drawbacks obtained. In a divine realm, for example, no expenses are incurred to exact retribution, the innocent never are punished, and corruption and abuse are nonexistent. Unfortunately, this possible world differs from the world we inhabit. We must sympathize with citizens who balk when asked to fund an institution that has the sole objective of realizing retributive justice. Persons might reasonably prefer to use their tax dollars for any number of other worthy purposes.[116] I conclude that the value of realizing retributive justice, by itself, is insufficient to justify the creation of an institution of criminal justice with the formidable drawbacks I have described. Something else needs to be said on behalf of criminal law and punishment.

This difficulty is not resolved if we hold, with Moore, that society has not only the right, but also the duty to realize retributive justice by imposing deserved punishment.[117] The same problem resurfaces. The legal moralist burden is to show not only that the imposition of punishment is a duty but also that it is a duty of sufficient magnitude to justify the creation of an institution with the three

---

112. See The Innocence Project: "Causes and Remedies of Wrongful Convictions," *http:www.innocenceproject.com/causes/index.php*. See also "Symposium: The Faces of Wrongful Conviction," 37 *Golden Gate University Law Review* 1–217 (2006).
113. See, for example, Anthony V. Bouza: *Police Unbound: Corruption, Abuse, and Heroism by the Boys in Blue* (Amherst, N.Y.: Prometheus Books, 2001).
114. For earlier thoughts, see Douglas Husak: "Why Punish the Deserving?" 26 *Nous* 447 (1992).
115. Of course, they need not allege that the value of conforming to a principle of retributive justice is enormous, so that punishments must be imposed even though, as Kant supposed, civil society were about to dissolve. See Immanuel Kant: *Metaphysical First Principles of Right* (Cambridge: Cambridge University Press, 1996), p.474.
116. The difficulty of showing that the amount of the value that punishment produces is sufficient to offset the drawbacks that inevitably result when an institution of criminal justice is created can be solved only by locating part of the justification of criminal law and punishment within political philosophy rather than moral philosophy. Another way to express my objection to legal moralism is that it emphasizes only the moral dimension and neglects the political dimension of criminal justice.
117. *Op. cit.*, note 80, p.91.

drawbacks I have recounted. Unless we have some views about the stringency of this duty—about the extent of the value of realizing retributive justice—we will be unable to assess any number of questions that have recently arisen. Consider, for example, the controversy about proposals to repeal statutes of limitations for rape prosecutions.[118] DNA evidence now enables us to identify perpetrators of rape years after their crimes were committed. Should we prosecute persons we now know to have committed rape decades ago? Retributivists may offer different answers to this question, depending on the relative importance they assign to the principle of retributive justice. Theorists who believe that the realization of retributive justice is of crucial significance are likely to think that statutes of limitations should give way in the face of reliable evidence about the identity of rapists. If the value of attaining retributive justice is small, however, the case for repealing statutes of limitations is weaker. Even if we have a duty to attain retributive justice by punishing culpable wrongdoers, we still must assess the stringency of that duty.

What is needed to answer the problem I have posed is some additional value punishment can be expected to attain—a value which, when added to the value of attaining retributive justice, will justify the creation of an institution of criminal law and punishment. This value, I submit, may be found in the theory of substantial state interests my theory of criminalization contains. Means that directly further substantial state interests, like the prevention of harm to others, clearly are worthy of tax resources. We must run the risks of abuse and corruption unless we can find some better way to achieve our important ends. The furtherance of these objectives (hopefully) will offset the drawbacks of punishment and give citizens ample reason to create a system of criminal law.[119] If I am correct, consequentialist considerations play an indispensable role in the justification of criminal law and punishment and the sufficiency thesis of legal moralism is false.

One final route to my conclusions might be taken. Let us stipulate that culpable wrongdoers have negative desert. Just as one might suppose that the state of affairs in which persons with negative desert are made to suffer is intrinsically good, he also might suppose that the state of affairs in which persons with positive desert are made to prosper is intrinsically good. Perhaps there is an asymmetry between negative and positive desert, so that the intrinsic value of depriving persons with negative desert is greater than the intrinsic value of rewarding persons with positive desert.[120] Still, there is some intrinsic value, however slight, in rewarding persons with positive desert. We would be unlikely to infer, however, that only the state could possibly achieve this intrinsic good by conferring rewards on persons with positive desert. Nor would we think that the extent of this intrinsic good is sufficient to give taxpayers adequate reasons to create institutions that reward persons with positive desert. By parity of reasoning, we should not assume

---

118. See Veronica Valdivieso: "DNA Warrants: A Panacea for Old, Cold Rape Cases?" 90 *Georgetown Law Journal* 1009 (2002).
119. For a challenge to whether good consequences suffice to offset the drawbacks of punishment, see David Wood: "Retribution, Crime Reduction and the Justification of Punishment," 22 *Oxford Journal of Legal Studies* 301 (2002).
120. Claims about the asymmetry of positive and negative desert are made frequently. See, for example, J. L. A. Garcia: "Two Concepts of Desert," 5 *Law and Philosophy* 219 (1986).

that only the state can possibly achieve the (alleged) intrinsic good of imposing deprivations on persons with negative desert, or that the extent of this intrinsic good is sufficient to give taxpayers adequate incentives to create institutions of criminal justice. Only the attainment of some additional good—which my theory of criminalization requires—can complete the process of justifying criminal law and punishment.

Arguably, my criticisms are forceful only against Moore's particular version of legal moralism rather than against that tradition more generally. Admittedly, wrongdoing *does* appear to have a special salience in explaining what the criminal law should proscribe.[121] Perhaps some other commentator who calls himself a legal moralist can adopt whatever account is given of the public–private distinction and show why private wrongs are not candidates for criminalization. He might demonstrate that intrinsic value, and not merely the absence of disvalue, is produced by justified punishments. Perhaps he might make room for consequentialist considerations in explaining why the state should create a system of criminal justice, notwithstanding its enormous drawbacks. No commentator has emerged to defend such a theory, however, or to explain why this alternative should be characterized as a version of legal moralism if it differs from Moore's account in the ways I have indicated. Moreover, notice that such a theory is less problematic precisely because it more closely resembles the theory I have sketched. In any event, my claim is not that no better theory of criminalization than mine can *possibly* be defended. I have no idea how such a claim could be supported. I allege only that no better theory presently exists.

If I am correct, legal moralism—like the previous two accounts of criminalization I have surveyed—is inferior to my view. Unless I have neglected to examine a viable competitor, I conclude that the minimalist theory of criminalization I have defended is superior to any of the alternatives found in the long history of legal philosophy. The implementation of this theory will do a better job than its rivals in furthering the cause of justice by combating the problem of overcriminalization from which we presently suffer.

---

121. That is, wrongfulness does not appear to function only as a constraint on what the state should criminalize. It is plausible to believe that conduct should be criminalized *because* it is an act of culpable wrongdoing.

Table of Cases

Bibliography

Abrams, Norman. "The New Ancillary Offenses," 1 *Criminal Law Forum* 1 (1989).

Adler, Matthew. "Expressive Theories of Law: A Skeptical Overview," 148 *University of Pennsylvania Law Review* 1363 (2000).

Alexander, Larry. "Deontology at the Threshold," *37 San Diego Law Review* 893 (2000).

——. "Insufficient Concern: A Unified Conception of Criminal Culpability," 88 *California Law Review* 931 (2000).

——. *Is There a Right of Freedom of Expression?* New York: Cambridge University Press, 2005.

——. "The Philosophy of Criminal Law," in Jules Coleman and Scott Shapiro, eds. *The Oxford Handbook of Jurisprudence & Philosophy of Law.* Oxford: Oxford University Press, 2002, p.815.

Alldridge, Peter. "Dealing with Drug Dealing," in A. P. Simester and A. T. H. Smith, eds. *Harm and Culpability.* Oxford: Clarendon Press, 1996, p.239.

Alschuler, Albert W. "Straining At Gnats and Swallowing Camels: The Selective Morality of Professor Bibas," 88 *Cornell Law Review* 1412 (2003).

American Bar Association. *The Federalization of Criminal Law* (1998), p.20.

Anderson, David. "The Deterrence Hypothesis and Picking Pockets at the Pickpockets' Hanging," 4 *American Law & Economic Review* 295 (2002).

Anderson, Elijah. *Streetwise: Race, Class, and Change in an Urban Community.* Chicago: University of Chicago Press, 1990.

Arneson, Richard. "The Principle of Fairness and Free-Rider Problems," 92 *Ethics* 624 (1982).

Ashutosh, Bhagwat. "Purpose Scrutiny in Constitutional Analysis," 85 *California Law Review* 297 (1997).

Ashworth, Andrew. "Is the Criminal Law a Lost Cause?" 116 *Law Quarterly Review* 225 (2000).

Ashworth, Andrew. *Principles of Criminal Law.* Oxford: Clarendon Press, 4th ed., 2003.

Ashworth, Andrew and Lucia Zedner. "Defending the Criminal Law: Reflections on the Changing Character of Crime, Procedure, and Sanctions" (forthcoming).

Ashworth, Andrew and Michael Redmayne. *The Criminal Process.* Oxford: Oxford University Press, 3rd ed., 2005.

Bak-Boychuk, Alexandra. "Liar Liar: How MPC §241.3 and State Unsworn Falsification Statutes Fix the Flaw in the False Statement Act (18 U.S.C. §1001)," 78 *Temple Law Review* 453 (2005).

Barak, Aharon. *Purposive Interpretation in Law.* Princeton: Princeton University Press, 2005.

Barkow, Rachel E. "Administering Crime," 52 *U.C.L.A. Law Review* 715 (2005).

——. "Recharging the Jury: The Criminal Jury's Constitutional Role in an Era of Mandatory Sentencing," 152 *University of Pennsylvania Law Review* 33 (2003).

Barkow, Rachel E. "Separation of Powers and the Criminal Law," 58 *Stanford Law Review* 989 (2006).

Barnett, Randy E. "Curing the Drug-Law Addiction: The Harmful Side Effects of Legal Prohibition," in Jeffrey Schaler, ed. *Drugs: Should We Legalize, Decriminalize, or Deregulate?* Amherst, N.Y.: Prometheus Books, 1998, p.155.

———. "Restitution: A New Paradigm of Criminal Justice," in Randy Barnett and John Hagel, III, eds. *Assessing the Criminal: Restitution, Retribution, and the Legal Process.* Cambridge: Ballinger Pub. Co., 1977, p.349.

———. *Restoring the Lost Constitution: The Presumption of Liberty.* Princeton: Princeton University Press, 2004.

Bateman, Tracey. "Annotation, Validity, Construction, and Application of State Statutes Prohibiting Sale or Possession of Controlled Substances Within Specified Distance of School," 27 *A.L.R. 5th* 593 (2000).

Bayles, Michael. "Criminal Paternalism," in J. Roland Pennock and John W. Chapman, eds. *Nomos XV: The Limits of Law.* New York: Lieber-Atherton, 1974, p.174.

Beale, Sara Sun. "The Many Faces of Overcriminalization: From Morals and Mattress Tags to Overfederalization," 54 *American University Law Review* 747 (2005).

———. "What's Law Got to Do with It? The Political, Social, Psychological and Other Non-Legal Factors Influencing the Development of (Federal) Criminal Law," 1 *Buffalo Criminal Law Review* 23 (1997).

Becker, Gary "Crime and Punishment: An Economic Approach," 76 *Journal of Political Economy* 169 (1968).

Becker, Lawrence C. "Criminal Attempts and the Theory of the Law of Crimes," 3 *Philosophy and Public Affairs* 262 (1974).

Bennett, William. "The Plea to Legalize Drugs Is a Siren Call to Surrender," in Michael Lyman and Gary Potter, eds. *Drugs in Society.* Cincinnati: Anderson Pub. Co., 1991, p.339.

Bentham, Jeremy. *Principles of Morals and Legislation.* London: Methuen, 1970.

Berman, Harold. *Soviet Criminal Law and Procedure.* Cambridge: Harvard University Press, 2nd Ed., 1972.

Berman, Mitchell N. "Punishment and Justification" (forthcoming).

Bianchi, Herman. "Abolition: Assensus and Sanctuary," in Antony Duff and David Garland, eds. *A Reader on Punishment.* Oxford: Oxford University Press, 1994, p.336.

Bibas, Stephanos. "Plea Bargaining outside the Shadow of Trial," 117 *Harvard Law Review* 2463 (2000).

Bilionis, Louis D. "Process, the Constitution, and Substantive Criminal Law," 96 *Michigan Law Review* 1269 (1998).

Binder, Guyora. "Punishment Theory: Moral or Political?" 5 *Buffalo Criminal Law Review* 321 (2002).

Black, Donald. *The Behavior of Law.* London: Academic Press, 1976.

Blackstone, William. 4 *Commentaries on the Laws of England* (1765–1769).

Blendon, Robert J. and John T. Young: "The Public and the War on Illicit Drugs," 279 *Journal of the American Medical Association* 140 (1998).

Blumstein, Alfred and Joel Wallman, eds. *The Crime Drop in America.* Cambridge: Cambridge University Press, 2000.

Boardman, William S. "Coordination and the Moral Obligation to Obey the Law," 97 *Ethics* 546 (1987).

Boaz, David. "The Consequences of Prohibition," in David Boaz, ed. *The Crisis in Drug Prohibition.* Washington, D.C.: Cato Institute, 1990, p.1.

Bouza, Anthony V. *Police Unbound: Corruption, Abuse, and Heroism by the Boys in Blue.* Amherst, N.Y.: Prometheus Books, 2001.

Braithwaite, John and Philip Pettit. *Not Just Deserts*. Oxford: Oxford University Press, 1990.

Brickey, Kathleen F. "Enron's Legacy," 8 *Buffalo Criminal Law Review* 221 (2004).

——. "Federal Criminal Code Reform: Hidden Costs, Illusory Benefits," 2 *Buffalo Criminal Law Review* 161 (1998).

Brown, Darryl K. "Rethinking Overcriminalization" (forthcoming).

Brownwell, Kelly D. and Katherine Battle Horgen. *Food Fight*. New York: McGraw-Hill, 2004.

Burgh, Richard. "Do the Guilty Deserve Punishment?" 79 *Journal of Philosophy* 193 (1982).

Bushman, Brad J. and Angela D. Stack. "Forbidden Fruit Versus Tainted Fruit: Effects of Warning Labels on Attraction to Television Violence," 2 *Journal of Experimental Psychology* 207 (1996).

Calabresi, Guido and A. Douglas Melamed. "Property Rules, Liability Rules, and Inalienability: One View of the Cathedral," 85 *Harvard Law Review* 1089 (1972).

Chemerinsky, Erwin. *Constitutional Law: Principles and Policies*. New York: Aspen, 1997.

Cheng, Edward K. "Structural Laws and the Puzzle of Regulating Behavior," 100 *Northwestern University Law Review* 655 (2006).

Christopher, Russell L. "Deterring Retributivism: The Injustice of 'Just' Punishment," 96 *Northwestern University Law Review* 843 (2002).

——. "The Prosecutor's Dilemma: Bargains and Punishments," 72 *Fordham Law Review* 93 (2003).

Coffee, John C. "Does 'Unlawful' Mean 'Criminal'?: Reflections on the Disappearing Tort/Crime Distinction in American Law," 71 *Boston University Law Review* 193 (1991).

Cohen, Jay S. *Overdose*. New York: Jeremy P. Tarcher/Putnam, 2001.

Colb, Sherry F. "Freedom from Incarceration: Why Is This Right Different from All Other Rights?" 69 *New York University Law Review* 781 (1994).

Coleman, Jules. "Crimes and Transactions," 88 *California Law Review* 921, 925 (2000).

——. *The Practice of Principle*. Oxford: Oxford University Press, 2001.

——. *Risks and Wrongs*. Cambridge: Cambridge University Press, 1992.

——. "Tort Law and the Demands of Corrective Justice," 67 *Indiana Law Journal* 349 (1992).

Conner, Toni L. "Juvenile Curfews: Political Pandering at the Expense of a Fundamental Right," 109 *West Virginia Law Review* 459 (2007).

Cook, Philip J. and Jens Ludwig. *Gun Violence: The Real Costs*. New York: Oxford University Press, 2000.

Cottingham, John. "Varieties of Retribution," 29 *Philosophical Quarterly* 116 (1979).

Darley, John M. "On the Unlikely Prospects of Reducing Crime by Increasing the Severity of Prison Sentences," XIII *Law and Policy* 189 (2005).

Darrow, Clarence. *The Story of My Life*. New York: Charles Scribner's Sons, 1932.

Davis, Kenneth Culp. *Discretionary Justice*. Urbana: University of Illinois Press, 3rd ed., 1976.

Davis, Michael. "Why Attempts Deserve Less Punishment than Complete Crimes," 5 *Law and Philosophy* 1 (1986).

Demleitner, Nora V. "'Collateral Damage': No Re-Entry for Drug Offenders," 47 *Villanova Law Review* 1027 (2002).

——. "Preventing Internal Exile: The Need for Restrictions on Collateral Sentencing Consequences," 11 *Stanford Law & Policy Review* 153 (1999).

Denno, Deborah W. "The Perils of Public Opinion," 28 *Hofstra Law Review* 741 (2000).

——. "Why the Model Penal Code's Sexual Offense Provisions Should Be Pulled and Replaced," 1 *Ohio State Journal of Criminal Law* 207 (2003).

Devlin, Patrick. *The Enforcement of Morals*. London: Oxford University Press, 1965.

Diamond, John L. "The Myth of Morality and Fault in Criminal Law Doctrine," 34 *American Criminal Law Review* 111 (1996).

Dimock, Susan. "Retributivism and Trust," 16 *Law and Philosophy* 27 (1997).

Dixon, Nicholas. "Boxing, Paternalism, and Legal Moralism," 27 *Social Theory and Practice* 323 (2001).

———. "Why We Should Ban Handguns in the United States," 12 *St. Louis University Public Law Review* 243 (1993).

Dolinko, David. "Some Thoughts about Retributivism," 101 *Ethics* 537 (1991).

Dolovich, Sharon. "Legitimate Punishment in Liberal Democracy," 7 *Buffalo Criminal Law Review* 307 (2004).

Dressler, Joshua. *Understanding Criminal Law*. Lexis/Nexis, 4th ed., 2006.

Dripps, Donald A. "The Liberal Critique of the Harm Principle," 17 *Criminal Justice Ethics* 3 (1998).

———. "Overcriminalization, Discretion, Waiver: A Survey of Possible Exit Strategies," 109 *Penn State Law Review* 1155 (2005).

Dubber, Markus Dirk. *The Police Power: Patriarchy and the Foundations of American Government*. New York: Columbia University Press, 2005.

———. "The Possession Paradigm: The Special Part and the Police Power Model of the Criminal Process," in Antony Duff and Stuart Green, eds. *Defining Crimes: Essays on the Special Part of the Criminal Law*. Oxford: Oxford University Press, 2005, p.91.

———. "Toward a Constitutional Law of Crime and Punishment," 55 *Hastings Law Journal* 509 (2004).

Duff, R. A. "Crime, Prohibition, and Punishment," 19 *Journal of Applied Philosophy* 97 (2002).

———. *Criminal Attempts*. Oxford: Clarendon Press, 1996.

———. "Criminal Responsibility, Municipal and International" (forthcoming).

———. "Criminalising Endangerment," in Antony Duff and Stuart Green, eds. *Defining Crimes: Essays on the Special Part of the Criminal Law* Oxford: Oxford University Press, 2005, p.43.

———. "Democratic Criminal Responsibility" (forthcoming).

———. *Punishment, Communication, and Community*. Oxford: Oxford University Press, 2001.

———. "Punishment, Communication, and Community" in Matt Matravers, ed. *Punishment and Political Theory*. Oxford: Hart Pub. Co., 1999, p.48.

———. "Theorising Criminal Law: A 25th Anniversary Essay," 25 *Oxford Journal of Legal Studies* 353 (2005).

———. *Trials and Punishments*. Cambridge: Cambridge University Press, 1986.

Dworkin, Gerald. "Devlin Was Right: Law and the Enforcement of Morality," 40 *William & Mary Law Review* 927 (1999).

Dworkin, Ronald. "Liberty and Moralism," in Ronald Dworkin. *Taking Rights Seriously*. Cambridge: Harvard University Press, 1977, p.240.

———. "Lord Devlin and the Enforcement of Morals," in Ronald Dworkin. *Taking Rights Seriously*. Cambridge: Harvard University Press, 1977, p.240.

———. *Taking Rights Seriously*. Cambridge: Harvard University Press, 1977.

———. "Why Efficiency?" 8 *Hofstra Law Review* 563 (1980).

Dwyer, Joel. *The Perpetual Prison Machine*. Boulder: Westview, 2000.

Earlywine, Mitch. *Understanding Marijuana: A New Look at the Scientific Evidence*. Oxford: Oxford University Press, 2002.

Edmundson, William A. *The Duty to Obey the Law*. Lanham, Md.: Rowman & Littlefield, 1999.

Edwards, Rem B. "Why We Should Not Use Some Drugs for Pleasure," in Stephen Luper-Foy and Curtis Brown, eds. *Drugs, Morality, and the Law*. New York: Garland Pub. Co., 1994, p.183.

Ellis, Dorsey D. "An Economic Theory of Intentional Torts: A Comment," 3 *International Review of Law and Economics* 45 (1983).

Ely, Amie N. "Note: Prosecutorial Discretion as an Ethical Necessity: The Ashcroft Memorandum's Curtailment of the Prosecutor's Duty to 'Seek Justice,'" 90 *Cornell Law Review* 237 (2004).

Fagan, Jeffrey. "Do Criminal Sanctions Deter Drug Offenders?" in Doris MacKenzie and Craig Uchida, eds. *Drugs and Criminal Justice: Evaluating Public Policy Initiatives.* Thousand Oaks: Sage Publications, 1994, p.188.

Fahrenthold, David A. "In N.H., a Beer in the Belly Can Get Youths Arrested," *The Washington Post* (Sunday, February 5, 2006), p.A8.

Farmer, Lindsay. *Criminal Law, Tradition and Legal Order: Crime and the Genius of Scots Law.* Cambridge: Cambridge University Press, 1997.

Farrington, David P. "Developmental Criminology and Risk-Focused Prevention," in Mike Maguire, Rod Morgan, and Robert Reiner, eds. *Oxford Handbook of Criminology.* 3rd ed., 2002, p.657.

Federal Bureau of Investigation. *Crime in the United States.* (2005).

Feinberg, Joel. "The Expressive Function of Punishment," in Joel Feinberg. *Doing and Deserving.* Princeton: Princeton University Press, 1970, p.95.

———. *Harm to Others: The Moral Limits of the Criminal Law.* Oxford: Oxford University Press, 1984.

———. *Harm to Self: The Moral Limits of the Criminal Law.* New York: Oxford University Press, 1986.

———. *Harmless Wrongdoing: The Moral Limits of the Criminal Law.* New York: Oxford University Press, 1988.

———. *Offense to Others: The Moral Limits of the Criminal Law.* New York: Oxford University Press, 1985.

Fellner, Jamie. "Punishment and Prejudice: Racial Disparities in the War on Drugs," 12:2 *Human Rights Watch* (May 2000).

Finkelstein, Claire O. "Is Risk a Harm?" 151 *University of Pennsylvania Law Review* 963 (2003).

———. "Positivism and the Notion of an Offense," 88 *California Law Review* 335 (2000).

Finnis, John. *Natural Law and Natural Rights.* Oxford: Clarendon Press, 1980.

Fisher, George. *Plea Bargaining's Triumph: A History of Plea Bargaining in America.* Stanford: Stanford University Press, 2003.

Fitzgerald, P.J. "A Concept of Crime," *Criminal Law Review* 257 (1960).

Fletcher, George P. *Basic Concepts of Criminal Law.* New York: Oxford University Press, 1998.

———. "Disenfranchisement as Punishment: Reflections on the Racial Uses of Infamia," 46 *UCLA Law Review* 1895 (1999).

———. "Dogmas of the Model Penal Code," 2 *Buffalo Criminal Law Review* 3 (1998).

———. "The Fall and Rise of Criminal Theory," 1 *Buffalo Criminal Law Review,*" 275 (1998).

———. *The Grammar of Criminal Law: American, European, International.* New York: Oxford University Press, 2007.

———. *Rethinking Criminal Law.* Boston: Little, Brown and Co., 1978.

Fuller, Lon. *The Morality of Law.* Cambridge: Harvard University Press, 1968.

Gainer, Ronald. "Federal Criminal Code Reform: Past and Future," 2 *Buffalo Criminal Law Review* 45.

Garcia, J. L. A. "Two Concepts of Desert," 5 *Law and Philosophy* 219 (1986).

Gardner, John. "On the General Part of the Criminal Law," in Antony Duff, ed. *Philosophy and the Criminal Law.* Cambridge: Cambridge University Press, 1998, p.205.

Gardner, John and Stephen Shute. "The Wrongness of Rape," in Jeremy Horder, ed. *Oxford Essays in Jurisprudence.* 4th Series, 2000, p.193.

Garland, David. *Mass Imprisonment in the United States: Social Causes and Consequences.* London: Sage, 2001.

Gewirth, Alan. "Are There Any Absolute Rights?" 31 *Philosophical Quarterly* 1 (1981).

Golash, Deirdre. *The Case against Punishment.* New York: New York University Press, 2005.

Goodin, Robert E. *Utilitarianism as a Public Philosophy.* Cambridge: Cambridge University Press, 1995.

Gottlieb, Stephen E. "Compelling Governmental Interests: An Essential But Unanalyzed Term in Constitutional Adjudication," 68 *Boston University Law Review* 917 (1988).

——. "Introduction: Overriding Public Values," in Stephen E. Gottlieb, ed. *Public Values in Constitutional Law.* Ann Arbor: University of Michigan Press, 1993, p.2.

——, ed. *Public Values in Constitutional Law.* Ann Arbor: University of Michigan Press, 1993.

Gottschalk, Marie. *The Prison and the Gallows: The Politics of Mass Incarceration in America.* New York: Cambridge University Press, 2006.

Green, Hillary. "Undead Laws: The Use of Historically Unenforced Criminal Statutes in Non-Criminal Legislation," 16 *Yale Law and Policy Review* 169 (1997).

Green, Leslie. "Law, Co-ordination, and the Common Good," 3 *Oxford Journal of Legal Studies* 299 (1983).

Green, Stuart P. "Cheating," 23 *Law and Philosophy* 137 (2004).

——. *Lying, Cheating, and Stealing: A Moral Theory of White-Collar Crime* (Oxford: Oxford University Press, 2006.

——. "Why It's a Crime to Tear the Tag Off a Mattress: Overcriminalization and the Moral Content of Regulatory Offenses," 46 *Emory Law Journal* 1533 (1997).

Green, Thomas Andrew. *Verdict According to Conscience: Perspectives on the English Criminal Trial Jury, 1200–1800* Chicago: University of Chicago Press, 1985.

Gross, Hyman. *A Theory of Criminal Justice.* New York: Oxford University Press, 1979.

Gross, Samuel R., et al. "Exonerations in the United States 1989 through 2003," 95 *Journal of Criminal Law and Criminology* 523 (2005).

Gunther, Gerald. "The Supreme Court, 1971 Term—Forward: In Search of Evolving Doctrine on a Changing Court: A Model for a Newer Equal Protection," 86 *Harvard Law Review* 1 (1972).

Hall, Tia. "Music Piracy and the Audio Home Recording Act," *Duke Law and Technology Review* 23 (2002).

Halvorsen, Victor. "Is It Better That Ten Guilty Persons Go Free Than That One Innocent Person Be Convicted?" 23 *Criminal Justice Ethics* 3 (2004).

Hampton, Jean. "The Moral Education Theory of Punishment," 13 *Philosophy and Public Affairs* 208 (1984).

Harcourt, Bernard E. "The Collapse of the Harm Principle," 90 *Journal of Criminal Law and Criminology* 109 (1999).

——. "Should We Aggregate Mental Hospitalization and Prison Population Rates in Empirical Research on the Relationship between Incarceration and Crime, Unemployment, Poverty, and Other Social Indicators?" (forthcoming).

Hardy, I. Trotter. "Criminal Copyright Infringement," 11 *William & Mary Bill of Rights Journal* 305 (2002).

Hare, R.M. "What Is Wrong with Slavery," 8 *Philosophy & Public Affairs* 103 (1979).

Harel, Alon. "Why Only the State May Punish: On the Vices of Privately-Inflicted Sanctions for Wrongdoing," *Cardozo Law Review* (forthcoming).

Harris, David. "Car Wars: The Fourth Amendment's Death on the Highway," 66 *George Washington Law Review* 556 (1998).

Harsanyi, John C. "Morality and the Theory of Rational Behaviour," in Amartya Sen and Bernard Williams, eds. *Utilitarianism and Beyond*. Cambridge: Cambridge University Press, 1983, p.39.

Hart, H. L. A. *Law, Liberty, and Morality*. New York: Vintage Books, 1963.

——. *Punishment and Responsibility*. Oxford: Oxford University Press, 1969.

Hart, Henry M., Jr. "The Aims of the Criminal Law," 23 *Law & Contemporary Problems* 404 (1958).

Hasen, Richard L. and Richard H. McAdams. "The Surprisingly Complex Case against Theft," 17 *International Review of Law and Economics*," 367 (1997).

Hawkins, Keith. *Law as Last Resort: Prosecution Decision-Making in a Regulatory Agency*. Oxford: Oxford University Press, 2002.

Heyman, Gene M. "Is Addiction a Chronic, Relapsing Disease?" in Philip B. Heyman and William N. Brownsberger, eds. *Drug Addiction and Drug Policy*. Cambridge: Harvard University Press, 2001, p.81

Holmes, Oliver W. "The Path of the Law," X *Harvard Law Review* 457 (1897).

Hooker, Brad. *Ideal Code, Real World: A Rule-Consequential Theory of Morality*. Oxford: Oxford University Press, 2000.

Horder, Jeremy. "Crimes of Ulterior Intent," in A. P. Simester and A. T. H. Smith, eds. *Harm and Culpability*. Oxford: Clarendon Press, 1996, p.153.

——. *Excusing Crime*. Oxford: Oxford University Press, 2004.

Huigens, Kyron. "What Is and Is Not Pathological in Criminal Law," 101 *Michigan Law Review* 811 (2002).

Hunt, Alan. *Governing Morals: A Social History of Moral Regulation*. Cambridge: Cambridge University Press, 1999.

Hurd, Heidi. "What in the World Is Wrong?" 5 *Journal of Contemporary Legal Issues* 157 (1994).

Husak, Douglas. "Already Punished Enough," 18 *Philosophical Topics* 79 (1990).

——. "The 'But Everybody Does That!' Defense," 10 *Public Affairs Quarterly* 307 (1996).

——. "Crimes outside the Core," 39 *Tulsa Law Review* 755 (2004).

——. "The Criminal Law as Last Resort," 24 *Oxford Journal of Legal Studies* 207 (2004).

——. *Drugs and Rights*. Cambridge: Cambridge University Press, 1992.

——. "Guns and Drugs: Case Studies on the Principled Limits of the Criminal Sanction," 23 *Law and Philosophy* 437 (2004).

——. "Is the Criminal Law Important?" 1 *Ohio State Journal of Criminal Law* 261 (2003).

——. "Justifications and the Criminal Liability of Accessories," 80 *Journal of Criminal Law and Criminology* 201 (1989).

——. "Legal Paternalism," in Hugh LaFollette, ed. *Oxford Handbook of Practical Ethics*. Oxford: Clarendon Press, 2002, p.387.

——. *Legalize This!* London: Verso, 2002.

——. "Liberal Neutrality, Autonomy, and Drug Prohibitions," 29 *Philosophy and Public Affairs* 43 (2000).

——. "A Liberal Theory of Excuses," 3 *Ohio State Journal of Criminal Law* 287 (2005).

——. "Limitations on Criminalization and the General Part of Criminal Law," in Stephen Shute and A. P. Simester, eds. *Criminal Law Theory: Doctrines of the General Part*. Oxford: Oxford University Press, 2002, p.13.

——. "Omissions, Causation, and Liability," 30 *Philosophical Quarterly* 316 (1980).

——. "Partial Defenses," XI *Canadian Journal of Law & Jurisprudence* 167 (1998).

——. *Philosophy of Criminal Law*. Totowa, N.J.: Rowman & Allanheld, 1987.

——."Reasonable Risk Creation and Overinclusive Legislation," 1 *Buffalo Criminal Law Review* 599 (1998).

——."Retribution in Criminal Theory," 37 *San Diego Law Review* 959 (2000).

——. "The Serial View of Criminal Law Defenses," 3 *Criminal Law Forum* 369 (1992).

——. "On the Supposed Priority of Justification to Excuse," 24 *Law and Philosophy* 557 (2005).

——. "Why Punish the Deserving?" 26 *Nous* 447 (1992).

Husak, Douglas and Andrew von Hirsch. "Culpability and Mistake of Law," in Stephen Shute, John Gardner, and Jeremy Horder, eds. *Action and Value in Criminal Law*. Oxford: Clarendon Press, 1993, p.157.

Husak, Douglas and Stanton Peele. "'One of the Major Problems of Our Society': Imagery and Evidence of Drug Harms in U.S. Supreme Court Decisions," 25 *Contemporary Drug Problems* 191 (1998).

Hylton, Keith N. "The Theory of Penalties and the Economics of Criminal Law," 1 *Review of Law and Economics* 1 (2005).

"Investigating Enron," *Wall Street Journal* (November 30, 2001), p.A14.

Jackson, Robert H. "The Federal Prosecutor," 24 *Journal of the American Judicature Society* 18 (1940).

Jacobs, James B. *Can Gun Control Work?* Oxford: Oxford University Press, 2002.

——. *Drunk Driving: An American Dilemma*. Chicago: University of Chicago Press, 1989.

Jacobs, James B. and Kimberley Potter. *Hate Crimes: Criminal Law & Identity Politics*. New York: Oxford University Press, 1998.

——. "Keeping Guns Out of the 'Wrong' Hands: The Brady Law and the Limits of Regulation," 86 *Journal of Criminal Law and Criminology* 93 (1995).

Jareborg, Nils. "Criminalization as Last Resort (*Ultima Ratio*)," 2 *Ohio State Journal of Criminal Law* 521 (2005).

——. "What Kind of Criminal Law Do We Want?" in Annika Snare, ed. *Beware of Punishment*. Oslo: Scandanavian Research Council for Criminology, 1995, p.17.

Jenkins, Philip. *Moral Panic: Changing Concepts of the Child Molester in Modern America*. New Haven: Yale University Press, 1998.

Jung, Heike. "Criminal Justice: A European Perspective," *Criminal Law Review* 237 (1993).

Junker, John M. "Criminalization and Criminogenesis," 19 *UCLA Law Review* 697, 700 (1972).

Kadish, Sanford. "The Crisis of Overcriminalization," 374 *Annals of the American Academy of Political and Social Science* 157 (1967).

Kadish, Sanford and Stephen Schulhofer. *Criminal Law and Its Processes*. New York: Aspen, 7th ed., 2001.

Kagan, Shelly. *The Limits of Morality*. Oxford: Clarendon Press, 1991.

Kahan, Dan. "The Secret Ambition of Deterrence," 119 *Harvard Law Review* 414 (1999).

——. "What Do Alternative Sanctions Mean?" 63 *University of Chicago Law Review* 591 (1996).

Kant, Immanuel. *Metaphysical First Principles of Right*. Cambridge: Cambridge University Press, 1996.

Kaplow, Louis and Steven Shavell. *Fairness versus Welfare*. Cambridge: Harvard University Press, 2002.

Katyal, Neil Kumar. "Conspiracy Theory," 112 *Yale Law Journal* 1307 (2003).

Katz, Leo. "Is There a Volume Discount for Crime?" (forthcoming).

——. "Villany and Felony: A Problem Concerning Criminalization," 6 *Buffalo Criminal Law Review* 451 (2003).

King, Ryan S. and Mark Mauer. "The War on Marijuana: The Transformation of the Drug War in the 1990s" (May 2005), *http://www.sentencingproject.org/pdfs/waronmarijuana.pdf.*

Kleck, Gary. *Targeting Guns: Firearms and Their Control.* New York: Aldine De Gruyter, 1997.

Klein, Susan R. "Redrawing the Criminal-Civil Boundary," 2 *Buffalo Criminal Law Review* 679 (1999).

Kleinig, John. "Criminally Harming Others," 5 *Criminal Justice Ethics* 3 (1986).

Klevorick, Alvin K. "On the Economic Theory of Crime," in J. Roland Pennock and John W. Chapman, eds. *Nomos XXVII: Criminal Justice.* 1985, p.289.

Koenig, Thomas and Michael Rustad. "'Crimtorts' as Corporate Just Deserts," 31 *University of Michigan Journal of Law Reform* 289 (1998).

Kopel, David and Christopher C. Little. "Communitarians, Neorepublicans, and Guns: Assessing the Case for Firearms Prohibition," 56 *Maryland Law Review* 438 (1997).

Kramer, Donald T., et al., eds. *Rights of Prisoners.* Colorado Springs: McGraw-Hill, 2nd ed., 1993.

Kramer, Matthew H. "Legal and Moral Obligation," in Martin P. Golding and William A. Edmundson, eds. *The Blackwell Guide to the Philosophy of Law and Legal Theory.* Oxford: Blackwell Publishing, 2005, p.179.

Lacey, Nicola. "Contingency, Coherence, and Conceptualism" in Antony Duff, ed. *Philosophy and the Criminal Law.* Cambridge: Cambridge University Press, 1998, p.9.

——. *State Punishment.* London: Routledge, 1988.

LaFave, Wayne R. *Criminal Law.* St. Paul: West Pub. Co, 3d.ed, 2000.

Lee, Youngjae. "The Constitutional Right Against Excessive Punishment," 91 *University of Virginia Law Review* 677 (2005).

Leshner, Alan. "Addiction Is a Brain Disease, and It Matters," 278 *Science* 45 (1997).

Lewis, David. *Convention.* Cambridge: Harvard University Press, 1969.

Lichtenberg, Illya. "Police Discretion and Traffic Enforcement: A Government of Men?" 50 *Cleveland State Law Review* 425 (2002–2003).

Liptak, Adam. "Debt to Society Is Least of Costs for Ex-Convicts," *New York Times* (February 23, 2006), p.A1.

——. "To More Inmates, Life Term Means Dying Behind Bars," *New York Times* (Sunday, October 2, 2005), p.A:1.

Logan, Wayne. "The Ex Post Facto Clause and the Jurisprudence of Punishment," 35 *American Criminal Law Review* 1261 (1998).

Luna, Eric. "Drug Exceptionalism," 47 *Villanova Law Review* 753 (2002).

——. "The Overcriminalization Phenomenon," 54 *American University Law Review* 703 (2005).

——. "Overextending the Criminal Law," in Gene Healy, ed. *Go Directly to Jail: The Criminalization of Almost Everything.* Washington D.C.: Cato Institute, 2004, p.1.

——. "Principled Enforcement of Penal Codes," 4 *Buffalo Criminal Law Review* 515 (2000).

Lungren, Daniel. "Legalization Would Be a Mistake," in Timothy Lynch, ed. *After Prohibition.* Washington, D.C.: Cato Institute, 2000, p.179.

Lynch, Gerald E. "Towards a Model Penal Code, Second (Federal?): The Challenge of the Special Part," 2 *Buffalo Criminal Law Review* 297 (1998).

——. "Revising the Model Penal Code," 1 *Ohio State Journal of Criminal Law* 219 (2003).

Mabbott, J. D. "Professor Flew on Punishment," in H. B. Acton, ed. *The Philosophy of Punishment.* Macmillan: St. Martin's Press, 1969, p.115.

———. "Punishment," in H. B. Acton, ed. *The Philosophy of Punishment.* Macmillan: St. Martin's Press, 1969, p.39.

MacGoun, Robert J. and Peter Reuter. *Drug War Heresies.* Cambridge: Cambridge University Press, 2001.

Mackenzie, Mary Margaret. *Plato on Punishment.* Berkeley: University of California Press, 1981.

Marshall, S. E. and R. A. Duff. "Criminalization and Sharing Wrongs," XI *Canadian Journal of Law & Jurisprudence* 7 (1998).

Massaro, Toni M. "Shame, Culture, and American Criminal Law," 89 *Michigan Law Review* 1880 (1991).

Massey, Calvin. "The New Formalism: Requiem for Tiered Scrutiny?" 6 *University of Pennsylvania Journal of Constitutional Law* 945 (2004).

McCabe, Neil Colman. "State Constitutions and Substantive Criminal Law," 71 *Temple Law Review* 521 (1998).

McCloskey, H. J. "A Non-Utilitarian Approach to Punishment," 8 *Inquiry* 249 (1965).

McEvoy, Suzanne P., et al. "Role of Mobile Phones in Motor Vehicle Crashes Resulting in Hospital Attendance: A Case-Crossover Study," *British Medical Journal* (July 2005) 10.1136/38537.

McWilliams, Peter. *Ain't Nobody's Business If You Do.* Los Angeles: Prelude Press, 1993.

Meares, Tracey. "Social Organization and Drug Law Enforcement," 35 *American Criminal Law Review* 191 (1998).

Meitl, P.J. "The Perjury Paradox: The Amazing Under-Enforcement of the Laws Regarding Lying to Congress," 25 *Quinnipiac Law Review* 547 (2007).

Menlowe, Michael and Alexander McCall Smith, eds. *The Duty to Rescue.* Hanover, Vt.: Dartmouth Pub. Group, 1993.

Michaels, Alan C. "Acceptance: The Missing Mental State," 71 *Southern California Law Review* 953 (1998).

———. "Constitutional Innocence," 112 *Harvard Law Review* 828 (1999).

Mill, John Stuart. *On Liberty.* E.P. Dutton: Everyman's Edition, 1951.

Miller, Eric J. "Embracing Addiction: Drug Courts and the False Promise of Judicial Interventionism," 65 *Ohio State Law Journal* 1479 (2004).

Mitchell, Melissa J. "Comment: Cleaning Out the Closet: Using Sunset Provisions to Clean up Cluttered Criminal Codes," 54 *Emory Law Journal* 1671 (2005).

Moohr, Geraldine Szott. "Defining Overcriminalization Through Cost-Benefit Analysis: The Example of Criminal Copyright Laws," 54 *American University Law Review* 783 (2005).

Moore, Michael S. *Act and Crime.* Oxford: Oxford University Press, 1993.

Moore, Michael S. *Legal Causation* (forthcoming).

———. *Placing Blame.* Oxford: Clarendon Press, 1997.

Morris, Herbert. "A Paternalistic Theory of Punishment," 18 *American Philosophical Quarterly* 263 (1981).

———. "Persons and Punishment," 53 *Monist* 474 (1968).

Morse, Stephen J. "Reasons, Results, and Criminal Responsibility," *University of Illinois Law Review* 363 (2004).

———. "Uncontrollable Urges and Irrational People," 88 *Virginia Law Review* 1025 (2002).

Murphy, Jeffrie G. "Marxism and Retribution," 2 *Philosophy and Public Affairs* 217 (1973).

———. "Retributivism, Moral Education, and the Liberal State," 4 *Criminal Justice Ethics* 3 (1985).

———. "The State's Interest in Retribution," 5 *Journal of Contemporary Legal Issues* 283 (1994).

Murphy, Jeffrie and Jules Coleman. *The Philosophy of Law.* Totowa, N.J: Rowman & Allanheld, 1984.

Murphy, Jeffrie J. and Jean Hampton. *Forgiveness and Mercy.* Cambridge: Cambridge University Press, 1988.

Musto, David F. *The American Disease: Origins of Narcotic Control.* Oxford: Oxford University Press, 3rd ed., 1999.

Nadelmann, Ethan. "Drug Prohibition in the United States: Costs, Consequences, and Alternatives," 245 *Science* 939 (1989).

———. "Thinking Seriously about Alternatives to Drug Prohibition," in Jefferson Fish, ed. *How to Legalize Drugs.* Northvale, N.J.: Jason Aronson, 1998, p.578.

Nagin, Daniel S. "Deterrence and Incapacitation," in Michael Tonry, ed. *The Handbook of Crime and Punishment.* Oxford: Oxford University Press, 1998, p.345.

Natapoff, Alexander. "Underenforcement," 75 *Fordham Law Review* 1715 (2006).

New Jersey Commission to Review Criminal Sentencing. *Report on New Jersey's Drug-Free Zone Crimes and Proposal for Reform* (December 2005).

Nino, C. S. "A Consensual Theory of Punishment," 12 *Philosophy and Public Affairs* 289 (1983).

Nolan, James L., Jr. *Reinventing Justice: The American Drug Court Movement.* Princeton: Princeton University Press, 2001.

Note. "Criminal Liability for Possession of Nonusable Amounts of Controlled Substances," 77 *Columbia Law Review* 596 (1977).

———. "Desuetude," 119 *Harvard Law Review* 2209 (2006).

———. "Making Sense of Hybrid Speech: A New Model for Commercial Speech and Expressive Conduct," 118 *Harvard Law Review* 2836 (2005).

Nozick, Robert. *Anarchy, State, and Utopia.* New York: Basic Books, 1974.

O'Neill, Michael Edmund. "When Prosecutors Don't: Trends in Federal Prosecutorial Declinations," 79 *Notre Dame Law Review* 221 (2003).

O'Sullivan, Julie R. "The Changing Face of White-Collar Crime: The Federal Criminal 'Code' Is a Disgrace: Obstruction Statutes as Case Study," 96 *Journal of Criminal Law and Criminology* 643 (2006).

Oberdiek, John. "Lost in Moral Space: On the Infringing/Violating Distinction and Its Place in the Theory of Rights," 23 *Law and Philosophy* 325 (2004).

Osler, Mark. "This Changes Everything: A Call for a Directive, Goal-Oriented Principle to Guide the Exercise of Discretion by Federal Prosecutors," 39 *Valparaiso Law Review* 625 (2005).

Packer, Herbert. *The Limits of the Criminal Sanction.* Stanford: Stanford University Press, 1968.

Parfit, Derek. *Reasons and Persons.* Oxford: Oxford University Press, 1984.

Parker, Jeffrey S. "The Economics of Mens Rea," 79 *Virginia Law Review* 741 (1993).

Peele, Stanton and Charles Buffe, with Archie Brodsky. *Resisting 12-Step Coercion.* Tucson: Sharp Press, 2000.

Perkins, Rollin M. and Ronald N. Boyce. *Criminal Law.* Mineola, N.Y.: Foundation Press, 3rd ed., 1982.

Peston, Maurice. *Public Goods and the Public Sector.* London: Macmillan, 1972.

Pilcher, Susan. "Ignorance, Discretion and the Fairness of Notice: Confronting 'Apparent Innocence' in the Criminal Law," 33 *American Criminal Law Review* 32 (1995).

Podgor, Ellen S. "Do We Need a 'Beanie Baby' Fraud Statute?" 49 *American University Law Review* 1031 (2000).

Podgor, Ellen S. "Jose Padilla and Martha Stewart: Who Should Have Been Charged with Criminal Conduct?" 109 *Penn State Law Review* 1059 (2005).

Posner, Richard A. "An Economic Theory of the Criminal Law," 85 *Columbia Law Review* 1193 (1985).

Price, Zachary. "The Rule of Lenity as a Rule of Structure," 72 *Fordham Law Review* 885 (2004).

Prothrow-Stith, Deborah and Michaele Weissman. *Deadly Consequences.* New York: Harper-Collins, 1991.

Railton, Peter. "Alienation, Consequentialism and the Demands of Morality," 13 *Philosophy and Public Affairs* 134 (1984).

Rakoff, Todd D. "Contracts of Adhesion: An Essay in Reconstruction," 96 *Harvard Law Review* 1174 (1983).

Rawls, John. *Political Liberalism.* New York: Columbia University Press, 1993.

———. "Two Concepts of Rules," 64 *Philosophical Review* 3 (1955).

Raz, Joseph. "Autonomy, Toleration, and the Harm Principle," in Ruth Gavison, ed. *Issues in Contemporary Legal Philosophy.* Oxford: Oxford University Press, 1987, p.313.

———. "Free Expression and Personal Identification," in Joseph Raz. *Ethics in the Public Domain: Essays in the Morality of Law and Politics.* Oxford: Clarendon Press, 1994, p.146.

———. *The Morality of Freedom.* Oxford: Clarendon Press, 1986.

———. *Practical Reasons and Norms.* Princeton: Princeton University Press, 2nd ed., 1990.

Reiff, Mark R. *Punishment, Compensation, and Law.* Cambridge: Cambridge University Press, 2005.

Richards, David. *Sex, Drugs, Death, and the Law: An Essay on Human Rights and Overcriminalization.* Totowa, N.J.: Rowman & Littlefield, 1982.

Ripstein, Arthur. "Beyond the Harm Principle," 34 *Philosophy & Public Affairs* 215 (2006).

———. "Prohibition and Preemption," 5 *Legal Theory* 235, 259 (1999).

Roberts, Julian V., et al. *Penal Populism and Public Opinion.* New York: Oxford University Press, 2002.

Robinson, Paul H. *Criminal Law Defenses.* St. Paul, Minn.: West Pub. Co., 1984.

Robinson, Paul H. *Structure and Function in Criminal Law.* Oxford: Oxford University Press, 1997.

Robinson, Paul H. and Michael T. Cahill. "The Accelerating Degradation of American Criminal Codes," 56 *Hastings Law Journal* 633 (2005).

———. "Can a Model Penal Code Second Save the States from Themselves? 1 *Ohio State Journal of Criminal Law* 169 (2003).

———. *Law without Justice.* New York: Oxford University Press, 2006.

Robinson, Paul H. and John M. Darley. "Does Criminal Law Deter? A Behavioural Science Investigation," 24 *Oxford Journal of Legal Studies* 173 (2004).

———. *Justice, Liability & Blame.* Boulder: WestviewPress, 1995.

———. "The Role of Deterrence in the Formulation of Criminal Law Rules: At Its Worst When Doing Its Best," 91 *Georgetown Law Journal* 949 (2003).

Robinson, Paul H., et al. "The Five Worst (and Five Best) American Criminal Codes," 95 *Northwestern University Law Review* 1 (2000).

Ross, H. Laurence. *Confronting Drunk Driving.* New Haven: Yale University Press, 1992.

Ross, Jacqueline E. "Damned Under Many Headings: The Problem of Multiple Punishment," 29 *American Journal of Criminal Law* 245 (2002).

Roth, Nelson E. and Scott E. Sundby. "The Felony-Murder Rule: A Doctrine at Constitutional Crossroads," 70 *Cornell Law Review* 446 (1985).

Schauer, Fredrick. *Playing by the Rules.* Oxford: Clarendon Press, 1991.

Scheck, Barry, Peter Neufeld and Jim Dwyer. *Actual Innocence*. (New York: Signet, 2001).

Schonsheck, Jonathan. *On Criminalization*. Dordrecht: Kluwer Academic Publishers, 1994.

Schulhofer, Stephen J. "Two Systems of Social Protection," 7 *Journal of Contemporary Legal Issues* 69 (1996).

Schulhofer, Stephen J. and Ilene H. Nagel. "Plea Negotiations under the Federal Sentencing Guidelines: Guideline Circumvention and Its Dynamics in the Post-*Mistretta* Period," 91 *Northwestern University Law Review* 1284 (1997).

Segal, Uzi and Alex Stein. "Ambiguity Aversion and the Criminal Process," 81 *Notre Dame Law Review*1495 (2006).

Segev, Re'em. "Justification, Rationality and Mistake: Mistake of Law Is no Excuse? It Might Be a Justification!" 25 *Law and Philosophy* 31 (2006).

Shafer-Landau, Russ. "Can Punishment Morally Educate?" 10 *Law and Philosophy* 189 (1991).

———. "Liberalism and Paternalism," 11 *Legal Theory* 169 (2005).

Shavell, Steven. *Foundations of Economic Analysis of Law*. Cambridge: Belknap Press of Harvard University Press, 2004.

Shedler, Jonathan Jack Block. "Adolescent Drug Use and Psychological Health," 45 *American Psychologist* 612 (1990).

Sher, George. *Beyond Neutrality*. Cambridge: Cambridge University Press, 1997.

———. "On the Decriminalization of Drugs," 22 *Criminal Justice Ethics* 30 (2003).

———. *In Praise of Blame*. Oxford: Oxford University Press, 2006.

Shiner, Roger A. "The De- and Re-construction of Criminal Law Theory" (forthcoming).

———. *Freedom of Commercial Expression*. Oxford: Oxford University Press, 2003.

Shute, Stephen. "With and without Constitutional Restraints: A Comparison between the Criminal Law of England and America," 1 *Buffalo Criminal Law Review* 329 (1998).

Sigler, Mary. "By the Light of Virtue: Prison Rape and the Corruption of Character," 91 *Iowa Law Review* 561 (2006).

Simester, A. P. "Is Strict Liability Always Wrong?" in A.P. Simester, ed. *Appraising Strict Liability*. Oxford: Oxford University Press, 2005, p.21.

Simester, A. P. and Andrew von Hirsch. "Rethinking the Offense Principle," 8 *Legal Theory* 269 (2002).

———, eds. *Incivilities: Regulating Offensive Behaviour*. Oxford: Hart Pub. Co., 2006.

Simester, A. P. and G. R. Sullivan. *Criminal Law: Theory and Doctrine*. Oxford: Hart Pub. Co., 2000.

Simester, Andrew and G.R. Sullivan: *Criminal Law: Theory and Doctrine*. Oxford: Hart Pub. Co., 3rd ed., 2007.

Simmons, A. John. *Justification & Legitimacy: Essays on Rights and Obligations*. Cambridge: Cambridge University Press, 2001.

———. *Moral Principles and Political Obligations*. Princeton: Princeton University Press, 1979.

Simons, Kenneth. "The Relevance of Community Values to Just Deserts: Criminal Law, Punishment Rationales, and Democracy," 28 *Hofstra Law Review* 635 (2000).

———. "Rethinking Mental States," 72 *Boston University Law Review* 463 (1992).

Singer, Richard. "The Model Penal Code and Three Two (Possibly Only One) Way Courts Avoid Mens Rea," 4 *Buffalo Criminal Law Review* 139 (2000).

———. "The Resurgence of Mens Rea III—The Rise and Fall of Strict Criminal Liability," 30 *Boston College Law Review* 337 (1989).

Singer, Richard and Douglas Husak. "Of Innocence and Innocents: The Supreme Court and *Mens Rea* Since Herbert Packer," 2 *Buffalo Criminal Law Review* 859 (1999).

Slobogin, Christopher. "The Civilization of the Criminal Law," 58 *Vanderbilt Law Review* 121 (2005).

———. "Is Justice Just Us? Using Social Science to Inform Substantive Criminal Law," 87 *Journal of Criminal Law & Criminology* 315 (1996).

Smith, Stephen D. "Is the Harm Principle Illiberal?" 51 *American Journal of Jurisprudence* 1 (2006).

Soper, Philip. *The Ethics of Deference*. Cambridge: Cambridge University Press, 2002. *Sourcebook of Criminal Justice Statistics*. (2005).

———. "Legal Theory and the Claim of Authority," 18 *Philosophy & Public Affairs* 209 (1989).

Standen, Jeffrey. "An Economic Perspective on Federal Criminal Law Reform," 2 *Buffalo Criminal Law Review* 249 (1998).

Steiker, Carol S. "Punishment and Procedure: Punishment Theory and the Criminal-Civil Divide," 85 *Georgia Law Journal* 775 (1997).

Stephen, James. 2 *A History of the Criminal Law of England*. 1883.

Stern, Nat. "In Defense of the Imprecise Definition of Commercial Speech," 58 *Maryland Law Review* 89 (1999).

Strader, J. Kelly. *Understanding White Collar Crime*. Lexis-Nexis, 2d.ed, 2006.

Stuart, Don. *Charter Justice in Canadian Criminal Law*. Toronto: Carswell, 4th ed, 2006.

Stuntz, William J. "Correspondence: Reply: Criminal Law's Pathology," 101 *Michigan Law Review* 828 (2002).

———. "Local Policing After the Terror," 111 *Yale Law Journal* 2137 (2002).

———. "The Pathological Politics of Criminal Law," 100 *Michigan Law Review* 506 (2001).

———. "Plea Bargaining and Criminal Law's Disappearing Shadow," 117 *Harvard Law Review* 2548 (2004).

———. "The Political Constitution of Criminal Justice," 119 *Harvard Law Review* 780 (2006).

———. "Substance, Process, and the Civil-Criminal Line," 7 *Journal of Contemporary Legal Issues* 1 (1996).

Suk, Jeannie. "Criminal Law Comes Home," 116 *Yale Law Journal* 2 (2006).

Sullum, Jacob. *Saying Yes: In Defense of Drug Use*. New York: Tarcher/Putnam, 2003.

Sunstein, Cass. "On the Expressive Function of Law," 144 *University of Pennsylvania Law Review* 2021 (1996).

Sweet, Robert W. and Edward A. Harris. "Moral and Constitutional Considerations in Support of the Decriminalization of Drugs," in Jefferson Fish, ed. *How to Legalize Drugs*. Northvale, N.J.: Jason Aronson, 1998, p.430.

Symposium. "The Faces of Wrongful Conviction," 37 *Golden Gate University Law Review* 1–217 (2006).

Tadros, Victor. *Criminal Responsibility*. Oxford: Oxford University Press, 2005.

———. "The Distinctiveness of Domestic Abuse: A Freedom-Based Account," in Green, Stuart and R.A. Duff, eds. *Defining Crimes: Essays on the Special Part of Criminal Law*. Oxford: Oxford University Press, 2005, p.119.

———. "Politics and the Presumption of Innocence," 1 *Criminal Law and Philosophy* 193 (2007).

Taylor, James Stacey, ed. *Personal Autonomy*. Cambridge: Cambridge University Press, 2005.

Temkin, Jennifer. *Rape and the Legal Process*. Oxford: Oxford University Press, 2d.ed, 2002.

Ten, C. I. *Crime, Guilt, and Punishment*. Oxford: Clarendon Press, 1987.

The Innocence Project: "Causes and Remedies of Wrongful Convictions," *http:www. innocenceproject.com/causes/index.php.*

Thomas, George. *Double Jeopardy: The History, the Law.* New York: New York University Press, 1998.

Thompson, Sandra Guerra. "The White-Collar Police Force: 'Duty to Report' Statutes in Criminal Law Theory," 11 *William & Mary Bill of Rights Journal* 3 (2002).

Thomson, Judith. "Some Ruminations on Rights," 19 *Arizona Law Review* 45 (1977).

Tonry, Michael. *Malign Neglect: Race, Crime, and Punishment in America.* New York: Oxford University Press, 1995.

——. *Thinking about Crime: Sense and Sensibility in American Penal Culture.* New York: Oxford University Press, 2004.

Tyler, Tom. *Why People Obey the Law.* New Haven: Yale University Press, 1990.

Valdivieso, Veronica. "DNA Warrants: A Panacea for Old, Cold Rape Cases?" 90 *Georgetown Law Journal* 1009 (2002).

van Zyl Smit, Dirk. *Taking Life Imprisonment Seriously.* The Hague: Kluwer Law International, 2002.

Von Hirsch, Andrew. "Extending the Harm Principle: 'Remote' Harms and Fair Imputation," in A. P. Simester and A. T. H. Smith, eds. *Harm and Culpability.* Oxford: Clarendon Press, 1996, p.259.

——. *Past or Future Crimes?* New Brunswick, N.J.: Rutgers University Press, 1987.

Von Hirsch, Andrew and Andrew Ashworth. *Proportionate Sentencing.* Oxford: Oxford University Press, 2005, p.141.

Von Hirsch, Andrew and Nils Jareborg. "Gauging Criminal Harm: A Living-Standard Analysis," 11 *Oxford Journal of Legal Studies* 1 (1991).

Von Hirsch, Andrew, Kay A. Knapp and Michael Tonry. *The Sentencing Commission and its Guidelines* (Boston: Northeastern University Press, 1987).

Von Hirsch, Andrew, et al., eds. *Restorative Justice & Criminal Justice: Competing or Reconcilable Paradigms?* Oxford: Hart Publishing, 2003.

Waldron, Jeremy. *Law and Disagreement.* Oxford: Clarendon Press, 1999.

——. "Legislation and Moral Neutrality," in Jeremy Waldron. *Liberal Rights: Collected Papers.* Cambridge: Cambridge University Press, 1993, p.151.

Waldron, Jeremy. *The Dignity of Legislation.* Cambridge: Cambridge University Press, 1999.

Walker, Samuel. *Popular Justice: A History of American Criminal Justice.* New York: Oxford University Press, 2nd ed., 1999.

Walzer, Michael. *Arguing About War.* New Haven: Yale University Press, 2004.

Weinrib, Ernest J. *The Idea of Private Law.* Cambridge: Harvard University Press, 1995.

Wenar, Leif. "The Nature of Rights," 33 *Philosophy & Public Affairs* 223 (2005).

Wertheimer, Alan. *Consent to Sexual Relations.* Cambridge: Cambridge University Press, 2003.

Westen, Peter. *The Logic of Consent.* Burlington, Vt.: Ashgate, 2004.

——. "Two Rules of Legality in Criminal Law," 26 *Law and Philosophy* (2007).

Whitman, James Q. *Harsh Justice: Criminal Punishment and the Widening Divide between America and Europe.* Oxford: Oxford University Press, 2003.

——. "A Plea against Retributivism," 7 *Buffalo Criminal Law Review* 85 (2003).

Williams, Bernard. "A Critique of Utilitarianism," in J. C. C. Smart and Bernard Williams, eds. *Utilitarianism: For and Against.* Cambridge: Cambridge University Press, 1973, p.77.

Williams, Glanville. *Criminal Law: The General Part.* London: Stevens & Sons, 1961.

——. "The Definition of Crime," 8 *Current Legal Problems* 107 (1955).

Williams, Glanville. "The Problem of Reckless Attempts," *Criminal Law Review* 365 (1983).

———. *Textbook of Criminal Law*. London: Stevens & Sons, 1983.

Wilson, James Q. "Drugs and Crime," in Michael Tonry and James Q. Wilson, eds. *Drugs and Crime*. Chicago: University of Chicago Press, 1990, p.522.

———. "Against the Legalization of Drugs," 89 *Commentary* 21, 26 (1990).

———. *The Moral Sense*. New York: Free Press, 1993, p.94.

Wolfgang, Marvin E. and Neil Alan Weiner, eds. *Criminal Violence*. Beverly Hills: Sage Pub. Co., 1982.

Wood, David. "Retribution, Crime Reduction and the Justification of Punishment," 22 *Oxford Journal of Legal Studies* 301 (2002).

———. "Retributive and Corrective Justice, Criminal and Private Law," in Peter Wahlgren, ed. *Perspectives on Jurisprudence: Essays in Honor of Jes Bjarup*. Stockholm Law Faculty. 48 Scandanavian Studies in Law, 2004, p.541.

Yaffe, Gideon. "Conditional Intent and *Mens Rea*," 10 *Legal Theory* 273 (2004).

Zaibert, Leo. *Punishment and Retribution*. Burlington, Vermont: Ashgate Pub. Co., 2006.

Zimmer, Lynn and John Morgan. *Marijuana Myths, Marijuana Facts*. New York: Lindesmith Center, 1997.

Zimring, Franklin E. *American Juvenile Justice*. New York: Oxford University Press, 2005.

———. *The Great American Crime Decline*. Oxford: Oxford University Press, 2006.

Zimring, Franklin E. and Gordin Hawkins. *Crime Is Not the Problem: Lethal Violence in America*. New York: Oxford University Press, 1997.

Zlotnick, David M. "The War Within the War on Crime: The Congressional Assault on Judicial Sentencing Discretion," 57 *Southern Methodist University Law Review* 211 (2004).

Index